THE FORMATION
OF HISTORICAL
THEOLOGY

A Study of Ferdinand Christian Baur

Ferdinand Christian Baur

A Study of
Ferdinand Christian Baur

THE FORMATION
OF HISTORICAL
THEOLOGY

PETER C. HODGSON

HARPER & ROW, PUBLISHERS
New York

FIRST EDITION

LIBRARY OF CONGRESS CATALOG CARD NUMBER: 66-15039

C-Q

To Eva

CONTENTS

EDITOR'S PREFACE

The history of the making of modern theology is, in many ways, the history of the development of the historical approach to its materials and methods. In a time when those materials and methods were under constant pressure to vindicate their right to a place among scholarly disciplines, theologians came increasingly to rely on the historical character of their materials and on the historical precision of their methods for such vindication. So it was that historical erudition came to be identified as an indispensable element of constructive theology.

No one contributed more to that identification than Ferdinand Christian Baur. There were probably a few men in the nineteenth century whose stature in the area of constructive theology was greater, but not very many. There were perhaps a few whose eminence in the field of historical-theological scholarship was greater, but not very many. There was certainly none within Continental Protestantism who ranked as high in both historical scholarship and theological creativity. Indeed, the competence of this phenomenal scholar enabled him to make contributions of far-reaching importance to the study of the New Testament as well as to historical and systematic theology. Taking up a suggestion that had come from Schleiermacher, apparently for the first time, Baur argued against the authenticity of the Pastoral Epistles, as well as of other letters bearing the name of Paul, and set the lines for the debate over these issues ever since. Similarly, his work on the Gospel of John turned the discussion of the life of Jesus into a new direction.

Yet it is for his pioneering work in historical theology that Baur is best remembered, and properly so. All three of the traditional fields of theological scholarship—the biblical, the systematic, and the Church-historical—became for him functions of his research and writing as a historical theologian. He applied to his research an almost unbelievable amount of industry and a truly dazzling array of historical and linguistic equipment. His burrowing in the sources occupied most of the waking hours of a working day that began early and ended late. By his ability to match "secular" historians point for point with his learning and accuracy, Baur brought to the work of the Church historian and historical theologian a new respect and dignity, for which all of us are in his debt. A contemporary of the great Leopold von Ranke, Baur occupies in the development of his discipline a place similar to that of the Berlin master in his.

It is a neat bit of historical irony (whose subtle twist Baur would probably have appreciated) that this craftsman of historical scholarship has acquired a reputation in the textbooks as the man who trimmed the facts of Christian history and theology to fit the Procrustean bed of Hegelian dialectics. This has enabled several generations of theologians—less erudite than he in their historical scholarship, perhaps also less honest about their own philosophical presuppositions—to dismiss Baur as little more than a philosopher in the cloak of the historical theologian. The accidents of translation into English, whose significance for the history of British and American theology has yet to be assessed, conspired to deprive Baur of his proper role in an English-speaking world that might have benefited from his books. As a study of the bibliography of this volume will show, very little of Baur has ever been translated into English. Nor can he be said to have exercised a large measure of influence on the development of historical theology in America, despite its German inspiration.

This monograph by Peter C. Hodgson is the first full-length study of Baur to appear in English. By a careful study of Baur's historical productivity, Mr. Hodgson explores the intricate relation between scholarly research and theological-philosophical presuppositions in Baur's interpretation of the development of dogma, thus setting the controverted question of Baur's Hegelianism into the proper context. To make that context as comprehensive as it must be for so many-faceted a scholar as Baur, the author has worked not only with Baur's published works on historical theology, but with his sermons and manuscripts as well. The result is itself a fine example of the historical-theological method for which Baur was contending. No series of books on "Makers of Modern Theology" would be complete without a volume on Ferdinand Christian Baur. With such a volume, not only the series, but historical-theological scholarship and intellectual history generally, is provided with new and valuable insights into the development of Christian thought during the modern period.

JAROSLAV PELIKAN

Yale University

AUTHOR'S PREFACE

This work represents an inclusive attempt to understand Ferdinand Christian Baur (1792–1860) and his conception of the nature of historical theology—its necessity, its dogmatic principles, its methodology, and its contents and results. The question which underlies the presentation concerns the place historical study should occupy in Christian theology, or the relation between historical knowledge and faith.

The chief sources for this study are Baur's major books, monographs, and published lectures. Relatively few of his journal articles have been used, since they represent for the most part source-critical studies, the results of which have usually been incorporated into later books and lectures. Extensive use of the journals would be required if a study were to be undertaken of the development of Baur's critical conclusions, or if his research on a special topic were to be examined. The several articles which have been used in this study are of peculiar significance for the development of Baur's critical method or for the articulation of his theological perspective. In addition to the published materials, I have also worked with Baur's unpublished manuscripts—letters, sermons, academic opinions, lecture manuscripts—now deposited in the University of Tübingen Library. My wife assisted in this project, for which I am extremely grateful.

A new monograph on Baur by Wolfgang Geiger, *Spekulation und Kritik: Die Geschichtstheologie Ferdinand Christian Baurs* (München: Chr. Kaiser Verlag, 1964), has been published too recently to be taken into account in the present volume. However, a conversation with Dr. Geiger in the summer of 1963 indicates that his interpretation of Baur and evaluation of his significance differ considerably from mine. The reader is thus provided the opportunity of reading these two works and reaching his own conclusions.

All quotations from Baur's writings cited in the text have been translated by me, for which I assume full responsibility. Only two of Baur's works were translated into English (*Paulus* and *Das Christenthum und die christliche Kirche der drei ersten Jahrhunderte*), but these translations, long out of print, are not useful because of their wooden style and theological insensitivity. Nevertheless, when quotations from these works are cited, the correspond-

xi

ing page numbers of the English translations have been provided.
I am also responsible for the translation of other passages quoted
from works written in German. Plans are under way to publish
a volume of Baur's writings in translation in *A Library of Protestant
Thought* (Oxford University Press). Included will be *Die Epochen
der kirchlichen Geschichtschreibung* and the lengthy introduction
to *Vorlesungen über die christliche Dogmengeschichte.*

A word needs to be said about the translation and meaning of
some terms. The difficult and crucial term *Geist* is translated as
"Spirit." It is capitalized when it refers either to the divine Spirit,
the Spirit of God, or to that quality of Spirit which God and man
share in common and which is sometimes described by Baur as
the inner dynamic foundation of the historical process. It is not
capitalized when it seems clearly to refer to empirical, finite human
spirit. When *Geist* refers to the divine Spirit or to human spirit
as personal agency, it is regarded as a personal noun, and the pronouns which refer to it are given in translation as personal pronouns. When it refers to Spirit as a quality, the pronouns which
refer to it are given as impersonal. In German, of course, these
distinctions are not made, so the decision in every instance rests
with the interpretation of the translator. *Wissenschaft* is translated
as "science" but is intended throughout in its broader German sense
as knowledge acquired through the imaginative or speculative ex-
ercise of the mind as well as its critical discipline. *An sich* is
rendered as "implicit." The translations and meanings of a number
of other terms used more or less systematically by Baur are explained (in some instances in footnotes) on pages where a discussion of their systematic usage is to be found: *Idee* (pp. 92–93),
Denken (p. 92), *Erscheinung* (p. 122), *Auffassung* (p.167),
Betrachtung (p. 167), *Darstellung* (p. 168). The sense in which
Baur used *Aufhebung* (usually left untranslated) and its related forms is explained on pp. 139–40. The meaning of the
term "supernatural," as used throughout this work, is explained
in a footnote on p. 5). Baur's use of the term "positivity"
(*Positivität, das Positive*) in the sense of "facticity" or "historicity"
is discussed on pp. 127–31. For the distinction intended in the
use of the terms "catholic" and "Catholic" throughout the latter
part of the book, see p. 130, n. 142. Finally, the conception and
character of "historical theology" (or, to use Baur's more technical
term, "historical-critical theology") is in a sense the question before
this work as a whole and the concluding chapter in particular.

I am grateful to Yale University and the William J. Garland
Trust for a grant which made it possible to work with the Baur
manuscripts at the University of Tübingen in the summer of 1963.
Trinity University in San Antonio, Texas, made a research grant
available to me and assisted in other ways in 1964 to expedite
preparation of the manuscript for the press. *Church History* has

granted permission to make use of material included in my article, "The Rediscovery of Ferdinand Christian Baur: A Review of the First Two Volumes of His *Ausgewählte Werke*," published in the June 1964 number.

I am indebted to many persons in the preparing and writing of this book and in the study of the problems with which it is concerned. Two great scholars and teachers, both recently dead, whose memory I shall cherish, were engaged in different ways with the relationship of Christian faith and historical scholarship and helped to shape my interest in it: Professors E. Harris Harbison of Princeton University and H. Richard Niebuhr of Yale University. Professor Paul Schubert of Yale first concretely directed my interest to a study of Baur. Professor William R. Farmer of the Perkins School of Theology has read portions of the manuscript, as have two of my former colleagues in the Department of Religion at Trinity University, Professors Guy H. Ranson and William O. Walker, Jr. I am also indebted to my colleagues in the Divinity School at Vanderbilt University for assistance in reading proofs and offering constructive comments on the manuscript in its final phase. Mr. Clifford A. McKay, a graduate student in theology at Vanderbilt, has rendered valuable assistance in preparing the index.

Dr. Klaus Scholder, editor of Baur's *Ausgewählte Werke in Einzelausgaben*, currently being published by the Friedrich Frommann Verlag, Stuttgart, very graciously received my wife and me while we worked at the University of Tübingen in the summer of 1963, and I benefited greatly from our conversations on Baur. In addition, he discovered and furnished duplicates of the excellent engraving which serves as the frontispiece of this book; the original is in the Tübinger Stift. During the same period, Dozent Dr. Heinz Liebing generously permitted me to make use of some material prepared by a seminar of his on Baur at the University of Tübingen, and also read portions of the manuscript. Professor Jaroslav Pelikan, editor of this series, has given encouragement and guidance beyond the call of duty as an editor, and I am especially grateful to him. Finally, my deepest appreciation is expressed to Professor Hans W. Frei of Yale. He served as a faithful and inspiring adviser to this project when it took the form of a dissertation presented to the Faculty of the Graduate School of Yale University for the Ph.D. degree in 1963. He made it his own project in more ways than one. Since then he has offered further suggestions which have helped to guide me in the complete revision and rewriting which have ensued in preparing it for the press. To him goes a special word of thanks for many hours of conversation, and for the encouragement, guidance, and criticism at every stage along the way without which this work could not exist in its present form.

To Eva, who already knows more than can here be said, this book is dedicated.

PETER C. HODGSON

Vanderbilt University
January, 1966

ABBREVIATIONS

ADB / *Allgemeine deutsche Biographie*
BAT / *Bengels Archiv für die Theologie und ihre neueste Literatur*
BWKG / *Blätter für Württembergische Kirchengeschichte*
CH / *Church History*
E.T. / English translation
ETh / *Evangelische Theologie*
JBW / *Jahrbücher der biblischen Wissenschaft*
JDT / *Jahrbücher für deutsche Theologie*
PJ / *Preussische Jahrbücher*
PK / *Protestantische Kirchenzeitung für das evangelische Deutschland*
SHZ / *Sybels historische Zeitschrift*
TJ / *Theologische Jahrbücher*
TL / *Theologische Literaturzeitung*
TSK / *Theologische Studien und Kritiken*
TZT / *Tübinger Zeitschrift für Theologie*
U.B.T. / Universitätsbibliothek Tübingen
WZMLU / *Wissenschaftliche Zeitschrift der Martin-Luther-Universität Halle-Wittenberg*, Gesellschafts- und sprachwissenschaftliche Reihe
ZKG / *Zeitschrift für Kirchengeschichte*
ZNTW / *Zeitschrift für die neutestamentliche Wissenschaft*
ZPK / *Zeitschrift für Protestantismus und Kirche*
ZTK / *Zeitschrift für Theologie und Kirche*
ZWT / *Zeitschrift für wissenschaftliche Theologie*

⁓

(For explanation of occasional use of asterisks
in citing Baur's sermons, see p. 110, n. 69.)

THE FORMATION
OF HISTORICAL
THEOLOGY
A Study of Ferdinand Christian Baur

1 ✳ THE AUTHOR OF
HISTORICAL THEOLOGY

THE CONTINUING CONTROVERSY OVER BAUR

Ferdinand Christian Baur, professor of theology at the University of Tübingen from 1826 until his death in 1860, was one of the most important and controversial, and has become one of the most neglected and misunderstood, theologians of the nineteenth century. Emanuel Hirsch has written, for example, that "the true author of historical-critical theology . . . is not [Strauss] but his teacher, Ferdinand Christian Baur, the greatest and at the same time the most controversial theologian to be produced by German evangelical Christianity after Schleiermacher."[1] Baur's greatness consisted in his unequivocal recognition of the radically historical nature of the Christian Church and Christian faith, and in his concomitant desire to relate historical-critical study *internally* rather than externally to the contents of dogmatic affirmation. He thought this to be possible by developing a method for historical understanding appropriate to a critical *and* theological study of the Church and its founding events, a study which he claimed to be an intrinsically proper and necessary theological discipline. The underlying thesis of this book is that Baur's conception of the place and significance of historical study in Christian theology is of importance for contemporary discussion of the relation between faith and history.

The controversy over Baur has concerned chiefly three matters: the extent to which he was a disciple of Hegel, his alleged tendency to neglect the concrete realities of history in favor of general theories and dialectical processes, and finally, his fundamental endeavor to explicate the "truth" of Christianity by means of historical-critical theology.

[1] Emanuel Hirsch, *Geschichte der neuern evangelischen Theologie im Zusammenhang mit den allgemeinen Bewegungen des europäischen Denkens,* Vol. V (Gütersloh: C. Bertelmanns Verlag, 1954), p. 518. Cf. a similar estimate of Baur by Wilhelm Dilthey, quoted below, p. 36.

Baur thought himself more profoundly influenced by Schleiermacher than by any other modern thinker. Yet he has come
to be known as an Hegelian who supposedly forced historical
facts to suit the fancy of an a priori dialectical scheme. Most brief
secondary treatments of Baur refer to him categorically as an
"Hegelian" and mention his "dialectical" historical patterns, such
as the antithesis between the Petrine (Judaizing) and Pauline
parties in the early Church. Two examples will suffice. In his
History of the Christian Church, Williston Walker writes: "All
historical progress, Baur felt, with Hegel, must be through the
three stages of thesis, antithesis, and synthesis." The New Testament books "must display the biases of the various aspects of this
development" in primitive Christianity.[2] Or, in an introduction to
Acts in *The Interpreter's Bible*, G. H. C. Macgregor writes that
"Baur reconstructed early Christian history according to the Hegelian presupposition of a thesis and an antithesis resolving themselves after conflict in a synthesis."[3] Such patterns of oversimplifi-
cation have been repeated by several generations of textbooks and
commentaries, both in German and in English, just as these
statements reflect an attitude toward Baur which originated with
some of his own contemporaries.

In his own time, Baur was dismissed by extreme critics as representing a totally "Hegelian," i.e., "pantheistic" or "atheistic,"
perspective in theology, and as constructing his historical interpretations a priori out of philosophical dialectic, for which reason
alone his critical challenge to the traditional view of the historical
inerrancy of the earliest Christian writings could be disregarded.[4]
In more recent times, this sort of argument has been advanced most
energetically by Ernst Barnikol, in defense of a return to the older
orthodoxy.[5] More serious critics of Baur's Hegelianism, such as
Ernst Troeltsch and Christoph Senft, have objected that Baur's
"dialectical-constructive idealism" tended to obscure the vitality

2 Williston Walker, *A History of the Christian Church* (New York: Charles
Scribner's Sons, 1918), p. 536.
3 G. H. C. Macgregor, "Introduction to the Acts of the Apostles," *The Interpreter's Bible*, Vol. IX (New York: Abingdon Press, 1954), p. 12.
4 Such is the argument of Samuel Berger, *F. C. Baur, les origines de l'école
de Tubingue et ses principes, 1826–1844* (Strasbourg: Berger-Levrault, 1867),
pp. 71–72; and of A. B. Bruce, "Ferdinand Christian Baur and His Theory of
the Origin of Christianity and of the New Testament Writings," *Living Papers
Concerning Christian Evidences, Doctrine, and Morals*, Vol. VII (Cincinnati,
Chicago, and St. Louis: Cranston & Stowe, 1886), pp. 4, 9, 11, 15–16, 21–25,
30, 32–40, 49. Baur himself replied to similar criticisms in some of his polemical writings, which will be discussed below, most important of which was *Die
Tübinger Schule und ihre Stellung zur Gegenwart* (Tübingen: L. F. Fues,
1859; 2d ed., 1860). Citations are from the second edition of this work.
5 Ernst Barnikol, "Das ideengeschichtliche Erbe Hegels bei und seit Strauss
und Baur im 19. Jahrhundert," *WZMLU*, Vol. X:1 (February 1961), esp. pp.
281, 288. Barnikol's polemic is defended, not by a critical study of Baur's own
writings, but by lengthy quotations from his opponents and critics.

and freedom of the interaction of "historical powers,"[6] or that he vitiated the objective knowledge of the historical past for which he strove by regarding the past, like Hegel, as ultimately "bare" and "empty," as only a moment in the ever present process of thought, as only a step into the present.[7]

Two rather different components may be distinguished in such criticisms. The first is that Baur shared Hegel's theological perspective. Although Baur insisted that he was fundamentally a student of Schleiermacher in theology, it is true that he preferred Hegel to Schleiermacher at one specific and important point: it seemed to Baur that Hegel's doctrine of God, specifically of the Trinity, involved God's self-mediation in historical process. Therefore history is intrinsic to the doctrine of God in Hegel's thought, whereas in Schleiermacher's theology, history remains simply a necessary presupposition of Christian consciousness which cannot be elucidated. At this point, Baur chose Hegel, and so he was driven to a panentheistic view of history as the concrete filling out of the idea of reconciliation. At the same time, however, Baur did not remain an uncritical or slavish adherent to Hegel's panentheism. His own radically historical orientation and specifically his Christology, would not permit him to. Unlike Hegel, Baur understood the significance of the particularity and positivity of Jesus for the history of redemption. Therefore, it was in Christology that Baur first and most decisively broke with Hegel, but this break later brought him to raise some questions concerning Hegel's doctrine of God and the world.[8]

The second component in the criticism of Baur's Hegelianism concerns the alleged apriorism and philosophical construction in his historical studies. Here we can anticipate several factors which must be considered when evaluating this criticism. First, we have Baur's direct and unequivocal testimony that his critical procedure was in no way a priori. Although he believed that history as it appears in events and in their interpretation is the outward patterning of an inward idea, the idea of reconciliation, the self-mirroring

---

[6] Ernst Troeltsch, "Adolf v. Harnack und Ferd. Christ. v. Baur," *Festgabe für D. Dr. A. von Harnack, zum siebzigsten Geburtstag* (Tübingen: J. C. B. Mohr, 1921), pp. 282–83, 286–91. In this essay, Troeltsch argues that the perpectives of both Baur and Harnack (acknowledged as his foremost mentors in historical theology and as the two great Protestant "scientific" theologians of the nineteenth century) must be preserved in the work of the historical theologian. He also suggests that Harnack himself was more deeply influenced by the romantic-idealist tradition ending with Baur than he was by rationalism. For further discussion of the relation between Baur and Harnack, see below, p. 277, n. 34.

[7] Christoph Senft, *Wahrhaftigkeit und Wahrheit: Die Theologie des 19. Jahrhunderts zwischen Orthodoxie und Aufklärung* (Tübingen: J. C. B. Mohr, 1956), pp. 76–78. See below, p. 183.

[8] On Baur's relation to Hegel, see below, pp. 54–66; on his panentheism and his understanding of the relation between God and history, pp. 134–42.

of God in free human acts, he also insisted that independent critical or positive historical research alone determines the shape of our understanding of the way these events are connected and the direction in which they move. Second, by "speculation" in historical knowledge, Baur meant the critical attempt to elicit meaning and rationality *from* history rather than to impose it on history. Third, his original discovery of theological opposition in primitive Christianity (e.g., the Petrine-Pauline antithesis) antedated his acquaintance with Hegel's philosophy by several years and was the result of purely critical investigations. Fourth, Baur never believed that historical process could be divided into neat triads of "thesis, antithesis, synthesis," as becomes manifestly clear when the total structure of his periodization of church history is examined. Finally, he insisted that historical study of the Church is at once a speculative (philosophical-theological) and an empirical (objective, critical) procedure, that these are two components in the same process of understanding, that methodological priority can be given to neither, and that neither may be sacrificed to the other.[9]

The second common criticism of Baur, that he neglected the concrete realities of history, such as historical individuals, in favor of general theories and dialectical processes, focuses attention on his Christology, or more specifically on the religious and historical significance, or lack of it, which he attributed to Jesus. Critics such as Gerhard Uhlhorn, Karl Hase, I. A. Dorner, A. B. Bruce, Albrecht Ritschl, and Heinrich Ewald claimed that Baur treated Jesus as a "purely natural" phenomenon, that for him the primitive faith in Jesus as the Christ had no foundation in the life of Jesus itself, that therefore Christianity did not begin with Jesus but rather first arose out of the conflict between Paulinism and Judaism.[10] Similarly, Baur was accused of neglecting the significance of other important figures in church history, such as Constantine, Charlemagne, and Luther, and of making them mere pawns in the unfolding of the "idea" in historical process. We shall examine these charges at some length below in our treatment of Baur's historically explicated Christology and of his understanding of the relation between individuals and the historical process of which they are a part.[11]

The criticisms of Baur's Christology mentioned above point to the third and perhaps most fundamental difficulty which many

9 See below, pp. 200–201, also pp. 22, 148, 161–67, 178–79, 189–90, 196, 207–212, 251–56.

10 Cf. Baur, *Die Tübinger Schule*, p. 12; Gerhard Uhlhorn, "Die älteste Kirchengeschichte in der Darstellung der Tübinger Schule," *JDT*, III (1858), 280–349; Karl Hase, *Die Tübinger Schule. Ein Sendschreiben an Herrn Dr. Ferdinand Christian von Baur* (Leipzig: Breitkopf und Härtel, 1855), p. 60; I. A. Dorner, *History of Protestant Theology Particularly in Germany, Viewed According to Its Fundamental Movement and in Connection with the Religious, Moral, and Intellectual Life*, George Robson and Sophia Taylor, trans. (Edinburgh: T. & T. Clark, 1871), II, 410–14; Bruce, *op. cit.*, pp. 5, 9, 12–14, 35. For Ritschl and Ewald, see below, p. 7, n. 22, 23.

11 See below, pp. 221–37, esp. pp. 221–23; and pp. 186–88.

interpreters have had with Baur, namely, his endeavor to explicate the "truth" of Christianity by means of historical-critical theology. The objection which often lurks behind criticisms of Baur's "Hegelianism" is that he considered Christianity as an historical phenomenon, to be subjected to the canons of historical-critical research, and that he believed that such study has an essential place among the theological disciplines, since it is a means of access to the truth and meaning of the Christian faith. The fear was that such a procedure would "naturalize" Christianity, rob it of its supernatural or miraculous foundation, treat it in "secular" categories rather than as *Heilsgeschichte,* and produce a Jesus who was purely the result of his natural environment, in no sense divine. It was believed that such a view was the inevitable result of an Hegelian *Weltanschauung* combined with a critical study of the New Testament documents, and that therefore neither modern philosophy nor historical criticism should be permitted a place in Christian dogmatics.[12] In our time, it is more common to say that historical study can know nothing of the truth of Christianity for faith and that therefore the attempt to consider Christianity in purely historical terms results in epistemological confusion. With respect to this criticism, it should be pointed out first that Baur did not consider historical-critical theology to have "naturalized" Christianity in the sense of robbing it of its divine foundation and reality, although he did believe that the "supernatural"[13] and the "miraculous" could no longer be accepted as valid theological categories. He sought rather to work out a theory of history and a mode of historical understanding which could, by means of eliminating the disjunction between secular history and *Heilsgeschichte,* enable the historical theologian to take account of the full divine-human reality of Christianity.[14] In the second place, however, it is true that Baur tended to absorb the function of dogmatics into historical theology to an extent which would find little acceptance today. *All* theology tended to become historical theology, which meant that normative or nonhistorically conditioned dogmatic statements were no longer possible. At the same time, Baur did not believe

12 Cf. Heinrich Beckh, "Die Tübinger historische Schule, kritisch beleuchtet," *ZPK,* Neue Folge, LXXIV (1864), 231–36, 242; Barnikol, "Das Erbe Hegels," *WZMLU,* X:1, 281, 288; and Bruce, *op. cit.,* pp. 5, 9, 12–14.

13 Throughout this work, the term "supernatural" will be used to describe that which happens through the operation of an agency or force above, outside, and in contradiction to the order of nature and history. It was given this definition in the controversy with rationalism, and Baur used it in this sense. As such, a "supernatural" occurrence is "miraculous," these terms being virtually synonymous in the theological vocabulary of Baur's day. On the question of miracle and the supernatural, see below, pp. 190–96, esp. pp. 192–93. Baur's rejection of supernaturalism does not mean that he denied the existence of God as an other than finite, transcendent being, but it does mean that God's revelation and action in nature and history must not be understood as occurring "supernaturally."

14 See below, pp. 127–31, 145–48, and 161–69.

that historical theology had emasculated the absoluteness or universality or divinity of Christianity, but rather had rendered its absolute truth intelligible in a new way. The possibilities and limitations in his procedure at this point will be explored in the concluding chapter of this book.[15]

Despite the controversy which has surrounded Baur from the very beginning, he has in fact been one of the most neglected and misunderstood of modern theologians. Although something of a minor Baur-renaissance is now appearing in Germany—signaled, for example, by a five-volume reprint edition of his major works,[16] and by a new monograph[17]—the most numerous and important studies still consist of shorter-length essays.[18] Until recently, only two books have appeared on Baur, both in German, both over fifty years old, and both more descriptive of the contents of his writing than interpretive.[19] In English nothing of significance has been written, aside from an early essay by Mark Pattison[20] and a recent article in which Baur is studied in connection with Ritschl.[21].

How is this neglect and misunderstanding of a major figure to be explained? In the first place, none of Baur's most important students developed and perpetuated the lines of his own work: David Friedrich Strauss, Eduard Zeller, and Albrecht Ritschl all went their own rather different ways. Despite the common reference to a "Tübingen School," there were in fact very few students who fully shared Baur's perspective and extended it creatively; among them might be listed Adolf Hilgenfeld, Albert Schwegler, and Otto

15 See below, pp. 261–71, 279–84; see also pp. 172–74.

16 Ausgewählte Werke in Einzelausgaben, Klaus Scholder, ed. (Stuttgart-Bad Canstatt: Friedrich Frommann Verlag [Günther Holzboog], 1963–). The following two volumes have been published: Vol. I, Historisch-kritische Untersuchungen zum Neuen Testament, with an introduction by Ernst Käsemann; and Vol. II, Die Epochen der kirchlichen Geschichtschreibung (1852), Dogmengeschichtliche Vorreden aus den Jahren 1838–1858, with an introduction by Ernst Wolf.

17 Wolfgang Geiger, Spekulation und Kritik: Die Geschichtstheologie Ferdinand Christian Baurs (München: Chr. Kaiser Verlag, 1964),

18 The best of these are Eduard Zeller's essay, "Ferdinand Christian Baur," first published in PJ in 1861 and reprinted in his Vorträge und Abhandlungen geschichtlichen Inhalts (Leipzig: Fues's Verlag [L. W. Reisland], 1865), pp. 354–434; and Emanuel Hirsch's discussion of Baur in his chapter, "Die Ausbildung der historisch-kritischen Theologie," op. cit., V, 518–52.

19 G. Fraedrich, Ferdinand Christian Baur: Der Begründer der Tübinger Schule als Theologe, Schriftsteller, und Charakter (Gotha: Friedrich Andreas Perthes, 1909), and Ernst Schneider, Ferdinand Christian Baur in seiner Bedeutung für die Theologie (München: J. F. Lehmanns Verlag, 1909).

20 "Present State of Theology in Germany" (1857), published in Essays by the Late Mark Pattison, Henry Nettleship, ed., Vol. II (Oxford: Clarendon Press, 1889), chap. xvi. Mention should also be made of the sympathetic treatment in R. W. Mackay, The Tübingen School and Its Antecedents: A Review of the History and Present Condition of Modern Theology (London: Williams & Norgate, 1863).

21 Philip Hefner, "Baur versus Ritschl on Early Christianity," CH, XXXI:3 (September 1962), 259–78.

Pfleiderer, but none of these was the equal of Baur in historical and theological ability. After the death of his colleague Friedrich Heinrich Kern in 1842, Baur found himself all but isolated within the Tübingen theological faculty and in academic theology in German generally. During his own lifetime he had become an extremely controversial figure, and after his death the polemical caricatures that were intended to discredit his position gained almost universal acceptance.

In dogmatics, Baur's position was quickly displaced by the antimetaphysical perspective of the Ritschlians.[22] His conception of historical understanding was, with minor but important exceptions, replaced by a growing positivism. In Church history and history of dogma, Baur's work was eclipsed, although not necessarily surpassed, by that of Adolf Harnack and others. Finally, in New Testament theology, his pioneering studies were quickly forgotten with the discovery of the significance of eschatology by Johannes Weiss and the argument for Markan priority and the two-document hypothesis by Heinrich Julius Holtzmann and others, which very quickly became a dogma in German and British circles. Baur, following J. J. Griesbach, had defended the priority of Matthew and the dependence of Mark on both Luke and Matthew.[23] Furthermore, the radical conclusions of some of his New Testament studies were unacceptable to many, and his "tendency criticism"[24] was caricatured by his opponents. At the end of the century, disaffection with Schleiermacher, Hegel, and synthesizing theology generally, i.e., with any attempt to hold faith together in an internal relation with philosophical and historical science, had become all but universal; likewise, disenchantment had spread with respect to the entire

[22] Ritschl himself, in an essay published the year after Baur's death, "Über geschichtliche Methode in der Erforschung des Urchristenthums," *JDT*, VI (1861), 429–59, forcefully attacked Baur's Christology and some aspects of his historical methodology. This essay, coming as it did from a former student, may well have contributed materially to the misunderstanding of Baur and to disenchantment with his theological direction. See below, p. 62, n. 92, and p. 277, n. 34.

[23] Heinrich Ewald's vicious personal attack on Baur and his study of the Gospels in "Ursprung und Wesen der Evangelien," *JBW*, I (1848), 113 ff., and II (1849), 180 ff., appears to have done as much as any other single factor to discredit the critical and theological integrity of the Tübingen School. Thereafter, German and British New Testament scholars tended to see Baur through Ewald's eyes. Cf. the comments by Ewald's student Julius Wellhausen, in *Heinrich Ewald, Beiträge zur Gelehrten-Geschichte Göttingens* (Berlin, 1901), p. 66, and William Sanday's article on the Gospels in Smith's *Bible Dictionary*, 1891. William R. Farmer, in *The Synoptic Problem: A Critical Analysis* (New York: The Macmillan Co., 1964), chaps. i and ii, defends the Griesbach hypothesis and Matthean priority, and shows that the two-document hypothesis was never really proved by Holtzmann and his predecessors. The reassessment of the Synoptic problem and its history provided by this book makes it clear that Baur's option, and his arguments, must be seriously considered rather than cursorily dismissed as "disproved." I examine Baur's treatment of the Synoptic problem below, pp. 154–56, 214–17.

[24] See below, pp. 196–201.

historical-critical approach in theology, as expressed by Albert Schweitzer. In the process, Baur became increasingly forgotten, identified as the author of an outdated "school" which furnished Hegelianized interpretations of all aspects of the Church's early history and subsequent development. Baur was simply not a part of the main stream of theological liberalism at the end of the nineteenth century, and consequently the twentieth century scarcely came to know him.

In addition to these difficulties, American theologians have faced some further barriers in the way of an unprejudiced understanding of Baur: very few Americans studied theology at Tübingen in the nineteenth century; as I noted in the Preface, only two of Baur's works have been translated into English (*Paulus* and *Das Christenthum und die christliche Kirche der drei ersten Jahrhunderte*), and the translations, which have long been out of print, were burdened by a wooden and theologically insensitive Victorian English; and finally, the literature on Baur in English has, with few exceptions, been prejudiced and uninformed. Consequently, what is needed for a reappraisal of Baur and his significance is a fresh start, from the very beginning.

BAUR'S LIFE: THE INTEGRATION OF PIETY AND CRITICISM

Ferdinand Christian Baur was born on June 21, 1792, in the Württemberg village of Schmiden, near Stuttgart. His father, Christian Jakob Baur (1755–1817), was called in 1800 as pastor at Blaubeuren, a small village at the southern foot of the Swabian Alps, two miles from Ulm, where the young Baur spent most of his boyhood. His mother, Eberhardine Regine Gross, was, like her husband, an industrious, pious, hard-working, serious-minded person, marked by a touch of melancholy. The young Baur was shaped in the virtues his parents thought appropriate and developed as a serious lad, having little need for companionship and possessed of a natural shyness or reserve which never left him even when he had achieved a position of importance and controversy.[25]

Baur was instructed by his father until the age of thirteen (1805), at which time he entered the lower theological seminary

---

25 Virtually nothing is known of Baur's childhood and early education other than what is reported by his son-in-law Eduard Zeller in "Ferdinard Christian Baur," *Vorträge und Abhandlungen,* p. 357; and in *Allgemeine deutsche Biographie,* Vol. II (Leipzig: Duncker und Humblot, 1875), p. 172. See also *Neue deutsche Biographie,* Vol. I (Berlin: Duncker und Humblot, 1952), p. 670. Zeller's monograph in *Vorträge und Abhandlungen* is generally excellent and serves as the foundation for most later studies of Baur, but Zeller is not an entirely unbiased interpreter. There were some aspects of Baur's thought which he never succeeded in fully understanding, and although he had access to Baur's literary estate, he did not make full use of it. He suppressed, especially, whatever information was relevant to the break between Strauss and Baur (see below, pp. 81–84).

in Blaubeuren, where he began his training in Greek, Hebrew, and Latin as well as New Testament exegesis, rhetoric, history, philosophy, Bible, and other subjects.[26] Between 1807 and 1809, he studied at the Maulbronn Kloster. In the autumn of 1809, he enrolled in the University of Tübingen and spent five years in the evangelical-theological seminary (the "Stift") as a philosophical and theological student. Although the leader of the old Tübingen School, Gottlob Christian Storr, had died four years before Baur's arrival, his influence was still very much felt in the theological faculty, which after his death adopted an unproductive and negative attitude toward the theological problems stirred up by the impact of rationalism, and later dismissed Schleiermacher's *Glaubenslehre* as pantheistic when it appeared in 1821.[27] An exception, however, was the teacher who most influenced Baur by force of personality as well as integrity of scholarship, Ernst Gottlieb Bengel. Bengel was one of the most open-minded supernaturalists of Storr's old school, touched deeply by Kantian philosophy and rational criticism. He awakened Baur's interest in historical theology, which was further stimulated by contact with the classical historians— Herodotus, Thucydides, Livy, and Tacitus—and by study of Barthold Niebuhr's *Römische Geschichte*. We also know that he was impressed by the hermeneutical procedure in the work of the classical scholar F. A. Wolf and in Schleiermacher's Plato research. Exactly when Baur engaged in these studies, which helped to liberate him from the old-Tübingen treatment of history and revelation, is uncertain; it may have been while he was still a student, but it is just as likely that it was not until after he had joined the Blaubeuren faculty in 1817.[28]

In a letter to Eduard Zeller, Friedrich August Baur suggests that his brother first came under the influence of Fichte and especially Schelling while still a student in Tübingen.[29] Following this suggestion, Zeller adds that A. K. A. von Eschenmayer, who was called to the philosophical faculty in Tübingen in 1812, may have first introduced Baur to Schelling's thought.[30] This suggestion is plausible, if for no other reason than that Eschenmayer, at least

[26] The content of Baur's first formal education in Blaubeuren has been described in an article by Karl Bauer, "Zur Jugendgeschichte von Ferdinand Christian Baur (1805–1807)," *TSK*, XCV:3/4 (1923–24), 303–313.

[27] Cf. Baur in K. Klüpfel, ed., *Geschichte und Beschreibung der Universität Tübingen* (Tübingen: L. F. Fues, 1849), pp. 397–98.

[28] Cf. Zeller, *ADB*, II, 172–73; Eberhard Pältz, "F. C. Baurs Verhältnis zu Schleiermacher" (unpublished doctoral dissertation, University of Jena, 1955; abstract by the author in *TL*, LXXXI:9 [September 1956], 571); and Heinz Liebing, "Historisch-kritische Theologie: zum 100. Todestag Ferdinand Christian Baurs am 2. Dezember 1960," *ZTK*, LVII:3 (1960), 306. Baur's brother, Friedrich August Baur, did not believe that these new contacts were made until after the student days. Cf. F. A. Baur to Eduard Zeller, 12 Jan. 1861 (U.B.T., Md 750, x).

[29] F. A. Baur to Eduard Zeller, 12 Jan. 1861 (U.B.T., Md 750, x).

[30] Zeller, *ADB*, II, 173.

in early days, was a critical admirer and student of Schelling and even contributed to the latter's move away from his early absolute idealism in a direction possibly significant for Baur's later appropriation of Schelling's view of history and historical study.[31] However, Eschenmayer did not begin lecturing in Tübingen until the summer semester of 1812, whereas Baur had completed his two years of philosophical study the previous winter and would not have heard Eschenmayer lecture in the normal course of his studies.[32] Nevertheless, one of Baur's closest friends, Ludwig Friedrich Heyd,[33] who entered the University as a theological student one year later than Baur, would have heard Eschenmayer lecture, and visited Schelling twice during a year-long trip in 1816. And for other reasons Baur would have been familiar with Schelling's name, if not his philosophy, at an early date: not only did they have mutual acquaintances, but an uncle of Schelling on his mother's side was prelate in Blaubeuren from 1795 to 1810, and Schelling's father was prelate in Maulbronn when Baur and Heyd were students in the Maulbronn Kloster.[34]

From this evidence, it seems clear that Baur must have known of Schelling, perhaps was generally familiar with the content of his philosophy from an early date, even if he had not actually read his work or appropriated his thought before 1818. This was the year in which he published, in Bengel's *Archiv für die Theologie*, a critical review of G. P. C. Kaiser's *Die biblische Theologie, oder Judaismus und Christianismus nach der grammatisch-historischen Interpretations-Methode*. In this essay, Baur showed himself still largely under the influence of Bengel and the old-Tübingen supernaturalism.[35] He argued that the connection between Judaism and Christianity must be treated in an historically comprehensive way, that revealed religion must be treated under categories drawn from studies in philosophy of religion and history of religions; and he gave evidence of having already done considerable study in history of religions and undertaken philosophical analyses of the essence and major forms of religion. But he still held out for a supernaturally inspired, suprahistorically mediated revelation of unique

---

31 Cf. Wilhelm Windelband, *Die Geschichte der neueren Philosophie*, Vol. II (2d ed.; Leipzig: Breitkopf und Härtel, 1899), pp. 346–47.

32 Cf. Ernst Kleucker, "Ferdinand Christian Baurs Schellingskenntnis zur Zeit der 'Kaiserrezension' (1818)." Seminararbeit (Doz. Dr. Heinz Liebing), Universität Tübingen, Sommersemester 1962.

33 Later Heyd became paster in Markgröningen and a student of Württemberg history. He remained a close friend and confidant until his death in 1842. Baur's letters to Heyd reveal his personality and family life, his opinions, hopes, and disappointments, more clearly than any other correspondence.

34 Kleucker, *op. cit.*

35 But Kleucker suggests that a study of certain phraseology in this review shows a developing interest in Schelling on Baur's part, without actually having read any of Schelling's writings; this interest may have led to a study of Schelling immediately thereafter. Cf. Fraedrich, *op. cit.*, p. 12.

religious truth, and thus drew back from treating Christianity in a fully "historical-critical" mode. As Zeller suggests, the scientific equipment of this young theologian was already impressively displayed, but the theological results were essentially those of Bengel's "rational supernaturalism."[36]

In any case, it is certain that Baur studied Schelling intensively —specifically, the *System des transzendentalen Idealismus* (1800) —shortly after assuming his teaching position at Blaubeuren in 1817.[37] Schelling's influence was clearly present in Baur's first major work, *Symbolik und Mythologie, oder die Naturreligion des Alterthums* (1824–25). The *Philosophische Untersuchungen über das Wesen der menschlichen Freiheit* (1809) was analyzed at some length in *Die christliche Gnosis*.[38] Finally, Baur showed himself to have been deeply impressed by the critique of historical empiricism and pragmatism in Schelling's *Vorlesungen über die Methode des akademischen Studium* (1803).[39] Schelling's early thought—his conception of history as revelation and his delineation of an historical method that would have access to the full scope of historical reality thus understood—maintained a lasting influence on Baur. After Schelling's retirement from public life in 1812, Baur was both curious and sceptical about the content of the new "philosophy of revelation" being developed in the Munich and Berlin lectures. He asked Heyd, who had heard Schelling lecture in Munich in 1833, why everything was so secretive and what the content of this important new work was supposed to be.[40] Later, he regarded Schelling's appearance in Berlin as one of "unexampled arrogance," almost as though it were intended to ridicule Hegel by imitating his dialectic; furthermore the new philosophy was obscure and contradictory in its understanding of revelation as somehow supernaturally mediated.[41]

Before concluding this discussion of Baur's education and his early theological orientation, it should be pointed out that it would be wrong to suggest that Baur learned nothing of lasting value from the old-Tübingen theologians or to dismiss his Swabian pietistic family heritage. Karl Barth rightly claims that throughout his life Baur shared with these theologians their interest in an

---

[36] Zeller, *Vorträge und Abhandlungen,* pp. 379–81; and *ADB,* II, 173.

[37] Cf. F. A. Baur to Eduard Zeller, 12 Jan. 1861 (U.B.T., Md 750, x).

[38] Cf. Baur, *Die christliche Gnosis, oder die christliche Religions-Philosophie in ihrer geschichtlichen Entwiklung* (Tübingen: C. F. Osiander, 1835), pp. 611 ff.

[39] Cf. Baur, *Die Epochen der kirchlichen Geschichtschreibung* (Tübingen: L. F. Fues, 1852), p. 248.

[40] Baur to L. F. Heyd, 18 Oct. 1833 (U.B.T., Md 619r, 13).

[41] Baur to L. F. Heyd, 30 Nov. 1841 (U.B.T., Md 750, ii, 6, 29); cf. Baur, *Geschichte der christlichen Kirche,* Vol. V: *Kirchengeschichte des neunzehnten Jahrhunderts,* Eduard Zeller, ed. (Tübingen: L. F. Fues, 1862), pp. 383–384.

objective theological truth in history against rationalistic subjectivism.[42] Only, for Baur, this interest did not exclude but rather was strengthened by critical-historical study. His respect for the old-Tübingen theology was revealed by his veneration of his beloved teacher Bengel,[43] and by his friendship with J. C. F. Steudel, the only representative of the old school who remained on the faculty after its reconstitution in 1826, who served as one of Baur's colleagues until his death in 1837.

Steudel had originally opposed Baur's call to Tübingen but welcomed him on his arrival with the assurance that they could work together.[44] The relationship between them was close, except for an incident in the summer of 1831: as editor, Steudel opposed the inclusion in the *Tübinger Zeitschrift für Theologie* of an article by Baur on the origin of Passover and circumcision rites on the grounds that, by virtue of its critical content, it ran counter to the *Zeitschrift's* position that the Bible contains divine revelation. If the article was to be published, Steudel insisted that, "as a matter of conscience," he serve as redactor. Baur vigorously resisted this arrangement and threatened to withdraw entirely from the *Zeitschrift;* but the matter was settled amicably and the article appeared the following year, uncensored.[45] Baur remarked that there was "something tragic" in Steudel's futile and increasingly personal polemic against Schleiermacher, Hegel, and later Strauss—a debate for which he was not equipped with his supernaturalistic categories.[46] The tragedy was that he defended his viewpoint with a true, noble, and authentic piety, and that such an irreconcilable clash between piety and criticism was both futile and needless. Throughout his last years, writes Baur, Steudel remained upright, well-meaning, and honest, a man full of friendship and love for his opponents, one who faced his sudden death with great courage of faith.[47]

Upon completion of his theological studies in the autumn of 1814, at the age of twenty-two, Baur served as vicar in two parishes,

42 Karl Barth, *Die protestantische Theologie im 19. Jahrhundert* (3d ed.; Zürich: Evangelischer Verlag AG., 1960), p. 452.

43 Cf. Baur in Klüpfel, *op. cit.,* p. 396.

44 Baur to L. F. Heyd, 19 Sept. 1826 (U.B.T., Md 750, ii, 6, 6).

45 Baur to L. F. Heyd, 1 Oct. 1832 (U.B.T., Md 619r, 11); Baur to F. A. Baur, 25 Aug. 1831 (U.B.T., Md 750, ii, 1, 4). Cf. Baur, Über die ursprüngliche Bedeutung des Passahfestes und des Beschneidungsritus," *TZT,* VI:1 (1832).

46 In a letter to Strauss, thanking him for having sent a copy of the first volume of his *Streitschriften* ("Herr Dr. Steudel, oder die Selbsttäuschungen des verständigen Supranaturalismus unserer Tage" [1837]), Baur writes: "I have immediately read it *uno tenore* and believe that, in title, tone, and content, you are in the right. As much as I must nevertheless sympathize with my friend Steudel, I can only acknowledge that it is an incomparable masterpiece of a devastating polemic. Keep it up." Baur to D. F. Strauss, 10 April 1837 (U.B.T., Md 750, ii, 7, 1).

47 Baur in Klüpfel, *op. cit.,* pp. 416–22. Cf. Baur to L. F. Heyd, 13 Nov. 1837 (U.B.T., Md 750, ii, 6, 17).

Rosswaag and Mühlhaufen, and then as an assistant in the lower theological seminary in Schönthal. In 1816 he returned to Tübingen as a *Repetent* in the Stift or seminary.[48] In November of 1817, he became a professor in the seminary at Blaubeuren, where for ten years he taught the Greek and Roman prose writers, including some of the classical historians: Livy, Tacitus, Herodotus, and Thucydides. He even began a translation of Thucydides' *History of the Peloponnesian Wars*, and several years later wrote an essay in which he compared Eusebius, as the father of Church historiography, with Herodotus, the father of secular historiography.[49] He also lectured in ancient history,[50] mythology, and later, Plato.[51] This was a period for intensive reading and study, liberated from the rather narrow perspective of the old-Tübingen theology. A collection of reading notes from this period shows that Baur became familiar with many contemporary works in ancient history, classical philosophy, mythology, linguistics, and history of religions, by such authors as Heilmann, Schleiermacher, Schlegel, Osiander, Creuzer, Hug, and Wolf.[52]

However, the work which had by far the greatest theological impact on Baur during this period was the first edition of Schleiermacher's *Glaubenslehre*, which appeared in 1821–22. In a letter to his brother, Baur described in enthusiastic terms the liberating influence the *Glaubenslehre* exercised on him personally. No other theological work, he wrote, had appealed to him as deeply and as fundamentally as this one; none other possessed the richness of content, the dialectical skill, the organic structure, and the significance for true Christian faith of this one. The primacy which Schleiermacher afforded to religious self-consciousness frees the believer from the external and arbitrary authority of supernaturally mediated revelation and verbally inspired scriptural texts.

But the enthusiasm of new discovery was already tempered by Baur's critical eye. He did not understand how "idealism" and "pantheism," freedom and determinism, could be held together so

---

[48] Zeller, *ADB*, II, 172–73; *Worte der Erinnerung an Ferdinand Christian von Baur* (Tübingen: L. F. Fues, 1861), p. 84.

[49] In 1826 Baur's translation of the first two books of Thucydides was rejected by the editor of the series in which it was to appear, C. N. Osiander, on the grounds that the translation was too literal. Baur to L. F. Heyd, 19 Aug. 1826 (U.B.T., Md 750, ii, 6, 5), and 19 Sept. 1826 (U.B.T., Md 750, ii, 6, 6). On Herodotus, see Baur's Latin *Programma, Comparatur Eusebius Caesariensis, historiae ecclesiasticae parens, cum parente historiarum, Herodoto Halicarnassensi* (Tubingae, 1834).

[50] A manuscript containing Part I of these lectures, "Von der Erschaffung der Welt bis auf die Römer," is deposited in the University of Tübingen Library (U.B.T., Mh II 166, q). The Introduction, in which Baur discusses the conception, sources, methods, values, and uses of history, is especially valuable.

[51] Wilhelm Lang, "Baur und Strauss," in *Von und aus Schwaben: Geschichte, Biographie, Litteratur*, Vol. III (Stuttgart: W. Kohlhammer, 1866), p. 9.

[52] U.B.T., Mh II 166, p2, 112.

neatly as the unspoken philosophical presuppositions of the dogmatic system. He also was alarmed lest the historical foundation
of the Christian faith, the person and work of Jesus of Nazareth, be
dissolved into a mode of subjective religious self-consciousness—
a fear which anticipated his later criticism that Schleiermacher's
Christology loses grasp of the possibility and the necessity of the
historical Jesus. "If the major elements which concern the person
of the Redeemer are themselves derived from religious self-
consciousness, then the outward history of Jesus could be taken
as a history of the internal development of religious self-consciousness, and I could think of the person of Christ as the Redeemer only
as a certain form and potency of self-consciousness, which would
therefore appear in an outward history only because the natural development of self-consciousness must necessarily so form itself
once in its highest perfection. Therefore, Christ is in every man,
and the outward appearance of Jesus is not the original fact [for
this *Glaubenslehre*]."[53]

Zeller rightly suggests that the *Glaubenslehre* enabled Baur to
achieve theological maturity by freeing him once and for all "from
the supernaturalism of the Tübingen School" and by enabling him
to bring his own theological perspective into greater clarity. It is
interesting to note that this freedom did not come until he had
reached the age of thirty.

Although in the course of certain of his doctrinal determinations he
confronted [Schleiermacher's] system with an autonomous criticism
and permitted Hegel's philosophy greater influence, and although he
went far beyond Schleiermacher in historical criticism, nevertheless
he had been so fundamentally penetrated by the spirit of this system
and remained so true to its doctrine that, if he can be named as the
disciple of a predecessor, it would be of Schleiermacher above all
others. . . . [Hegel's] influence did not have as great or as lengthy an
effect as that of Schleiermacher's system. Schleiermacher's thought
encountered him before he had reached the crucial point of his own
striving. Hegel's furnished the mature man, who had already sought
his own way autonomously, something more in the way of an under-
pinning and a scientific formulization of that which he already
possessed substantively.[54]

53 Baur to F. A. Baur, 26 July 1823 (U.B.T., Md 750, ii, 1, 1).
54 Zeller, *Vorträge und Abhandlungen*, 361, 364–65. Cf. also Zeller, *ADB*,
II, 173. This judgment is undoubtedly influenced to some extent by Friedrich
August Baur's statement, expressed in a letter concerned with his brother's
theological development, that Schleiermacher represented the "greatest influence on his inner course of development." F. A. Baur to Eduard Zeller, 12
Jan. 1861 (U.B.T., Md 750, x). Heinz Liebing, in "Ferdinand Christian Baurs
Kritik an Schleiermachers Glaubenslehre," *ZTK*, LIV:2 (1957), 225–43, dis-
putes Zeller's judgment by arguing that Baur never really was deeply influenced by the *Glaubenslehre*, even from the beginning. We shall examine
Baur's relation to Schleiermacher below, pp. 43–54.

The influence of both Schleiermacher and Schelling was clearly felt in Baur's first major publication, *Symbolik und Mythologie, oder die Naturreligion des Alterthums* (three volumes, 1824–25), which, in presupposition and content, reveals the final and decisive break from the old supernaturalism. Baur was indebted to Schleiermacher for his definition and typology of religion, and to Schelling for his conception of revelation. On the other hand, it is generally agreed that there was no evidence of Hegelian influence or categories in this work. Baur's philosophical orientation at this stage was clearly idealistic, but it was an idealism shaped by Schelling, Fichte, Schleiermacher, and Plato. Even the famous statement which prefaced this work, that "without philosophy, history remains . . . eternally dead and dumb,"[55] reflected the influence of the above-named thinkers and especially Baur's studies in ancient history and classical historiography, but not Hegel.[56]

The purpose of *Symbolik und Mythologie* was to provide a comparative, "scientific" analysis of nature religion, the basic categories of which are symbol and myth, in order to show the relations and distinctions between the nature religions and the historical religions, specifically Christianity. Baur argued for the necessity of a general theory of religion in relating and interpreting the various religions, and drew his definition and categorization of religion primarily from Schleiermacher. He attempted to understand, from a *religionsgeschichtlich* standpoint, the unity of all religions as different manifestations of divine revelation in history, a revelation which is no longer to be interpreted in terms of a distinction between nature and supernature, or history and superhistory, since nature and history themselves—and here he showed his appropriation of Schelling—are media of divine revelation.[57]

Toward the beginning of his Blaubeuren career, on April 30, 1821, Baur married Emilie Becher (1802–1839), the nineteen-year old daughter of Gottlob Benjamin Becher, court physician in Stuttgart. She was a woman, according to the testimony[58] of Eduard Zeller, her son-in-law, of vital and receptive nature, although frail physically, who complemented her husband's scholarly seriousness with her practical qualities and was a devoted mother to her children. Their deep and happy relationship was ended by her untimely death, the result of a fatal illness, in November 1839, which dealt

[55] *Symbolik und Mythologie, oder die Naturreligion des Alterthums*, 2 Vols. in 3 Parts (Stuttgart: J. B. Metzler, 1824–25), I, xi–xii. This statement is sometimes taken as a hallmark of Baur's "Hegelianism."

[56] See also Baur, "Geschichte des Alterthums" (U.B.T., Mh II 166, q), pp. 12–17, and below, p. 97, n. 29; pp. 162–63.

[57] The content of *Symbolik und Mythologie* is discussed briefly below, pp. 97–98. See also Zeller, *Vorträge und Abhandlungen*, pp. 382–85. Baur remarks rather bitterly that on the basis of this work he already has been called a "pantheistic (!) ideologue" and has been accused of overthrowing "all the foundations of religion and morality." Baur to L. F. Heyd, undated, apparently fall 1825 (U.B.T., Md 750, ii, 6, 3).

[58] Zeller, *Vorträge und Abhandlungen*, p. 361; and ADB, II, 173.

a severe blow to Baur's sensitive spirit.[59] She bore five children, two sons and three daughters (one of whom died in infancy), including Emilie Caroline (1823–1904), who married Eduard Zeller in Bern in 1847.[60]

In the summer of 1826, after the death of Bengel, the Württemberg educational ministry decided that the evangelical theological faculty at Tübingen needed an essential reform. On the strength of his *Symbolik und Mythologie*, but after some consideration and delay,[61] Baur, who was by then thirty-four, and his close friend and colleague on the Blaubeuren faculty, Fredrich Heinrich Kern (1790–1842), were called and appointed *ordentlich* professors. At first, Baur had some misgivings about his ability to fill this new and important position,[62] but later he expressed general satisfaction with the new situation, except for the lack of colleagues interested in matters of historical criticism.[63] At the same time that Baur and Kern were brought from Blaubeuren, Christian Friedrich Schmid, who had joined the faculty in 1821, was elevated to *ordentlich* professor. Schmid's orientation was pietistic, and he became increasingly antagonistic toward speculative theology and historical criticism as the years went on. Including Steudel, the evangelical faculty was now comprised of four *ordentlich* professors and remained unchanged until Steudel's death in 1837. The division of labor was as follows: Steudel taught dogmatics, apologetics and Old Testament exegesis (for the latter he was joined by Julius Mohl, professor of oriental literature on the philosophical faculty); Kern also taught dogmatics and apologetics and in addition Christian ethics; Schmid was responsible for homiletics, catechism, and pedagogy; and Baur covered the historical disciplines other than

---

59 See Baur's expressions of grief and loss in letters to Ludwig Friedrich Heyd, dated 6 Nov. 1839 and 24 Mar. 1840 (U.B.T., Md 619r, 23 and 25). The feeling for his wife is further reflected in a sermon eight years after her death at the marriage of his daughter, Emilie Caroline, to Eduard Zeller, in which he asks his daughter to preserve the memory of her mother, "this serene and unbiased, just and upright, pure and unpretentious spirit, far from all striving for vain appearance, living in the simple, pure, unadorned love of truth and right." Sermon at the Wedding of Emilie Caroline Baur and Eduard Zeller, 22 June 1847 (U.B.T., Md 750, iv, 6).

60 The others were Ferdinand Friedrich, born while the Baurs still lived in Blaubeuren, who later published some of his father's lectures posthumously and became a professor at the Maulbronn Seminary; a second daughter, born in 1829; a third daughter, born in 1831, who died a little over a year later; and Albert Otto, born in 1834, who survived several severe illnesses during infancy. Information concerning Baur's children and family life during the period from 1824 to 1840 is found in various letters to L. F. Heyd and F. A. Baur (e.g., U.B.T., Md 619r, 9, 11, 20, 25; Md 750, ii, 1: 4, 7, 8, 9; Md 750, ii, 6, 1).

61 K. A. Osiander was also considered; and Baur was opposed, at least initially, by Steudel. Baur to L. F. Heyd, 19 Aug. 1826 (U.B.T., Md 750, ii, 6, 5).

62 Cf. Baur to L. F. Heyd, 30 Apr. 1826, 19 Aug. 1826, and 19 Sept. 1826 (U.B.T., Md 750, ii, 6: 4, 5, 6).

63 Baur to L. F. Heyd, 17 Dec. 1826 (U.B.T., Md 750, ii, 6, 7), and 1 Oct. 1832 (U.B.T., Md 619r, 11).

Old Testament—Church history, history of dogma, and New Testament history, exegesis, and theology. He also taught symbolics and Protestant Church law,[64] and in earlier years he shared ethics with Kern. In 1828, Steudel founded the *Tübinger Zeitschrift für Theologie,* co-edited by the other members of the faculty, as the successor to journals published by K. C. Flatt and Bengel, and as an organ of the "new" Tübingen theologians.[65]

Baur's inaugural dissertation at Tübingen, presented early in 1827, was devoted to a study of Schleiermacher's theology, and especially his Christology, as a form of Christian Gnosticism.[66] It was one of Baur's most important theological documents, since it contained the germ of so many of his later ideas. In the thorough study which preceded it, he launched his investigations of Gnosticism which were to continue for many years and worked out his basic criticism of Schleiermacher's theological system, which was never significantly altered thereafter. The contents of this work will be examined when we study Baur's analysis of Schleiermacher's "ideal rationalism" and Christology.[67]

Baur found his scholarly home upon his call to Tübingen in the autumn of 1826, where he remained for thirty-four years, until his death in 1860. His life assumed the regulated patterns of scholar and teacher without further external change. However, during the 1830's he was considered for two other theological positions in German universities—for Schleiermacher's chair in Berlin and for Ullmann's in Halle—but he received calls to neither. The possibility of a call to the former is indicated in a letter to Heyd,[68] but already Baur's associations with Strauss had gained him a bad reputation in ecclesiastical circles in Prussia.[69] His call to Halle, which appears to have been a more serious matter, was blocked by the conservative Lutheran party of the *Evangelische Kirchenzeitung,* and by an opinion delivered against him by Neander and Twesten, because of the "hypercriticism" allegedly evident in his *Die sogenannten Pastoralbriefe.*[70]

[64] Cf. U.B.T., Mh II 166, n, o.

[65] Baur in Klüpfel, *op. cit.,* pp. 402–405, 407.

[66] *Primae Rationalismi et Supranaturalismi historiae capita potiora. Pars I. De Gnosticorum Christianismo ideali* (January 1827). *Pars II. Comparatur Gnosticismus cum Schleiermacherianae theologiae indole* (Easter 1827). *Pars III. Exponitur praesertim Arianismi indoles rationalis* (Pentecost 1828). (Tubingae: Hopferi de l'Orme, 1827–28). Baur provided a review of the first two parts, "Anzeige der beiden academischen Schriften von Dr. F. C. Baur," in TZT, I (1828), 220–64, which is almost as detailed as the original, and which has been used for the present study, since it is more readily available.

[67] See below, pp. 43–47, 50.

[68] Baur to L. F. Heyd, 20 Aug. 1834 (Md 750, ii, 6, 15).

[69] Cf. Wilhelm Lang, "Ferdinand Baur und David Friedrich Strauss," PJ, CLX (April–June 1915), 492–93.

[70] Baur writes: "From day to day it becomes less healthy in science and in life, and one has only to proceed so as not to lose courage entirely." Baur to F. A. Baur, 29 July 1836 (U.B.T., Md 750, ii, 1, 14). See also Lang, "Baur und Strauss," PJ, CLX, 493–94.

In Halle itself, Tholuck opposed the call to Baur, and the two exchanged letters on the matter. Baur insisted that what had been rumoured to Tholuck concerning his lectures on Acts—that he applied to the New Testament literature generally the mythical elements he had found in Acts, and that he rejected "the entire history of miracle"—was absolutely untrue. He also denied that critical theology "demolishes" rather than "upbuilds" the faith of the Church; that which may appear externally to be destructive may in truth be upbuilding. "In addition," he added, "I am lecturing on Christian symbolics, whereby I have opportunity enough to express my dependence on our Protestant faith and doctrines—and really thus to express myself without reservation."[71] Although Baur earlier indicated to Heyd that he was satisfied with his present position and had no desire to leave Tübingen,[72] despite the unpleasant incident with Steudel in 1831 already mentioned, it appears from this correspondence that Baur would have seriously considered a call either to Berlin or to Halle at this time. Later, after assuming directorship of the evangelical theological seminary (the Stift) upon Steudel's death in 1837, his roots were too deeply planted in Tübingen to leave.

In addition to his duties as director of the Stift, Baur was appointed Rector of the University for the year 1841–42. This was a position which entailed a number of burdensome ceremonial activities, including a speech delivered at a University festival celebrating the twenty-fifth year in the reign of King Wilhelm I of Württemberg.[73] The speech concerned the political and theological significance of the twenty-five years from 1816 to 1841. In it Baur extolled the liberality and beneficence of the Württemberg regime, pointed to the growing sense of national (i.e., German) unity and identity, and then argued for the place of Hegelian speculation in scientific theology and for a more open attitude on the relation of historical criticism to faith. The speech was not well received by the pietists, and after some consideration Baur reversed his earlier decision to allow it to be published.[74] At the same time the King availed himself of the opportunity to suggest to Baur that theologians ought not to dabble in metaphysics or to engage in

71 Baur to F. A. G. Tholuck, early summer 1836, rough draft (U.B.T., Md 750, ii, 9, 1).
72 Baur to L. F. Heyd, 1 Feb. 1833 (U.B.T., Md 619r, 12).
73 Baur to L. F. Heyd, 13 Sept. 1841 (U.B.T., Md 619r, 29).
74 The speech was, however, published posthumously by Baur's son: "Über die geschichtliche Bedeutung der fünfundzwanzig Jahre 1816–1841. Rede zur Feier des Gedächtnisses der fünfundzwanzigjährigen Regierung seiner Majestät des Königs Wilhelm von Württemberg am 31. Oktober 1841 auf der Universität zu Tübingen." Printed in Ferdinand Friedrich Baur, ed., Gratulationsschrift des Gymnasiums zu Tübingen für die vierte Säcularfeier der Universität Tübingen, 9–11 August 1877 (Tübingen: L. F. Fues, 1877), pp. 3–22. Cf. also Baur to L. F. Heyd, 30 Nov. 1841 (U.B.T., Md 750, ii, 6, 29).

polemical disputes with one another.[75] On the whole, it was an unhappy occasion.

Baur's other major nonacademic function at Tübingen was that of serving as morning preacher (*Frühprediger*) in the University Church (the Stiftskirche) on Sundays and festival days, an office to which members of the evangelical-theological faculty were officially appointed. There were three such preachers, who were ranked according to their seniority on the faculty, and each of whom preached once every four or five Sundays. Baur was appointed a *Frühprediger* upon his arrival in Tübingen in 1826 and obtained the rank of *erste Frühprediger* apparently upon the death of Kern in 1842, who had been the senior member of the faculty since 1837; he retained this office and rank until his death in 1860.[76] When, in the midst of an academic dispute over whether to call Zeller to the faculty, Schmid questioned the propriety of a speculative theologian also serving as a Christian preacher, Baur vigorously defended the combination of the two offices. "I am not merely a teacher of theology," he pointed out, "but also a preacher";[77] and in another context he insisted that the scientifically trained theologian, by virtue of his ability to distinguish the essential content of the Christian faith from unessential or superfluous forms, is especially well equipped to serve a pastoral call.[78]

Baur's sermons are very useful for clarifying certain aspects of his own theological perspective and will be employed for this purpose in the chapters to follow.[79] In general, they were Christocentric in focus; almost always they started with an exposition of the

---

[75] Baur to L. F. Heyd, 11 Nov. 1841 (U.B.T., Md 619r, 30).

[76] Cf. U.B.T., Mh 969; and *Worte der Erinnerung an Dr. Johann Tobias Beck* (Tübingen: J. J. Heckenhauer, 1879), p. 24. Baur preached regularly, then, for thirty-four years. This contradicts Zeller's testimony in *ADB*, II, 174, that Baur preached for a period of twenty years. Unfortunately, none of the sermons are dated. I do not know how to reconcile these data other than to suggest that Zeller was perhaps referring to the nearly nineteen years that Baur served as *erste Frühprediger*. There are 221 sermons in Mh 969. If Baur preached ten to twelve times a year, this would account for eighteen to twenty-two years of preaching. It is entirely possible, however, that the collection in Mh 969 is not complete; and internal evidence seems to indicate that the sermons cover a wider range of years. The signature in which the sermons are contained states that these are sermons preached by Baur in the Stiftskirche between 1826 and 1860.

[77] Gutachten of 12 Apr. 1841 (U.B.T., Md 750, v, 4).

[78] Gutachten of 27 June 1839 (U.B.T., Md 750, v, 3). See below, pp. 96–97.

[79] See below, especially pp. 110–18. Because of the very time-consuming and costly process involved, it has been possible to study in detail only a relatively small but representative selection of the 221 sermons in U.B.T., Mh 969. These sermons are written in an exceedingly miniscule and difficult script; I am indebted to the services of Dr. Gustave Celmins in transcribing a microfilmed selection of them into modern German typescript. The patterns of consistency in this selection are sufficient to convince me that I can discuss with relative confidence the major themes and emphases in Baur's sermons, but with no pretense to an exhaustive coverage of details.

meaning of Jesus' teaching ministry or reconciling work as described in the Gospel text designated by the Württemberg lectionary; and then they moved to a personal or contemporary
application of this meaning or perhaps a description of the Christian life as it is shaped by it. They reflected a careful integration
of piety and criticism, although Baur did not bring his critical
studies of the New Testament literature directly into his sermons.
He was concerned with the religious content, not the historical
authenticity, of the passages which his sermons exegeted. The
later sermons disclosed a growing interest in the person and work
of Jesus in addition to the content of his teaching; they were also
more simply and directly written and adhered to a standard format.[80]

After he had become settled into the academic routine at Tübingen, the rest of Baur's life was the story of his writing and of the
development of theological and critical perspectives. His literary
productivity began, for the most part, only after he had reached
his mid-forties, which was relatively late for a scholar of his
magnitude and output. The earlier years had been ones of careful
preparation. It has generally been considered that two dates, 1835
and 1847, marked important turning points in his literary and
theological development.[81] The work in which Baur first made
explicit use of Hegelian categories and in which he evidenced a
thorough study of Hegel's philosophy of religion was *Die christliche
Gnosis*, published in 1835, when Baur was forty-three. And in 1847
a monograph appeared in the *Theologische Jahrbücher*, "Über
Prinzip und Charakter des Lehrbegriffs der reformierten Kirche, in
seinem Unterschied von der lutherischen." Zeller claims this article
marked a transition in Baur's thought to a stronger interest in the
moral and cultic content of religion as opposed to the ideological
or doctrinal, and a greater emphasis on subjective human freedom
against a divine determinism which expresses itself in laws of
historical development—in both cases a break with the characteristically Hegelian emphases of the years 1835–47, during which
Baur produced his epoch-making treatises in history of dogma and
brought his monographs on Paul together for the publication of

---

80 Although none of the sermons are dated, it is possible to designate most
of them as early or late in the period from 1826 to 1860 on the basis of such
considerations as type of paper, handwriting, literary style, content, and
especially the Gospel text on which the sermons are based. A new edition
of the *Gesangbuch für die Evangelische Kirche in Württemberg* was published
in 1841, containing a new lectionary in addition to the old one continued
from the 1791 edition of the *Gesangbuch*. Sermons based on the new lectionary are obviously post–1841, but sermons based on the 1791 lectionary may
also be late, when other indications point in this direction. Any precise dating
of specific sermons is impossible.

81 Zeller, *Vorträge und Abhandlungen*, pp. 378 ff.; Otto Pfleiderer, "Zu
Ferdinand Christian Baur's Gedächtnis," PK, XXXIX:25 (June 1892), 565–
573; August Baur, "Ferdinand Christian Baur," PK, XXXIX:29, 30 (July
1892), 661–67, 691–99; and Fraedrich, *op. cit.*, pp. xv–xix.

Paulus. With respect to the first date, it is clear that it did mark the beginning of Hegel's influence on Baur, although his interest in the use of philosophy or "speculation" in historical study can be traced back to his first contacts with Schelling and the classical historians. It would be wrong to suggest, however, that Baur's interest in a speculative interpretation of historical development ceased in 1847. This interest was actually brought to its culmination in the volumes on Church history published during the 1850's, although the interpretive categories found in this work had been refined and were now more distinctly Baur's own.

It is not certain, therefore, that the second date possessed as much significance as Zeller attributes to it. It is true that the moral and cultic aspects of religion had a larger place in the Church history than they did in the monographs on history of dogma, which of course reflected a difference in subject matter as well as theological perspective. But it is not true that Baur's interest in subjective moral freedom as an essential component of authentic humanity suddenly appeared for the first time in 1847. As early as 1823, he criticized the deterministic elements in Schleiermacher's system.[82] His own theological anthropology, worked out for the most part in the middle period, 1835–47, focused on the structures of human freedom. In his debate with the Catholic theologian J. A. Möhler, for example, he tried to show that authentic moral freedom does not consist of arbitrary subjectivism but of a special mode of internally mediated dependence on God. True Christian freedom, as exemplified above all by Paul, is a freedom-in-dependence. This also marks the authentic principle of Protestantism, although it is anticipated by pre-Augustinian developments in the Christian doctrine of man. This aspect of the Reformation became the object of intensive research in 1847, but it did not mark a radically new departure in Baur's appreciation of freedom or interpretation of the Reformation.[83]

[82] Baur to F. A. Baur, 26 July 1823 (U.B.T., Md 750, ii, 1, 1). Cf. also "Anzeige der beiden academischen Schriften," TZT, I, 258.

[83] Cf. *Geschichte der christlichen Kirche,* Vol. II: *Die christliche Kirche vom Anfang des vierten bis zum Ende des sechsten Jahrhunderts in den Hauptmomenten ihrer Entwicklung* (2d ed.; Tübingen: L. F. Fues, 1863), p. 124; *Kirchengeschichte,* V, 313–15; "Das christliche des Platonismus oder Sokrates und Christus," TZT, X:3 (1837), 26; *Paulus, der Apostel Jesu Christi. Sein Leben und Wirken, seine Briefe und seine Lehre. Ein Beitrag zu einer kritischen Geschichte des Urchristenthums,* Eduard Zeller, ed., 2 Vols. (2d ed.; Leipzig: Fues's Verlag, 1866–67), II, 297–99 (*Paul, the Apostle of Jesus Christ, His Life and Work, His Epistles and His Doctrine. A Contribution to a Critical History of Primitive Christianity,* trans. from the 2d German ed. by A. Menzies, 2 Vols. [London & Edinburgh: Williams & Norgate, 1875–76], II, 272–74); *Die christliche Lehre von der Versöhnung in ihrer geschichtlichen Entwicklung von der ältesten Zeit bis auf die neueste* (Tübingen: C. F. Osiander, 1838), pp. 285–88; and *Lehrbuch der christlichen Dogmengeschichte* (1st ed.; Stuttgart: Becher's Verlag, 1847), pp. 202–205. One of the items in Zeller's argument that 1847 marks an important transition in Baur's evaluation of freedom is that before this date he had attacked

The thesis which underlies the following survey of Baur's major writings is that throughout his Tübingen career his fundamental viewpoint remained unchanged, while his categories, emphases, and data were continually being modified and revised. Like the historical process he studied, Baur was not a static thinker; he was always moving forward, never satisfied with the results achieved. But it can be argued that he moved within a consistent framework of interpretation, that a basic continuity underlay the various periods of his theological development. This continuity was provided by a conviction about the irreducibly historical nature of the Christian Church, its Gospel and its faith, a conviction which was present in his earliest writings and which was continued and strengthened to the final stroke of his pen.

During his early years at Tübingen Baur published several important monographs in the newly founded *Tübinger Zeitschrift für Theologie*. Among them was his first examination of miracle, specifically in Acts and Paul, which fully anticipated his mature treatment of the subject.[84] Then, in 1831 "Die Christuspartei in der korinthischen Gemeinde" appeared, in which Baur first enunciated his famous thesis of a conflict between Petrine (Judaizing) and Pauline parties in the primitive Church and employed what later came to be known as "tendency criticism" to reach a judgment concerning the authenticity of the Corinthian Epistles as products of Pauline thought. This article was published well before Baur first read Hegel, and its thesis, more complex than is generally recognized, rested on several years of intensive research with the New Testament writings.[85]

Baur's studies in early Christian literature were interrupted in 1832 by the appearance of J. A. Möhler's *Symbolik oder Darstellung der dogmatischen Gegensätze der Katholiken und Protestanten*. This work, by a colleague on the faculty of Catholic theology who hitherto had been a sympathetic student of modern Protestantism,

Pelagianism (in *Die christliche Lehre von der Dreieinigkeit und Menschwerdung Gottes in ihrer geschichtlichen Entwicklung*, Vol. I: *Das Dogma der alten Kirche bis zur Synode von Chalcedon* [Tübingen: C. F. Osiander, 1841], pp. xvii–xviii), whereas later he defended Pelagius against Augustine (in *Kirchengeschichte*, II, 124). An examination of these passages, however, indicates that this change results from a reappraisal of Pelagius' understanding of freedom, which Baur had earlier regarded as merely an empty, arbitrary subjectivism, not a new discovery of the necessity of freedom for faith. In the earlier writing, Baur defends the Reformation view of freedom against Pelagius. The change represents a shift in historical judgment, not in theological viewpoint.

84 See below, pp. 195–96.

85 Preparation began as early as 1826, when Baur first lectured on Acts and Corinthians and began to develop a new critical method for dealing with the New Testament texts. Cf. Wilhelm Lang, "Baur und Strauss," *Von und aus Schwaben*, III, 10. Early in 1830 Baur indicated that he already was engaged in the research which led to the 1831 article. Cf. Baur to L. F. Heyd, 5 Feb. 1830 (U.B.T., Md 619r, 10).

was in fact intended as a polemical contrast between the objective purity of Catholic dogma and the hopelessly arbitrary subjectivism of the Protestant faith. Baur, who had been lecturing on Protestant symbolics in the evangelical seminary,[86] quickly responded with a work of his own, *Der Gegensatz des Katholicismus und Protestantismus nach den Principien und Hauptdogmen der beiden Lehrbegriffe* (first published in the *Tübinger Zeitschrift für Theologie* in 1833 and then as a book in 1834), in which he contrasted Catholicism and Protestantism according to their "root principles." In addition, he argued that Protestant idealism represents an authentic continuation of the Reformation spirit (against Möhler's charge to the contrary), but also, from a *religionsgeschichtlich* perspective, shows some marked similarities to ancient Christian Gnosticism, whereas modern Catholicism is analogous to the religious temper of early Jewish Christianity. Seen from this point of view, there is both the need and the possibility for a mediation between these two religious tendencies.[87]

One of the themes touched on briefly in *Der Gegensatz des Katholicismus und Protestantismus*, "the parallel between Protestantism and Gnosticism," was taken up and expanded in *Die christliche Gnosis, oder die christliche Religions-Philosophie in ihrer geschichtlichen Entwiklung* (1835). It was in connection with this work that Baur apparently first read Hegel's *Vorlesungen über die Philosophie der Religion,* published by Marheineke in 1832, which was probably his first direct contact with Hegel's thought.[88] In a letter written in February 1835 Baur indicated that, in connection with his work on *Die christliche Gnosis,* which by then had continued "for more than a year," Hegel's *"Religionsphilosophie* has especially occupied me this winter [1834–35] and in many respects attracts me. Thus I am likely to come up against the fact that I am not able to find in it the atrocities customarily attributed to it."[89] This is the first mention of Hegel in any of Baur's correspondence, and the tone of the letter seems to indicate that Hegel's work represented a fresh discovery. Later, Baur specifically stated that Hegel's philosophy was brought under consideration and influenced

[86] Cf. Baur to L. F. Heyd, 1 Feb. 1833 (U.B.T., Md 619r, 12).

[87] Cf. Baur, *Der Gegensatz des Katholicismus und Protestantismus nach den Principien und Hauptdogmen der beiden Lehrbegriffe. Mit besonderer Rücksicht auf Herrn Dr. Möhler's Symbolik* (2d ed.; Tübingen: L. F. Fues, 1836), pp. xxiii–xxvi; Baur, *Kirchengeschichte,* V, 309–317; Zeller, *ADB,* II, 175; and Zeller, *Vorträge und Abhandlungen,* pp. 397–99. The exchange between Möhler and Baur continued until 1836.

[88] Baur may first have learned about Hegel through Strauss, who, having spent the winter of 1831–32 in Berlin, returned to Tübingen for the summer semester, where as a Privatdozent he gave philosophical lectures reflecting Hegel. Cf. Lang, "Baur und Strauss," *PJ,* CLX, 477.

[89] Baur to F. A. Baur, 15 Feb. 1835 (U.B.T., Md 750, ii, 1, 9). The handscript for the first part of the second sentence ("thus I am likely to come up against the fact that") is unclear; the reading given here follows the transcription in Lang, "Baur und Strauss," *PJ, loc. cit.*

his own work for the first time in *Die christliche Gnosis*.[90] This evidence would seem to indicate the winter of 1834–35 (and perhaps the preceding months as well) as the period in which Baur first studied Hegel's philosophy.[91]

Die christliche Gnosis represented a return to the thesis first expounded in Baur's inaugural dissertation, that there are marked similarities between ancient Gnosticism and modern Protestant philosophies of religion. Now a full-scale historical treatment was provided, beginning with the concept and origin of *gnosis*, and continuing with types of pagan and Jewish religious speculation, a classification of Christian Gnostic systems, the conflict between Gnosticism and Church doctrine, and the transition from old Gnosticism to the "modern philosophies of religion." To the latter were now added—in addition to Schleiermacher—Boehme, Schelling, and especially Hegel. The work was intended as both a defense and an internal critique of Christian Gnosticism or philosophy of religion.[92] It made evident the extent to which Hegel's doctrine of God and his philosophical formulation of the truth of reconciliation had deeply impressed Baur; but at the same time he was alert to the danger present especially in Hegel's Christology of dissolving the positive, historical foundations of the Christian faith into a higher dialectic of thought.

The same year that *Die christliche Gnosis* was published, 1835, also witnessed the appearance of Strauss's *Das Leben Jesu*, which immediately stirred up an intense public controversy and brought about Strauss's dismissal from Tübingen as a Privatdozent. Baur, who had been Strauss's teacher both in Blaubeuren and in Tübingen, protested this cursory abridgment of academic freedom; and in December 1835 he tendered his resignation from the Evangelische Verein when the president of that organization accepted on its behalf Eschenmayer's bitter and unprincipled *Streitschrift* against Strauss, "Der Ischariotismus unsere Tage." In the academic opinion which accompanied his resignation, Baur insisted that critical, "scientific" theology is not inimical to faith and that it

90 Baur in Klüpfel, *op. cit.*, p. 407.

91 Zeller claims that Hegelian influences are to be detected for the first time in the treatment of Protestant doctrine in the first edition of *Der Gegensatz des Katholicismus und Protestantismus* (1833). However, this runs counter to Baur's own testimony; and it is perhaps significant to note that, in a second edition of *Der Gegensatz*, published in 1836, a new section appears, "the Hegelianism of recent Catholic theologians," which was not found in the first edition. Liebing, in "Historisch-kritische Theologie," *ZTK*, LVII:3, 308, raises the possibility that Baur may have been familiar with some of Hegel's writings as early as *Symbolik und Mythologie*, but offers no evidence. On this question, see below, p. 97, n. 29.

92 See below, pp. 66–70. In a letter to F. A. Baur, 21 May 1835 (U.B.T., Md 750, ii, 1, 10), Baur makes it clear that, although he has sought to find "a satisfying side" in Hegel's thought in *Die christliche Gnosis*, the work is not to be understood as a wholesale endorsement of Hegelianism.

must be allowed to pursue the truth, without the limitation of dogmatic presuppositions.[93]

With respect to the *content* of Strauss's book, namely, its attack on the historicity of the Jesus of the Gospels, Baur remained silent, since, as he later remarked, he lacked at that time the "necessary deeper studies" by which to reach a judgment on this, the most difficult of all critical questions connected with the New Testament.[94] In this case, the "necessary deeper studies" involved investigation of the theological tendencies of the apostolic and postapostolic ages (provided in *Paulus*, 1845, and numerous articles) and examination of the literary sources of the Gospel story (a series of studies culminating in *Kritische Untersuchungen über die kanonischen Evangelien*, 1847) before Baur was in a position to furnish, eighteen years later, his own alternative to Strauss's portrayal of the historical Jesus in *Das Christenthum und die christliche Kirche der drei ersten Jahrhunderte*, 1853, and in his lectures in New Testament theology of the same years.[95] With respect to the validity of Strauss's historical *method*, however, Baur made it clear almost immediately, in an article published in May 1836, that he had serious questions about it and wished to dissociate himself from it.[96] Baur's criticism of Strauss's method and the subsequent relationship between the two men will be discussed in the next chapter.[97]

Because of his sympathetic treatment of Hegel in *Die christliche Gnosis* and his silence with respect to the content of Strauss's *Das Leben Jesu*, Baur was thereafter associated with the Hegelian "school" by some of his contemporaries,[98] although he replied almost immediately that he was not the follower of any one philosophical system and that he had learned a great deal of importance for theology from Hegel without becoming a disciple.[99] By the time he read Hegel, Baur was a mature scholar in his own right,

[93] Gutachten of 20 Dec. 1835 (U.B.T., Md 750, v, 1).

[94] *Kirchengeschichte*, V, 396–97.

[95] Baur discussed the life of Jesus in his lectures on Church history in the 1840's, but examination of lecture manuscripts and student notes from this period reveals that his treatment of Jesus underwent considerable modification and enrichment before he published the first volume of Church history lectures in 1853. In the 1843–44 lectures, the discussion of Jesus was limited to four brief topics: his relation to his historical environment, chronology of his ministry, his intention to found a Church, and extracanonical sources. Cf. U.B.T., Mh II 156, Mh II 166 h.

[96] "Abgenöthigte Erklärung gegen einen Artikel der *Evangelishen Kirchenzeitung*, herausgegeben von D. E. W. Hengstenberg, Prof. der Theol. an der Universität zu Berlin. Mai 1836," *TZT*, IX:3 (1836), 179–232. The objections against Strauss are first raised in a letter from Baur to L. F. Heyd, 10 Feb. 1836 (U.B.T., Md 619r, 16).

[97] See pp. 73–84.

[98] E.g., by Hengstenberg in the *Evangelische Kirchenzeitung*; Cf. Zeller, *Vorträge und Abhandlungen*, p. 364.

[99] "Abgenöthigte Erklärung," *TZT*, IX:3, 225. See below, pp. 65–66.

in his mid-forties, and the influence of Hegel was, as might be expected, only critically and cautiously assimilated. In fact, Baur belonged to none of the Hegelian schools ("left," "right," or "center") in the narrower sense;[100] but he did contribute a number of review articles to a journal published by the Hegelian circle in Berlin, the *Jahrbücher für wissenschaftliche Kritik*, between 1834 and 1841. The *Jahrbücher* was a weekly journal, founded in 1827, consisting entirely of critical reviews of new publications. It ceased publication in 1846. The years in which Baur contributed to it, 1834–41, would seem to mark rather precisely the period during which he was most deeply influenced by Hegel or at least chose to associate himself openly with the Hegelians.

In the years between 1838 and 1843, Baur published his two great monographs in the history of dogma: *Die christliche Lehre von der Versöhnung in ihrer geschichtlichen Entwicklung von der ältesten Zeit bis auf die neueste* (1838), and *Die christliche Lehre von der Dreieinigkeit und Menschwerdung Gottes in ihrer geschichtlichen Entwicklung* (three volumes, 1841–43). The influence of Hegel was felt especially in the first of these works, an historical study of the doctrine of atonement, for Baur was convinced that Hegel had provided the most recent and satisfying speculative interpretation of the meaning of reconciliation between God and man, and that the history of the development of the doctrine must be viewed from the perspective provided by his explication of it. The detailed contents of the volume, however, including Baur's periodization of the development of the doctrine, rested on his studies in the history of dogma which reached back to 1826, the year that he began lecturing in this discipline. The same was true for the second of the monographs, the study of the doctrines of the Trinity and incarnation, where the Hegelian perspective was somewhat less apparent. In both volumes, however, the tendency to describe the development of dogmatic concepts through the dialectical movement of Spirit (although critical historical research alone can establish the empirical patterns of this movement), and the use of "speculation" to achieve critical objectivity, reflected the impetus given to Baur's historical studies by Hegel's philosophy.[101] This impetus was never lost, although it was gradually assimilated into a fuller, more mature and independent methodology. The periodization of the development of dogma worked out in these two monographs became, with some significant modifications, the foundation for Baur's treatment in *Lehrbuch der christlichen Dogmengeschichte* (1847) and in his

100 See below, pp. 71–73, and Zeller, *ADB*, II, 175.
101 Heinz Liebing suggests that Baur's productivity in the years following *Die christliche Gnosis* can be explained in part by the fact that he found "peace" in Hegel's philosophy as an answer to the methodological questions with which he had been struggling. Cf. "Historisch-kritische Theologie," *ZTK*, LVII:3, 311.

lectures on history of dogma, published posthumously, 1865–67.[102]

In the midst of his dogmatic-historical studies, Baur continued his research into the history and literature of the early Church and Paul. In 1835 he published *Die sogenannten Pastoralbriefe des Apostels Paulus*, in which he challenged for the first time the Pauline authorship of the Pastoral Epistles by arguing that the heretics mentioned in them were Gnostics, probably Marcionites, thus precluding, by the necessarily late date of the Epistles, the possibility of their having been authentic Pauline letters.[103] A year later he published his second major monograph on Paul, "Über Zweck und Veranlassung des Römerbriefs und die damit zusammenhängenden Verhältnisse der römischen Gemeinde," in the *Tübinger Zeitschrift für Theologie*. Then in 1845 these and other monographs on the Pauline literature were brought together with a discussion of Paul's life and works and an extensive and fundamental analysis of his theology to produce one of Baur's major works, the most important contribution to Pauline studies of the nineteenth century, his *Paulus, der Apostel Jesu Christi*. A partial revision of this work and of his lectures on Paul in New Testament theology had been completed before his death in 1860, and a second edition was published posthumously by Zeller in 1866. Among the ancient theologians, Paul was Baur's first love, and he managed to think and write from within the Pauline theological framework brilliantly at the same time that he sought to elucidate its central meaning through categories of interpretation borrowed from Schleiermacher and Hegel, in a way analogous, perhaps, to Bultmann's "existentialist" interpretation of Paul's theology.

The decade following *Die christliche Gnosis* was a productive period for Baur from a literary point of view; but it was an unhappy one, not only because it brought the death of his wife in 1839 and of his two most trusted friends, Heyd and Kern, in 1842, but also because it was filled with continuing faculty controversy concerning the appointment of a successor to Steudel's chair and with polemical debates respecting the value of "scientific" theology for faith. Following Steudel's sudden death in November 1837, Eduard Elwert was first considered for the chair in dogmatics but was rejected by the Academic Senate because he was too "Schleiermacherian."[104] Instead, the Senate preferred one of Baur's former students, I. A. Dorner, presently a Privatdozent, "on account of his more Christian direction," as Baur ironically put it.[105] Baur was not impressed by Dorner's ability in dogmatics; he was con-

---

[102] The way in which Baur worked out his periodization of the historical development of dogma, and its significance for the study of this discipline, are discussed below, pp. 245–51.

[103] Cf. *Paulus*, II, 109–110 (E.T., 99–100).

[104] Gutachten of 12 April 1841 (U.B.T., Md 750, v, 4).

[105] *Ibid.*

vinced that behind the critical and scientific façade an older supernaturalism lurked, and he took as evidence the fact that during
the brief period he lectured in dogmatics in 1838 Dorner attracted
only five students.[106] After further discussion, it was decided to
invite Elwert, who had assumed a pastorate, to lecture on an
interim basis from 1839 until the end of 1840, at which time he
became too ill to continue.[107] Meanwhile, Baur proposed as a per-
manent replacement for the chair one of his former Blaubeuren
students, Christian Märklin, now a pastor in Calw and a close
friend of Strauss's. His scientific ability had been demonstrated,
so Baur claimed, by his *Reform des protestantischen Kirchen-
wesens;* but a more recent critical study, *Die Pietisten,* published
in 1839, had aroused the opposition of the pietistic party in the
Württemberg Church.[108] Kern, who had originally favored Märklin, now joined Schmid in opposition; and in a session of the
Academic Senate on June 20, 1839, the call to Märklin was de-
feated by twenty votes to seven. This was a bitter blow to Baur,
who quickly addressed an academic opinion to King Wilhelm of
Württemberg, expressing his judgment that the opposition to Märklin in fact reflected opposition to all nonpietistically oriented theology, i.e., to any form of scientific or speculative theology.[109]

Following this unhappy confrontation, the issue was allowed to
rest undecided for another year and a half, until in February 1841,
Baur and Kern proposed Eduard Zeller for the chair, but apparently
without much hope for success since Zeller was already considered
an "Hegelian" on the basis of lectures in dogmatics he had read
as a Privatdozent in 1839–40.[110] Schmid opposed Zeller on the
ground of his Hegelianism, and he was rejected by the Academic
Senate on February 25, 1841, although Baur had insisted that
Zeller was by no means a slavish disciple of Hegel, that indeed
his chief virtue was his scholarly freedom and integrity.[111] Two
other candidates for the position, Karl Ullmann and J. T. Beck,
were considered and rejected in 1841, until the call was finally
extended to M. A. Landerer, who accepted and was appointed
ordentlich professor in 1842.[112]

106 *Ibid.*
107 *Ibid.;* Baur to Heyd, 13 Feb. 1841 (U.B.T., Md 619r, 27).
108 Gutachten of 29 May 1839 (U.B.T., Md 750, v, 2).
109 Gutachten of 27 June 1839 (U.B.T., Md 750, v, 3).
110 Baur to L. F. Heyd, 13 Feb. 1841 (U.B.T., Md 619r, 27).
111 Gutachten of 12 Apr. 1841 (U.B.T., Md 750, v, 4).
112 Baur to L. F. Heyd, 16 June 1841 (U.B.T., Md 619r, 28); *Worte der
Erinnerung an J. T. Beck,* p. 24; Baur in Klüpfel, *op. cit.,* p. 424. Little is
known of the relation between Landerer and Baur, but apparently it was not
close. Shortly after the latter's death, Landerer delivered one of several
speeches in his honor. The speech was an essentially negative criticism of
Baur's treatment of Christianity as a "purely historical" phenomenon. Cf.
Worte der Erinnerung an Baur, pp. 32–83. As a representative of the Mediating Theology, Landerer sought to relate scientific study to the unchanged
content of the older dogmas; like Schleiermacher, he believed the absoluteness of Christianity to rest on the supernatural birth of Jesus, a position Baur

No sooner had Steudel's chair been permanently filled, however, than Baur's most trusted friend and colleague on the faculty, Kern, was suddenly taken ill and died in February 1842. The loss was a severe blow to Baur, who had known Kern since they were both students in the Maulbronn Seminary in 1807; they had been "yoked" together as teaching colleagues for twenty-six years, first in Blaubeuren, then in Tübingen. He was in Baur's judgment a teacher of clarity and critical content, an excellent lecturer, an earnest preacher, and a man of liberality and mildness.[113] Baur again proposed Zeller, who was no more acceptable to the educational ministry now than he had been a year before. The choice then settled between two candidates, Dorner (supported by Schmid) and J. T. Beck (supported by Baur). In its initial vote, the Academic Senate favored Dorner by two votes; but Baur apparently managed to reverse the decision by an opinion directed specifically to a criticism of Dorner's historical and theological method.[114] Although Beck's *heilsgeschichtlich* treatment of the Bible represented a rather different perspective than that of historical-critical theology, he was brought to Tübingen essentially through Baur's efforts, where he was appointed *ordentlich* professor in 1842. The two men lived and worked together in peace and friendship. Baur treasured not only Beck's originality and independence, but also his scientific sense, for the latter's "biblical realism" contained a critical as well as a positive element.[115] Indeed, in an analogous way, Baur's own approach to the Bible was positive as well as critical.

The contrast between the positive or constructive element in his own historical-critical studies of the New Testament writings and Strauss's "negative-critical" or "dialectical" method was one of Baur's chief concerns in the introduction to his *Kritische Untersuchungen über die kanonischen Evangelien* (1847). He also discussed two other methods earlier used for the study of the Gospels: the "dogmatic" approach (based on the theory of spiritual inspiration and later, verbal infallibility), and the "abstract literary" approach (represented by the theory of a "Proto-Gospel").[116] Historical-critical theology, on the other hand, considered the Gospels as historical-theological products and brought historical as well

rejected. Cf. *The New Schaff-Herzog Encyclopedia of Religious Knowledge*, Samuel M. Jackson, ed. (New York & London: Funk and Wagnalls, 1910), VI, 406–407.

113 Baur in Klüpfel, *op. cit.*, p. 425; Baur, ed., *Worte der Erinnerung an Dr. Friedrich Heinrich Kern* (Tübingen: L. F. Fues, 1842), pp. 7–28; and Baur to L. F. Heyd, 16 Jan. 1842 (U.B.T., Md 750, ii, 6, 30). Heyd also died in the same year.

114 Gutachten of 6 May 1842 (U.B.T., Md 750, v, 5). Cf. Baur in Klüpfel, *op. cit.*, p. 425.

115 *Die Religion in Geschichte und Gegenwart* (1st ed.; Tübingen: J. C. B. Mohr, 1909), I, 995; (2d ed., 1927) I, 844–45; (3d ed., 1957), I, 954. Cf. also *Worte der Erinnerung an J. T. Beck*, p. 24.

116 See below, pp. 151–56.

as literary criticism fully to bear upon them, as was done brilliantly and in pioneering fashion by this work. It was structured as a quest for the most historically authentic sources of knowledge about the ministry and teaching of Jesus.[117] Baur began at what he considered to be the furthest point, the Gospel of John, and then moved through Luke[118] and Mark before concluding with Matthew, which he judged to be the earliest of the Gospels and the one which contains the most reliable traditions about Jesus.[119]

The ministry and teaching of Jesus became the direct object of study for the first time in the introductory chapter of *Das Christenthum und die christliche Kirche der drei ersten Jahrhunderte* (1853). Jesus was studied at greater length in *Vorlesungen über neutestamentliche Theologie*, but, significantly, Baur never wrote a separate "life of Jesus."[120] In *Das Christenthum*, he explained the historical theologian's interest in Jesus as the founder of Christianity, in whose person and teaching Christianity has its "definite beginning," since it is in his life that the idea of reconciliation, as Baur understood it from Schleiermacher and Hegel, is fully realized, originally and definitively.[121] This book, which constituted the first volume of Baur's Church history, is generally regarded as his *magnum opus*, the culmination of his life's work. Dilthey, for example, writes:

It is Baur's maturest work. . . . [Earlier] as he explored the sources of Christian history, he was successful in making fruitful use of Hegel's methods and historical categories for the history of the Christian world-view. Now, deepening himself in the totality of the appearances of the life of Christianity, he took a new step. He let go of the categories which he had adopted from Hegel, not to return to the external and purely mechanical limitations of previous church histories, but to build out of the materials his own authentic historical categories for the sake of representing the different modes of expression of the world-historical power of Christianity. . . . This book is perhaps the most penetrating attempt ever made to comprehend an historical phenomenon through analysis of its essential forms of manifestation.[122]

---

117 Cf. *Kritische Untersuchungen über die kanonischen Evangelien, ihr Verhältniss zu einander, ihren Charakter und Ursprung* (Tübingen: L. F. Fues, 1847), p. 571.

118 The chapters on John and Luke, which constituted the greater bulk of the work, were revisions of earlier studies of these two Gospels, which appeared in the *Theologische Jahrbücher* in 1844 and 1846.

119 See below, pp. 212–20.

120 In the New Testament lectures he said that "it cannot be the task of New Testament theology to provide a critical history of the life of Jesus." *Vorlesungen über neutestamentliche Theologie*, F. F. Baur, ed. (Leipzig: Fues's Verlag, 1864), p. 85.

121 See below, pp. 221–37.

122 Wilhelm Dilthey, "Ferdinand Christian Baur," *Gesammelte Schriften*, Vol. IV: *Die Jugendgeschichte Hegels und andere Abhandlungen zur Geschichte des deutschen Idealismus* (2d ed.; Leipzig and Berlin: B. G. Teubner, 1925), pp. 429–30. Cf. also Otto Pfleiderer, *The Development of*

In the preface to the first edition of *Das Christenthum*, Baur himself acknowledged a broadening of interests, to consider for the first time the place of Church institutions, worship, ethics, and missionary activity in the life of the Church in addition to dogma, which had preoccupied him in the decade following *Die christliche Gnosis*.[123]

The most impressive single quality of the Church history as a whole was its attempt to provide an interpretation of the total historical development of the Church, an interpretation which was organic to the Church's historicity and illuminated the various periods through which it had passed. In this respect alone, Baur's work has never been paralleled. The development was understood in terms of the different modes of relation between the idea of the Church (the reconciliation of God and man through Jesus Christ) and the historical forms (dogma, institutions, worship, ethics, faith) in which the idea has been realized.[124] The categories for this interpretation were worked out in *Die Epochen der kirchlichen Geschichtschreibung*, which was published in 1852, the year prior to the first edition of *Das Christenthum*.[125] The *Epochen* was singularly important for a statement of Baur's mature historical method and theology of the Church, and its examination of various types of methods used in writing Church history has never been surpassed.[126]

Die christliche Kirche vom Anfang des vierten bis zum Ende des sechsten Jahrhunderts (Volume II of the total work) was published in 1859. Baur brought out a second, only slightly altered, edition of the first volume in 1860. In this year he also prepared Volume III, *Die christliche Kirche des Mittelalters*, the materials for which had been reworked for many years, for the press; but he died before it could be published. It appeared the next year, 1861, and in form and content was Baur's own work throughout. In 1862, Zeller edited and published Volume V, *Kirchengeschichte*

Theology in Germany Since Kant, and Its Progress in Great Britain Since 1825, J. Frederick Smith, trans. (London: Swan Sonnenschein & Co., 1890), pp. 287–88; and Zeller, *Vorträge und Abhandlungen*, pp. 426, 432.

[123] *Geschichte der christlichen Kirche*, Vol. I: *Das Christenthum und die christliche Kirche der drei ersten Jahrhunderte* (3d ed., ident. with the 2d ed.; Tübingen: L. F. Fues, 1863), p. vi (*The Church History of the First Three Centuries*, trans. from the 3d German ed. by A. Menzies, 2 Vols. [London & Edinburgh: Williams & Norgate, 1878–79], I, x).

[124] See below, pp. 121–24, 251–56.

[125] Prior to this date, an earlier version of *Die Epochen* served as an extended introduction to Baur's lectures in Church history, similar to the lengthy introduction to his lectures in history of dogma which was included in the posthumously published edition of the latter work. Cf. U.B.T., Mh II 166 h. Of course, the introduction to the Church history was thoroughly revised and expanded before being published as a separate volume; in particular the last section, containing Baur's categories for interpreting the historicity of the Church, was not found in earlier lecture manuscripts.

[126] Cf. Hirsch, *op. cit.*, V, 524; and below, pp. 150–60.

des neunzehnten Jahrhunderts, based on lectures given for the first time during the 1850's. Finally, in 1863, Baur's son, Ferdinand Friedrich, edited and published *Kirchengeschichte der neueren Zeit, von der Reformation bis zum Ende des achtzehnten Jahrhunderts,* as Volume IV of the total work. The basic lecture manuscripts employed for the printed edition predated 1845,[127] but it had been heavily revised during the author's subsequent use of it: it was interleaved with new sheets, there were numerous marginal corrections, some sections were crossed out and others added, etc. In addition, the major structural divisions of the work were imposed on it in F. F. Baur's hand. There is reason to believe that, had Baur lived, he would have completely rewritten this work for the press, bringing it into greater structural continuity with the earlier volumes.

F. F. Baur was also responsible for editing and publishing his father's *Vorlesungen über die christliche Dogmengeschichte* (three volumes in four parts, 1865–67). Baur lectured in the history of dogma a total of seventeen times during the thirty-four year period from 1826 to 1860. Although the editor gave no indication of the date of the manuscripts from which the printed edition was made, it is probable that they were written during the period between 1843 and 1847, just before Baur published the first edition of his *Lehrbuch der christlichen Dogmengeschichte* (1847).[128] If this dating is correct, the *Vorlesungen* cannot then be taken as representative in every respect of the latest stage in Baur's thinking, a point which is important for my later argument.

During the period when he was writing the Church history, Baur also continued his studies in New Testament and primitive Christianity with monographs in the *Theologische Jahrbücher* (to 1857) and the *Zeitschrift für wissenschaftliche Theologie* (from 1858 to 1860). The emphasis was on the refinement of the Pauline studies (resulting in a partial revision of *Paulus* and of lectures on Paul's theology in 1860), the clarification and refinement of his interpretation of the Johannine question and the Synoptic problem,

127 This can be determined by comparing the manuscript used for the press, U.B.T., Mh II 166 k, with notes of these lectures made by a student during the period 1843–45, Mh II 156, and with an earlier manuscript version of the material now found in Vols. I–III of the Church history, Mh II 166 h. F. F. Baur states in the preface that parts of these lectures remained unchanged from 1827–28, the first year they were given, but he does not indicate the date of the manuscript used for the press.

128 This period can be determined with reasonable certainty by comparing the structure and contents of (*a*) a set of student notes from Baur's lectures taken in 1842–43 (U.B.T., Mh II 154), (*b*) the first edition of the *Lehrbuch der Dogmengeschichte* (1847), (*c*) the second edition of the *Lehrbuch* (1858), (*d*) the printed edition of the *Vorlesungen* (published posthumously, 1865–1867), and (*e*) some of the manuscripts from which this printed edition was made (U.B.T., Mh II 166 m). All the evidence from this comparison points to the fact that the *Vorlesungen* manuscripts were written sometime between the student notes of 1842–43 and the first edition of the *Lehrbuch,* which came from the press in the fall of 1846.

and the historical investigation of Jesus (culminating in lectures on the teaching of Jesus and an article on Jesus' use of the title, "Son of Man," in 1860). Some of the most important later work on Jesus and Paul was contained in the *Vorlesungen über neutestamentliche Theologie*, lectures which were given during the years 1852–60 and were published posthumously by F. F. Baur in 1864. The section on the theology of Paul was newly reworked in 1860 and provides the only source for Baur's latest interpretation of the Apostle's thought, since the revision of the 1845 edition of *Paulus*, which was also under way at the time, had not reached the third and last part, where Baur examined Paul's theology. Mention should finally be made of *Die Tübinger Schule und ihre Stellung zur Gegenwart* (1859; 2d ed. 1860), a response to an attack by Gerhard Uhlhorn,[129] which contained an important summary of the aims, methods, and results of historical-critical theology and served as a fitting conclusion to Baur's life work.

Baur carried his heavy schedule of research, writing, lecturing, preaching, and administration without physical disability until the end. He had never been seriously ill until on July 15, 1860, he suffered a stroke which prevented all future lecturing. He partially recovered, but was afflicted with recurring eye-failure, a disability which weighed upon him heavily. On November 29, while attending a session of the Academic Senate, he suffered a second, more severe stroke, which brought his death on Sunday, December 2.[130] Burial followed on the fifth; the many who attended the funeral and followed the coffin to the grave testified, claims Zeller, not only to the teacher and scholar, but especially to the man, whose personal attributes aroused "the most general honor and love."[131]

In concluding this survey of Baur's life and works, a word should now be said about the man himself. He was, above all else, a dedicated critical scholar. The foundation of his speculative and interpretive genius was a relentless study of the texts. His capacity for sustained and exhaustive research is reflected in this rather dramatic example offered by Zeller: "Summer and winter he arose at 4:00 A.M., and in winter he customarily worked for several hours in an unheated room out of consideration for the servants, although on especially cold nights the ink froze; and thereafter the regular midday or evening walk was invariably the single long interruption in this scholarly day of work."[132]

[129] In "Die älteste Kirchengeschichte in der Darstellung der Tübinger Schule," *JDT*, III, 280–349.

[130] There is extant a letter to a friend and former student, Friedrich Theodor Vischer, written in an almost illegibly feeble hand on the morning of the fatal stroke, in which Baur expressed general dissatisfaction with his physical condition. Baur to F. T. Vischer, 29 Nov. 1860 (U.B.T., Md 750, ii, 8).

[131] Zeller, *ADB*, II, 174; and *Vorträge und Abhandlungen*, pp. 363, 371–72. Cf. also *Worte der Erinnerung an Baur*, p. 88.

[132] Zeller, *Vorträge und Abhandlungen*, p. 363. Baur's brother-in-law, Robert von Mohl, a jurist and from 1827 to 1846 a colleague at Tübingen, wrote of

With respect to the way in which his personal life was absorbed into his scholarly passion, both Dilthey and Zeller compared Baur with Kant. Dilthey, for example, writes: "[Baur] was of an wholly objective nature. Nothing in the way of personal necessities or struggles is to be noted in his investigations of Christianity. To study the nature and history of Christianity moved him as a mighty *scientific problem* of the heart. . . . A strong sense of duty and a noble and ideal drive to do research—a drive which became a passion—ruled his mind. Like another great scholar who was exclusively moved by the work of his life, he was in his relations in life passionless, patient, almost conservative. . . ."[133] Similarly, Zeller describes Baur's total dedication to his material, his lack of concern with himself and his accomplishments, his totally unassuming nature, and the rigorous moral sensitivity and integrity which embodied and paralleled the qualitative level of his historical investigations. The work and the person were one.[134]

Baur's letters to Heyd and to his brother were filled mostly with scholarly matters. However, one receives the impression from them of a man of deep sensitivity, rigorous integrity, disarming modesty, and genuine good will. He was also a devoted husband and father, and the letters from 1824 to about 1840, during the period when his wife was alive and his family gathered together, contained many references to them. Following that, his life seems to have been caught up more completely in his work.

Baur possessed a mind of originality, independence, and self-criticism. Although he learned deeply from many sources, his was too restless, independent, and creative a spirit to be made the disciple of any school or philosophy. He was never satisfied with the results attained; he tested every new claim and presupposition and used every discovery as a step for further investigation. He always remained a student, willing to learn anew and ready to correct or discard his own results when convinced of their inaccuracy.[135] His love for truth never let him shrink back from results attained through honest research. Dilthey is right in claiming that he allowed the positive religious convictions of his youthful years to remain standing exactly so far as scientific historical research had not demonstrated their untenability[136]—again a mark of the unity existing between the man and his work, a unity which excluded the compartmentalization of religious belief and critical research.

He was as critical of his contemporaries as he was of himself. He possessed remarkable perspective by which to judge the impli-

---

him that, of all the men he knew, Baur was the least experienced in mundane, practical matters and was a "true child" in daily life. He conformed to the typical picture of a German scholar. *Lebenserinnerungen von Robert von Mohl* (1902), I, 192 (quoted in K. Bauer, *op. cit.*, p. 312).

133 Dilthey, *op. cit.*, pp. 413–14. Italics his.
134 Zeller, *Vorträge und Abhandlungen*, pp. 372, 374.
135 Cf. *ibid.*, pp. 374, 428–29.
136 Dilthey, *op. cit.*, p. 414.

cations and significance of contemporary theological tendencies; his lectures on nineteenth-century Church history contained some brilliant insights. No theological contemporary was exempted from his critical acumen. Every theological assertion, every historical interpretation, every methodological procedure was carefully scrutinized, probed for its strengths and weaknesses. He also became caught up in the controversies of his time, especially as they centered on his own work; and when he encountered bigotry and illiberalism he responded sharply, unsympathetically, and impatiently. There was a tinge of hypersensitivity and of hypercriticism in some of his writings. But he became milder as the years wore on, and his polemic was always directed at the material, never the person.[137]

Beyond the critical passion, Baur was possessed of a quiet confidence that Christian truth and the shape of the historical past, whatever it should prove to be, are congruent; in other words, that Christian truth is mediated by the historically real. To the unshakable historical and religious scepticism of Dilthey, this attitude was both peculiar and enviable: "No subjective passionateness drove him to an utterance on questions on which the peaceful light of his research had not yet fallen; the darkness in which he let them remain was not that of scepticism but of a peaceful preliminary acknowledgement."[138] Thus Baur felt that Christianity would not suffer from the critical investigation of its origin and history; rather, its true nature—its divine-human reality—would thereby be brought to light. For him there was no contradiction between religious piety and critical objectivity; these attitudes were two sides of the same coin. Truth was a matter of both heart and head. The historical and religious truth of Christianity was the most important single question for Baur, personally, and his own attitude toward this question was profoundly positive, not negative.[139] This attitude was revealed by the words with which for many years he concluded his lectures in Church history, words addressed directly to his students:

Whoever is convinced of the divine Spirit of Christianity will also be convinced that all free movements must eventually, as our own time shows, lead back to the acknowledgment of the one God. . . .

May this be the impression with which the whole image of the preceding ages stands before your minds, and may this also draw you for the future to the science [Church history] with which your first acquaintance has now been completed. May this be the impression with which you come down the common path out of the dark night of the centuries to the splendid morning of your own lives and see yourselves now placed at the point at the end of the long course at

137 Cf. Zeller, *Vorträge und Abhandlungen*, p. 367, 373.
138 Dilthey, *loc. cit.*
139 Cf. Pfleiderer, "Zu Baur's Gedächtnis," *PK*, XXXIX:25, 572.

which you yourselves may enter as actual members into the living
sphere of activity of the Christian Church, the point at which each
may see himself called to contribute his own gift, according as he
has seen what has been done by others before him, also on his own
part, according to the measure of his power and knowledge, his love
and spirituality, to the great structure [of the Church]! To bring before
you and to leave with you such an impression was at the very least
the desire and the attempt by which above all I have been guided
in these lectures.[140]

Those who studied under Baur testified to his greatness as a
teacher more in terms of the impact of his personality than of
special capacities as a speaker. Zeller writes that there were no
spectacular effects in his lectures and that he never spoke extem-
poraneously; he worked from a carefully prepared manuscript
which he closely followed in early years and from which he only
gradually freed himself.[141] But his listeners had the impression
that before them stood a man who truly lived in the material and
let it speak for itself, that everything he said was "the expression
of an innermost, duly acquired conviction, the result of a consci-
entious search for the truth."[142] His eloquence was in the quality
and integrity of his historical analysis. Most important "was the
fact that one could participate in the spiritual work of a teacher
who until the end of his life remained and intended to remain a
student himself."[143] By virtue of his scholarly and personal integrity he exerted an influence on students, Pfleiderer remarks,
"of the depth and intensity of which the present generation can
form no idea."[144] Dilthey's brief if perhaps extravagant words are
the most expressive: "He was the greatest theologian of our century. He was a man of great character and a scholar in the grand
style, both in *a single* person."[145]

140 *Geschichte der christlichen Kirche*, Vol. IV: *Kirchengeschichte der
neueren Zeit, von der Reformation bis zum Ende des achtzehnten Jahrhunderts*, F. F. Baur, ed. (Tübingen: L. F. Fues, 1862), pp. 678–79.
141 Zeller, *Vorträge und Abhandlungen*, p. 376.
142 Lang, "Baur und Strauss," *Von und aus Schwaben*, III, 8.
143 Zeller, *Vorträge und Abhandlungen*, p. 377.
144 Pfleiderer, *The Development of Theology in Germany*, p. 233.
145 Dilthey, *op. cit.*, p. 431. Italics his.

2 * THE NEED FOR AN HISTORICAL THEOLOGY

THE THEOLOGICAL SITUATION IN THE EIGHTEENTH AND NINETEENTH CENTURIES

Baur's understanding of the purpose and significance of historical-critical theology is shaped by his analysis of the theological situation of his own time. In his judgment, the "modern" or contemporary period in Protestant theology has its beginning around the middle of the eighteenth century, when the Protestant conception of "faith," understood as an act of religious consciousness which mediates authentically between the objective truth of the Gospel and the subjectivity of human spirit,[1] is brought for the first time into a productive encounter with critical or "scientific" thought, both historical and philosophical. Three subdivisions within the modern period can be distinguished according to different ways in which this encounter was realized.[2]

The first of these divisions dates from about 1750 to 1815 and can be characterized as a period of "revolution" because of the theological crisis and transformation occasioned by the challenge of rationalism and the impact of historical-critical study for the first time on the biblical documents. The second period, from 1815 to 1830, is one of reaction and synthesis or mediation—reaction

---

[1] See below, pp. 175, 255–56.

[2] In Baur's analysis, the "modern" period (1750 to about 1850) is the second of two periods in post-Reformation Church history and history of dogma. The first is that of old Protestantism or Protestant scholasticism, which runs from the end of the Reformation to the beginning of the eighteenth century. The first half of the eighteenth century marks a transition between old and modern Protestantism. Cf. *Kirchengeschichte*, IV, vii, ix–xx, 476, 572; and *Vorlesungen über die christliche Dogmengeschichte*, F. F. Baur, ed., Vol. III: *Das Dogma der neueren Zeit* (Leipzig: Fues's Verlag, 1867), pp. 298–99. The lectures on which the former work is based originally carried the history of the Church through the third decade of the nineteenth century, until they were replaced in the 1850's by a new series of lectures on the nineteenth century. It was in this new series that the further division of the modern period into three parts was first made; cf. *Kirchengeschichte*, V, 3–9.

to the extremes of Protestant rationalism, for which the objective historical norms of Christian thought were largely submerged or transformed by subjective rationalistic criteria, and attempted synthesis or mediation between the requirements of critical, speculative reason on the one hand and the positivity of the Christian Church, its Gospel, and its theology, on the other. The two great figures in this period are Schleiermacher and Hegel.[3] Great and unequaled though their intellectual achievements are, they fail to produce a completely satisfactory synthesizing theology. With respect to faith and critical historical knowledge, the mediation between them is imperfect because of the failure of this period to argue along historical-critical lines for the historicity of the Gospel and the Church (it rather attempts a *speculative* demonstration of the necessity of certain historical events), and because of its "Gnostic" tendency toward historical docetism (thus precluding, among other things, the possibility of an authentic connection between the ideal and the historical).

The third period in "modern" theology, from about 1830 through the middle of the century, represents a falling apart of the attempted synthesis and in one form or another rejects as untenable all attempts to mediate between faith and truly critical thought, thus repudiating, in Baur's judgment, the peculiarly historical quality of faith which is the Protestant heritage.[4] This dissolution is marked by the disintegration of the Hegelian school into right and left wings, the negative results of Strauss's methodologically invalid historical criticism, the failure of the Mediating theologians and New Testament scholars to further the work of Schleiermacher, Hegel, and "scientific" theology, and the revival of Protestant conservatism in the forms of Confessionalism and Orthodoxy. In this context, only historical-critical theology would

---

3 In *Kirchengeschichte*, V, Hegel's thought is actually not considered until the beginning of the third period, since it was not until after his death in 1831 that his influence was really felt in theological circles. In 1832 the posthumous publication of his lectures began. But his thought clearly belongs to the second period, bringing it to a climax and anticipating, by virtue of the ambiguity in the direction of his Christology, the dissolution to follow. Thus, in a sense Hegel marks the transition between the two periods while also standing in the second. In *Kirchengeschichte*, V, there is a curious neglect of Hegel, who is referred to as the most important philosopher of the day— "next to the presently disregarded . . . Schelling" (p. 348). In this work, Baur devotes only eight pages to Hegel (less space than that given to Kant, Fichte, or Schelling), while Schleiermacher receives fifty-three pages. In the lectures on history of dogma, Hegel receives much more attention; but these lectures are based on manuscripts which date from an earlier period than the lectures in nineteenth-century Church history (see above, p. 32). Whatever the reasons for this later neglect of Hegel, we are forced to draw our materials for Baur's analysis of his thought from other sources than *Kirchengeschichte des neunzehnten Jahrhunderts*.

4 This interpretation, which is fully developed in *Kirchengeschichte*, V, is anticipated as early as 1836 in a letter to F. A. G. Tholuck (U.B.T., Md 750, ii, 9, 1), and in Baur's Gutachten of 27 June 1839 (U.B.T., Md 750, v, 3).

appear to answer the real theological need of the day (although Baur never directly makes this claim), by furthering more adequately the mediation between faith and historical science already anticipated but never realized in the second period. Baur believes this mediation to be a possibility because—and here he proves himself to be a true representative of the nineteenth century—there is ultimately no necessary hostility between the Church and the world, between the faith of the Church and the critical-speculative "sciences" of the world. For what constitutes the "idea" of the Church—the reconciliation of God and man—can be and is also present in the life of the world, indeed as the substance of the world's life.[5] The truth of faith and the truth of thought are ultimately one, in content, if not in form.

The task now is to examine the thesis outlined above by studying in greater detail Baur's interpretation of the course of theology in the modern period. I shall concentrate on his analysis of and relation to his most important contemporaries, especially Schleiermacher, Hegel, and Strauss. What follows is essentially a presentation of Baur's interpretation, although I shall occasionally offer critical comments regarding the accuracy of his insights.

FIRST PERIOD: RATIONALISM

General Characteristics of Protestant Rationalism

Baur's analysis of the period of Protestant rationalism, which he regards as the product of a spiritual revolution in the life of the German nation in the eighteenth century, related to but not specifically within the German Lutheran Church,[6] focuses on two major considerations. The first is his conviction that theological rationalism authentically embodies the material principle of the Reformation—the primacy of faith and free subjectivity in the actualization of the Christian Gospel[7]—so that there is a genuine continuity between old and new forms of Protestantism. The second is that the mutual relationship between theology and philosophy which had become a possibility when the Reformation secured the freedom of philosophical thought from dogmatic limitations, reaches a certain completion in this period. In both considerations, there is the potential danger that subjective rationalism will absorb the objective content and historical positivity of Christian theology. We shall examine Baur's interpretation of the second factor—the relationship between theology and philosophy—in the

---

[5] *An Herrn Dr. Karl Hase. Beantwortung des Sendschreibens "Die Tübinger Schule"* (Tübingen: L. F. Fues, 1855), pp. 102–103.

[6] See *Lehrbuch der Dogmengeschichte* (1st ed.), p. 243; *Kirchengeschichte*, IV, 611–12; *Kirchengeschichte*, V, 2, 39–40; and *Dogmengeschichte*, III, 18, 298–300.

[7] See below, pp. 255–56.

next chapter,[8] where it helps to illuminate his general understanding of the place of dogmatics in relation to religion and philosophy.

With respect to the first factor, Baur insists that the break with the old Protestant creeds in the eighteenth century is by no means complete, but that our relation to them is now different by virtue of the impact of free critical thought in their interpretation and appropriation.[9] Indeed, in the modern period (and this applies to the nineteenth century as well as to the eighteenth), the "Protestant principle" comes into its own in a way unparalleled since the Reformation itself, for it is now freed from the antirational bonds of the scholasticism of the sixteenth and seventeenth centuries. Thus, "the movement of dogma beginning anew in the eighteenth century is nothing other than the freer development of the Protestant principle, whose tendency is . . . always to comprehend itself more purely in the universality of its original idea. This is indeed the goal toward which Protestant theology in its most recent period of development has always more decisively striven."[10] The striving for self-consciousness and freedom of spirit which so penetrates theological rationalism is nothing other "than the return to the principle of Protestantism," the "innermost nature" of which is "the principle of autonomy, the liberation from and renunciation of everything wherein the self-conscious spirit cannot know its own specific nature and become one with itself."[11] The objective content of dogma is now mediated through and congruent with the subjective consciousness of the believer.

The investigations which led Baur to the conviction that a fundamental continuity exists between old and modern forms of Protestantism were first undertaken for his response to Möhler in *Der Gegensatz des Katholicismus und Protestantismus*. If Catholicism and Protestantism are not distinguished from the beginning according to their respective principles of heteronomy and autonomy (rather than according to Möhler's contrast between objective truth and arbitrary subjectivism), then Strauss would be right in claiming that Protestant orthodox theology is closer to Catholicism than it is to Protestant rationalism; and there would then be no defense against Möhler's charges respecting the nature of Protestantism.[12] In fact, Eduard Zeller is unhappy with Baur's attempt to bridge the gap between the Reformers on the one end and Schleiermacher and Hegel on the other. He is not convinced that the history of post-Reformation Protestantism holds together. He writes that, were he to have defended modern Protestantism against Möhler, he would have argued that it is an essentially new form of religious consciousness, necessitated by the spirit of the

8 See below, pp. 93–97.
9 *Dogmengeschichte*, III, 306.
10 *Lehrbuch der Dogmengeschichte* (1st ed.), pp. 244–45.
11 *Kirchengeschichte*, V, 40.
12 *Ibid.*, p. 313.

times, and that there are no essential connections between it and older Church doctrine, either Protestant or Catholic.[13] But it is clear that Baur's entire conception of the history of the Church's development is opposed to this attitude.

An important element in the rebirth of free subjectivity in eighteenth-century Protestantism is the rise of the historical-critical method. The very essence of criticism consists of a self-relatedness in freedom, whereby the interpreter obtains a definite point of orientation. It is a point which provides a criterion of interpretation free from the external authority of the old dogmas. But in this period of subjective rationalism, the interpreter is not free from his own subjectivity, not free to penetrate to the objective content of historical occurrences, which explains the limits and arbitrariness of historical criticism in the eighteenth century. Although criticism arises in the period of subjective idealism, it must move beyond this period in order to grasp and to interpret that which is real.[14]

Finally, Baur is aware of the danger in focusing exclusively on the subjectivity of religious experience. According to rationalism, in the conviction of one of its spokesmen, Lessing, the truth of the Christian religion is freed from all externals; it is immanent; its truth rests only in reason, and reason itself is purely subjective.[15] But to dissolve an historically mediated faith into subjective rational truth is to vitiate not only the heritage of Protestantism but of the Christian Church as a whole, throughout its entire history. Thus, while retaining the authentic emphasis on free subjectivity in the theological Enlightenment and its striving for an internal congruence between faith and reason, it is necessary to press on to an awareness of the objectively historical content of Christian faith without returning to the old supernaturalism. Religion exists at the point of congruence of authority and freedom; we shall return to this view of religion, and to Baur's understanding of the distinction between religion and philosophy, in Chapter III.[16]

The Christology of Rationalism

The danger of subjectivism is most apparent, according to Baur, in the Christology of the Enlightenment theologians, a danger anticipated by the abandonment of the doctrine of the *communicatio idiomatum* in the dogmatics of Protestant scholasticism, which led to an almost exclusive emphasis on the humanity of Jesus and to a loss of the reality of the incarnation. This point

---

[13] Eduard Zeller, "Ferdinand Christian Baur," *Vorträge und Abhandlungen*, pp. 397–99.

[14] *Dogmengeschichte*, III, 306. See below, pp. 153–56.

[15] *Ibid.*, p. 312.

[16] See below, pp. 93–97, 127–31.

of view is taken over decisively by the rationalist dogmaticians (e.g., von Gabler, Ammon, de Wette), with the consequence that the divinity attributed to Christ is for them at best an "empty representation," a subjective appearance, or an aesthetic or moral ideal which as the infinite Ought never existed in reality. The founder of Christianity becomes a hero of humanity and a purely human phenomenon; everything else in the Gospel stories is regarded as a mythical product of the authors. In this and other respects, the true antecedents of Strauss are to be found in the rationalists, not Hegel.[17]

The Christology of the rationalist dogmaticians is taken up and brought to its completion, according to Baur, by Kant. In this as in so many other respects, Kant's philosophy is the first to bring to full consciousness the tendency and spirit of his time; in his thought the strengths and limitations of theological rationalism are fully realized.[18] For Kant, the whole process of atonement, when the allegorical form is unclothed, falls into the sphere of moral consciousness or intentionality. The raw subjectivism of the pre-Kantian rationalists is thus seemingly exchanged for a new kind of objectivity, since the reality of reconciliation is grounded in the universal, necessary, and objective principles of practical reason; it resides in the absolute idea of moral freedom and the possibility of an implicitly good intention conditioned by this idea. But in fact the Kantian viewpoint is unable to shake off its subjectivist character. For the objectivity of reconciliation resides only in the objectivity of an ideal, which remains unobtainably distant and never achieves historical reality.[19] Thus the "Christ," or the "Son of God," remains an ideal in the moral consciousness of mankind and can never be realized in an historically decisive (if not absolute) fashion in a single, definite individual. All the predicates applied to the Son of God in orthodox Church doctrine really refer to the ideal of moral perfection; and God himself is only the idea of the moral world-rule. To the question whether the speculative idea of the God-man can be identified in any sense with the historical individual in whom theology sees the unity of God and man realized, Kant—and with him, Schelling —replies "No."[20] Kant does not deny the bare factuality of the historical Jesus and his death on a cross. But he sees a purely external and accidental connection between the forgiveness of sins and this death; it parallels the external connection between the thing in itself (der Ding an sich) and its image (Bild). This image (namely, the historical death of Jesus) actually represents the

17 *Dogmengeschichte*, III, 516–22.

18 *Ibid.*, pp. 333–34. Cf. the similar judgment of Karl Barth: "It was in this man and in this work that the eighteenth century saw, understood and affirmed itself in its own limitations." *From Rousseau to Ritschl*, Brian Cozens, trans. (London: SCM Press, 1959), p. 150.

19 *Versöhnung*, pp. 580–84.

20 *Dogmengeschichte*, III, 523–26.

sensualizing of the moral idea.[21] If one can talk about the necessity of the death of Jesus at all, it is a rational necessity which man can find only in himself.[22] Even when Kant attempts to regard the history of Christianity as the objective mediation of rational faith, he comes to the conclusion that the whole course of the Christian Church has only a corrupting effect on the purely rational idea of atonement, and he concludes his *Religion innerhalb der Grenzen der blossen Vernunft* with a completely irreconcilable opposition between the objectivity of history and the subjectivity of the idea of atonement.[23]

The theologians who follow Kant and write under his influence (Tieftrunk, Stäudlin, Schmid, Daub, Röhr, Wegscheider, and others) are unable to reproduce the moral depth of his Christology and his striving for an objective—albeit abstract and historically unrealized—conception of moral freedom in relation to God. Fichte, especially, accentuates the subjectivity of Kant's critical idealism. He speaks more sharply against the positive content of religion than anyone else of his time; although, says Baur, his position is already fully anticipated in Kant's *Religion*.[24] This is the theological situation at the end of the first period in modern theology. It is suddenly transformed by the appearance of Schleiermacher's *Glaubenslehre* in 1821.

SECOND PERIOD: SCHLEIERMACHER AND HEGEL

Schleiermacher

Schleiermacher's "Ideal Rationalism." Although rationalism had probed the subjective elements in religious experience and been richly productive of philosophical ideas, it had at the same time been indifferent, in Baur's words, to "everything positive and ecclesiastical."[25] The beginning of the second period in modern theology is marked by a change in this attitude and by the beginning of an effort to relate the positive (i.e., concretely historical) and ecclesiastical content of Christianity to the criteria of reason and religious consciousness. However, the two elements in this relationship are not "internally mediated" but rather brought together artificially or externally.[26] Hence, in terms of the relation between

21 *Versöhnung*, pp. 592–93.

22 *Ibid.*, pp. 605–608.

23 *Ibid.*, p. 630. Baur contrasts this position with Schleiermacher's completely different estimation of the historical, mediatorial function of the Church.

24 *Dogmengeschichte*, III, 337; and *Kirchengeschichte*, V, 174–78.

25 *Kirchengeschichte*, V, 112–13.

26 *Ibid.*, p. 174. In the Catholic Church there is no question of a mediation at all but rather of a "restoration" of the old order. *Ibid.*, pp. 112, 175. The German Catholic Church alone has felt—if only slightly and temporarily—the impact of theological enlightenment, idealism, and historical criticism in such centers as Tübingen, Bonn, Munich, and Freiburg. See *ibid.*, IV, 570, and V, 310.

faith and historical knowledge, the mediation tends to break down in the direction either of a subjective or abstract idealism, which is unable to account for the necessity or reality of the historical, or of a return to a supernatural conception of historical revelation, which not only destroys the subjective freedom and rationality of faith but also vitiates the historical itself. The latter represents the failure, for example, of the "rational supernaturalism" of Baur's former teacher, Ernst Gottlieb Bengel. A truly internal mediation is achieved for the first time by Schleiermacher's *Glaubenslehre*, which ends the old and fruitless debate between rationalism and supernaturalism by providing new categories and a new starting point for theological knowledge, while at the same time it restores the Church to its rightful place as the historical mediator of Christian faith.

In his inaugural dissertation, *Primae Rationalismi et Supranaturalismi*, Baur distinguishes between two types of rationalism: "ordinary rationalism," the rationalism of the *Aufklärung*, which is based solely on the authority and autonomy of reason; and "ideal rationalism," which is based on "historical forms proper to supernaturalism" as well as on the facts of consciousness and the ideas of reason, such that the latter cannot appear apart from a temporal-historical course of development.[27] It is as an expression of "ideal rationalism," which is the characteristic form of Christian philosophy of religion or "Gnosticism," that Schleiermacher's *Glaubenslehre* provides the most complete and successful attempt at mediation between the supernaturalism of the old Church doctrines and the claims of reason. In this respect, the *Glaubenslehre* is a masterful and epoch-making work; yet, in so far as it attempts to couch the claims of Christian faith for a positive and historically mediated authority in *supernatural* terms, the mediation between faith and reason cannot be perfect and eventually will fall apart.[28] An authentic mediation will have to renounce a supernatural conception of historical events.

Whereas the previous attempts at mediation had favored the rational side of Christianity, Schleiermacher's at first appears to favor the supernatural.[29] He claims to be completely independent of philosophical presuppositions and to base his *Glaubenslehre* solely on the doctrinal creeds of the Reformed and Lutheran Churches. Although on the one hand Christianity represents a natural form of human development, on the other it occupies such a high and peculiar level of that development that it differs from all that goes before it not only relatively and gradually but also

[27] "Anzeige der beiden academischen Schriften," *TZT*, I, 223.

[28] *Kirchengeschichte*, V, 182. Cf. *Dogmengeschichte*, III, 341–43; and *Versöhnung*, p. 626.

[29] On Baur's understanding of the term "supernatural," and his rejection of "supernaturalism," see above, p. 5, n. 13, and below, pp. 190–96, esp. pp. 192–93.

essentially and specifically; its "natural form is at the same time supernatural." In the absolute and wholly peculiar significance which it attributes to the historical Jesus, in its complete identification of him with the idea of redemption, so that he differs qualitatively from all other human beings, this *Glaubenslehre* shows that its rationalism is not of the "ordinary" variety. Yet it remains a rationalism, since the redemptive peculiarity it attributes wholly, absolutely, supernaturally to Jesus can and must be understood from within the inner nature of the human spirit.[30]

It would in fact be a great mistake to suppose that Schleiermacher's "ideal rationalism" is fundamentally supernaturalistic, or that Schleiermacher intended to preserve the supernatural mode of perception along with the substance of Church doctrine.[31] For the *Glaubenslehre* possesses a speculative foundation, despite Schleiermacher's protestations to the contrary.[32] This foundation is Spinoza's conception of the immanence of God and the world, a conception which, in Baur's view, is "scarcely to be avoided in the modern view of the world," although Schleiermacher does not share Spinoza's notion of absolute substance, nor is he to be regarded as a "pantheist," at least in the same sense Spinoza is.[33] For a theory of immanence such as that appropriated by Schleiermacher, the ordinary distinctions between natural and supernatural disappear: that which is apparently supernatural is at the same time natural because of the broadened conception of the natural in its congruence, but not identity, with the divine. The conse-

[30] *Kirchengeschichte*, V, 183; and "Anzeige der beiden academischen Schriften," *TZT*, I, 224–25.

[31] *Kirchengeschichte*, V, 183–84. Baur suggests that Schleiermacher speaks as though he regards the Gospel accounts of the birth, resurrection, and ascension as descriptions of supernatural events because he wants to let his *Glaubenslehre* appear more orthodox than it really is. *Ibid.*, p. 188.

[32] Baur first makes this charge in his inaugural dissertation of 1827, to which Schleiermacher replies in his second *Sendschreiben an Lücke*, 1829. In the reply he argues that, although a true philosopher can be and remain a true believer, both piety and philosophy can exist without the other. This remains the case with his *Glaubenslehre*, wherein, despite his "philosophical dilettantism," his maxim remains the same: no influence from philosophy on the *content* of dogmatics. This maxim is necessary because unfortunately the relation between philosophy and religion has not been a happy and free one. Whether he has succeeded in this is another question (one he does not argue), although this has been his goal. *Schleiermachers Sendschreiben über seine Glaubenslehre an Lücke*, Hermann Mulert, ed. (Giessen: Alfred Töpelmann, 1908), pp. 65–68. Schleiermacher defends himself only indirectly by arguing that the introduction to the *Glaubenslehre*, in which philosophical considerations are definitely present, does not contribute anything to the *dogmatic content* of the work. *Ibid.*, pp. 54–56. For Baur's rejoinder to this defense in *Die christliche Gnosis*, see below, p. 47.

[33] *Dogmengeschichte*, III, 344–46; Baur to L. F. Heyd, 17 Dec. 1826 (U.B.T., Md 750, ii, 6, 7). Baur, of course, shares this Spinozistic conception of immanence with Schleiermacher. It serves as the speculative foundation for his historical-critical theology. He learned it prior to and apart from Hegel, although Hegel's view is certainly co-ordinate with it. See below, pp. 134–42.

quence of this view is that "absolute miracle, miracle in the proper sense of the word, is abolished," since there is no longer the need for a miraculous (i.e., nonnatural, nonhistorical) conception of the mediation of the divine. This mediation becomes natural, historical, without on the one hand losing its revelatory capacity or on the other returning to an ordinary rationalism which excludes entirely the transcendent and the objective by virtue of its subjectivism. Absolute miracle, suggests Baur, is the most immediate consequence of ordinary or traditional theism. If God is thought of as an extraworldly absolute will, one must give a practical proof of this will in the world, which consists in demonstrating that an exclusively transcendent principle breaks into the course of the world; this can happen only supernaturally, miraculously. But the speculative basis of Schleiermacher's *Glaubenslehre* is not that of ordinary theism.[34]

In his inaugural dissertation, Baur argues that the basic mark of Schleiermacher's "ideal rationalism" is that the first of the three dogmatic forms (the feeling of absolute dependence or of God-consciousness as a mode of self-consciousness) provides the foundation for the second and the third (Church-world and God) and thus of the *Glaubenslehre* as a whole.[35] The potentiality for pious God-consciousness is there as a kind of primal human possibility before it is excited or actualized by the believing community.[36] The individual precedes the community, and thus also the historical Jesus, as the norm for Christian faith. If only those sentences constitute the authentic content of Christian dogmatics which describe the inner condition of the soul and which proceed directly from self-consciousness, then it is difficult to see how the historical and ecclesiastical character of Christianity is an essential and necessary part of this *Glaubenslehre*, whose historical side is greatly subordinated to the philosophical and the idealistic.[37]

Schleiermacher replies to this criticism by asserting that it is illegitimate to make judgments about the *dogmatic* foundation of the *Glaubenslehre* on the basis of material found in the introduction, whose purpose is only to assign Christianity its appropriate place among the different possible modifications of the common human consciousness.[38] In response, Baur rejects the notion that

34 *Dogmengeschichte*, III, 345; *Kirchengeschichte*, V, 184; *Lehrbuch der Dogmengeschichte* (1st ed.), p. 257; *Die christliche Gnosis*, p. 641.

35 In this respect Baur compares the structure of Schleiermacher's dogmatic system with that of Origen's *De principiis*. *Lehrbuch der christlichen Dogmengeschichte* (3d ed., identical with the 2d; Leipzig: Fues's Verlag [L. W. Reisland], 1867), p. 77.

36 Here Baur cites §§ 3–5 from the introduction to the second edition of the *Glaubenslehre*.

37 "Anzeige der beiden academischen Schriften," *TZT*, I, 244–47. Essentially the same argument is repeated elsewhere by Baur, e.g., in *Versöhnung*, pp. 631–32, and in *Lehrbuch der Dogmengeschichte* (1st ed.), p. 257.

38 Schleiermacher, *Sendschreiben an Lücke*, pp. 54–56.

the introduction is not a part of the dogmatics, since the whole content of the introduction is ordered under and defended by the three forms of dogmatics: self, God, world. The very purpose Schleiermacher attributes to the introduction, that of assigning to Christianity its appropriate place among the different possible modifications of consciousness, depends on a particular dogmatic concept of piety; and the assignment itself depends on "the redemption accomplished by Jesus of Nazareth" as that which alone distinguished Christianity from other religions. Schleiermacher clearly states, in the introduction and elsewhere, that the second and third dogmatic forms, the world and God, are functions of the first. This means that the archetypal or ideal Christ (the subjective experience of redemption) is prior to and determinative of the historical Jesus, who, as the founder of the community, can only be introduced in conjunction with the Church as the second dogmatic form (the constitution of the world in relation to redemption). Jesus himself, his person and work, are treated directly as functions of pious consciousness. The basic defect of the *Glaubenslehre* is that Schleiermacher nowhere explains how he moves from the first to the second form, or from the consciousness of redemption to an historical individual. "With what right, therefore, does this dogmatics regard its Christ as at the same time historical when it represents him as archetypal?"[39]

Critique of Schleiermacher's Christology: Failure to Mediate between the Ideal Christ and the Historical Jesus. The basic problem in Schleiermacher's Christology, as Baur sees it, is that the *Glaubenslehre* does not *start* with the historical Jesus, in terms of a critical analysis of the Gospel stories, where alone he can be found, and therefore never really succeeds in getting to him.[40]

[39] *Die christliche Gnosis*, pp. 647–52 (these pages represent a long footnote, devoted specifically to a response to Schleiermacher's defense in the second *Sendschreiben*). On a formal basis, it seems clear that Baur has the better of the argument. Schleiermacher does not develop a general theory of religion independently of his Christian dogmatic presuppositions. And in terms of the formal structure of the *Glaubenslehre*, sentences concerning the Church (and its founder, Jesus of Nazareth) can only be regarded as functions of pious self-consciousness. It can be argued, and perhaps rightly, that the *material* basis of this dogmatics lies in the eternal divine decrees which Schleiermacher draws from the Reformed creeds, and that he seriously intends that the historical Jesus, as the actualization of those decrees, should be the authoritative basis of Christian faith. He fully intends to, and in fact does —no matter how "desperately" (Barth)—get to the historical Jesus. The only question is how. Here Baur is quite right in pointing out that Schleiermacher cannot, on the basis of his formal dogmatic structure, answer that question satisfactorily. And since he cannot, he can hold the ideal and the historical Christ together only by fiat, not by exposition. The same problem would seem to plague the existentialist theology of Bultmann and others.

[40] Baur structures the problem this way as early as his inaugural dissertation of 1827. See "Anzeige der beiden academischen Schriften," *TZT*, I, 240–42.

He does start, as we have seen, with the archetypal or ideal Christ, with the idea of reconciliation or pious God-consciousness. This starting place is most clearly evident in Schleiermacher's *Weihnachtsfeier* (1806). Here the "ideal Christ" is defined as ideal or authentic humanity, true or universal manhood, "man-as-such" (*der Mensch an sich*), man reconciled with God, the "idea" of God-man unity. Men—factual, empirical men—will be redeemed only when *der Mensch an sich* "arises" in humanity, i.e., when mankind becomes authentically human in perfect reconciliation and unity with God. This happens in and through the Church as the community of reconciliation. Through this process, the ideal Christ as authentic manhood achieves factual, historical reality. The only problem is that in this work Schleiermacher does not show *how* "man-as-such" arises in humanity through the Church.[41]

Having started with the ideal Christ, Schleiermacher in his later work introduces the agent through whom the historical process of the realization of true manhood is initiated and fulfilled. He moves in his dogmatics from the ideal Christ to the historical Jesus in two ways. The first way is to argue both dogmatically and speculatively—in both cases, nonhistorically—that the ideal Christ is *identical* with the historical Jesus in such a way that the whole ideality of reconciliation is completely actualized in this one man and that the historical appearance and person of Jesus must be regarded as miraculous and supernatural. With Schleiermacher, the *dogmatic* argument predominates, whereas Hegel tries to establish the necessity of the historical Jesus primarily in a speculative way. The dogmatic argument is not so much an argument as it is an assertion of faith, namely, that God-consciousness is completely actualized in one historical figure, Jesus Christ, in a totally ahistorical fashion. This is the one miracle (in the "absolute" sense) which Schleiermacher allows, who in this respect remains loyal to the language and thought of orthodox Christology. Jesus Christ is a dogmatic truth and fact, not an historical one; he completely shatters historical categories.[42] The *speculative* argument is employed because Schleiermacher realizes that he can never provide historical proof for the absolute, primal, or achetypal God-consciousness of Jesus. He rather asserts, on what are in fact philosophical grounds, that "it was impossible to attain [the] higher life" of complete God-consciousness "out of the natural order which had its beginning in Adam." Our original capacity for God-consciousness was so weakened by sin that it could not be restored apart from a completely new act of creation, Jesus Christ, whose perfection is communicated to us.[43]

41 *Kirchengeschichte*, V, 211–12.
42 Cf. *Dogmengeschichte*, III, 354, 527; and *Versöhnung*, p. 620.
43 *Die christliche Gnosis*, pp. 638–42. The quotation from Schleiermacher is from *The Christian Faith*, trans. from the 2d German ed., H. R. Mackintosh and J. S. Stewart, eds. (Edinburgh: T. & T. Clark, 1928), § 89, p. 367.

According to Baur, this first group of arguments fails on three counts: (1) The miraculous identity of the ideal Christ with the historical Jesus cannot be established by dogmatic propositions;[44] nor is such a conception of the Redeemer compatible with the immanental world-view Schleiermacher shares with Spinoza. Such a world-view eliminates the disjunction between the natural and the supernatural so as to make it both possible and necessary to understand Jesus' redemptive significance in entirely historical categories. This is in fact what Schleiermacher does in the *Glaubenslehre*, where the focus is on Jesus as the first and most complete historical manifestation of pure God-consciousness and as the founder of the Christian community, and where Jesus' *supernatural* birth, resurrection, and ascension are matters of relative indifference.[45] (2) The speculative argument fails because on Schleiermacher's principles the ideal Christ possesses its reality apart from any outward historical expression. There is no speculative necessity that it be historically actualized in order to repair the supposed damage of sin, or that, if it is actualized, it be so archetypally in a single individual rather than in a multitude or indeed in the race as a whole.[46] (3) It is impossible for the idea of reconciliation (the ideal Christ) to be actualized archetypally in a *single* individual. Such an actualization would vitiate both the ideal, by causing it to be exhausted and relativized in a single instance, and the historical, by causing it to lose all connection with other historical events, thus shattering its historicity.[47] Baur suggests that Schleiermacher's Christology represents a new form of Arianism, since on the one hand it relativizes the idea by identifying it absolutely with a single individual, this being equivalent to a doctrine of radical subordinationism, and on the other it tends to exalt the historical manifestation of Jesus in such a way that a docetic figures emerges. The result is that Jesus is neither true God nor true man.[48] Schleiermacher thus fails to get to the authentic historical Jesus because of his illicit attempt to identify the idea of reconciliation archetypally with the historical Jesus; in his dogmatics the historical Jesus is not a *possibility*. We shall discover that the *way* in which Baur criticizes Schleiermacher at this point is of fundamental importance for the development of his own positive Christology.[49]

The second way Schleiermacher attempts to move from the ideal Christ to the historical Jesus is to argue from the effects of reconciliation in the religious life of the community to the cause. "The whole of Schleiermacher's Christology rests on the inference from

---

44 *Die christliche Gnosis*, pp. 653–55.
45 *Dogmengeschichte*, III, 528; and *Kirchengeschichte*, V, 186.
46 *Die christliche Gnosis*, pp. 646–55.
47 *Dogmengeschichte*, III, 531–32.
48 *Versöhnung*, p. 623.
49 See below, pp. 101–109.

effect to cause."[50] The effect of sinless God-consciousness is historically mediated by a community existing through time and must proceed from a single individual, who on the one hand possesses the sinlessness and perfection presupposed by the effect, and who on the other hand stands in such a relation to the community that he can mediate his personal attributes to it (i.e., he is its founder, and he is truly human so that there can be an authentic relation between him and us).[51] Baur acknowledges that Schleiermacher has correctly understood the historical relationship between the founder and the community. The only difficulty is that his argument is put "backward." To understand an historical process, one must start with its beginning point, in which the idea to be realized in the process is first clearly, definitely, and definitively expressed, not with its goal or its sequence of effects.[52] In the case of the experience of pious consciousness in the Christian community, there is no historical *necessity* that its ultimate cause be a *single* founder or that it be the *particular* founder claimed by Christian faith.

Baur's conclusion can be stated thus: in terms of the nature of Schleiermacher's argument from the ideal Christ to the historical Jesus, he fails to provide for the *possibility* of an authentically historical Jesus; in terms of the direction of the argument, he fails to provide for the *necessity* of the historical Jesus. On the one hand, he fails to explain correctly the relation between the ideal and the historical, a relationship in which they can *neither be separated nor totally identified.*[53] On the other hand, he does not realize that in order to get to the historical Jesus, one must *start* with him, and that means starting with the only historical sources available, the Gospels. Baur makes this fact abundantly clear in a statement from his inaugural dissertation, which describes *in nuce* what he later comes to regard as the Christological task of historical-critical theology: "Whether the person of Jesus of Nazareth really possesses the attributes which belong to the established concept of the Redeemer is in fact a purely historical question, which can be answered only through an historical investigation of the literary sources of the Gospel stories, sources which surely nowhere in the introduction to this Christian *Glaubenslehre* are brought forward as the proper sources of knowledge for Christianity."[54]

50 *Versöhnung*, p. 620.
51 *Dogmengeschichte*, III, 528–30.
52 See below, pp. 188–90.
53 See below, pp. 104–107.
54 Anzeige der beiden academischen Schriften," *TZT*, I, 242. For interpretations of Baur's criticism of Schleiermacher's Christology which differ in varying respects from the one presented above, the reader is referred to the following: Heinz Leibing, "Ferdinand Christian Baurs Kritik an Schleiermachers Glaubenslehre," *ZTK*, LIV:2, 236; Eberhard Pältz, "F. C. Baurs Verhältnis zu Schleiermacher," *TL*, LXXXI:9, 570–72; Zeller, *Vorträge und Abhandlungen*, pp. 389–90. Dilthey is right in suggesting that by freeing

Schleiermacher's Doctrine of the Church: Key to His Theological Genius. For the young Baur, the most exciting aspect of Schleiermacher's thought had been the primacy he afforded to religious consciousness as a new starting place for Christian dogmatics, one which could free the believer from the external authority of Protestant scholasticism.[55] Later the focus of his enthusiasm broadened. He writes, for example, that the section on the Church in the *Glaubenslehre* is "one of the most beautiful parts of the artistically ordered whole. In a *Glaubenslehre* whose principle is the Christian consciousness based on the Christian community, the doctrine of the Church must possess a wholly other significance and position than the supernaturalists and the rationalists could give it."[56]

Of crucial importance for Baur's development of his own theology of the Church, structured on the relationship between idea and manifestation,[57] is Schleiermacher's discussion of the relation between the invisible and the visible Church.[58] The institutions dealt with under "the essential and invariable features of the Church"—Holy Scripture, ministry of the Word, Baptism, Lord's Supper, power of the keys, and prayer—are the principle organs of the invisible Church, the instruments of the Holy Spirit, representing the power at work within the visible Church as the active, dynamic element in its historical life. But these spiritual institutions have no reality apart from historical embodiment, nor can the Church's historical life be isolated from these invisible institutions. The Church exists historically only at the point of congruence of invisible and visible elements. To account for its historical existence one cannot simply describe its outward and mutable structures—its plurality and fallibility—but must also take account of its inward and invisible elements. The implication this would seem to have for Baur is that the critical historian must under-

---

himself from the supernaturalism of Schleiermacher's God-man, Baur was able to leave the question as to who Jesus was up to "unprejudiced historical research," and that "this bold step cuts to the heart of Schleiermacher's system." Wilhelm Dilthey, "Ferdinand Christian Baur," *Gesammelte Schriften*, IV, 416.

Strauss appropriates Baur's criticism of Schleiermacher's Christology against Schleiermacher himself in *The Life of Jesus Critically Examined*, trans. from 4th German ed. by George Eliot (2d ed.; London: Swan Sonnenschein & Co., 1892), § 148, and against Hegel and the Right-Hegelians in *Streitschriften zur Vertheidigung meiner Schrift über das Leben Jesu und zur Charakteristik der gegenwärtigen Theologie* (new ed. in one vol.; Tübingen: C. F. Osiander, 1841), III, 68, 126. But Strauss draws from this criticism the opposite conclusion from that drawn by Baur: namely, that the historical Jesus has at best only an accidental connection with the ideal Christ.

[55] Cf. Baur to F. A. Baur, 26 July 1823 (U.B.T., Md 750, ii, 1, 1).

[56] *Dogmengeschichte*, III, 606.

[57] See below, pp. 121–24.

[58] Cf. *The Christian Faith*, § 148, pp. 676–81. The entire treatment of "the mutable element characteristic of the Church in virtue of its coexistence with the world," §§ 148–56, is relevant here.

stand the Church with respect to its "invisibility" as well as its "visibility," if he is to succeed in grasping the full historical reality which confronts him. But on the other hand he is not to confuse the invisible and the visible; they are distinct but not separable.[59]

The Church has a specific and very important function in Schleiermacher's theology. As we have already seen, the brilliance of the *Glaubenslehre* rests in the fact that it develops the whole content of Christian faith from the expressions of Christian consciousness. When Christian consciousness is thus set above even Scripture as the source of religious knowledge, then faith cannot be something merely externally given but has an inner point of contact in the consciousness of the believer. "Schleiermacher's *Glaubenslehre* has its great historical significance in the fact that it is the first thoroughgoing attempt to establish the content of the Christian faith as an original property of the human spirit, as something not brought into it externally but as something which has sprung forth from its innermost depths."[60] Contrary to the rationalist separation of reason and faith, for Schleiermacher the specific content of Christian faith already exists immanently in the consciousness of the subject and therefore is internally at one with reason by virtue of the fact that it is only a form and modification of a universal religious consciousness. "Christianity cannot contain what is not rational in itself."[61] But at the same time the definite and specific content of Christian consciousness is "mediated" through the "historically given" by the Church without conflicting with the "immediacy" of religious consciousness.[62] There must be a perfect congruence between that which is mediated historically and that which is possessed immediately or immanently, i.e., between authority and freedom—this is the genius of the Protestant conception of faith.

On the one hand, the Christian consciousness, as the principle of rational thought, has for its principle the "I" of self-consciousness; on the other it rests on the idea of the community, which belongs to the nature of religion. . . . The individual is determined in his religious consciousness through the community of which he is a member. The community stands over against subjective consciousness as the power of objectivity, as the sphere in which the religious consciousness and life of the individual alone possess their objective reality and truth. But the religious community has this objective meaning . . . only because the Spirit works in it. As the common Spirit forming the communal consciousness of the faithful, this Spirit is the Holy Spirit. If religious truth were not to become an historically given, objectively

---

59 Cf. *Dogmengeschichte*, III, 606–608.
60 *Kirchengeschichte*, V, 208.
61 *Ibid.*
62 *Ibid.*, p. 209. The verb used here by Baur for "mediation" is *mitteilen*, but he also uses *vermitteln*.

real truth through the power of this Spirit in the religious community, whose principle he is, then it would be valid for the believer only as something subjective, not as an objective truth.[63]

Thus the function of the Church, as Baur interprets Schleiermacher, is to serve as the historical mediation of that which is "objectively true" for Christian faith.

To serve this function properly, the Church must be adequately related to that objective or ideal truth which it mediates historically, and this mediation must be explained theologically. But this is where Schleiermacher fails: he lacks an adequate doctrine of God. The basic difficulty is that God is "for him the emptiest abstraction, only the point at which the different relations of the feeling of dependence have their final presupposition."[64] This abstraction is the result of the fact that Schleiermacher lacks an objective knowledge of God; God remains only an implicate of the subjective experience of dependence. Furthermore, the *Glaubenslehre* excludes the notion of the personality of God. For, "personality exists only where Spirit distinguishes itself as subject from objectivity or from its other";[65] whereas for Schleiermacher the totality of being is simply observed as "God" in its unity and as "world" in its multiplicity. There is no doctrine of internal relations, and thus no notion of God as Spirit or as triune.[66] The Holy Spirit is understood only as the common Spirit of the community, not as the objective Spirit of God, related internally to the Father and the Son. This means that the community, the Church, of which the Spirit is the principle, is not after all objectively grounded in the being of God, but has its reality only in a common Spirit, which is the collective consciousness of the faithful, the Spirit of humanity in its authentic self-consciousness or subjectivity.

Therefore, although Schleiermacher strives for objectivity in his doctrine of the Church, we return to the fact that the pious God-consciousness of the individual is the real center of his thought, not the piety transmitted from the Mediator through the community. The Holy Spirit as the common Spirit of the community certainly has as his presupposition for Schleiermacher the being of God in Jesus Christ. But Schleiermacher is unable to explain this presupposition because of his failure to start with the historical Jesus and because of his abstract, empty, subjective conception of God, which excludes any understanding of the relation betweeen Son and Spirit.[67] It also excludes a theological understanding of

[63] *Ibid.* For the above exposition, see also *Dogmengeschichte*, III, 351–52, and *Versöhnung*, pp. 630–31.

[64] *Dogmengeschichte*, III, 346; cf. p. 352, and *Lehrbuch der Dogmengeschichte* (1st ed.), p. 257.

[65] "Persönlichkeit ist nur, wo sich der Geist als Subject von der Objectivität, oder dem Anderen seiner, unterscheidet." *Kirchengeschichte*, V, 203.

[66] *Ibid.*

[67] *Ibid.*, pp. 209–211; and *Versöhnung*, pp. 631–33.

the historical process itself, which remains for Schleiermacher only a necessary presupposition of Christian consciousness and cannot be elucidated. It is primarily in this respect that Hegel's doctrine of God represents an important advance beyond Schleiermacher's theology, which remains ultimately unable to explain the mediation between subjectivity and objectivity, freedom and authority, which his doctrine of the Church presupposes.

The necessary progression from Schleiermacher to Hegel is that the historical process, which is merely presupposed by Schleiermacher and is left entirely undetermined with respect to its beginning and end points, is comprehended in its principle and is transposed into the nature of God himself. The historical process, in which Christianity comes to historical manifestation, is simply an element of the general process which is the life-process of God himself, in which the idea of God explicates itself in the distinction of its moments. This also explains why the same problem, which Schleiermacher sought to resolve through the principle of Christian consciousness, now for the first time comes to its complete solution. The content of Christian faith is no longer merely set indefinitely in consciousness or feeling; it becomes the immanent content of thought itself. For the content of Christian faith is the divine Trinity. The triune nature of God is itself the totality of the moments in which the divine life-process itself consists. As triune, God is the Absolute Spirit mediating himself with himself in the process of thought. Historical Christianity is simply an element of the same course in which the process immanent to the nature of God explicates itself historically.[68]

Hegel

Hegel's Understanding of God and the World. The major factor in Hegel's advance beyond Schleiermacher, as Baur sees it, is his doctrine of the Trinity or of the self-relatedness of the Absolute Spirit.

Hegel's philosophy is the philosophy of the Absolute Spirit. That is, the principle of this philosophy is not God in his unmediated identity with nature, as in Schelling, nor the consciousness of the "I" which never proceeds out of itself but always draws back into itself, which is Schleiermacher's standpoint, but God as Spirit, as the Absolute Spirit mediating himself with himself in thought as the element of Spirit. . . . God as Spirit has a definite, concrete content; God as Spirit is thought itself. But thought is, according to its nature, a self-distinguishing in which a distinction is also a unity. It is therefore only the logical form of thought when God distinguishes himself from that other which is not himself, the world, as the Infinite is distinguished from the finite. But this distinction between God and the world, or

68 *Dogmengeschichte*, III, 352–53. Cf. also *Lehrbuch der Dogmengeschichte* (1st ed.), p. 257; (3d ed.), pp. 354–55. See below, pp. 134–35, 145–48.

between the Infinite and the finite, is also one which is implicitly over-come [*an sich aufgehoben*[69]], in that God, as God in the absolute sense, the true Infinite, is not the Infinite for himself but simply the unity of the finite and the Infinite, so that the finite also belongs to the concept of God. For without the distinction of finite and Infinite, God would not be a self-distinguishing God and thus also not a think-ing God.[70]

With this statement, the dogmatic content of the doctrine of the Trinity, first formulated by the Council of Nicea, is brought into full rational clarity and penetrated by understanding. Hegel's interpretation is anticipated in important ways by the movement in Christian thought from Augustine through Anselm to St. Thomas and Duns Scotus.[71] His achievement is made possible by means of an analysis of the nature of "Spirit" (*Geist*). The Trinity *is* Spirit, the life of Spirit, or more precisely, the life of the Absolute Spirit.[72]

In the quoted paragraph, Baur precisely summarizes Hegel's understanding of the relation between God and the world; but he also expresses the ambiguity which emerges in Hegel's thought at this point. As the Absolute Spirit, God's life-process-in-thought nec-essarily involves an essential and internally mediated relationship not only to himself but also to that which is other than himself, the world. God appears to possess no independent substantiality apart from the world; at the same time the world becomes a part of the divine process of life and therefore tends to have no inde-pendent substantiality of its own. Hegel's system provides a vision of the internal relations between things. It is a form of panenthe-ism. But since God and the world achieve reality only together, Hegel's panentheistic system is open to the charge of either "athe-ism" or "acosmism"; i.e., either God tends to be absorbed or taken or merged (*aufgehoben*) into the cosmos and the sole reality is human spirit, or the cosmos tends to be absorbed or taken or merged into God and the sole reality is the divine Spirit.[73]

---

[69] For Baur's use of *Aufhebung*, see below, pp. 139–40.

[70] *Dogmengeschichte*, III, 349–50; cf. also 533.

[71] Cf. *Die christliche Lehre von der Dreieinigkeit und Menschwerdung Gottes in ihrer geschichtlichen Entwicklung*, Vol. I: *Das Dogma der alten Kirche bis zur Synode von Chalcedon* (Tübingen: C. F. Osiander, 1841), p. 827; and Vol. II: *Das Dogma des Mittelalters* (1842), pp. 376–83, 389–90, 398–99, 661.

[72] *Lehrbuch der Dogmengeschichte* (1st ed.), p. 257.

[73] Cf. Stephen D. Crites, "The Problem of the 'Positivity' of the Gospel in the Hegelian Dialectic of Alienation and Reconciliation" (unpublished Ph.D. dissertation, Dept. of Religion, Yale University, 1961), pp. 81–105. The term panentheism is used here to describe the view that God interpenetrates every-thing without cancelling the relative, independent existence of the world of entities. It suggests a mediating position between pantheism, with its extreme immanence of God and the world, and traditional theism. For Hegel's (and Baur's) panentheism, the root reality is the divine Spirit or Subject, not cosmic Substance, as with Spinoza's pantheism, or cosmic Process. "Acosmism," on

Baur rejects the charge of atheism in the process of contrasting Hegel with Feuerbach, who represents a breakdown of the Hegelian synthesis and cannot properly be considered an Hegelian at all.

Everything which for Hegel has a double side, an objective and a subjective, has for Feuerbach only a single side, the subjective, which for him is the totality of things. Therefore, everything in religion is only subjective; there is nothing in it which is objective. Feuerbach stands completely within the viewpoint of Hegelian philosophy in that he seeks to comprehend the essence of religion as a process of self-consciousness. But for Hegel this process is only the subjective side of the Absolute Spirit determining himself in terms of finite consciousness. Against this, Feuerbach regards everything objective as transcendent. Therefore he has the same tendency as Hegel, in that for him everything transcendent must be immanent, everything eternal, temporal. But for Hegel the Universal-as-such still has its objective reality, while for Feuerbach all truth lies only in the sensual and actual, only in that which man is immediately.[74]

Although it is true, according to Hegel, to say that God "is not the Infinite for himself but simply the unity of the finite and the Infinite, so that the finite also belongs to the concept of God"; and although it is true that God would not be God, i.e., a "thinking" and thus a self-distinguishing Spirit, without such a relationship to the finite; nevertheless, the relationship between the divine Spirit and human spirit must remain an untranscended one in the sense that God cannot be collapsed into a mode of human self-consciousness, as in the thought of Feuerbach. Hegel attempts to keep the distinction clear in this direction.

But does the distinction remain clear in the other direction? Is there the danger that human spirit be collapsed or taken up into the divine Spirit in such a way that man himself, and the cosmos, are divinized by virtue of being identified with God, or conversely, that man loses his subjective freedom and autonomy and becomes simply a mode of divine consciousness? This is not atheism but acosmism. Baur suggests tentatively in his later writings that Hegel leaves himself open to this second danger. The passage quoted above continues: "If one can say, according to Hegel, that God is everything and man is nothing, in so far as for Hegel man has the truth of his nature only in God, then, on the other hand, according to Feuerbach, man is everything and God is nothing."[75] Once the distinction is blurred in the first direction, then it can become

---

the other hand, is taken to mean the denial of the real existence of the cosmos apart from God or as other than a mode of the divine being. Acosmism, then, is a form of pantheism. The systematic use of these terms will be preserved in the following discussion, but they are not used by Baur himself.

[74] *Kirchengeschichte*, V, 393.
[75] *Ibid.*

blurred in the second, and it is no longer meaningful to distinguish between God and man. Although Hegel's theology is definitely not a subjective egoism, and although Hegel wants definitely to preserve the objective reality of the divine being, nevertheless, if he allows man and the cosmos to be *aufgehoben* into this objective divine being, then he is open to the reversal of this *Aufhebung* and the deleterious consequences which flow from it. His acosmism can be inverted into an atheism.

As a proper consequence of the proposition that man cannot move out beyond himself and that all truth and reality reside in what man himself is immediately conscious of, Feuerbach's doctrine makes the transition from the Hegelian philosophy out of which it has proceeded to communistic and other practical tendencies, whose principle is a subjective egoism which denies everything universal and objective. This is the point at which everything which belongs in theory and practice to the most extreme aberrations of the time also appears in its connection with "science" and with the highest spiritual striving of the time. The principle of the time is the self-consciousness of man as the absolute power over all and as the most immediate point wherein man lays hold of himself. If, however, one does not establish —and this is the major point in Hegel—the truth of self-consciousness in the Universal, which all subjective thinking and willing has as its necessary presupposition, then everything which gives unity and connection to life dissolves into the raw dominance of egoism.[76]

Baur here seems to be suggesting that the Hegelian position is open to the Feuerbachian inversion precisely because of the way in which it conceives the relation between God and man, precisely because human spirit can be *aufgehoben* in divine Spirit. Thus it is possible to say that Feuerbach's doctrine does, in a certain sense, "proceed" from Hegelian philosophy, although it represents a grotesque and tragic distortion of it. And therefore the "most extreme aberrations of the time" are, in a certain sense, connected with "the highest spiritual striving of the time." The seeds of the breakdown of the Hegelian synthesis are already planted in the *way* in which Hegel conceives the relation between God and man. The relation itself is not wrong. His speculative panentheism provides the categories by which the "unity and connection" of life and of history can be fruitfully and newly understood. But there is an unstable element in this understanding which will permit its breakdown into either a pantheistic monism or a subjective, atheistic egoism. The history of the post-Hegelians—Feuerbach, Strauss, Bruno Bauer—is the history of this dissolution.

It is instructive to note that the section relating Hegel and Feuerbach appears only in *Kirchengeschichte des neunzehnten Jahrhun-*

76 *Ibid.*, pp. 393–94.

derts, which dates from the last period of Baur's career, and which is curiously lacking in a positive discussion of Hegel's theology.[77] It may be that this criticism came into focus only relatively late, in light of Baur's continuing concern for the subjective freedom and moral autonomy of man against any form of theological determinism,[78] his development of new and more independent categories of historical interpretation, and his increasing critical interest in the life and teaching of Jesus. Perhaps it was Feuerbach himself, whose *Das Wesen des Christentums* appeared in 1841, who opened Baur's eyes to the possibility of inverting Hegel's theology into anthropology. Or, more generally, perhaps it was the dissolution of Hegel's synthesis in the post-Hegelian period which caused Baur to raise some questions about the synthesis itself.

Finally, for Baur, evidence that seeds of dissolution were already present in Hegel's thought is to be found in the ambiguity in his Christology with respect to the historicity of Jesus Christ, an ambiguity which becomes the basis of controversy between the "left" and "right" wings of his followers. This ambiguity Baur discovered quite soon after his initial reading of Hegel, while his criticism of the latter's acosmism developed more slowly and tentatively.

Critique of Hegel's Christology: the "Aufhebung" of the Historical Jesus. Baur shares the Christological presuppositions which are expressed in Hegel's doctrine of reconciliation. As a *speculative* development and statement of Church doctrine,[79] he finds it illuminating and of constructive importance for his own position. It is the completion of the idea of reconciliation suggested in Schleiermacher's notion of "God-consciousness." Baur rightly notes that the doctrine of atonement is organic to Hegel's system, by virtue of the fact that atonement is part of the immanent process of the divine nature mediating itself with itself. The objective truth of atonement is thus to be found in the Trinity. The finite subject knows himself to be reconciled by virtue of the fact that reconciliation is an act eternally self-completed in the nature of God. The whole content of Hegel's doctrine of reconciliation consists in this metaphysically expressed fact.

This is the highest metaphysical standpoint on which one can and must place oneself if the reality of reconciliation is not finally to fall into merely the subjectivity of consciousness. Only in so far as man is implicitly, in the idea of the Triune God itself, reconciled with God, can there be a reconciliation for subjective, finite consciousness. This most highly objective aspect of the doctrine is in no way foreign to the ecclesiastical doctrine of reconciliation either, in so far as the relation-

[77] See above, p. 38, n. 3.
[78] See above, pp. 20–21.
[79] Cf. *Versöhnung*, p. 713.

ship in which the Son stands to the Father in the work of redemption
and reconciliation has its necessary foundation, in the final analysis,
only in the relationship between the Father and the Son conditioned
through the idea of the Trinity. The only lack [in the ecclesiastical
doctrine] is that this relationship has not been brought to true metaphysical expression.[80]

This passage shows why Baur considers Hegel's speculative doctrine of reconciliation to be the wholly authentic development of
the traditional Church doctrine and why he thus essentially adopts
it as his own.[81]

The transition from Hegel's doctrine of atonement to his
Christology is described by a passage in which Baur shows how
for Hegel the "external" or "outward" (*äusser*) reconciliation of
God and man in the historical event of the incarnation is based on
the divine idea of reconciliation contained "implicitly" (*an sich*)
in the Godhead.

Christianity itself is nothing other than the revelation and external
realization of the mystery of redemption existing eternally in God.
However, that which is realized externally is, according to its principle,
already existing [*vorhanden*] implicitly; and it can rightly be said that
the whole of historical reality is nothing other than the consciousness
in time of that which exists as an eternal idea in God. . . . This is
the reason why every view which places the true nature of Christianity
only in its external, factual objectivity is completely untenable. That
God became man in Christ is incontestably the most essential fact
of Christianity. But how can this happen if human nature does not
implicitly possess the receptivity for the divine, and if on the other
side there is not an essential determination of God to reveal himself
in human nature and to become man? Or how would the redemption
and reconciliation of man with God through the death of Jesus be
effective if God were not already implicitly reconciled with man and
at one with him, for reconciliation is nothing other than the re-establishment of unity with God?[82]

It is the case that the outward event of atonement depends on the
eternal idea of reconciliation contained in the Godhead. But the

[80] *Ibid.*, p. 713. Cf. also *Die christliche Gnosis*, p. 716, and *Die christliche
Lehre von der Dreieinigkeit und Menschwerdung Gottes*, Vol. III: *Die neuere
Geschichte des Dogma, von der Reformation bis in die neueste Zeit* (Tübingen:
C. F. Osiander, 1843), p. 968.

[81] However, at the end of the *Versöhnung*, pp. 738–42, the following cau-
tionary note is added: "One would badly misinterpret the above remarks if
one thought they were intended to argue simply that the most recent speculative doctrine of the atonement and the Christology connected with it represent
the final solution, satisfactory in every respect, to the great mystery with
which the human spirit has been occupied for so many centuries. . . ." The
purpose of Baur's defense of Hegel has been to counterbalance unjustified
and one-sided criticism of his atonement theory and to place it in its true
relation to the historical development of the dogma.

[82] *Ibid.*, p. 725. Italics mine.

inverse dependence is equally essential in Hegel's view, according to Baur: God achieves "true reality" only through the *historical mediation* of the relationship between himself and man which exists implicitly and eternally in the divine trinitarian life; God lives historically.[83] But why should reconciliation be mediated in the way it is? Why should Jesus of Nazareth be the focus of the movement of God to man and of man to God? And if we do not hold to the precise way in which reconciliation is mediated historically, are we not in fact in danger of allowing the positivity of this mediation to be forgotten? There is in fact no speculative or dogmatic need, in Hegel's thought, that Jesus of Nazareth be considered essential to the process of reconciliation.

On the one hand, the whole thrust of Hegel's theory of atonement is to exclude the possibility that a single individual could be considered as the complete or total embodiment of God-man unity, for this unity in its archetypal reality is a divine idea that cannot be exhaustively identified with any particular historical individual or event, but only with "true humanity." As we have observed from his criticism of Schleiermacher, Baur is in accord with this conclusion. In this respect, he can be regarded as a left-wing Hegelian. But on the other hand, Hegel's speculative atonement theory also excludes any essential or special significance to the "peculiar history" of Jesus of Nazareth for the redemption of mankind, and with this Baur is not in agreement.[84] For Hegel, it is important only that reconciliation be mediated historically; how, when, by whom, and by what are irrelevant matters. Hegel was among the most historically oriented of philosophers, yet possessed a strange lack of interest in critical questions such as these.[85] This weakness becomes especially evident in his treatment of the historical Jesus.

If we examine Hegel's Christology closely, Baur suggests, we discover that it distinguishes three moments in the understanding of who and what Jesus Christ is. A transition is effected between the first and the second, and between the second and third moments, which results finally in a complete absorption (*Aufhebung*) of the historical Jesus into a purely speculative idea of reconciliation. The consequence is a docetic and Gnostic Christology.[86]

The first moment is that of purely external, merely historical observation, which sees in Jesus Christ only an ordinary man, a martyr to the truth, a Socrates. The fact that Hegel's Christology

[83] Cf. *Ibid.*, p. 726.

[84] *Dreieinigkeit*, III, 961–63, 970.

[85] Cf. Strauss, *Streitschriften*, III, 61–62; and Crites, *op. cit.*, p. 197.

[86] The basic text for this interpretation is *Die christliche Gnosis*, pp. 711–21, although Baur amplifies it in later writings which also will be introduced into the discussion. It is interesting to note that, as with his interpretation of Schleiermacher, the basic lines of Baur's criticism of Hegel's Christology were clearly developed in the first major writing in which he discussed Hegel's thought.

starts here shows how seriously his philosophy of religion had intended to appropriate the full content of Christian faith, even to the point of affirming that God has appeared in the flesh, that he has been revealed objectively and positively in the unity of divine nature with a single human subject.[87] In order for men to become certain of redemption, "God must appear as a single man, and indeed as an immediately and sensuously perceived individual."[88] All this is maintained with the full weight of ecclesiastical expression. The only question is the sense in which it is to be taken. For, as Baur immediately adds: "The whole nature of this process would be completely misunderstood if one thought that [for Hegel] God has become man really, factually, and objectively. Rather he becomes man in a definite, single individual only in the representation [*Vorstellung*] which men have made of this fact. It is *the faith of the world* that the Spirit is there as a self-consciousness, i.e., as a real man."[89]

It is at this point that we move to the second moment in the understanding of who Jesus Christ is, that of faith, into which the first moment is taken up (*aufgehoben*). In faith, Jesus is no longer regarded as an ordinary man but as the God-man.

It is the death of Christ which constitutes this transition to the religious dimension, for Christ is the God-man only in that he overcomes death, kills death, negates the negation, denies the finite and evil as something foreign to him, and thus reconciles the world with God. The apprehension of this death is the stone of proof on which faith must above all be authenticated, for the Spirit cannot come before Christ has disappeared according to the flesh, until his immediate sensual presence has ceased. In short, Christ is the God-man only through the mediation of faith. Whatever lies behind faith as the historically given, objective reality, on the assumption of which merely external historical consideration can come to faith, remains concealed in a secret into which we are not to penetrate; for the question is not whether Christ in himself, according to his objective appearance, was the God-man, but only how it was established that he was believed to be the God-man. . . . Thus Christ is everything that he is as the God-man only in and through faith. The God-man is the object of faith, not the necessary presupposition of faith. What faith has for its presupposition is not Christ as the God-man but rather as mere man, as human sensuous appearance.[90]

---

[87] *Ibid.*, p. 711.
[88] *Dogmengeschichte*, III, 534.
[89] *Ibid.* Italics mine.
[90] *Die christliche Gnosis*, pp. 712–13. This quotation is more cautious and perhaps fairer to Hegel than the preceding one, which is from a later work, the *Vorlesungen über die christliche Dogmengeschichte*. In *Die christliche Gnosis*, Baur seems to acknowledge the ambiguity in Hegel's Christology, namely, that Hegel could not make up his mind as to whether Jesus *was*, or was only *believed to be*, the God-man. Later, in the *Dogmengeschichte*, he

As with Kant, the outward historical fact of Jesus of Nazareth is not denied, but it is of no significance to faith and can even act as a sensuous burden to it. Without actually denying the existence of Jesus, Hegel severs all essential or internal connections between the Christ of faith and the Jesus of history. And thus it would not matter if *this particular* Jesus had not existed. But Baur himself rejects the notion that faith can emerge autonomously, apart from a specific historical event and person as its source and presupposition; for it is his fundamental conviction that faith is based on and mediated by the historically real, and the historically real can be apprehended only by critical research.

Hegel's philosophy of religion regards Christ as the God-man only in his relation to faith, without expressing more definitely what objective point of contact faith has in the real appearance of Christ[91] as its presupposition. But how could faith in him as the God-man have arisen without his having also been in some fashion objectively what faith claimed for him? The necessary presupposition in any case is that the implicit truth, the unity of divine and human nature, must first come to concrete truth and self-conscious knowledge in Christ, and be expressed and learned from him as truth. Herein consists, therefore, the peculiar excellence of Christ.[92]

Baur goes on to point out that for faith, properly understood, there can be no separation between historical form and religious content, since the content is perfectly mediated by the form: "Form and content are inseparably bound together. The truth of the content can exist in absolutely no other form than the original, i.e.,

---

suggests that, behind the ambiguity, Hegel's position is that Jesus was not in fact the God-man. In other words, the left-wing Hegelians have properly interpreted Hegel's real meaning on this point. See below, p. 72.

91 When unmodified, the term "Christ" is customarily used by Baur as a proper name to refer to Jesus of Nazareth (the "historical Christ"), not as a title to refer to the Messiah, or as a conceptual term to refer to the idea of reconciliation or of God-manhood (the "ideal Christ").

92 *Die christliche Gnosis*, p. 717. This conviction underlies the later development of Baur's historically oriented Christology. Zeller substantiates the fact that this passage represents Baur's criticism *against* Hegel in the midst of an exposition of Hegel's Christology. Ritschl, in "Über geschichtliche Methode in der Erforschung des Urchristenthums," *JDT*, VI, 434–35, 438, had accused *Baur* of claiming that faith in the God-man does not have the historical Jesus as its presupposition. He referred to the passage on pp. 712–13 of *Die christliche Gnosis*, quoted earlier, as though this were Baur's own opinion and not his exposition of Hegel. Zeller, in a reply to Ritschl in "Die historische Kritik und das Wunder," *SHZ*, VI (1861), 359–60, points out that in this and other instances Ritschl confused Baur's own theology with his exposition of Hegel. Zeller then cites this passage from p. 717 of *Die christliche Gnosis* as an example of Baur's criticism of Hegel's Christology. A. B. Bruce, "Ferdinand Christian Baur and His Theory of the Origin of Christianity and of the New Testament Writings," *Living Papers*, VII, 9, manifests the same confusion as Ritschl in reading *Die christliche Gnosis*.

the form given externally-historically, with which faith has also received its content directly. Every elevation [*Erhebung*] of the content over this form serves at once to establish the disjunction
between form and content. It places the archetypal Christ over the
historical, and the once-begun disjunction runs its course until
finally the pure content is also the pure form in the naked idea."[93]
Baur makes the same point against the *Aufhebung* of the historical
Christ into the Christ of faith very forcefully in his *Dogmengeschichte:* by surrendering the objective historical reality of Jesus
as a "bare representation," faith becomes merely subjectively determined, a function of self-consciousness; and Hegel's philosophy of
religion loses the objective basis for which it has striven.[94]

The third moment in the understanding of Jesus Christ, according to Hegel, is conceptual or philosophical. For the faith of the
congregation, the appearance of the God-man is still *represented*
as an historical fact, if only as a "mere representation." But speculative thought does away with all representations. Speculatively understood, reconciliation is not an event which occurs temporally
but is only an eternal act of the Godhead; "what the Spirit is and
does is no history."[95] As we already have observed, Baur does not
object to the use of speculation in probing the meaning of redemption. Nor does he object to the assertion that the fundamental possibility and reality of reconciliation is grounded in the eternal
self-relatedness of God. But he does object to what is implied in the
third moment of Hegel's Christology, namely, that the historical
mediation of reconciliation, which Hegel himself sees elsewhere as
an implicate of his doctrine of God, is *aufgehoben* into an ahistorical, abstract dialectic of thought. Baur asks:

Can everything human and personal in the appearance of Christ, indeed everything typal and archetypal [*alles Bildliche und Urbildliche*]
in his person, be more strongly and decisively laid aside? The idea tears
itself free in its spiritual purity from every earthly, sensual hull; and all
facts of history, on which faith still depends, appear only as the turbid
reflex of the external process of Spirit,[96] which, from the highest standpoint of consideration, is itself only a game of distinctions lacking in
seriousness. But if we once again descend from this most abstract
height of speculation, which itself leaves far beneath it every docetism
of the Gnostic world-view, into that sphere in which the distinction
comes into its own, and the Spirit, driven through the inner negativity
of the idea, accomplishes the never-resting work of world history, then

[93] *Die christliche Gnosis*, p. 720.
[94] *Dogmengeschichte*, III, 353–55. For further documentation of this point,
see *Dreieinigkeit*, III, 971; and *Die christliche Gnosis*, pp. 715, 720–21.
[95] *Die christliche Gnosis*, pp. 714–15.
[96] "The facts of the history of Christ retain a figurative [*bildlich*] significance, relating to the essence of Spirit, as with the Gnostics" (Baur's footnote).

what high, well-to-be-marked significance even this philosophy of religion allows to the historical appearance of Christ![97]

In other words, the implication of Hegel's *Aufhebung* of the historical Jesus, not only into the faith of the congregation but also and finally into abstract speculative thought, is that it vitiates the most essential and authentic insights of his own philosophy of religion respecting the historicity of the divine life. Ultimately, this *Aufhebung* is only the most complete expression of what Baur refers to as Hegel's Gnosticism. In Hegel's philosophy of religion, "there is in one word the same separation of the historical and the ideal Christ as that produced by Gnosticism as the necessary result of its speculative comprehension of Christianity."[98] To this matter we shall return below.

Baur's Relation to Hegel. Baur discovered in Hegel's doctrine of God and his philosophy of history an objective basis for interpreting Christianity as an historical process and for understanding speculatively the meaning of reconciliation. But at the same time he seems to have become aware, tentatively, of the acosmic tendencies in Hegel's panentheism; and from the first he criticized Hegel's *Aufhebung* of the historical Jesus, first into the faith of the congregation, and then into an abstract dialectic of thought. Thus, although Hegel's theology calls for the historical mediation of God-man unity as a "necessary" part of the divine life itself, it in fact fails, in Baur's view, to provide an understanding of and an emphasis on historical actuality commensurate with its own systematic requirement. It manifests a curious indifference to the details of the historical past and to the methodology of historical criticism. As Strauss observed, "Hegel was personally no friend of historical criticism. It annoyed him . . . to see the heroic figures of antiquity . . . assailed by critical doubts."[99] He believed that the history written by historians "occupies itself with truths which *were* truths,"[100] whereas the philosopher is interested in the always-present dialectic of Spirit. The task of the philosopher of history is to take the *meaning* of the past up into this present dialectic, not to study the past as past. Hegel regards historical positivity as brute factuality, bearing no intrinsic relation to the meaning, idea, or concept temporarily ingredient in it. Positivity, in fact, is a form of spiritual self-estrangement and thus represents only the second moment of the dialectic of Spirit; the historical is the highest form

97 *Ibid.*, p. 716.

98 *Ibid.*, pp. 710–11; cf. pp. 720–21.

99 Strauss, *Streitschriften*, III, 61–62. Cf. Crites, *op. cit.*, p. 197: "Hegel is the most historically-oriented of philosophers, yet ends by calling radically into question the ultimate authority and even the authenticity of history as such."

100 G. W. F. Hegel, *Lectures on the Philosophy of Religion*, Vol. I, trans. from the 2d Ger. ed. by E. B. Speirs and J. B. Sanderson (London: Routledge & Kegan Paul, 1895), p. 41. Italics his.

of *representation*, which, with religion, must eventually be *aufgehoben* in pure thought.[101]

While appropriating Hegel's doctrine of the Trinity, his understanding of reconciliation, and some of his categories for interpreting the historical process, Baur rejects this attitude toward history itself, and along with it Hegel's Christology. The whole thrust of Baur's life work is to investigate critically and to interpret imaginatively events of the human past and the historical process itself as the continuum through which God mediates himself to man and actualizes the fellowship between himself and man. Consequently, Baur denies being an Hegelian, while at the same time he insists on Hegel's theological importance: "I am not a disciple of any philosophical system, because I well know how deceptive it is to make oneself dependent on human authority; but likewise I have the conviction that there is a great deal for theology to learn from Hegel. . . .[102] Baur objects, furthermore, to the use of "Hegelianism" as a label to discredit his historical investigations. He notes that his critics do not attack his critical results or his handling of the historical materials, and he asserts that his alleged Hegelianism "is nothing other than . . . the scientific consideration of the subject matter [*die wissenschaftliche Betrachtung der Sache*], as opposed to a thoroughly unscientific procedure, evidencing a complete lack of philosophical thought."[103]

Baur rejects Hegel's negative attitude toward historical positivity and his Christological docetism. But are not precisely these attitudes implied in Hegel's panentheistic view of the relation between God and the world, which Baur at least initially accepted? For in the Hegelian scheme God remains "free" and therefore sovereign in the relation to the cosmos by which he achieves his own spirituality only if the cosmos itself is absorbed into the divine life, i.e., only if the world and history are ingredient within God. And if this is the case, then it would appear that the positivity of the Gospel, of the historical Jesus, is indeed *aufgehoben*. But this is just what Baur will not allow. Thus there appears to be an inconsistency in his tentative acceptance of Hegel's doctrine of God and his simultaneous rejection of Hegel's Christology. Later he seems to have become aware that his own claim for the historical Jesus could

[101] On Hegel's view of history, as sketched above, see Crites, *op. cit.*, pp. 197–98, 203–204, 234–36, 241–44. Cf. also Hegel, *Encyclopedia of Philosophy*, Gustav Emil Mueller, trans. (New York: Philosophical Library, 1959), §§ 71–80, 207, 442–49, 465, 468–77; and Hegel, *The Philosophy of History*, J. Sibree, trans. (New York: Dover Publications, 1956), pp. 415–16.

[102] "Abgenöthigte Erklärung," *TZT*, IX:3, 225. Two of Baur's students, Pfleiderer and Zeller, corroborate this testimony of independence from Hegel. Zeller, for example, writes that Hegel was never an "infallible authority" for Baur, who "in his later years made himself increasingly independent of Hegel's influence, to which he had never unconditionally surrendered." Cf. "Die historische Kritik und das Wunder," *SHZ*, VI, 371–72.

[103] *Dreieinigkeit*, I, xviii; cf. iv–vi, xxii.

not be reconciled with Hegel's acosmic panentheism. But he never was able to resolve this systematic inconsistency, which also plagued his own dogmatic understanding of the relation between God and history.[104]

Gnosticism, Ancient and Modern

We have already noted that Baur advances the thesis in *Die christliche Gnosis* that there are marked similarities between ancient Christian Gnosticism and modern Protestant philosophies of religion, specifically those of Boehme, Schelling, Schleiermacher, and Hegel. We have also suggested that this work is intended as both a defense and an internal critique of Christian Gnosticism or philosophy of religion. Since it represents the general framework within which Baur critically analyzes the thought of the great mediating theologians of the second period in modern theology, it will be illuminating to look briefly at Baur's study of Gnosticism, not only in *Die christliche Gnosis* and his inaugural dissertation, *De Gnosticorum Christianismo ideali*, but especially in *Das Christenthum und die christliche Kirche der drei ersten Jahrhunderte*, where he draws together into a sixty-page summary statement the conclusions from several monographs devoted to this study.[105]

By "Gnosticism" Baur means "philosophy of religion," either mythical-allegorical in method, as represented by the ancients, or speculative, as exemplified by modern philosophers of religion. On the one hand it is concerned to develop an ideal principle of interpretation of the world-historical process. But on the other hand it does not consist of pure or abstract thought but of *religious* knowledge, concerned with redemption. Gnosticism is philosophy of religion in the sense that it stands between the abstraction of pure philosophy and the historical concreteness of pure religion. It is thus an "ideal rationalism."[106] As such, nonheretical Gnosticism has a legitimate place in Christian theology, whose concern is to penetrate the object of faith by knowledge or *gnosis*.[107]

Baur's principle concern is with Christian Gnosticism, which is, however, closely related to the two other major forms of Gnosticism: pagan and Jewish. The earliest of the authentically Chris-

---

104 See below, pp. 134–42.

105 In addition to the works mentioned above, Baur's studies of Gnosticism, as listed in a footnote in *Das Christenthum*, p. 178 (E.T., I, 187), include monographs in *Theologische Studien und Kritiken* and *Zeitschrift für speculative Theologie* (both 1837). Baur also refers to his discussion of Gnosticism in *Lehrbuch der Dogmengeschichte* and *Die Tübinger Schule*.

106 *Das Christenthum*, pp. 178–83, 185–88 (E.T., I, 187–92, 195–97); and *Die christliche Gnosis*, pp. vii–viii.

107 Cf. *Lehrbuch der Dogmengeschichte* (3d ed.), p. 75: "The Alexandrine theologians, Clement and Origen, also regarded the Gnostics as heretics. But they were so far from rejecting the essence of *gnosis* along with the heretical *gnosis* that they declared it to be a necessary demand of Christian perfection to proceed from faith to knowledge. According to their view, neither can faith exist without knowledge, nor knowledge without faith."

tian Gnostic systems are pagan in character, by virtue of their symbolic and mythical mode, and can be regarded as expressions of Christian paganism. Their chief exponents are Basilides of Alexandria and Valentinus, the latter having come to Rome from Alexandria, possibly as a student of Basilides, around A.D. 140.[108] A second form of Christian Gnosticism is essentially Jewish in character and is represented by the Pseudo-Clementine Homilies.[109] A third form is a purely Christian Gnosticism, disengaged from foreign elements entirely, although rightly declared heretical by the Church. Here Baur's prime example is Marcion, whom he places in Rome between 140 and 150, as a possible student of Valentinus. Marcion's opposition of law and Gospel, based on the general antithesis of the two principles of matter and spirit, Demiurge and God, represents the strictest dualism of any of the Gnostic systems. He consequently severs all essential connections between Christianity and its religious antecedent, Judaism, except in so far as the kingdom of the Demiurge must necessarily precede God's revelation in Christ. In this latter respect he shares the tendency of other Gnostic systems to comprehend the stages of religious history "speculatively."[110] Baur further notes that Marcion is the most decidedly docetic of the Gnostics.[111] Finally, as the prime representative of a purely Christian Gnosticism, Marcion is a fanatical and dedicated Paulinist, although one who destroys in his appropriation of Pauline antinomianism Paul's uncompromising loyalty to the positivity of the Gospel and to the unity of Old and New Testaments.[112]

There are two major distinguishing marks of the Gnostic world-

[108] *Das Christenthum*, pp. 195–96, 198–201, 204–213 (E.T., I, 205, 207–210, 213–22).

[109] *Ibid.*, pp. 217–25 (E.T., I, 228–35).

[110] *Ibid.*, pp. 216–17 (E.T., I, 226–27). Baur's classification of Marcion as a Gnostic, against the judgment of later historians of dogma such as Harnack, follows from his determination of the two major distinguishing marks of Gnosticism as its metaphysical dualism and its speculative representation of the stages of religious history (see below), characteristics which he believes to be central to Marcion's thought.

[111] *Ibid.*, p. 230 (E.T., I, 239).

[112] "It is self-evident that this [remark] is not to be understood in the sense which Ritschl, *Entstehung* (2d ed., p. 311), imputes to me, as though Paulinism developed generally into Marcionism and the pure, basic ideas of Paul had been preserved in this heresy. He could also have spared himself the further remark that monotheism and the . . . recognition of the unity of the Old and New Testaments are such inseparable provisions of the purely Pauline view that Marcion's agreement with Paul, even though intended by him, proves in truth to be only outward and apparent. It is well known that Marcion was not only a Paulinist but a Gnostic; on that account, however, his antinomianism still remains authentically Pauline, and he is entitled to a place in the history of Paulinism." *Ibid.*, pp. 77–78 (E.T., I, 82). That place is primarily due to his canon—which he collected out of loyalty to Paul and on the basis of his understanding of him—and to his heretical interpretation of Paul, which forced a reaction on the part of the Church instrumental to its historical definition and development. Cf. *Paulus*, I, 279 (E.T., 249).

view. The first is its endeavor to comprehend and represent the
stages of religious history according to speculative principles of
development.[113] The second is its metaphysical dualism between
matter and spirit, the real and the ideal, the historical and the
archetypal, which marks all Gnosticism as an offspring of paganism. The process of world-historical development is constituted
by the interaction of the dualistic principles on each other. Matter
is the opposite of spirit, into which the latter dirempts itself in
the process of self-realization. The development terminates with
the return of spirit to itself as pure spirit, but then the whole
process repeats itself. The infinite abyss between spirit and matter
is filled with the emanations and projections of spirit, which constitute the aeons, the forms of spirit objectivizing itself, the arche-
types of the finite world. Concomitant with this dualism is a
determinism which excludes moral freedom. Finally, as Baur notes
significantly, the dualism of spirit and matter excludes a true
doctrine of creation; rather, the Demiurge is the artificer of matter,
and spirit emanates from its first principle.[114]

Because of its dualism, the Christology in Christian Gnostic
systems is invariably docetic,[115] since, in order to free the spiritual
from the material or psychical, the Redeemer must come into as
little contact as possible with the latter; the two principles repudiate each other and are incompatible.[116] In contrast to some earlier,
materialistic versions of Gnosticism, Christian Gnosticism gives
precedence to the ideal or spiritual. "The concrete, the individual,
the personal, is in every case lost in the universality of the concept; the Gnostic Christ merely represents a principle, the spiritual
principle which underlies all forms and stages of development."[117]
"The body of Christ lacks the concrete reality of a human body";
fact becomes "only the figurative [bildlich] reflex of the idea."[118]
Its docetism is the clue to Gnosticism's fundamentally rationalistic
tendency, a rationalism which excludes the historical foundation
of the Christian Gospel.

We need only to strip off the symbolic-mythical cloak in which Gnostic
supernaturalism wraps itself, and to take the forms in which it per-

---

113 *Das Christenthum*, p. 226 (E.T., I, 236).

114 *Ibid.*, pp. 183–85 (E.T., I, 193–95).

115 Baur first clearly states this in his inaugural dissertation. Christian
Gnosticism is a form of "ideal rationalism" which holds fast to the historical
character of Christianity; but in fact the whole temporal course which it
represents falls completely into the sphere of consciousness. "Christ is actually
not an historical and human person but a rational idea. Christianity is not
a free act of the will of God but the result of a development conforming to
nature. Without doubt, this establishes . . . the docetism of the Gnostics. . . .
Everything outwardly real, objectively historical, and truly human in Christ
according to the biblical story is regarded by them only as a deceptive illusion." "Anzeige der beiden academischen Schriften," *TZT*, I, 236–38.

116 *Das Christenthum*, p. 230 (E.T., I, 240).

117 *Ibid.*, pp. 231–32 (E.T., I, 241).

118 *Ibid.*, p. 234 (E.T., I, 243).

sonifies its concepts for what they are in themselves, and the true kernel of the Gnostic world-view then emerges as a very transparent rationalism, based on the immanent self-consciousness of spirit. . . . Docetism can be considered simply as the point at which the rationalizing tendency implicitly present in Gnosticism came most visibly to its outward manifestation. . . . To the extent to which everything of importance rests on universal ideas of speculative or religious content, the historical reality of the facts of Christianity recedes.[119]

Not only is Gnosticism a thoroughgoing rationalism, but also its conception of salvation, in so far as it has one, stresses a natural cosmic process and understands the state of salvation as a mode of being or *gnosis*.[120]

In light of this docetic attitude, Baur asks whether, "through Gnosticism, the reality of the historical facts of Christianity and the historical character of Christianity generally are not thrown into doubt in a way which is incompatible with the Christian consciousness."[121] He answers that "the general character of Gnosticism is the evaporation or generalization of the positive content of historical Christianity,"[122] and argues that the ancient Church achieved its authentic historicity in the struggle first against the particularizing tendency of Judaism and then against the idealizing tendency of Gnosticism. The Church embraces in its essential being elements of both positivity and universality, of both authority and freedom; it exists historically at the point of congruence of these two factors. We shall examine later this aspect of Baur's theology of the Church;[123] for the time being it is enough to recognize that in his view it belongs to the *essence* of the Church to be historical, and that this is what Christian Gnosticism, ancient and modern, has failed to make clear.

The study of Gnosticism was one of Baur's lifelong interests. It was the unifying theme of his inaugural dissertation in 1827; it was the subject of a major monograph and of several shorter studies; it again occupied him in the last year of his life when he updated the section on Gnosticism for the second edition of *Das Christenthum* in 1860. Two things about it constantly attracted his attention. The first was its capacity to elucidate speculatively the implicit and universal truth of the Christian Gospel and its ability to provide a framework within which the historical development of the great religions could be adequately understood. The second was its inability to comprehend the historical foundation and substance of that Gospel. This inability could be traced,

---

[119] *Ibid.*, pp. 233–34; cf. p. 233 (E.T., I, 243; cf. p. 242); and "Anzeige der beiden academischen Schriften," *TZT*, I, 228–35.

[120] *Das Christenthum*, pp. 231, 234; cf. pp. 246–47 (E.T., I, 240–41, 244; cf. II, 2).

[121] *Ibid.*, p. 228 (E.T., I, 237–38).

[122] *Ibid.*, p. 234 (E.T., I, 243).

[123] See below, pp. 127–31.

in a word, to its pagan dualism—its dualism of spirit versus matter, the ideal against the real, freedom versus authority, the archetypal in opposition to the historical. But the very genius of Christianity, which precisely marks its advance beyond paganism, is its transcendence of this dualism and its holding together of the historical and the spiritual in an authentic union, which is not, however, a sheer identity. Thus as Baur sees it the basic heresy of the Christian Church has always been docetism in one form or another, and it is against docetism that his entire historical-critical theological program is postured. It is the docetism in the Christologies of Schleiermacher and Hegel which marks the focal point of the failure of these two great theologians. At the end of *Die christliche Gnosis*, Baur suggests that, if Christian philosophy of religion could shake off the pagan, docetic dualism which it still displays, then it could become a more adequate tool for conceptualizing the truth of the Christian Gospel.[124]

THIRD PERIOD: STRAUSS AND THE DISSOLUTION OF SYNTHESIS

Dissolution of the Synthesis: the Quest for an Authentic Mediating Theology

Beginning in the early 1830's, the synthesis attempted by Schleiermacher and Hegel between the authority of a positive, historically mediated religious tradition and freedom of consciousness and thought appears rapidly to be breaking down. Very quickly, as Strauss first notes in the *Streitschriften*, the Hegelian school splits into right and left wings, the right wing representing a return to a modern supernaturalism in which the criteria of critical thought, both speculative and historical, are sacrificed, and the left wing announcing that historical Christianity as it has been known must be given up. Strauss himself, with the negative results of his methodologically invalid historical criticism of the Gospel sources and later with his post-Christian *Glaubenslehre*, stands on the left wing. Also on the left wing of an Hegelianism which no longer could properly be called such are the avowedly atheistic Bruno Bauer and Ludwig Feuerbach, and recently, in addition, the *Deutschen Jahrbücher*, under the guidance of Bauer and Arnold Ruge. To the right of center is the so-called "Mediating Theology" of the Schleiermacherian and Right-Hegelian schools, which, in Baur's judgment, represents a return to the "new supernaturalism." Much further to the right are the Protestant Confessionalists and the "consensus dogmatics" of the Unionists. On the Catholic side, there is Möhler's *Symbolik*, which has the unfortunate purpose of making the distinction between Catholicism and Protestantism absolute. Finally, some of the more interesting

124 *Die christliche Gnosis*, pp. 739–40.

attempts at a mediating position in terms of a speculative theism, while suggestive, contain too much that is unclear or fantastical.

This, in brief, is the thesis by which Baur interprets the theological situation of his own time, especially as it is laid out in the lectures of the 1850's which constitute *Kirchengeschichte des neunzehnten Jahrhunderts*. This thesis also suggests, indirectly, the authentic task of historical-critical theology as Baur conceives it. Theology, he argues, must not move backward from where it stands at present, only forward. This movement ought to be from and beyond the standpoint of speculative theology, whereas most of the objections brought against speculative theology, from either the right or the left, have represented retrogression, not progression—i.e., retrogression to a pre-mediating position in which either Christianity is embraced apart from critical thought or consciousness and reason are made normative apart from Christian dogma.[125] In this situation, the authentic task of theology in the modern period is to further the mediation between the faith of the Church and the critical "sciences" already imperfectly initiated by speculative theology.

Right- and Left-Wing Hegelianism

In Baur's judgment, Hegel not only belongs to the second period in nineteenth century theology but also marks the transition to the third by virtue of the fact that his Christology contains a systematic ambiguity with respect to the positivity of the God-man.[126] The latter problem, in fact, provides the clue to the division between the post-Hegelian schools.

Hegel's Christology does not move beyond [the proposition] . . . that Christ becomes the God-man for the faith of the world. It is not concerned with what lies behind this faith objectively in connection with the person of Christ; and it separates this view of the person of Christ from that which is concerned only with what he is for faith and in faith, approximately as Kantian philosophy distinguishes between the unknown *Ding an sich* and the appearance which exists for consciousness alone. Either one can say that actually nothing objective corresponds to this faith, that the whole appearance and personality of Christ are only the fortuitous occasion from which faith in the God-man has developed, that the two therefore stand in a purely external relationship to each other [the left-wing position]. Or on the other side one can attempt to establish both as much as possible in an inner relationship to each other such that, with respect to his person, Christ is therefore held to be objectively what he is as God-man for faith [the right-wing position].[127]

[125] *Lehrbuch der Dogmengeschichte* (1st ed.), pp. 258–59.
[126] Cf. *Kirchengeschichte*, V, 348, and above, p. 38, n. 3.
[127] *Dreieinigkeit*, III, 971. Cf. also *Kirchengeschichte*, V, 356–59. The terms "left-" and "right-wing" are not used by Baur.

The distinction between left and right wings of the Hegelian school had already been made by Strauss in the *Streitschriften* several years before Baur's mention of it.[128] The basis of the division is the same: the unclarity in Hegel's Christology. But there is some disagreement between Strauss and Baur with respect to what constitutes the left wing. They agree that the left wing asserts, on both philosophical and historical grounds, that the ideal truth of reconciliation must in fact be separated from the historical Jesus, who can yield to the historian's critical judgment nothing of what faith claims for him.[129] But in addition, according to Strauss, the left wing claims that the truth of the Gospel narrative and the identity of the God-man cannot be demonstrated philosophically, as the Mediating theologians attempted, but only investigated historically.[130] Baur, however, does not include this second element in his definition of the left-wing position, nor does acceptance of it necessarily entail the left-wing conclusion with respect to the ahistoricity of the God-man. Baur shares with Strauss the conviction (in fact he is the original source of it) that the positive truth of the Gospel narrative is not a matter of philosophical necessity but of historical investigation. But it does not necessarily follow that such investigation will lead to the left-wing conclusion, shared by Strauss but not by Baur, that nothing positive corresponds to faith in the God-man. Given Strauss's definition of the left wing, Baur could be included partially within it; and this has led to considerable confusion in later interpretation.[131]

Although there is ambiguity in Hegel's Christology, Baur regards Strauss and the left wing as having correctly interpreted the real direction and implication of Hegel's position. Strauss's Christology is nothing other than the "strongest consequence" of the Hegelian;[132] and he was right in remarking that the "concluding dissertation" of his *Das Leben Jesu* would be "epoch-making" for the right understanding of Hegel's Christology.[133]

We have seen that Baur dissociated himself from the left wing. But he also regarded the right wing as at least partially untenable. The passage quoted earlier continues as follows: "On the other side [the right wing] one can attempt to establish both [objective reality and faith] as much as possible in an inner relationship to each other such that, with respect to his person, Christ is therefore held to be objectively what he is as God-man for faith. This second view permits different modifications, the extreme being when one, in this fashion, returns again to the God-man of ecclesi-

128 Strauss, *Streitschriften*, III, 94–95.
129 *Ibid.*, pp. 94–95, 126.
130 *Ibid.*, pp. 68, 126.
131 Eduard Zeller, for example, thinks that as a dogmatician Baur took the left wing into "unequally greater claim for himself than the right." "Ferdinand Christian Baur," *ADB*, II, 175.
132 *Dreieinigkeit*, III, 974; cf. pp. 971–73.
133 *Dogmengeschichte*, III, 537.

astical doctrine and accordingly *identifies point-blank* the ideal and the historical Christ."[134]

It is important to note the way in which Baur circumscribes his criticism of the right wing. He specifically dissociates himself from those elements of the right wing, namely the neo-Schleiermacherian and Right-Hegelian Mediating theologians, who would return to the old supernaturalism of Church doctrine in modern guise, and who accordingly attribute to the historical Christ supernatural characteristics by virtue of their *total identification* of the archetypal and the historical. But Baur suggests there may be another modification of the right-wing position which could hold the ideal and the historical together without a *sacrificium intellectus*. He asks if it is not possible to regard the historical Jesus more highly than Hegel and Strauss allow—if there is not perhaps a "mediating way" whereby the separation of the historical and the ideal Christ, which is the result of the speculative point of view, can be harmonized with or adjusted to the ecclesiastical doctrine of the God-man in at least an approximate manner.[135] The "mediating way" would neither separate nor totally identify the ideal and the historical. On the one hand, Baur agrees with the Mediating theologians that there is an inner relation between faith and the historical event, but disagrees with their interpretation of the relationship. On the other hand, he agrees with Strauss that Jesus of Nazareth cannot be demonstrated *speculatively* to be the God-man of faith, but at the same time he argues historically-critically that Jesus is in fact the original and authoritative exemplification of God-manhood. Thus, Baur cannot be identified with either left- or right-wing Hegelianism, a fact which Strauss appears to acknowledge in the *Streitschriften*.[136]

Strauss[137]

Strauss as a True Reflex of the Critical Consciousness of His Time. We have already observed that Baur concurs with Strauss's

[134] *Dreieinigkeit*, III, 971. Italics mine.

[135] *Ibid.*, p. 992. For another statement of this position, see below, p. 108, n. 59. At first, Baur thought that Strauss himself had come around to something like this viewpoint in his essay, "Vergängliches und Bleibendes im Christenthum," *Freihafens* (1838), which anticipated the position taken in the third edition of *Das Leben Jesu* (1839). Cf. *Dreieinigkeit*, III, 992–94. However, when Strauss returned to his original position in the fourth edition, Baur realized that he was merely accommodating himself to the winds of criticism. Cf. *Die kanonischen Evangelien*, p. 75.

[136] Although he mentions Baur's "Abgenöthigte Erklärung" in a footnote (*Streitschriften*, III, 103) he does not classify Baur in either left or right wing in his discussion of "different tendencies in the Hegelian School with respect to Christology."

[137] The correspondence between Strauss and Baur deposited in U.B.T., Md 750, i, 19, and Md 750, ii, 7, makes it possible to trace their relationship between 1835 and 1846. This task has been undertaken in the following articles, in which this correspondence has been published in whole or in part, and to which the reader is referred: Ernst Barnikol, "Der Briefwechsel

self-designation as a Left-Hegelian, although both also note that Strauss was excluded from the ranks of the left-Hegelians.[138] But the question as to the nature and validity of Strauss's "Hegelianism" is another matter, one we cannot examine here. Suffice it to say that his abstract, ahistorical idealism, his dogmatic naturalism, and his attempt to "correct" Hegel in the direction of an undialectical pantheism all spell death to the vitality and genius of Hegel's system. Baur, at least at first, did not see this side of Strauss's thought—the dogmatic and philosophical side—very clearly at all.[139] His personal friendship for Strauss was perhaps too deep to allow him to be convinced that behind the façade of historical criticism lay a philosophical mind which was ever more clearly breaking with the Christian faith and in fact repudiating the very synthesis of Church theology and "science" which Baur hoped to enhance, although this fact became increasingly clear to him after Strauss published his *Glaubenslehre* in 1841.

Although disagreeing with Strauss's critical method and results, and although indicating that he had begun his own historical investigations long before Strauss, proceeding from a wholly different standpoint, thus proving that he was not a disciple of his own student,[140] Baur always spoke of Strauss as a personal friend when he had occasion to do so. He did not deny the "heinous charge" of friendship leveled against him by the *Evangelische Kirchenzeitung*. In his many years of acquaintance with Strauss he had not observed any evidence of the "demonic nature" ascribed to him, out of "Christian charity," by his opponents.[141] Later Baur remarks that Strauss had been his student since the Blaubeuren days, that there had always been friendly communication between the two, and that they had discussed the contents of the forth-

---

zwischen Strauss und Baur," *ZKG*, 4. Folge X, LXXIII:1/2 (1962), 74–125 (the entire extant correspondence published); Wilhelm Lang, "Ferdinand Baur und David Friedrich Strauss," *PJ*, CLX (April–June 1915), 474–504; CLXI (July–September 1915), 123–44 (portions of the correspondence published with other items); and Adolph Rapp, "Baur und Strauss in ihrer Stellung zueinander und zum Christentum," *BWKG*, 3. Folge, LII (1952), 95–149; LIII (1953), 157; LIV (1954), 182–85 (portions of the correspondence published with other items).

138 Cf. Strauss, *Streitschriften*, III, 126; and Baur, *Kirchengeschichte*, V, 390.

139 In one of his earliest responses in the Strauss controversy, Baur writes: "It has not occurred to any of the more recent philosophers and critics to take from historical Christianity its historical Christ and to interpret his historical existence as a mere fable. . . . Even the mythical mode of conception allows the historical individual to stand with an inviolable kernel of his life and work, to which faith holds and must learn to hold." Gutachten of 20 Dec. 1835 (U.B.T., Md 750, v, 1). This was written to defend Strauss and speculative theology against the unjust attack of Eschenmayer. Later, as we have seen, Baur changed his mind about Strauss.

140 Cf. "Abgenöthigte Erklärung," *TZT*, IX:3, 185, 207; and *Kirchengeschichte*, V, 395.

141 "Abgenöthigte Erklärung," *TZT*, IX:3, 221.

coming *Das Leben Jesu,* which consequently came as no surprise to Baur when it was published.[142]

Baur's primary concern is with Strauss's historical-critical method, not with his philosophical and theological position. It would not be unfair to say that Baur is so preoccupied with this method that he does not see the purely philosophical function which it serves Strauss. He treats it with full seriousness, something which Strauss himself apparently did not do. In discussing Strauss's historical criticism, Baur first makes it clear that he defends the right and the necessity of such criticism, regardless of the results. Those who have erroneously associated him with Strauss have done so simply because they fear all critical theology as destructive of true faith.[143] The service of *Das Leben Jesu* is to show to the age that the historical-critical questions connected with the origin and development of Christianity can no longer be ignored.[144] The *positive* result of Strauss's criticism is to show "that the Gospel stories contain more or less mythical elements, that they cannot be taken so immediately as objective historical truth as customarily had been thought, that in any case one can penetrate to the true historical kernel of primitive Christianity only by means of historical criticism."[145]

Yet Strauss's *Das Leben Jesu* is only a way station on the path to an authentic historical-critical knowledge of the New Testament. It serves the purpose of clearing away as invalid all previous attempts at constructing an historical picture of the Gospel events; it reflects to its age the confusion and ignorance with which this task has been approached; the very negativity and scepticism of its results serve as a necessary mediation between a precritical age and an authentic historical method (for until faith has been tested by doubt it does not reach critical maturity); it reflects a new despair that Church theology and critical research cannot be held together. Such is Baur's argument in the introduction to *Kritische Untersuchungen über die kanonischen Evangelien.*

[Strauss] was hated because the spirit of the time could not endure its own picture, which he held up to it in faithful, clearly drawn outlines. . . . Let us frankly admit the facts of the case, and rest assured that, instead of going on forever with vague and empty polemics, it is time

---

[142] Baur in Klüpfel, ed., *Geschichte und Beschreibung der Universität Tübingen,* p. 410; and *Kirchengeschichte,* V, 396–97. Wilhelm Lang, who knew both Strauss and Baur, and had access to the latter's literary estate, claims that Baur never expressed personal unfriendliness toward Strauss publicly or in private correspondence, either before or after the bitter break of 1846 (see below). This is probably true; however, in two letters to Heyd, Baur seems to treat Strauss's recalcitrance with a tinge of sarcasm. Cf. Baur to Heyd, 13 Nov. 1836 (U.B.T., Md 619r, 18), and 16 June 1841 (U.B.T., Md 619r, 28).

[143] "Abgenöthigte Erklärung," TZT, IX:3, 184, 205, 208.

[144] Cf. *Paulus,* I, 4–5 (E.T., 2–3).

[145] *Dogmengeschichte,* III, 357–58.

to look at Strauss's criticism as *a product of its time,* and to understand how, in the *then* existing stage of criticism it was not only a possible but also a necessary phenomenon. What result could be reached from the investigations then carried on into the origin and mutual relation of the Gospels, except a purely negative one? One opinion was opposed by another, taken together the opinions were mutually contradictory and destructive, and any certainty was impossible. Nothing else remained than the renunciation of every positive insight. . . . It was, in fact, just as Strauss himself said, in the darkness produced by the extinguishing of all supposed historical lights by criticism, the eye had gradually to learn to distinguish individual objects. Strauss's work was intended to begin this process, by leading men out of the general darkness into a clear day of historical knowledge. But it introduced a new era not in virtue of this positive but of its negative side; its chief merit lay not in the knowledge which it brought to light, but in the lack of knowledge of which it made men conscious. . . . This is the truly historical importance of Strauss's critique. Its greatest merit will always consist in having shown the condition of historical knowledge of the Gospel story *at the time.* . . . When all our previous knowledge is self-contradictory and self-destructive, certain knowledge can only come from the examination and classification of details. But these details formed the limit of Strauss's criticism, beyond which one can proceed only if one regards the limitations of Strauss's criticism . . . not as belonging to the criticism of the Gospel stories in general but only to a certain moment in the history of the development of the same.[146]

From this passage, it is clear that Baur regards Strauss's work as belonging to a stage beyond which his own historical criticism has already proceeded. It is the "necessary" prolegomenon to a positive yet critical analysis of the New Testament writings. It is necessary because it shows that the synthesis achieved by the mediating period between faith and science did not rest on a sound historical-critical analysis of the texts. That period had short-circuited the historical way by means of speculation. The result of Strauss's purely negative criticism—which now becomes the mark of the post-Hegelian dissolution—is to throw into doubt the conviction achieved by Schleiermacher and Hegel that ecclesiastical faith and free research could be mediated with each other. Now it appears there is only the "hard choice" of throwing in one's lot with Strauss or of falling back into the arms of ecclesiastical orthodoxy.[147] In order to develop an authentic mediating theology,

---

146 *Die kanonischen Evangelien,* pp. 48–52. Italics mine. Parts of this passage are translated in Otto Pfleiderer, *The Development of Theology in Germany,* pp. 224–25.

147 *Die kanonischen Evangelien,* pp. 48–49. Cf. Baur to F. A. G. Tholuck, early summer 1836 (U.B.T., Md 750, ii, 9, 1), and Gutachten of 27 June 1839 (U.B.T., Md 750, v, 3).

it is necessary to move beyond, not only Schleiermacher and Hegel, but also Strauss and the theological dilemma he engendered.[148]

Strauss's "Negative Critical" or "Dialectical" Historical Method. Given the coincidence of two hypothetical conditions, first, that Christian truth-claims and Christian faith are absolutely dependent on a particular historical fact or facts and must be honestly instructed by the evidence produced by the critical investigation of these facts, and second, that an historian (for example, Strauss) has critically demolished the historical authenticity of that fact or those facts—then a work such as Strauss's *Das Leben Jesu* would indeed have had a devastating impact upon either the veracity or the character of the Christian faith. In the face of such circumstances, most apologists for the faith have questioned the first condition by asserting that Christian truth-claims are not absolutely dependent on a particular historical fact, or at least on that mode of historical facticity open to historical-critical investigation. Karl Barth, for example, is convinced that, for reasons both theological and historical, Strauss has shown that a life of Jesus ought not to and cannot be written. His was the life of Jesus to end all lives of Jesus; it did its negative, destructive work well. Its service was to show that the true Jesus Christ cannot be known by such methods, that therefore the Christian faith is not a matter for historical investigation. Strauss can be of service to us only when we no longer need to take him seriously. "Proper theology begins just at the point where the difficulties disclosed by Strauss and Feuerbach are seen and then laughed at."[149] It may be proper to laugh at Strauss's eclectic philosophizing. But it is not so easy or proper to laugh at the critical methods and critical conclusions of *Das Leben Jesu*. Baur came to realize that if Strauss were actually right with respect not only to his methods but also his conclusions in this and later works, then a very damaging case had been made against the historical positivity of the Christian Church, and thus also, in Baur's view, against the Christian faith, at least as it had hitherto been understood. Thus, in response to Strauss, Baur did not dispute the validity of the first condition, which he regarded as essentially true if Christianity is indeed an "historically given religion," but turned rather to a questioning first of Strauss's method and then later of his results.[150]

It is characteristic of Baur's careful and methodical procedure that he did not, as we have seen, immediately question the *results*

---

[148] A similar judgment on Strauss's historical significance is expressed in *Kirchengeschichte,* V, 379–80.

[149] Barth, *From Rousseau to Ritschl,* pp. 386–89. See below, p. 270, n. 24.

[150] For further discussion of this question, see chap. vi.

of Strauss's historical study, since, as he later described it, he lacked at the time the "necessary deeper studies" by which to reach a judgment on this most difficult question; it required, in fact, some eighteen years before Baur was prepared to offer in print his own positive analysis of the ministry and teaching of Jesus.[151] But he does question the validity of Strauss's historical method, and especially the negativity of his procedure, almost at once, in a letter to Heyd early in 1836: "What I most object to in the book is, next to the often damaging coldness especially toward the person of Jesus, the excessive negativity of the criticism. I believe, also from the critical standpoint, that a broader basis can be gained for the historical in the life of Jesus. . . . There appear to me some historical data here which are insufficiently valued in a positive sense." It is not plausible, Baur continues, that the high significance attributed to the person of Jesus is the product of mere chance or of arbitrary belief on the part of the primitive Church.[152]

Three months later, in May 1836, Baur published an article in which he defended the right of free criticism and its value for faith but distinguished his own "positive" method from Strauss's "negative" criticism and use of mythical criteria to question the historicity of the Gospels.[153] This criticism anticipated Baur's lengthy treatment of Strauss's "negative critical or dialectical" method in the introduction to *Kritische Untersuchungen über die kanonischen Evangelien* (1847). In this work the criticism of Strauss rests on three main points: his use of myth as the negative criterion of historical authenticity, his dialectical criticism of "stories" rather than of "writings" as a whole, and his arbitrary oscillation on matters of great critical import.

The first weakness is partially the consequence of the second.

---

151 See above, p. 25.

152 Baur to L. F. Heyd, 10 Feb. 1836 (U.B.T., Md 750, ii, 6, 16). Baur agrees with Heyd that the work possesses an arrogant or presumptive tone, especially in the preface to the second volume. But it must be remembered, suggests Baur, that when Strauss wrote this preface, in the summer of 1835, he was justly irritated by his recent dismissal as Privatdozent by the Studienrat. It is interesting to note in this connection that, as early as 1826, Baur objected to the "negativity" of de Wette's history of Israel. Baur to L. F. Heyd, 30 April 1826 (U.B.T., Md 750, ii, 6, 4).

153 "Abgenöthigte Erklärung gegen einen Artikel der *Evangelischen Kirchenzeitung*," TZT, IX:3, 200–208, *et passim*. Strauss was not happy with Baur's attempt to distinguish his own "positive" critical procedure from Strauss's "negative" method, and he indicated his displeasure in a letter to Baur in August 1836. It was, however, a polite letter, in which Strauss asked to be pardoned for "this sensitivity." Strauss to Baur, 19 August 1836 (U.B.T., Md 750, i, 19, 3). A week later Strauss wrote angry words to his friend Georgii: if Baur, "up to then" his "truest friend in the field of criticism," were to forswear association with him in order to obtain peace, "then it is all over with the friendship." But Strauss retracted these harsh words some two months later. Cf. Heinrich Maier, "Briefe von D. Fr. Strauss an L. Georgii," *Tübinger Universitätsschrift* (1912), p. 16 (quoted in Rapp, *op. cit.*, LII, 107–108).

By analyzing the isolated units of the Gospel tradition apart from the literary and historical context in which they are found, Strauss prepares the way for the application of mythical categories as the only criteria for determining the authenticity of these separate units. Myth is the sole category, indeed the only one necessary, in Strauss's critical apparatus. Myth is present, he believes, wherever contradiction or inconsistency exists between two or more accounts of the same event, whenever the outward course of an event is described as "miraculous" in the absolute sense, or whenever the inner kernel of an event is rationally unthinkable. Since Strauss ignores the literary purposes and theological "tendencies" of the writings in which the units of tradition are found, he possesses no criteria by which to judge whether the presence of contradiction and miracle marks the intention of the author or simply his passing on of unhistorical material. Consequently, the presence of mythical elements in the Gospel tradition is magnified way out of proportion. Almost everything in the Gospels is seen as mythical in its roots, and myth consequently becomes the tool of an essentially negative and abstract criticism.[154] It can readily be understood, therefore, why Baur dissociated himself from the very beginning from Strauss's use of the category of myth.

Where is my criticism supported in even a single place in my writing by the mythical view? Where do I reject even a single historical fact which is of importance for the critical judgment respecting [the Pastoral] Epistles solely on the ground that it is a miracle, or where do I argue solely and alone from the inner contradiction of the contents? Above all, I proceed from definite, historically advanced facts and seek on this foundation to draw together for the first time the different threads of my critical combinations into a single whole. This holding fast to the historically given is the characteristic mark of my criticism. . . . [155]

In the second place, as we already have seen, Strauss engages entirely in a dialectical criticism of the individual stories or pericopes in the Gospel accounts. He plays one off against the other on the basis of his canons of authenticity, thus reducing them all to the status of incredibility. The authenticity of the writings—the literary units—in which these stories are contained is then rendered dependent on the credibility of the stories: "Since the stories, on account of their general historical character—partly mythical, partly at least highly doubtful—could make only a very limited claim to credibility, so also only a negative judgment could be brought against the writings to the effect that, since they are neither eyewitnesses nor exact reports, they are also

[154] Cf. *Die kanonischen Evangelien*, pp. 41–46; and *Paulus*, I, 93 (E.T., 81), especially the whole of chap. iii of Part I, "Die Bekehrung des Apostels Paulus."

[155] "Abgenöthigte Erklärung," *TZT*, IX:3, 206.

very unreliable sources for the handing over of the Gospel story."[156]

In Baur's judgment, this is an entirely backward procedure. To examine the individual stories historically, one must first consider the literary context in which they are found. Only thus is one in a position to make judgments respecting the literary and theological intention of the stories for the mind of the writer. On the basis of their use, one can then determine their historical credibility and their mutual relationships. The Gospels are not haphazard collections of pericopes; they are theological treatises, and the first task of the interpreter is to start with the mind and intent of the author or authors, in so far as this can be determined from the writing as a whole. Only then is he able to move on to the detailed task of examining the units separately and in comparison with similar units in other Gospels. The fact that Strauss starts at the wrong place in his criticism of the Gospels and never moves beyond it marks his greatest failing.[157] Therefore Baur regards his own criticism as "more methodical" than Strauss's, since it starts at the place where the historian must start in order to reach a sound judgment about the life of Jesus. At the same time, it is "more conservative," since it succeeds in separating genuinely historical elements from the nonhistorical, and thus in preserving the positivity of the Gospel.[158]

Finally, for Baur the artificiality of Strauss's critical approach is revealed by his oscillating opinion regarding the historical credibility of the Fourth Gospel, as expressed in the first, third, and fourth editions of *Das Leben Jesu*. In the introduction to the third edition, he attempts to justify a new and more positive assessment of the historical Jesus on the ground that recent studies (de Wette's and Neander's) have now caused him to doubt his earlier doubt regarding the credibility of John—not that he is now entirely convinced of its authenticity, only that he is no longer convinced of its unauthenticity.[159] But in the fourth edition, this doubt about his doubt has disappeared again. Baur asks: "Can one express oneself any more weakly and uncertainly on a major question of New Testament criticism? . . . How could it be other-

---

[156] *Die kanonischen Evangelien*, pp. 42–43; cf. pp. 40–43.

[157] *Ibid.*, pp. 72–76. This criticism of Strauss is the basis for Baur's development of an alternative method for dealing with the Gospel texts; see below, pp. 196–201. Both Dilthey and Hirsch regard this as Baur's basic and most telling criticism of Strauss. Cf. Dilthey, *op. cit.*, pp. 420–21, and Emanuel Hirsch, *Geschichte der neuern evangelischen Theologie*, V, 523.

[158] *Kirchengeschichte*, V, 399. See also *Paulus*, I, vi–vii (E.T., vi–vii).

[159] Baur expressed surprise that in the third edition of *Das Leben Jesu* Strauss now argued for the historical authenticity of the Fourth Gospel, while his own investigations were leading him decisively in the other direction. Baur to D. F. Strauss, 29 May 1838 (U.B.T., Md 750, ii, 7, 2). This is the last letter from Baur to Strauss in their extant correspondence devoted to substantive theological matters. Following 1838, their correspondence declined in volume and turned largely to personal affairs until Strauss's bitter letter of 1846, in which the theological issue was engaged for the last time.

wise than that a criticism, which on such questions is so little in accord with itself, should only come to an entirely negative result?"[160]

Strauss's "Glaubenslehre" and the Open Break Between Baur and Strauss. Strauss intended *Das Leben Jesu* as the critical prolegomenon to a speculative reconstruction of Christology— which remained forever unwritten. This "inability to keep to a system"[161] is revealed again in his *Glaubenslehre* (1840–41), which also ends with entirely negative results and is not followed by the intended positive reconstruction. In this work, Strauss traces step by step the formation and development of each major dogma up to the height of its ecclesiastical expression, at which point the seeds of its dissolution are unveiled as well as the kernel of truth which it contains. Then the steps of decline are traced down to the present, where a new coat of paint on an old building is not to be confused with a genuine renovation. The history of dogma is thus its criticism.[162] At this point Baur raises the question whether "the negative result, which Strauss finds in the case of every dogma, is really to be perceived as the objective judgment of history itself. . . ."[163]

The purpose and consequence of Strauss's challenge is to pose the basic problem in modern theology, no longer as that of conflict between different theological systems and tendencies, but as that of a complete antithesis between Church theology and modern "science." In the face of such a challenge, the Confessionalists have discovered that it is far simpler to hold to the "factuality of the Church" and to regard the "ecclesiastical consciousness" as the limit at which all "scientific denials" must break down, than it is "to contend for the positivity of Christianity [*das Positive des Christenthums*] on scientific grounds."[164]

Baur's earliest criticism of Strauss's *Glaubenslehre* came in the introduction to his *Lehrbuch der Dogmengeschichte*, where he classified Strauss's work among the eighteenth century rationalist historians of dogma,[165] whose *Lehrbüchern* were "bound to dogmatics" (or, as Strauss rightly put it, to "antidogmatics"):

Rationalism has in itself, according to the nature of the case, no historical sense. The emptier its dogmatics is, the more it devotes itself to history in order to have an object for its criticism. Just this, however, is the one-sidedness and subjectivity of this dogmatic-historical standpoint, that the history of dogma should be conducive only of criticism. In such a relation with dogmatics, the history of dogma can never

---

160 *Die kanonischen Evangelien*, p. 75.
161 Barth, *From Rousseau to Ritschl*, pp. 365–66.
162 *Kirchengeschichte*, V, 403.
163 *Ibid.*, p. 404.
164 *Ibid.*, pp. 404–405.
165 See below, pp. 153–54.

come into its own. The most striking example of this is provided by Strauss's dogmatics [the *Glaubenslehre*]. Although this dogmatics, in a wholly different sense than is the case with ordinary *Lehrbüchern*, rests on the realization of the view that the history of dogma is also its criticism, it is also clearly to be seen from this work that history, considered only from the dogmatic standpoint, comes off badly. The major concern is not history itself but criticism. . . . Rationalism can relate itself to the history of dogma only negatively.[166]

Strauss reacted bitterly to the prepublication copy of this work which he received from Baur in the fall of 1846. In an angry letter he asserts that "the critical questions of concern today cannot be so peacefully handled from a purely historical standpoint if the dogmatic point is not *negatively* settled—I do not say, through me, but, however, through the actions aroused by me—fundamentally and in the inner consciousness even of the orthodox. The acknowledgement of this, and that therefore contemporary historical criticism must travel the road down which I have helped it—this is what I have never found from you, from the beginning up to the present."[167] Strauss asks: if Baur can acknowledge that an historical-critical treatment of dogma is in fact the result of an "antidogmatic" intention, as it is in the case of rationalism, then why can he not also recognize that his own "peaceful" handling of critical questions implies a "negative" stance dogmatically? Yet this is what Baur has never acknowledged. He perceives continuity and development, upbuilding and growth, in the history of dogma precisely where Strauss sees only atrophy and self-destruction. Furthermore, Baur views historical-critical study as a positive foundation for faith and dogmatics, while Strauss considers it as only destructive of Christian faith as it has been traditionally understood. Therefore Strauss concludes his letter by writing that "the affair lies between us even as it lies, and neither these lines nor an answer from you can make it otherwise." He suspects that Baur has expressed these "positive," even "conservative," convictions and has publicly dissociated himself from Strauss in order to protect himself and his position from official censure.[168]

Baur respected Strauss's desire not to receive a reply and wrote instead to Christian Märklin, asking him to communicate his response to Strauss and, if possible, to mediate the dispute. In the letter Baur restates the disagreement between himself and Strauss on the history of dogma and criticism of the Gospels, anticipating something of his characterization of Strauss's position in *Die kanonischen Evangelien*, which was to be published the following summer. He insists, however, that these are scientific, not per-

166 *Lehrbuch der Dogmengeschichte* (1st ed.), pp. 42–43.
167 Strauss to Baur, 17 Nov. 1846 (U.B.T., Md 750, i, 19, 19). Italics mine.
168 *Ibid.* As we have seen, Strauss harbored these suspicions as early as 1836; they are now finally expressed, openly and bitterly.

sonal differences, and that he "has never polemicized against him in any other interest than for the purpose of the scientific establishment of my view." Strauss demands "something impossible" if he insists that "one ought unconditionally to remain standing with his *Leben Jesu.*" Baur insists that he was not first helped to the "dogmatically free standpoint, . . . in which I stand," by Strauss and his book, and that his own position, critically and dogmatically, is an independent and autonomous one, although he will not deny that he has learned much from his former student in terms of an understanding of the future direction which criticism must take. He resents the implication that he has learned everything from Strauss and that in return Strauss has learned nothing from him. Finally, Baur "rejects with indignation" the implication that he has opposed Strauss with "impure motives."[169]

The result of this dispute seems to have been that Strauss and Baur each finally became clear on the dogmatic as well as the critical stance of the other. There was apparently no further correspondence between them, except for a final, conciliatory letter sent by Strauss to Baur in September 1860, prompted by the latter's first stroke, in which Strauss hints at an intention to return once again to a theological authorship.[170] The personal and private relation seems to have been terminated by the break of 1846, and Baur now saw fit to express himself objectively and critically on Strauss's position and its distinction from his own, in terms not only of method but now also of results, in lectures and publications over the next few years. Finally, during the last two months of his life Baur was prompted by an essay by Zeller[171] to stress more sharply than ever before the distinction between the "Tübingen criticism" and Strauss. In a letter to Zeller Baur writes:

The major point is still this, that Strauss brought an already long-established view of the unhistorical reality of miracle methodically and in principle to a purely negative view of history. However, he also remained there. Between his life of Jesus and his dogmatic "Concluding Dissertation" there lies an infinite cleft which he could never bridge by his standpoint of that time.[172] Only by means of a *wholly other*

169 Baur to Christian Märklin, 26 Nov. 1846 (Letters from Baur to Christian Märklin, Nos. 20785–20800, Schiller-Nationalmuseum, Marbach; cited in Barnikol, "Das Erbe Hegels," *WZMLU*, X:1, 297–98).

170 Strauss to Baur, 5 Sept. 1860 (U.B.T., Md 750, i, 19, 20). This letter is a curious and fascinating piece, but it is relevant to a study of Strauss, not of Baur. No reply to it is extant.

171 "Die Tübinger historische Schule," *SHZ*, IV (1860), 90–173. In this essay, Zeller did not clarify to Baur's satisfaction the distinction between himself and Strauss.

172 In other words, Strauss was unable to move from historical criticism to dogmatics, "to re-establish dogmatically that which has been destroyed critically" (as Strauss himself states the problem at the beginning of the "Concluding Dissertation," *The Life of Jesus*, p. 757). The reason is that his criticism provided no firm historical ground on which a dogmatic re-establishment of Christology could be executed.

criticism can his view descend from its negativity to a ground in which there is a true and real history. I believe this would have to be accentuated with yet more definite emphasis and should be designated as the main point of the distinction.[173]

Developments Following Strauss

Strauss both announces and exemplifies the dissolution of the theological synthesis achieved by Schleiermacher and Hegel. Following him, the effects of the dissolution spread throughout the theological world. On the far left, Feuerbach, Bruno Bauer, and Arnold Ruge move beyond the bounds of the Christian faith entirely, replacing it with a new atheism and (in Bauer's case) denying the historicity of Jesus.[174] More significant, however, is the failure of the so-called "Mediating Theology" of the Schleiermacherian and Right-Hegelian schools authentically to "mediate" between Church theology and critical-speculative science. For the Schleiermacher group, centered at Berlin and including in its ranks Nitzsch, Twesten, Ullmann, Lücke, and Umbreit, Schleiermacher's dogmatics has "ossified into the rigid forms of orthodoxy." Ullmann is the major defender of the Mediating Theology against Strauss. His *Das Wesen des Christenthums* (1845) represents a superficial combination of supernaturalism and rationalism. His language "holds to Schleiermacherian expressions and definitions, but it knows nothing of the general view, the *Weltanschauung*, by which they are borne in Schleiermacher and without which they have no meaning."[175] The "flat and weak" theology of the Schleiermacher party is represented by two journals, *Theologische Studien und Kritiken*, and *Deutsche Zeitschrift für christliche Wissenschaft und christliches Lebens*.[176]

The Right-Hegelian theologians include Liebner, Lange, Marheineke, Martensen, Conradi, Göschel, and Dorner.[177] In Baur's judgment, their failure at mediation can be seen especially in their Christology. In the first place, they attempt to deduce speculatively the necessity of an individual God-man; and in the second place, the God-man thus deduced is conceived as the absolute identity of the archetypal and the historical. They restore a supernatural conception of the person of Jesus and thus diminish or destroy his true humanity: for Dorner "Christ therefore stands as

---

[173] Baur to Eduard Zeller, 6 Nov. 1860 (U.B.T., Md 747, 19, 34, 168). Italics mine. Cf. also Baur to Eduard Zeller, 19 Oct. 1860 (U.B.T., Md 747, 19, 34, 167).

[174] Baur discusses Bruno Bauer's hypothesis concerning the Proto-Gospel as the original source of the mythical traditions about Jesus in *Die kanonischen Evangelien*, pp. 65–68. Cf. also *Kirchengeschichte*, V, 386–94. On Feuerbach, see above, pp. 56–58.

[175] *Kirchengeschichte*, V, 405–406; cf. also pp. 399–400, and *Dogmengeschichte*, III, 347–48.

[176] *Kirchengeschichte*, V, 424, 426.

[177] *Ibid.*, 406–407, 427.

much above humanity as man does above the animal kingdom."[178] Conradi and Göschel argue for the supernatural conception of Jesus on the basis that human nature does not contain in itself the capacity to produce the God-man. Baur responds that Jesus cannot exist as an authentic human being apart from the capacity of the human race to produce him.[179] With respect to Dorner, Baur acknowledges that, in his *Entwicklungsgeschichte der Lehre von der Person Christi* (1839), he has sought to modify the traditional Christology with respect to its understanding of the absolute coincidence of humanity and divinity in Christ; but he complains that Dorner's positive statement (that Christ's Godhead is possessed only *in potentia* or "in principle") is shrouded in unclarity, confusion, and contradiction. He also objects to Dorner's notion that Christ is the head and crown of a spiritual creation in the same way that man (represented by Adam) is head and crown of the natural creation, a distinction which results in what Baur regards as a new kind of docetism; and in any case, the Christ thus conceived is not necessarily a single individual, any more than "Adam" is necessarily a single individual.[180]

The Mediating theologians of this period have at least the virtue, however, of opposing the reactionary tendencies of the conservative Lutheran ecclesiastical parties, represented by their powerful organ, the *Evangelische Kirchenzeitung*, and of Confessionalism, represented by the Erlangen theologians J. C. K. Hofmann and A. Harless, and by their journal, the *Zeitschrift für Protestantismus und Kirche*. The Confessionalists, as we have seen, refuse entirely to face the challenge to theology of scientific criticism.[181] In addition, both the Confessionalists and the Lutheran parties bitterly oppose the idea advanced by the Mediating school of a unified German Protestant Church. Indeed, the controversy engendered by the question of Church union has done nothing but sharpen the awareness of ecclesiastical differences.[182] Symptomatic in another way of the dissolution of theological unity is Möhler's uncompromising attack on Protestantism and the consequent loss of any earlier hope of mediation between Catholic and Protestant tendencies.[183]

Finally, Baur turns his attention to a new expression of speculative theism, which, in opposition to the tendency toward a pan-

[178] *Dreieinigkeit*, III, 988.

[179] *Ibid.*, pp. 975–79, 983–86.

[180] *Ibid.*, pp. 963–65, 987–88. As we have seen above, pp. 27–29, Baur was not impressed by Dorner when he lectured in Tübingen as a Privatdozent, and apparently he never changed his mind. He was primarily acquainted with Dorner's early work as an historian, whereas Dorner's most impressive accomplishments came later as a systematic theologian. His *System der christlichen Glaubenslehre* was published in 1879–81, twenty years after Baur's death.

[181] See above, p. 81.

[182] *Kirchengeschichte*, V, 405, 409–411.

[183] See above, pp. 22–23.

theistic *Weltanschauung* in Schleiermacher and Hegel, attempts a new mediation of transcendence and immanence based on the notion of the absolute personality of God. Included here are I. H. Fichte's *Speculative Theologie* (1846), C. H. Weisse's *Philosophische Dogmatik* (Vol. I, 1855), and Richard Rothe's *Theologische Ethik* (1845).[184] Among these, Rothe's *Ethik* is the most important; it is one of "the most significant appearances in the area of systematic theology" of its time by virtue of the unity it achieves between the ethical and the religious, speculation and theology. In his awareness of the task, value, and independence of theological "science," Rothe is on a plane with Schleiermacher. But his "theosophical realism terminates finally in a very empty play of fantasy" respecting the relation of God and the world.[185] More serious difficulties plague Weisse's work;[186] but despite these shortcomings Baur seems to approve the effort to fashion a theism in which the transcendence and immanence of God are genuinely mediated. Unfortunately, he has nothing substantive to say about this possibility.

BAUR AND THE TÜBINGEN SCHOOL

Baur's interpretation of the history of modern theology, developing through three distinct phases from about 1750 to 1850, provides the context within which his own theological task is set. This task, to put it simply, is "to contend for the positivity of Christianity on scientific grounds,"[187] or, to describe it more generally, to mediate between theology and criticism. As we have observed earlier, Baur thought this mediation to be a possibility because there is no necessary hostility between the Church and the world —between the faith of the Church and the critical-speculative "sciences" of the modern world.

For Baur, the central theological task of his day is historical-critical in nature. That aspect of contemporary "scientific" thought with which above all Church theology must now come to terms is historical science. In the first place, historical study is the primary form in which the scientific spirit of the "present age" has been expressed and by means of which any critically defensible theology must verify its claim to credibility.

The chief endeavors of the [present] age in the higher realms of science are critical and historical. Everything which is to have value for the present is asked for its historical justification; everything found exist-

---

184 Rothe is usually regarded as a Mediating theologian (cf. Hirsch, *op. cit.*, V, 395 ff.), but is not treated by Baur as such.
185 *Kirchengeschichte*, V, 407–408.
186 *Ibid.*, pp. 408–409.
187 Which, as we have seen, is Baur's description of what the Confessionalists *failed* to do. *Ibid.*, p. 405.

ing is examined down to the roots of its existence; one seeks to return to the beginnings and the first elements in which everything is already decided, in order to achieve a clear insight into the whole from the discovered relations of the individual parts. . . . If this critical task is in so many areas of human knowledge the necessary spiritual process through which the consciousness of the present must be mediated with the past, where can it be of greater importance than where the present is connected most closely and immediately with the past, and where this connection is established in the innermost interests of our spiritual nature?[188]

Now that the tools for the "scientific" (i.e., in the vocabulary of German idealism, both critical and imaginative) study of the past have been developed, Christian theology has no choice other than to submit its historical claims to the scrutiny of this tool and to defend them by its use. In the second place, Schleiermacher and Hegel—the two great mediating theologians of the modern period —virtually ignored the historical use of scientific thought in their concentration rather on metaphysical and speculative arguments, and this is a major reason for the internal collapse of their mediating positions. Third, the historical-critical challenge posed to theology by Strauss and others could not responsibly be ignored. Finally, religion itself is a peculiarly historical phenomenon. This is especially the case with Christianity, which, as the above quotation intimates, is an "historically given religion," whose essential nature can be determined only through historical investigation.[189] Furthermore, the act of faith itself is historical in nature, and the relationship between faith and its object or content is an historically mediated and historically knowable relationship.[190] In any case, the historicity of Christianity is not of a special or esoteric nature, hidden from the scrutiny of the critical historian (although the historical study of Christianity also involves a theological commitment). Baur knew nothing of the later distinction in German theology between *Historie* and *Geschichte*.[191]

For these reasons Baur suggests in his lectures on the history of dogma that "theology in its most recent period of development could not remain standing" with Hegel, and that "the same result [the meditation of religious faith and critical thought] at which philosophy had arrived in *its way* must also be established in *the historical way* through historical criticism. If Christianity is what speculative consideration shows it to be, then history must also provide the same result. What the true nature of Christianity is in itself, as philosophy states it, must also allow itself to be

---

188 *Paulus*, I, 3–4 (E.T., 1–2).
189 See below, pp. 127–28, 237.
190 See below, pp. 175–77.
191 See below, p. 145.

authenticated historically."[192] Baur expresses himself similarly toward the end of the second edition of the *Lehrbuch der Dogmengeschichte*, where he is speaking of the future task of Protestant dogmatics: "Since Christianity itself, as an historical manifestation, belongs to the past, the highest task [for the present], on the solution of which everything else depends, can only consist in the ever purer and less prejudiced investigation of what Christianity originally and essentially is. The more certainly progress in this way is strengthened through an awakened and more active sense for historical research, . . . the more . . . the conditions are provided under which dogma can approach a new and rich epoch of its development."[193] This is the task which the Tübingen School and historical-critical theology have set for themselves.[194]

As such, historical-critical theology does not embrace the total theological task of the day but only a very important part of it. Whenever Baur describes the work of the Tübingen School in his own writings,[195] he limits himself to the development and major results of his historical research in the areas of New Testament, Church history, and history of dogma. Clearly, he does not regard himself primarily as a systematic or constructive theologian but as an historian—an historian of the Church and its theology —i.e., as an historical-critical theologian. The purpose of historical-critical theology is to investigate critically and interpret imaginatively the historical orgins, development, and "forms" of the Christian Church. As such, it is not to be confused with, nor is it a substitute for, systematic theology. By its very nature, it is misleading to refer to it as a theological "school." Baur disclaims being the founder of a new school and remarks that those who participate in the ongoing tradition of historical research scarcely constitute a special school. For this reason, it would not be a repudiation of the school or its methods and purposes if some of its conclusions were modified or reversed.[196]

---

192 *Dogmengeschichte*, III, 356. Italics mine. Such an attempt at an historical authentication has been undertaken, Baur thinks, by Strauss, but with entirely negative results. *Ibid.*, p. 356. Cf. also the following in a letter to Heyd regarding work on *Dreieinigkeit und Menschwerdung Gottes:* "I have again convinced myself through this work that one cannot better establish the truth of the newer theology than in historical fashion [*auf dem geschichtlichen Wege*]." Baur to L. F. Heyd, 13 Feb. 1841 (U.B.T., Md 619r, 27).

193 *Lehrbuch der Dogmengeschichte* (3d ed.), p. 357 (this material is not found in the first edition). Baur suggests that in this fashion the opposition between philosophical and ecclesiastical world-views can be overcome (see pp. 356–57).

194 The extent to which this proposal represents the "historicizing" of theology will be discussed below, pp. 268–69.

195 Baur in Klüpfel, *op. cit.*, pp. 407–408; *Kirchengeschichte*, V, 394–99; *An Hase; Die Tübinger Schule*, Part I.

196 Cf. *Kirchengeschichte*, V, 394–99; *Die Tübinger Schule*, pp. 56–60; and Baur in Klüpfel, *loc. cit.*

But even if historical-critical theology is not, strictly speaking, a theological school, it does embrace some dogmatic principles, and it does possess a specific historical methodology. It has a *point of view* and a *method* as well as results, and to these matters we turn our attention in the next two chapters.

3 * DOGMATIC PRINCIPLES OF AN HISTORICAL THEOLOGY

In Baur's view, it is not only justifiable but necessary to examine the theological presuppositions and principles of historical study, when the subject of that study is the history of the Christian Church and Christian thought. "The historian of dogma can take his position only from the standpoint of the most recent dogmatic consciousness. . . . Where else can he obtain the clear conception of the object whose historical movement is the problem with which he ought to concern himself, other than from the consciousness of the present? The historian can move back into the past only from the present."[1] "There can be no comprehensive work in Church history whose historical perspective does not wholly bear in itself the character of the theological standpoint shared by its author."[2] The theological historian who attempts to reconstruct the past from a previous theological standpoint, or who thinks he can write Church history or history of dogma without a theology of his own, fails on one of two counts. Either he writes a history which interprets the past from a viewpoint other than the present and which is therefore not only artificial but also fails to take advantage of new perspectives. Or he produces a work which does not participate internally in the historical life of the Church and which is blind to its own subjective principles. Baur, therefore, makes no secret of the fact that as an historian he is working within a theological and philosophical framework which has its roots in Schleiermacher and Hegel, and to a lesser degree, Schelling.

At the same time, Baur's dogmatic convictions are not only the presupposition but also the result of his historical-critical theology. The inverse relationship also holds: dogmatics depends on the study of the history of dogma as well as the history of dogma on dogmatics.[3] As with other aspects of Baur's thought, it is diffi-

[1] *Vorlesungen über die christliche Dogmengeschichte*, F. F. Baur, ed., Vol. I/1: *Das Dogma der alten Kirche von der apostolischen Zeit bis zur Synode in Nicäa* (Leipzig: Fues's Verlag, 1865), p. 12.

[2] *Epochen*, p. 5. See below, pp. 170–74.

[3] *Dogmengeschichte*, I/1, 3 ff. The question as to whether dogmatics remains in any sense "normative" at the same time that it is understood to be histori-

cult to break this unity apart so as to begin to elucidate it. There are no compelling or necessary reasons why we start where we do. With a thinker for whom unities are more vital than distinctions, any starting place is bound to be arbitrary.

Baur was not and did not intend to be a systematic theologian. He did not write a *Glaubenslehre* like some theological historians (e.g., Strauss, Ritschl, Troeltsch); nowhere does he draw together his dogmatic convictions into a convenient summary. Indeed, it is often difficult to distinguish his own theological viewpoint from material he is critically elucidating. Occasionally, direct clues are provided by footnotes or by statements of interpretation and judgment which make clear the perspective from which he is writing. His academic opinions and correspondence provide valuable clues, and his sermons are especially helpful in clarifying certain aspects of his Christology. His interpretation of the course of theology between 1750 and 1850, examined in the preceding chapter, is immensely helpful for our present purposes. But for the most part one must rely on the emergence of consistent patterns of conviction, interest, and intention from the corpus of his literature as a whole. The theological conceptions contained in the individual writings must be judged in terms of the total corpus and the patterns it contains, but this framework has its roots, of course, in the individual writings. Hence any attempt to present critically and systematically Baur's dogmatic convictions must remain a hazardous and experimental enterprise.

The present chapter is structured in such a way as to elicit some of the continuities which are implicit in Baur's thought. It is logical to start with his understanding of the place of dogmatics in relation to religion and philosophy. Then it is possible to turn to his "general theory" of religion, derived from comparative studies in the history of religions, according to which religion generally, and Christianity in particular, are to be understood as the actualization of the idea of reconciliation between God and man. Next, his Christology can be considered, which serves as the dogmatic center of his theology as a whole, since it is here that the historical mediation of reconciliation is most decisively enacted. His doctrine of the Church can then be treated as following from his Christological principles.[4] Finally, we may consider the foundation of Baur's historical theology, namely, his doctrine of God and his understanding of the relation between God and history. Here,

---

cally conditioned and therefore relative, in Baur's view, will be considered below, pp. 172–73, 268–69. For further discussion of the relation between history of dogma and dogmatics, see pp. 240–41.

[4] It is in this context, as a doctrine essentially related to and dependent upon his Christology, that Baur's anthropology would also find its appropriate place in a systematic exposition of his dogmatic position. However, since his doctrine of man is not organic to the argument of this chapter, it has been omitted. It is chiefly concerned with the structures of human freedom. For a very brief discussion of it, see above, pp. 20–21.

too, some of the weaknesses in his viewpoint will be brought to
light and criticized.

It should be stressed that Baur's dogmatic convictions are not
simply modifications of Schleiermacher and Hegel. In theology
as in historical study Baur went his own way, and he fashioned a
point of view which was distinctly his own. The two most important components in this point of view are his Christology and
his theology of the Church. Not only did he do his most independent and sustained thinking at these two points, but also they
are closest to the heart of his historical-critical theology, for they
are concerned with the origin and development of that internally
congruent series of historical manifestations whereby the idea of
reconciliation is actualized.

What does Baur mean by the *idea* of reconciliation? Before
continuing, we must take a closer look at one of Baur's most
important systematic categories: "idea"—for it becomes of constitutive importance in both his Christology and his doctrine of the
Church, as well as in his general definition of religion. An idea
(*Idee*) or a concept (*Begriff*) is an expression, form, or actualization of thought (*das Denken*).[5] Thought constitutes the "life" of
Spirit or the "nature" of Spirit; it is that whereby Spirit mediates
itself with itself in order to become thinking, free, self-conscious Spirit.[6] "The absolute idea is God as the Absolute Spirit,
who mediates himself with himself in the process of thought."[7]
By thought, Spirit—both divine and human—"moves" and "lives."
For both Baur and Hegel, thought is a process which transpires
concretely, historically. Therefore the expressions of thought—
ideas or concepts—constitute the life, the substantial reality, of
history. Although this terminology and usage is Hegelian, Baur
acquired "idea" as a category for the description of historical movement and life first from Schleiermacher[8] and Schelling, and used it
as such in the introduction to his *Symbolik und Mythologie*,[9]

5 Throughout this work, *das Denken* is translated as "thought." Were it
not for the awkward construction which would often result in English, the
term might better be translated as "thinking," in order to convey the distinction in German between this active verbal form and the substantival,
das Gedanke, or the past participial, *das Gedachte*. "Thought" (*das Denken*),
as used to describe the divine life by both Hegel and Baur, means "the process
of thinking" rather than "thoughts" in the sense of static, past, reified ideas.
6 *Dogmengeschichte*, I/1, 49–50. Cf. III, 353 (quoted above, p. 54).
7 *Lehrbuch der Dogmengeschichte* (1st ed.), p. 257.
8 Cf. Schleiermacher's distinction between nature and history in his philosophical ethics, *Entwürfe zu einem System der Sittenlehre*, Otto Braun, ed.
(Leipzig: Felix Meiner, 1927), Ms. VII (*Ethik*, 1816), Allgemeine Einleitung,
§ 46.
9 Cf. *Symbolik und Mythologie*, I, v, x–xii. "The idea at all times conditions the individual manifestations. Without the idea of religion, the essence of the individual forms of religion cannot be grasped. . . ." (p. x).
Cf. also Baur's lecture manuscript from the Blaubeuren period, "Geschichte
des Alterthums" (U.B.T., Mh II 166, q), p. 13, and Heinz Liebing, "Historisch-
kritische Theologie," ZTK, LVII:3, 307.

several years before his encounter with Hegel's philosophy of religion.

Idea as an historical category is not to be understood as the expression of an abstract rational process of logical dialectic. Spirit is not simply "mind"; it is the fundamental quality of nonmaterial life, described biblically by metaphors of light, such as "brilliance," "radiance," "glory" (*doxa*). The thought (or "thinking") which is the nature of Spirit in its life-process of self-relatedness is not therefore abstract and lifeless. It is concrete, historical, vital, moral, the mode of relatedness of Spirit (both divine and human) to itself and to other Spirits. According to Paul, thought (or knowledge, *gnosis*) is a relation of love; without love, knowledge is abstract, vain, "puffed up." Religion is knowledge in the sense that God knows man and man knows God in love. To know something is to exist in a relation of love to it.[10] If this Pauline idea can be considered normative for Baur, then it can be said that to think is to engage in an act or a relation of love. Such acts are the constitutive factor in divine-human history. An idea is an expression of an act or a relation of love. This would seem to be pre-eminently the case with the Christian idea of reconcilation, which is primarily soteriological (i.e., concerned with the divine act of love whereby the estranged relationship between God and man is healed, and with the human response to this act in faith, love, and moral obedience) rather than speculative or cosmological. Therefore the universalism of the Christian idea is always bound to the concrete historical acts in which salvation is actualized, and in this respect is fundamentally distinguished from Gnosticism and all forms of abstract idealism.[11]

THE RELATION OF PHILOSOPHY, THEOLOGY, AND RELIGION

Baur has sometimes been accused of collapsing the distinctions between philosophy, theology, and religion in a fashion similar to Hegel, so that theological and religious knowledge are ultimately taken up into a higher form of philosophical knowledge. In fact, however, he maintains an important distinction between philosophy and religion (or religious faith), while theology serves as the point of contact between them, but is not identified with either.

With respect, first, to the distinction between philosophy and religion, Baur describes it as follows:

Religion is distinguished from philosophy in that it cannot exist without a positive, historically given authority. Without such an authority, it would lack the character of objective truth, which must belong to it according to its concept. It can derive its truth only from an historically given beginning point, which possesses its definite authority in that it lies above and beyond the consciousness of every individual,

10 Cf. *Paulus*, II, 258–59 (E.T., 236–37).
11 Cf. *Das Christenthum*, pp. 230–31, 305–306 (E.T., I, 240–41; II, 62–63).

and which leads back to a higher divine causality. It introduces every individual into the circle of a total consciousness in which he possesses his significance only through the unity of the whole, to which he belongs as an individual, and in which he must subordinate his subjectivity to the objectivity standing over against him.[12]

Religion, as we shall observe more clearly in the next section, cannot be severed from its historical roots and historical manifestations; it is an essentially historical phenomenon. The content of religious faith cannot be separated from the historical forms through which it is mediated: "Form and content are inseparably bound together. The truth of the content can exist in absolutely no other form than the original, i.e., the form given externally-historically, with which faith has also immediately preserved its content."[13] Philosophical knowledge, by contrast, is abstract and universal; it is not mediated by specific historical events. This can be seen most clearly when Platonic philosophy is compared with the Christian religion. The Platonic ideas subsist in a realm of abstract transcendence; Plato's idea of God "has not yet descended from the area of philosophy and knowledge into that of religion and faith."[14] The *content* of religious and philosophical knowledge may indeed ultimately be identical (namely, the idea of reconciliation); but the *forms* through which this content is mediated are different in religion and in philosophy.[15]

Theology stands in a mediating relationship between philosophy and religion. Its tools of thought are philosophical in nature; but its subject matter or content is given by faith. The relation between philosophy and theology can be seen from the intimate and dialectical connection between the history of philosophy and the history of dogma. They are part of the same spiritual process: "The history of dogma, like the history of philosophy, is the history of human thought and investigation of the Absolute, of being-and-truth-in-itself, with the only difference that in the history of dogma thought moves wholly in the form of Christian dogma."[16] Indeed, so powerful and authentic was this form, as the dogmatic expression of the absolute religion and the absolute revelation, that for a long period in the history of the West, philosophy became the tool of theology and was given expression only in the form of Christian dogma. Only since the Reformation has philosophy been freed from its subservience to dogma, with the resultant possibility of a new and more authentic mediation between philosophy and

12 "Das christliche des Platonismus," *TZT*, X:3, 91; see also pp. 153–54.
13 *Die christliche Gnosis*, p. 720.
14 "Das christliche des Platonismus," *TZT*, X:3, 153–54. See below, p. 99. Baur suggests that Hegel's interpretation of Christianity has been influenced by Plato's philosophy of religion and shares its one-sidedness (cf. pp. 153–54). Cf. also *Lehrbuch der Dogmengeschichte* (3d ed.), p. 150.
15 *Die christliche Gnosis*, p. 717.
16 *Lehrbuch der Dogmengeschichte* (3d ed.), p. 16.

theology, one in which neither is surrendered to the other.[17] This possibility is brought to its completion in the philosophical theology of Hegel. "Philosophy and theology are reconciled with each other and become essentially one. Philosophy has become theology since it recognizes the content of theology as its own, and only in it does it have the element of its movement. Theology has become philosophy since the content common to both . . . no longer has the form of theology but of philosophy."[18]

The *content* common to philosophy and theology is theological, namely, the triune God, or the Absolute Spirit; the *form* common to both is philosophical, namely, the speculative employment of thought. Theology brings the philosophical use of thought freely to bear upon the unique and special content of faith, that content which is inseparable from the historical mediation of faith. This is theology's unique function, one which it does not share with philosophy, since the content or subject matter of philosophy is not given through a positive religious tradition, although ultimately it is concerned with the same truth.

Baur defends the use of speculation in theology against critics who are opposed to the appropriation of Hegelian and other philosophical categories in the work of the dogmatic theologian.[19] These categories enable the dogmatician to penetrate to the inner nature of the material with which he is dealing and to explicate it intelligibly.[20] They serve to relate historical faith in revelation to "thinking consideration" in such a way that both historical and philosophical investigations may freely result. They are not, however, inimical to biblical faith.[21] These categories do not represent the imposition of a particular philosophical bias on faith but rather the employment of disciplined, critical, "scientific" thought in the realm of theology.[22]

The task of dogmatics, I have suggested, is to bring thought to bear on the content of religion and religious faith, and thus to mediate between faith and thought (or between religion and philosophy).

Dogmatics is the science of faith [*Dogmatik ist die Wissenschaft des Glaubens*], and its task therefore is to mediate faith and knowledge [*Wissen*]. If faith and knowledge are to be mediated, then it stands to reason that each of these two elements in dogmatics has an equal right. . . . That which is true for faith naturally remains true also for knowledge; but it is another matter completely when faith is straight-

[17] *Ibid.*, pp. 16–19. Cf. also *Dreieinigkeit*, III, 11–15.

[18] *Lehrbuch der Dogmengeschichte* (3d ed.), pp. 355–56. Cf. also *Dogmengeschichte*, I/1, 60; III, 348, 355.

[19] On the place of speculation in historical theology, see below, pp. 162–67.

[20] Cf. Gutachten of 12 Apr. 1841 (U.B.T., Md 750, v, 4).

[21] Gutachten of 29 May 1839 (U.B.T., Md 750, v, 2).

[22] Cf. *ibid.*, and Gutachten of 27 June 1839 (U.B.T., Md 750, v, 3). Cf. also "Über die geschichtliche Bedeutung der fünfundzwanzig Jahre 1816–1841," pp. 17–18.

way presupposed as absolutely true. In this case, knowledge is reduced merely to the status of bringing the content of faith into a logical form, and any speculation . . . that knowledge also has its right against faith is excluded in advance.[23]

The content of faith is not something which is brought to dogmatics as absolutely given (either in Scripture or in the symbolical books); rather, it is the task of dogmatics, through the use of knowledge, to determine and express the content of faith for every new age.[24] This is by no means a new idea; the Church Fathers (above all Origen and Clement of Alexandria, but also Tertullian) recognized the necessary place of knowledge in faith; and the "critical principle" of Protestantism consists in bringing historical and philosophical thought, i.e., "scientific" thought, freely to bear on the content of faith.[25]

Finally, Baur maintains against his pietistic critics that scientific theology is not inimical to the religious life but instead makes an important contribution to it.

[It is said] that the more recent speculative theology, because it deviates in so many respects from biblical Christianity, i.e., from the letter of the Bible, abolishes the foundation of practical religiousness. . . . What is this other than the arrogant pietistic prejudice that everything which belongs to the calling of the practicing clergyman can be pursued only in pietistic fashion? The congregation too is destined not always to remain standing in its faith in the same spot, but, so far as it is able, to make progress, in order that it may better learn to distinguish between essentials and unessentials in matters of faith. But how can this happen other than through clergymen who possess the necessary scientific training alongside religious interests? And for what other purpose are all clergymen and pastors trained in the University, than that through their scientific training they are placed in the position to work all the more effectively in their practical calling?[26]

23 Gutachten of 12 Apr. 1841 (U.B.T., Md 750, v, 4). This opinion is directed against Schmid and the pietists, who believe that knowledge ought to be permitted only a subservient and apologetic status in relation to faith, and who therefore are opposed to having the chair in dogmatics filled by a "speculative" theologian, in this case Zeller. It is clear, however, that Baur would equally oppose the sacrifice of faith to knowledge in dogmatics.

24 Ibid.

25 Cf. Lehrbuch der Dogmengeschichte (3d ed.), pp. 75–77; and Gutachten of 29 May 1839 (U.B.T., Md 750, v, 2) and 27 June 1839 (U.B.T., Md 750, v, 3). For further discussion of the Protestant principle, see below, pp. 174–75; of the relation of faith and historical knowledge, pp. 175–81; and of Baur's conception of dogma and dogmatics, pp. 239–41.

26 Gutachten of 27 June 1839 (U.B.T., Md 750, v, 3). Cf. also Gutachten of 20 Dec. 1835 (U.B.T., Md 750, v, 1), and Baur to L. F. Heyd, 10 Feb. 1836 (U.B.T., Md 750, ii, 6, 16): "The most difficult problem surely remains the relationship [of criticism] to the people. . . . Yet it must be confessed that one learns more properly to distinguish the essential from the less essential of religion and Christianity also for the needs of the people only by this method of the critical interpretation of history."

The religious life in general, even for the layman, is not possible without the discipline and direction provided it by scientific theology. Baur does not mean to suggest, of course, that biblical faith can be abandoned as an "unessential," but rather that the laymen must learn to think critically about the Bible and to distinguish between letter and spirit, so as not to confuse the essential truths of Christianity with matters of less importance.[27] "Science," understood as critical and speculative thought, can help the Christian discern more clearly the central foundations of his religious life. Indeed, suggests Baur, "true science" is a product of life and is not alien to it; it represents the "noblest spiritual side of life."[28]

RELIGION AS RECONCILIATION

Three forms of a general theory of religion can be distinguished in Baur's writings; they reflect different stages in his theological development. The first is almost purely Schleiermacherian and is expressed in *Symbolik und Mythologie,* his first published work. In a chapter "on the concept of religion," it is defined as the feeling of absolute dependence on God, a feeling which discloses the relation between finite being and the Absolute, who is the absolute cause of all being and the ground of religious experience itself. Religion is distinguished from philosophy by virtue of the fact that the relation to the divine transpires in a mode of feeling as opposed to thought.[29] At the same time, Baur discloses his indebtedness to Schelling by suggesting that the unity of the religions is based on the fact that they are this-worldly revelations of the divine; religion *is* divine revelation.[30]

The second stage is Hegelian. In *Die christliche Gnosis* Baur writes that for philosophy of religion the history of religions is "not merely the history of divine revelations"—that is precisely the view of Schelling which Baur himself had expressed in *Symbolik und Mythologie*—"but these revelations are at the same time the process of development in which the eternal nature of the Godhead proceeds from itself in order to return to eternal unity with itself through this manifestation and self-estrangement."[31] Re-

[27] See below, pp. 177–78.
[28] Gutachten of 27 June 1839 (U.B.T., Md 750, v, 3). Cf. "Über die geschichtliche Bedeutung der fünfundzwanzig Jahre 1816–1841," pp. 20–21.
[29] *Symbolik und Mythologie,* I, 104–107. Baur acknowledges (p. vii) that this definition, as indeed his whole treatment of the relation between Christianity and the nature religions, is deeply influenced by the first edition of Schleiermacher's *Glaubenslehre.* On the basis of the distinction of feeling from thought as the mode of religious experience, it is almost certain that Baur had not read (or, if read, had not appropriated) Hegel when he wrote this work. Later Baur draws the distinction between religion and philosophy differently and attempts to moderate the distinction between feeling and thought.
[30] *Ibid.,* pp. vi–vii.
[31] *Die christliche Gnosis,* p. 22.

ligion, in other words, *is* the divine self-manifestation. It is "essentially a relation of Spirit to spirit, in which Spirit mediates himself with himself through the factuality of thought."[32] The second form is related to the first in that the locus wherein the divine self-manifestation is realized is subjective human consciousness. "Religion, according to its nature, is nothing other than the revelation and realization of being-in-itself [*das an sich Seyende*] for consciousness."[33]

The third stage represents the culmination of the first two in that now the combination of the idea of a divine process with that of subjective religious experience is expressed in the definition itself: the essence of religion is the idea of reconciliation or atonement between God and man.[34] Here the objective and subjective components of religion are mediated. Baur's clearest and final exposition of this definition is found in his treatment of Paul's theology in his New Testament lectures, where he suggests that the concept by which Paul expresses the reconciled relationship between God and man is "righteousness" (*dikaiosunē*): "*Dikaiosunē* is the highest concept for every religion, since it is the necessary presupposition under which alone man can truly be one with God. Only when man is as God intends him to be can a relationship of unity exist between God and man. . . . Since every religion has the task of bringing man into unity with God, . . . this is therefore the concept in which even Judaism and Christianity stand completely on the same ground with each other."[35]

If the essence of religion is the relationship of reconciliation between God and man, then the various religions can be distinguished according to their understanding of the way in which this relationship is mediated.[36] The basic contrast lies between nature and history as the media through which reconciliation is actualized, or between the oriental nature religions on the one hand and Christianity as the absolute historical religion on the other.[37] The Greek and Jewish religions mediate the transition from nature religion to Christianity.[38] In Judaism, religious consciousness rises above nature, and man exists as a free, personal agent in relation to a personal God. However, the mediating

[32] *Dogmengeschichte*, I/1, 49
[33] *Dreieinigkeit*, III, 968.
[34] *Versöhnung*, p. 1.
[35] *Neutestamentliche Theologie*, p. 133. The differentia between Judaism and Christianity for Paul is the way in which *dikaiosunē* is mediated.
[36] *Versöhnung*, pp. 3–5.
[37] This contrast is shown in *Symbolik und Mythologie, oder die Naturreligion des Alterthums*. "Symbol" and "myth" are nature images by which reconciliation with the Infinite, achieved through a static and external unity with nature, is represented. Cf. I, 28–31, 41–42, 148–56, 166; II/2, 454.
[38] *Ibid.*, II/2, 454. Baur also mentions Islam in this connection (I, 148), but does not discuss it.

factor between God and man is not a subjective God-consciousness but the consciousness of people and nation, whose essential determination is the law. The law serves as only an external and legal bond between God and man and permits only the consciousness of "requirement" in their relation rather than "satisfaction," although a movement in this direction can be seen in the prophetic spirit of Judaism.[39]

With respect to Greek religion, Baur devotes an entire monograph to the subject. The substance of his argument is that Christianity and Platonic religious philosophy (the most truly religious of the pagan philosophies) are similar in their envisionment of the idea of the Good, but that the contrast between them is that of historical reality versus abstract idea. Consequently, redemption or reconciliation is understood by Platonism as eternal recollection rather than temporal-historical renewal.[40] In addition, a substantial doctrine of God is lacking in Platonism, so that the divine is only an ideal form of the human; consequently, there is no need for an historical incarnation in order to effect redemption. "Therefore everything divine of the Platonic world of ideas still remains something other-worldly for human consciousness. It has not yet descended from the area of philosophy and knowledge into that of religion and faith. Out of the multiplicity of ideas the one divine Logos must first come to consciousness, and, on the other hand, the Logos must first become flesh, if the unity of the divine and the human is not to remain a unity that is merely surmised and ascertained, but is to become a truly revealed and factually certain one."[41]

Nevertheless, Plato *anticipates* the need for an historical authority as the mediation of religious truth, and it is just this concrete and authoritative function which Socrates serves in the Platonic dialogues. Hence there is a certain parallel in function between Socrates and Christ, which marks the Christian element in Platonism, despite the fact that the *teaching* of the Platonic Socrates embraces the disjunction of idea and reality.[42] In this respect Platonism anticipates the fundamental characteristic of all the higher (i.e., non-natural) religions, namely, their historical positivity.

[39] *Versöhnung*, pp. 3–5.
[40] "Das christliche des Platonismus oder Sokrates und Christus," *TZT*, X:3, 10–11, 33, 38–40.
[41] *Ibid.*, pp. 153–54. With these words the study ends. See also pp. 38–40, 81–82, 150–54.
[42] *Ibid.*, pp. 91 ff., 153. Baur states later that by means of this *religionsgeschichtlich* comparison he has in no way diminished the historical uniqueness of Jesus of Nazareth or denied him the role of the founder of Christianity, in whom God-manhood is most completely manifested, as he has been accused of doing by Uhlhorn. See *Die Tübinger Schule*, pp. 12–13.

JESUS CHRIST AND THE HISTORICAL
MEDIATION OF RECONCILIATION

The Christology of Historical-Critical Theology

We turn now to the way in which the idea of reconcilation, which constitutes the essence of religion according to Baur, is related to the doctrine of Jesus Christ, i.e., the way in which reconciliation is historically mediated specifically for Christian faith. Emanuel Hirsch suggests that in a single sentence Baur expresses the major Christological affirmation of historical-critical theology: "[Christianity] is everything that it is solely through the person of its founder."[43] Hirsch adds that this point of view must be distinguished both from the dogmatic Christology of the ancient Church and from the rational Christology of the *Aufklärung*. It is distinguished from the first "by its completely unmetaphysical nature" and from the second "by its rootedness in a condition of reality [*Wirklichkeitsverhältnis*] and its understanding of the manifold expression which this condition of reality has found."[44] That is, the categories of this Christology are historical, which free it with one stroke from the static metaphysical terminology with which the ancient Church sought to describe the relation between the divine and the human in Jesus Christ (two "natures," one "person") as well as from the abstract idealism of the Enlightenment.

The substance of Baur's Christology, therefore, is found in his critical investigations of the historical Jesus. Who Jesus was, as the one in whom God-manhood is originally and fully actualized, and his work as the founder of Christianity and the source of Christian life and thought, can be discovered and interpreted through historical-theological study of his life and teaching. For this purpose, Baur thought it possible to penetrate critically through the kerygmatic witness of the New Testament writings to the historical figure who stands at their source and center. He engages in such an investigation in *Das Christenthum* and in the lectures on New Testament theology, the results of which will be presented in Chapter V.

At the same time, certain dogmatic considerations are necessary to justify this Christological procedure. These are explored in the section immediately following, "the necessity, possibility, and actuality of Jesus Christ," where materials are drawn primarily from Baur's discussion and evaluation of current trends in Christology, especially the third volume of *Dreieinigkeit und Menschwerdung Gottes*. Baur's criticism of the Christologies of Schleiermacher and Hegel, as summarized above in Chapter II, is also

[43] *Das Christenthum*, p. 23 (E.T., I, 23). See below, pp. 221–23. Virtually identical statements are found in *Paulus*, II, 197 (E.T., 181) ("As an historical religion, Christianity depends wholly on the person of its founder"), and in "Das christliche des Platonismus," *TZT*, X:3, 90 (". . . Christianity depends on the person of its founder in its entire historical manifestation").

[44] Emanuel Hirsch, *Geschichte der neuern evangelischen Theologie*, V, 544.

relevant to the justification of his own procedure and indeed serves as the starting point for the present discussion.

Not only must an historical approach in Christology be justified dogmatically; it is also necessary to describe the content of such a Christology—the person and work of Jesus—in dogmatic as well as historical categories, in order to establish the theological framework in which the historical study of Jesus can be approached and to possess criteria by which to evaluate the significance and meaning of the ensuing historical investigations, which at the same time will either legitimate or falsify the dogmatic framework. An historically explicated Christology possesses both critical and dogmatic elements.

Some of the dogmatic elements in Baur's Christology will be discussed in the last two sections of this part of the chapter. Here the selection of materials with which to work is more difficult, since rarely in his published writings does Baur engage in purely dogmatic statements of his own about the person and work of Christ. Hence these two sections are based primarily on Baur's unpublished sermons, which are chiefly Christological in focus.[45] They have been supplemented by Baur's interpretation of the Pauline doctrine of the person and work of Christ, as it is found in *Paulus* and the lectures on New Testament theology. This has been done for several reasons. In the first place, Baur's interpretation of Paul's Christology is for the most part congruent with the Christology of his sermons and with clues to his constructive position found at the end of *Dreieinigkeit und Menschwerdung Gottes*. Wherever this congruence is found, we shall feel free to make use of the Pauline material in this context. Second, the direction in which Baur criticizes the Christologies of Schleiermacher and Hegel points toward his positive and sympathetic treatment of Pauline Christology. In the third place, Baur regards Paul's starting place in Christology—with the human life of Jesus rather than with the divine Logos as the substantial Person of the Incarnate—as necessary in post-Reformation Protestant Christology.[46] Finally, in Baur's judgment, no one has understood and interpreted Christ more fully, or given more adequate expression to Christian consciousness, than Paul, and therefore his theology possesses a normative significance for Christian thought and Christian faith.[47] For these reasons, in his study of Paul, Baur comes closest to giving direct expression to his own Christological convictions.

The Necessity, Possibility, and Actuality of Jesus Christ

The Historical "Necessity" of Jesus Christ. I have already discussed Baur's conviction that there can be no dogmatic or speculative demonstration (such as that attempted by Schleiermacher

---

[45] See above, pp. 19–20.
[46] See below, pp. 109–110.
[47] Cf. *Paulus*, II, 133, 295–302, 315 (E.T., 123, 270–77, 288).

and the Mediating theologians) of the necessity of the historical Jesus. But it is possible, in Baur's judgment, to press an *historical* argument for the necessity of a specific founder of a religious community. If the idea of reconciliation is to be historically actualized, then it must enter into the consciousness of humanity and historical tradition by means of a definite individual or a definite beginning point. The reason for this is not speculative but historical—it is required by the nature of historical development. In Baur's judgment, the goal toward which an historical process moves proceeds from a specific and definite beginning point in which the idea to be realized in the process is first clearly, definitely and definitively expressed. Hence a critical understanding of the beginning point is the most crucial part of understanding any historical process. This is one of the fundamental canons in Baur's historical method; as such it is a critical, methodological, and hermeneutical requirement.[48] Therefore, if it can be argued dogmatically-speculatively, as Baur thinks it can, that the idea of reconciliation must be historically actualized, since it is in this fashion that the divine life achieves self-actualization, then it must first be actualized in a specific historical individual (or, possibly, a group of individuals), who serves as the founder and beginning point of the historical process in which the idea is manifested.[49]

The question as to whether the Christian Church is the specific historical process wherein the idea of reconciliation is actualized depends first of all on the person of its founder. We cannot infer, as did Schleiermacher, a *specific* cause from the effects of reconciliation in the community. This is not an historical procedure. Such an argument could only establish a spectrum of possible causes. Rather, according to Baur's interpretive canon, in order to establish whether this historical community is a divine process, we must first examine and evaluate historically its actual cause or beginning point, which serves as the foundation and center of its meaning, and which cannot be merely hypothetically inferred from its effects without historical investigation. To summarize, if God lives historically, specifically, in the Christian Church, then there must be a specific individual who is the founder, actualization, and center of meaning of this Church.

But this statement does not tell *who* this individual is or indeed even whether he exists, for there is no necessity that the Church is in fact the historical community in which the divine life mediates itself. Nor does it rule out, in principle, the possibility that the beginning point may have been a *collegium* of individuals. Therefore, *whether such an individual exists, and who he is, is a question to be settled purely by historical research.* The faith of the Church asserts that Jesus of Nazareth is this man. This faith

48 See below, pp. 188–90.
49 Cf. *Dreieinigkeit*, III, 998.

can be substantiated or repudiated, not speculatively, but historically-critically. This does not mean that historical criticism is the source of faith, which has its roots instead in the posturing of religious consciousness. Historical criticism could produce evidence that Jesus of Nazareth existed and possessed the attributes of a Redeemer without inducing faith—the subjectively appropriated conviction—that this fact is to be religiously authoritative for me, that here God confronts me authoritatively. On the other hand, historical criticism could produce evidence that Jesus of Nazareth did not exist or that the redemptive attributes were entirely products of mythical tradition, without destroying faith that this particular man is in fact what the Church claims for him. But in the latter case, such faith would involve a *sacrificium intellectus*. In the former case, however, there is no necessary movement from the historical evidence to the actuality of faith. All that is being proposed is that *if* and *when* authentic faith comes into existence, since it is historically mediated, it must be honestly instructed and tested by the historical evidence.[50]

If we wish to get to the historical Jesus, we can only start with him, not with the faith of the community, or with speculative arguments, or (to put it in modern terms) with the present existential experience of the "eschatological event." We must start with Jesus, historically-criticially, by examination of the literary sources, the Gospels, wherein his story is told.[51] This fact, Baur suggests, has tended to be forgotten. "It is the great task of our age to investigate critically the primitive history of Christianity, its origin and first development, as it lies before us in the series of writings which form the content of our New Testament canon."[52] As we have seen, Baur first recognized this need in his criticism of Schleiermacher's *Glaubenslehre* in his inaugural dissertation of 1827. "Whether the person of Jesus of Nazareth really possesses the attributes which belong to the established concept of the Redeemer is in fact a purely historical question, which can be answered only through an historical investigation of the literary sources of the Gospel stories, sources which surely nowhere in the introduction to this Christian *Glaubenslehre* are brought forward as the proper sources of knowledge for Christianity."[53] Similarly, Baur claims that it is possible to move beyond that minimum required of the historical Jesus by a speculative system such as Hegel's (namely, that he is merely the fortuitous presupposition of faith and does not necessarily correspond to what faith claims for him) only by historical investigation. "It is no longer a speculative but only an historical question, to be settled

50 See below, pp. 175–81.
51 Cf. *Das Christenthum*, p. 24 (E.T., I, 24), and Gutachten of 20 Dec. 1835 (U.B.T., Md 750, v, 1).
52 *Paulus*, I, 3 (E.T., 1). With these words the work opens.
53 "Anzeige der beiden academischen Schriften," *TZT*, I, 242.

by means of historical criticism, how much beyond that minimum Christ is to be considered as the real content of self-consciousness, as it is also only an historically given truth that this definite individual, the person Jesus of Nazareth, actually has this high significance for the faith and self-consciousness of humanity."[54]

Properly speaking, therefore, the historical Jesus is "necessary," as Baur sees it, only if he in fact exists as the one possessing the attributes of a Redeemer. The actual existence of this particular Redeemer and founder cannot be deduced from what Baur regards as the necessary historical actualization of the idea of reconciliation, although the necessity of *some* particular beginning point of the process of actualization is implied by the necessity impinging upon the divine life. It is the task, then, of historical-critical theology to judge whether this particular Jesus of Nazareth is in actuality what the Church claims for him.

The Relation Between the Idea of the God-man and the Historical Jesus: the Historical Possibility of Jesus Christ. In one respect, however, Jesus cannot be what traditional Church dogma has claimed for him, according to Baur: he cannot be absolutely identical with the idea of the God-man (i.e., the ideal Christ or the idea of reconciliation), for this would vitiate not only the divine life itself, which can be perfectly or absolutely related only to the totality of manhood as such, but also the historical reality of the individual in whom such a divine idea would be absolutely achieved. *For there to be an authentic relationship between the ideal Christ and the historical Jesus, they must not be absolutely identified.* Baur shares this fundamental premise with Hegel's speculative theology, but it is an historical condition as well as a speculative one; the historical possibility of Jesus Christ depends upon it. We also have observed that Baur quarrels with Schleiermacher on this question.[55]

This point is most clearly argued at the end of *Dreieinigkeit und Menschwerdung Gottes*, where Baur criticizes the allegedly "new" Christology of the Mediating theologians.

There is already a crack [in their argument] if one says that the idea [of reconciliation] must determine absolutely the subjectivity of man, or appear in the individual absolutely, for this would mean nothing other than that the subject becomes absolutely one with the idea and that it must evaporate [*aufgehen*] completely into the idea. . . . However, just this is the docetism into which ecclesiastical Christology unavoidably devolves. If the finite is to be absolutely one with the Infinite, then it can only disappear into the Infinite and exist in it docetically. . . . [Furthermore] if one proceeds from the assumption

54 *Dreieinigkeit*, III, 974.
55 See above, pp. 49, 60.

that the idea must actualize itself, and if at the same time one establishes the complete and pure actualization of the divine idea or the perfect creation of human nature in the person of a [single] individual, then it cannot be seen how the impulse can proceed from this individual to a life actualizing itself in humanity. If the idea once succeeds to its absolute existence in a single, definite individual, then not merely the drive but also the possibility of actualizing itself in other individuals is taken away from the idea. . . . It is therefore clear that one cannot absolutely say that the idea must become absolutely real in a single, definite individual. So understood, the relationship of idea and reality would be placed only under the viewpoint of unity, and the idea would be the absolutely determining factor while the reality would be degraded to mere appearance. But the relationship of idea and reality also embraces in itself the element of distinction; and for this reason idea and reality can never be joined together in such absolute unity that the idea does not transcend every manifestation given in reality, indeed, every single individual; therefore the idea can actualize itself only in an infinite series of individuals. In every single individual the nonbeing of the idea must also be posited, *be it only as a minimum.* . . . As certainly as the idea of humanity must actualize itself, and as certainly as it is established essentially in the unity of God and man, just as certainly can it be actualized only by virtue of the fact that it enters into the consciousness of humanity at a definite point in a definite individual. However, no matter how highly in other respects one may place this individual, in virtue of the idea of this unity which comes to consciousness in him, he must still stand in a subordinate relationship to the idea; and a God-man in the sense of ecclesiastical doctrine embraces in itself an irresolvable contradiction.[56]

By insisting that just a *minimum* of the nonbeing of the idea of God-manhood remains in the person of Jesus—and that which distinguishes him from all other men, as we shall see, is precisely that the nonbeing of the idea is at its absolute minimum in him— Baur thinks he has preserved the authentic humanity of Christ from the incipient docetism and supernaturalism of traditional Christology and has thus rendered him knowable to the categories of historical-critical theology. He suggests, further, that the absolute unity of idea and reality is actualized only transhistorically, since an infinite series of individuals is not an historical reality. This unity becomes absolute when manhood as such is reconciled with God. The whole process of historical development is toward this goal, but the goal itself stands at the end of history, at the point where all things created return to God. This represents in fact Baur's eschatology. If the idea were totally actualized in

---

[56] *Dreieinigkeit*, III, 996–99. Italics mine. These words come at the conclusion of the work. Cf. also Gutachten of 20 Dec. 1835 (U.B.T., Md 750, v, 1), where Baur claims that his colleague Kern makes the same point.

Jesus Christ, then there would be no historical process and thus no Church, no redeemed community. By denying this total actualization, Baur seeks to preserve the reality of the Church as well as to avoid a docetic Christ, and thus to render both accessible to historical theology with respect to their divinity as well as their humanity, which are herewith conceived in their historical congruence.

At this point the question can be raised whether the method by which Baur sought to obtain these worthy ends was either necessary or theologically adequate. There is no reason why the idea of reconciliation, itself infinite, should be exhausted in a single instance of perfect manifestation, or why the distinction between divinity and humanity should necessarily disappear in a perfect union between them. At Chalcedon the Church affirmed that Jesus Christ is "made known in two natures, *inconfusedly, immutably, indivisibly, inseparably*; the difference of the natures by no means being annulled through the union, but rather the peculiarity of each nature being preserved and both concurring into one person and one substantial individual." To be sure, this formal, abstract statement requires elucidation in every age; but it contains no logical contradiction, and there is no reason why in principle the mode of relationship thus affirmed could not be elucidated in historical-theological categories, i.e., in nonsupernatural categories, adequate to describe the perfect unity-in-distinction of divine idea and human nature in Jesus Christ. Anything less than the full yet untranscended copresence of divine and human in Jesus Christ represents a dimunition of the Church's claim in faith, which means that Baur actually tends very slightly toward a different sort of Christological heresy—not a docetism which vitiates the humanity but an Ebionitism which vitiates the divinity of Christ, by withholding the idea from full and absolute ingredience in this one instance. Baur belongs to the Antiochene tradition of Christological interpretation, for which the Alexandrine solution is never able to free itself from the suspicion of docetism or Apollinarianism as well as from abstract, static, and even contradictory categories. In discussing the Christological controversy, Baur sympathetically treats the Antiochenes, e.g., Theodore of Mopsuestia, for having preserved the "reality of the human" in the person of Christ. But at the same time he is critical of their understanding the relation between the divine and the human as "only a moral unity," such as that between a husband and a wife. Of Nestorius he writes, "There is no true unity and union, but rather a bare concurrence"; and he criticizes Nestorius and Cyril of Alexandria equally.[57] Finally, one wonders whether there is any material significance for the historical categories in which Baur's Christology is fashioned in the distinction between the absolute God-manhood of Jesus Christ and the most intensive possible for

57 Cf. *Kirchengeschichte*, II, 107–112.

a single individual. For Baur, however, this distinction marks the crucial difference between a supernatural and an historical mode of comprehending the person of Christ.

The Historical Actuality of Jesus Christ. This distinction does not, however, reduce Jesus Christ to the level of a "religious genius," interchangeable with any number of other such geniuses, as, for example, Socrates. Although he is continuous with our manhood, distinguishable from us quantitatively, not qualitatively, a *primus inter pares*, nevertheless he is decisively distinct from every other man by virtue both of the intensity of the being of God in him and of his unique (nonduplicative) historical role.

This theological conviction is clearly expressed in Baur's academic opinion of 20 December 1835.

As the founder and author of a new spiritual life, as the one in whose person, history, and doctrine the most holy thing which humanity possesses, the content of the Christian faith, comes to consciousness, he remains always the one who has a value and significance which none other can share with him. . . . The newer theology . . . not only holds firmly to Christ as a single human individual but also becomes conscious of the God-man in him, since this theology, too, far from denying Christ, recognizes in him both the human and the divine, and wants to have neither without the other but rather both in the closest union. . . . That to which faith holds fast as historical fact it explains by the concept [of the God-man] and accordingly places the idea over the person without, however, annihilating the reality of the person and its connection with the idea. . . . This procedure is as old as Christianity itself, and already the simple proposition, *ho logos sarx egeneto*, accomplishes the same thing, since the Logos also is a concept, an idea, the divine reason, the divine Spirit; and in so far as the Logos was determined from eternity to be incarnate, it is the divine Spirit in its unity with the human, and the human in its unity with the divine.[58]

In the passage quoted earlier from *Dreieinigkeit und Menschwerdung Gottes*, and elsewhere, Baur suggests the category by which he will distinguish the being of God in the person of Jesus from that in all other men: in him the nonbeing of the idea of God-manhood is at its absolute minimum; he is the man most fully at one with God and therefore the most truly human of all men. In the midst of his Hegelian period, Baur writes: "The absolute idea is the essential unity of God and man, and Christ, moreover, can be thought of as representing in himself nothing other than the one who is penetrated by the idea in the most intensive fashion and who completes its reality up to the limit possible for a single individual. But at the same time it remains true

[58] Gutachten of 20 Dec. 1835 (U.B.T., Md 750, v, 1).

and incontestable that the individual stands under the idea."[59] He maintains essentially the same idea at the end of his career, during the completion of his historical studies of the person of Jesus: "As the relationship of the divine and the human may be more exactly determined in the person of Christ, the simple, fundamental perception remains that the relation of man to God, into which all other men are to come through the mediation of Christ, presents itself in him in its unity and completion [*Vollendung*]."[60]

Jesus is unique by virtue not only of the quality of his relationship to God but also of his historical role as the founder of the Christian community, i.e., as the one in whom the unity of God and man *first* appears in its concrete truth, and who therefore possesses universal significance for the destiny of man. This "peculiar excellence" of Christ can never be "taken up" into the faith of the community, Baur suggests in opposition to Hegel. "How could faith in him as the God-man have arisen, without his having also been in some fashion objectively what faith claimed for him? The necessary presupposition in any case is that the implicit truth, the unity of divine and human nature, must first come to concrete truth and self-conscious knowledge in Christ, and be expressed and learned from him as truth. Herein consists, therefore, the peculiar excellence of Christ."[61]

Reconciliation could not take place were it not for the implicit unity of God and man; it does not, therefore, imply an absolutely new creation, whereby human nature would be substantially altered, but rather a renewal of the original nature of man. Nevertheless, the historical mediation of this reconciliation in Jesus Christ, who for this reason has a universal significance for the race, is essential, for otherwise, as with Hegel, that which is implicit would never attain historical actuality.[62]

Christ has a universal significance if he presents in himself the unity of the divine and the human, not objectively as God-man in the ecclesiastical sense, but mediates it subjectively for the consciousness of humanity, in so far as through his person and history it first enters into the consciousness of humanity. Also, this historical position of the person of Christ gives him a specific value which none other can share with him. He is and remains in absolute fashion the one through whose

59 *Versöhnung*, pp. 623–24. In referring later in this work to the footnote in which this passage is contained and which is an early expression of Baur's own positive Christology, he writes that between the extremes of orthodox Christology and pure Ebionitism there is yet room enough "to vindicate in Jesus a value and nobility which specifically differentiates him from all other men and places him high above them" (p. 735). Cf. also "Das christliche des Platonismus," *TZT*, X:3, 38–39.

60 *An Hase*, p. 86. Presumably this is the "completion" possible for a single individual to achieve.

61 *Die christliche Gnosis*, p. 717.

62 *Dreieinigkeit*, III, 968–69.

mediation the idea of the unity of God and man, which determines Christianity as the absolute religion, has obtained its historical reality in the consciousness of humanity.[63]

This twofold significance of Christ—the uniqueness of his God-manhood, and his essential role in the redemption of humanity—can be seen more clearly when we turn directly to a dogmatic consideration of his person and work.

The Person of Jesus Christ

The Christological Focus on the Human Life of Jesus. Baur suggests that John and Paul represent two contrasting ways of approaching the Christological task. The Fourth Gospel, at least in the Prologue, starts "from above" with a metaphysical dualism of light and darkness; it posits the substance of the person of Christ as the divine Logos, not as human spirit; and it identifies the Jesus of history with the Logos in absolute fashion. Paul starts "from below" with the anthropological opposition of spirit and flesh; he posits the substance of the person of Christ as true human spirituality and "mounts up" to the divinity of Christ by discovering in him the most complete realization of God-manhood possible for a single individual.[64]

Baur used the Johannine language when contrasting Christianity with Platonism in 1837.[65] But thereafter he does not employ it in his published writings to express his own Christological position, while at the same time the Pauline language becomes increasingly normative for him. His Johannine studies, which began the next year and continued the rest of his life, convinced him of the historical unauthenticity and idealizing character of the Fourth Gospel.[66] In addition, he claims that the focal point in post-Reformation Protestant Christology has been to observe Christ "from below," as a truly human subject, and to perceive his divinity-in-humanity rather than vice versa. As such, Christ can possess the principle of his self-consciousness only within himself, not from beyond himself, as is the case with a Word-flesh Christology. This means that Christ can be divine only in so far as his human consciousness is itself the locus of the unity of the divine and the human, only in so far as "the empirical ego is also the absolute."[67] It is only in the human life of Jesus that we encounter both true God and true man. Beginning with the Reformation, "the entire manifestation [of Christ] has been comprehended as much as possible from the natural historical continuity in which it belongs. . . . If the unity of God and man, which is the absolute content of

---

63 *Ibid.*, p. 969.
64 *Die kanonischen Evangelien*, pp. 312–14.
65 Cf. "Das christliche des Platonismus," *TZT*, X:3, 38, 40, 48, 154.
66 See below, pp. 212–14.
67 *Dreieinigkeit*, III, 959–60.

Christianity, is to be perceived in the person of Christ, this can occur only under the presupposition that his humanity remains in its complete integrity and is regarded as the essential, substantial foundation of what he is as a whole."[68]

Nevertheless, Baur continued to use passages from the Fourth Gospel as texts for his sermons. Although, from an historical-critical standpoint, John is the least authentic of the Gospels, it can be seen from these sermons that in Baur's judgment it under-stands the meaning of Jesus' earthly ministry and death at least as fully as any of the others, and in this sense is radically oriented toward the historicity of the Logos. By virtue of a powerful theo-logical imagination, it interprets the significance of the earthly ministry of Jesus, even if it does not describe it historically. One of his most important sermons on the person of the Lord is based on a Johannine text; it shows that, for Baur, the focus of the Fourth Gospel is on the human life of Jesus—his suffering, death, and gathering of a community of disciples.[69] This is true despite the fact that Baur draws the distinction between John and Paul mentioned above in *Kritische Untersuchungen über die kanoni-schen Evangelien*, and despite the fact that he detects a docetic element at certain points in the Fourth Gospel, e.g., in the state-ment of the Prologue that "the Word became *flesh*" (not "man").[70]

The Unity of Godhead and Manhood in the Human Life of Jesus. It is in the human life of Jesus that his divinity is to be perceived. Baur believes this to be true especially for Paul, who stresses Christ's essential manhood, and whose subordinationist Christology is partially the function of an absolute doctrine of God.[71] The "human nature" with which Christ is essentially one is not a static, substantial quality but a mode of existence; specifically, it is a function of the relationship of the human subject to that which is other than himself. Man exists *kata sarka*, according to the flesh, when the constitutive relationship of his life is not with God but with finite things. This present "earthly existence" is by definition sinful, for it excludes man from the relationship with God whereby his authentic humanity is established. Man exists *kata pneuma*, according to the Spirit, when the constitutive relationship of his life is with God. Man is a spiritual being, whose destiny is to

68 *Epochen*, p. 262.
69 Sermon on Judica Sunday, Jn. 12:20–32* (U.B.T., Mh 969, 260–62). Cf. also Sermon on the 3rd Sunday after Epiphany, Jn. 4:5–14* (U.B.T., Mh 969, 142–44). Sermons marked with an asterisk are based on texts from a new lectionary added to the 1841 edition of the *Gesangbuch für die Evangelische Kirche in Württemberg*, and are therefore necessarily later than 1841. The unmarked sermons come both before and after this date. See above, p. 20, n. 80.
70 *Die kanonischen Evangelien*, pp. 233, 286, 373.
71 *Paulus*, II, 263, 267–68, 273 (E.T., 241, 245, 250); and *Neutestamentliche Theologie*, pp. 193–94.

enter the future, heavenly kingdom, by virtue of his relationship to God.[72]

Christ, of course, exists in the flesh—this marking his identity with all other men—but he does not live *according to* the flesh, i.e., according to the relationships of the flesh to finite, earthly objects. The objective principle of sin, of which flesh is the bearer, does not penetrate to his subjective consciousness or become in him a subjectively appropriated fact. Paul expresses Christ's oneness with humanity without sharing in human sin by referring to his earthly existence as a "likeness of the sin of flesh." What is rejected by the "likeness" (*homoiōma*) is not flesh itself, as the Gnostics interpreted Paul, but the *sin* of flesh or the existence *according to* the flesh.[73]

On the other hand, Christ is the only man to exist exclusively "according to the Spirit," i.e., according to the Spirit of God, or according to the principle of Christian consciousness. As such, he is the "second, heavenly man," as contrasted with the first, earthly man, Adam.[74] His human existence is totally determined by and congruent with his relationship to God. Human spirituality is properly defined by this relationship. "Spirit" is described by Paul in terms of metaphors of light; consequently, Christ's perfect imaging of the Spirit of God in his authentic human spirituality is outwardly manifested as his "glory" (*doxa*). He is the "Lord of glory," and those who behold his glory are transformed into his image.[75] Baur devotes an entire sermon to the theme that Jesus is "glorified" through his suffering and obedience unto death, for these actions mark the true determining relationship of his life, and it is through them that he establishes the community in which he will continue to be glorified after his death. By virtue of his obedience and humility, he is exalted to Lordship and to the glory of the Father. Furthermore, the name of the Father is glorified in the work of the Son, which consists in the enactment of divine love and reconciling grace through his suffering and death.[76]

It is precisely this "glory"—the glory of his earthly ministry—which is the outward mark and product of his divinity. Whoever

[72] Cf. *Neutestamentliche Theologie*, pp. 191–92, 187; and *Paulus*, II, 272–73 (E.T., 249–50). This "anthropological dualism" forms the basis of Paul's "philosophy of history"; see *Paulus*, II, 239–48 (E.T., 218–26). This distinction is also found throughout Baur's sermons, and will be further discussed below.

[73] *Neutestamentliche Theologie*, pp. 189–91; cf. *Paulus*, II, 169–70, 268–69, 273 (E.T., 156, 246, 250). See below, p. 211.

[74] *Neutestamentliche Theologie*, p. 187; cf. *Paulus*, II, 267–68, 272 (E.T., 245, 249).

[75] *Neutestamentliche Theologie*, pp. 187–89, and *Paulus*, II, 271–72 (E.T., 248–49).

[76] Sermon on Judica Sunday, Jn. 12:20–32* (U.B.T., Mh 969, 260–62). In this sermon Baur concentrates on John 12:23–26, and at one point compares this passage with Phil. 2:8–11.

can see the glory of his human life can also see his divinity. His divinity is manifest in his authentic human spirituality. The divinity is not this spirituality itself but rather the relationship by which he is spirit, namely, his perfect and determining relationship to the Spirit of God.[77] This relationship can be otherwise expressed as the idea of reconciliation, or the idea of God-manhood (of divine-human unity), or the principle of Christian consciousness, which is fully and originally actualized in the consciousness of Jesus. This relationship is not a human achievement but a divine gift. Christ is not authentically spirit, the "Lord of glory," by virtue of his natural birth, but rather implicitly, by virtue of the fact that the possibility of his spirituality and glorification is contained only in the divine idea of reconciliation. Baur suggests that this is what Paul means by Christ's preexistence—his "archetypal" humanity or spirituality, which is actualized only in his specific historical existence.[78]

By suggesting that the divinity of Christ can be perceived in the "glory" of his authentic manhood, Baur has provided the dogmatic framework within which the Christology of an historical-critical theology becomes possible. The copresence of God and man is not expressed in abstract and supernatural concepts but rather in a way congruent with historical understanding. The task of the historical theologian is to bring his critical tools and interpretive insights to bear on the human life of Jesus, thus to make manifest

[77] "Spirit" is here understood as a modality of the Absolute Spirit (or God in his triune being); he is the agent of the relationship between subject and object whereby the Absolute Spirit "lives." Used in this sense, "the Spirit of God" refers to the Third Person of the Trinity, or, in traditional language, to the Holy Spirit. The fact that the divinity of Jesus Christ, or the divine presence in Jesus Christ, is constituted by the Third Person of the Trinity rather than by the Second Person indicates a weakness or at least a peculiarity in Baur's doctrine of God to which I shall refer in other ways below. The Second Person, the divine Son, the mode of being wherein God exists in love for and as the object to himself, is not, for Baur, God in his self-objectivizing whereby he *adopts* humanity to be his other, but is simply humanity-as-such or humanity-as-reconciled, which is not in itself divine but which functions, nevertheless, as a mode of the divine being. Baur truncates the Trinity with respect to the Second, not the Third, Person. Therefore it is impossible for him to conceive the *divinity* of Jesus Christ as God in the modality of Son, for sonship is the task of the *humanity* of Jesus and of all men. The *divinity* of Jesus is constituted by his immediate and perfect relationship to "the Spirit of God," by the presence of the Spirit in him who is the agent of the idea of God-manhood or of divine-human unity. Baur also calls the Spirit of God, who is mediated to humanity through Jesus Christ, "the Spirit of Christ," referring to Pauline usage: "the Spirit of the Son" (Gal. 4:6), "the law of the Spirit of life in Christ Jesus" (Rom. 8:1). Schleiermacher, on the other hand, truncates the Third Person of the Trinity rather than the Second, since for him the Spirit is no longer the divine, Holy Spirit, the Spirit of God, but only the common spirit of the community, the collective consciousness of the faithful.

[78] *Paulus*, II, 271, 273–74 (E.T., 248, 250–51); and *Neutestamentliche Theologie*, pp. 188–89. Cf. also *Die Tübinger Schule*, pp. 32–33, quoted below, pp. 209–210.

the shape and reality of his glory—a reality which is constituted by the presence of the divine Spirit to human spirit.

From his sermons it is clear that Baur regards this human life, and the glory it manifests, as possessing the attributes and accomplishing the work of a Redeemer. For example, he suggests that the love of God and fellow man, as commanded in the law of the Old Testament, becomes a genuine possibility only

through the sending of the One in whom all are to find their Redeemer, . . . in whom the eternal love itself descends to us, so that we may perceive in him the visible image of the invisible Father. In him we become conscious of the fact that we also are a divine family, that there is a bond which brings earth together with heaven, and man with God, in the innermost relationship. . . . Therefore, only in him who was given by God for the forgiveness of our sins, and who has purchased us dearly through his reconciling death, can we grasp hold of the fatherly heart of God with almost childlike trust, which is the first condition on which love must rest.[79]

From this sermon we can perceive the close connection Baur maintains between the person of Jesus and his teaching and saving work. His work is described as a reconciling act which lays the foundation for the true and inward love of God. This work is accomplished through the person of Christ, in whom the bond of unity between God and man is actualized, and especially through his death, which heals the estrangement of this bond created by sin. The qualitative difference between Judaism and Christianity is to be seen in terms not simply of a radicalizing of the law but more especially of the connection into which this law is now brought with the person of the Redeemer—a connection which is made, according to Baur, in the teaching of Jesus itself, since Jesus responds to the question of the Pharisee concerning the great commandment with another question concerning the identity of the Christ (cf. Matt. 22:34–46).[80] That is to say, Jesus makes his person, and the work accomplished through his person, at least indirectly the subject of his teaching.[81]

[79] Sermon on the 18th Sunday after Trinity, Matt. 22:34–46 (U.B.T., Mh 969, 626–29). Cf. also Sermon on the 22nd Sunday after Trinity, Matt. 18:21–35 (U.B.T., Mh 969, 651–53); and Sermon on Palm Sunday (U.B.T., Mh 969, 295–97).

[80] Cf. Sermon on the 18th Sunday after Trinity, Matt. 22:34–46 (U.B.T., Mh 969, 626–29). It is the relationship between these two questions which provides the substance of this sermon.

[81] These connections are expressed or implied in other sermons as well; cf. Sermon on Misericordia Domini Sunday, John 10:11–18 (U.B.T., Mh 969, 317–19); Sermon on the 22nd Sunday after Trinity, Matt. 18:21–35 (U.B.T., Mh 969, 651–53); and "Predigt zur Vorbereitung auf das Säcularfest der Übergabe der Augsburgischen Confession bei Verlesung der 21 ersten Artikel derselben an II. Trinit. über das gewöhnliche sonntägliche Evangelium Luc. 15. 1–10. in der Stadtkirche, den 20. Juni 1830," *Feier des dritten Säcularfestes der Augsburgischen Confession auf der Universität Tübingen* (Tübingen: L. F. Fues, 1830), p. 94.

In most of Baur's sermons, however, it is not Jesus himself who is seen as the direct subject of his teaching but rather his proclamation of the good news of salvation. For example, in a sermon on Luke 4:16–22,[82] Baur does not develop the idea that Jesus is the one in and through whom the Gospel of the acceptable year of the Lord is enacted, but rather concentrates on the content of this Gospel, which is here described as freedom from sin and the gift of forgiveness and grace and thus as the source of all spiritual blessing. Of course the "glory" of Jesus—the earthly mark of his God-manhood—is to be seen in the exalted content of his teaching as well as in his suffering and death; and this teaching is given its authority by the person who teaches.

The message of Jesus is most characteristically described in Baur's sermons as the proclamation of a distinction between present and future life, earth and heaven, time and eternity, unessential and essential. In addition, Jesus exhorts his hearers to strive for the future and eternal life and provides them with the means for obtaining it—grace, forgiveness, his mediatorial work. Baur preaches on the Lukan version of the Beatitudes as follows:

Poverty of spirit is the first and most necessary mark of an authentic disciple of the Lord and therefore the necessary condition of an authentically Christian disposition in general. . . . The true greatness and dignity of the Christian consists in the fact that he does not merely see the visible but the invisible. Even now, as long as he is still engaged in his temporal pilgrimage, he lives not so much in the present world but much more in the future, to which everything present must be connected. . . . The whole content of his teaching consists in contrasting present and future so sharply that it becomes clear to us that to the extent to which a man possesses the one he does not possess the other.[83]

This is in fact the substance of Jesus' teaching concerning the kingdom of God: it is not an imminent, this-worldly reality, progressively breaking into history; it rather consists of a qualitatively different mode of relationship between God and man which stands in absolute contrast to, and is yet the fulfillment of, everything earthly and temporal. This qualitative distinction is expressed by Jesus in terms of a temporal distinction: future versus present. This "future" life is marked by freedom from earthly anxieties, by a radical purity of intention in all ethical actions, and by thankfulness toward God expressed in terms of love and forgiveness of one's neighbor. It is also a life beyond the vicissitudes of death. Although this life is a future reality, it also impinges upon the

---

[82] Sermon on the Sunday after Epiphany, Luke 4:16–22* (U.B.T., Mh 969, 108–109).

[83] Sermon on the 13th Sunday after Trinity, Luke 6:21–31* (U.B.T., Mh 969, 594–96). The point of course is that only those who are poor in spirit are free from dependence on things of this world and recognize the need for a future, eternal life, the gift of God.

present, and the Christian ought to posture his earthly life in accordance with it in so far as possible. Furthermore, the kingdom, thus described, is not miraculous or supernatural; for, as Baur carefully points out, continuity exists between present and future as well as discontinuity. For example, the kingdom represents the satisfaction of all authentic human longings. Yet it cannot be achieved by this longing; it is solely a divine gift.[84]

The major concern of almost all of Baur's sermons is to interpret the teaching of Jesus as contained in the Gospel text for the day; therefore, any attempt to summarize this interpretation in brief scope must prove to be unsatisfactory. More important is the fact that the exegesis of the teaching of Jesus as found in the sermons corresponds in its major elements with Baur's historical-critical treatment of his teaching in *Das Christenthum* and *Vorlesungen über neutestamentliche Theologie*, which is discussed in Chapter V.[85] This proves that although Baur does not bring his critical studies directly to bear on his sermons, a fundamental continuity exists between his critical and his homiletical pursuits.

The Reconciling Work of Jesus Christ

The Substance of His Saving Work. Christ came not simply to judge those who oppose him and have fallen into sin, but more especially to mediate the grace and forgiveness of God to them through his exemplification of divine-human unity and through his suffering and death.[86] "Can [the Christian] believe in his Lord and Redeemer without having the certainty that he has come also for him, that he has suffered and died for him, in order to secure for him anew the grace and fatherhood of God, and with this fatherhood to consecrate him to the blessed inheritance of his heavenly kingdom?"[87] It is this work which is suggested by the image of the good shepherd who lays down his life for his sheep, in whom "the full truth appears and everything is given which we must have to be blessed."[88]

This connection between the revelatory life and sacrificial death of Christ and his mediation of forgiveness is often stated in Baur's sermons without being developed in terms of a formal doctrine of atonement. His saving work is understood not so much in terms

---

84 Cf. *Ibid.*; Sermon on Palm Sunday (U.B.T., Mh 969, 295–97); Sermon on Rogate Sunday, John 16:23–33, Luke 11:9–13 (U.B.T., Mh 969, 350–52); Sermon on the 6th Sunday after Trinity, Matt. 6:19–34 (U.B.T., Mh 969, 500–502); Sermon on the 18th Sunday after Trinity, Matt. 22:34–46 (U.B.T., Mh 969, 626–29); Sermon on the 22nd Sunday after Trinity, Matt. 22:23–33* (U.B.T., Mh 969, 645–47); Sermon on the 22nd Sunday after Trinity, Matt. 18:21–35 (U.B.T., Mh 969, 651–53).

85 See pp. 224–28.

86 Sermon on Palm Sunday (U.B.T., Mh 969, 295–97).

87 Sermon on the 13th Sunday after Trinity, Luke 6:20–31* (U.B.T., Mh 969, 594–96).

88 Sermon on Misericordia Domini Sunday, John 10:11–18 (U.B.T., Mh 969, 317–19).

of the satisfaction of a divine requirement or the substitution of
the life of Jesus for the penalty to be paid by sinful man as it is
in terms of bringing eternal life to man through the re-establishment of the estranged relationship between God and man.[89] As
the bringer of eternal life he may be described in Johannine
imagery as the good shepherd, the bread of life, the word of life.[90]
The life he brings is a consequence of the fact that in him God
himself has drawn near and revealed his fatherly and eternal love
to us; the Son mediates the Father to us and us to the Father.[91]
He establishes the reconciled relationship between God and man
by virtue of his coming into the world, his enactment of this relationship in his own life, his revelation of the forgiveness and
mercy of God, and his reconciling death. "That which we must
consider as greatest and most unique about the sending of our
Lord, his teaching, and his establishment [of a community], is
concerned simply with giving us the strongest reassurance of the
grace of love which God will not withhold from sinful men, and
with specifying a new and blessed relationship between God and
man, by means of a new and open trust in God and the proof of
every open access to the fatherly mercy of God."[92]

Death and Resurrection. The saving work of Christ becomes universally efficacious through his death and resurrection, which mark
the transition from his earthly ministry to his universal and eternal
lordship in the life of the community. For example, the justification of man accomplished through the death of Jesus is univer-
salized and completed through his resurrection: "Next to the death
of Christ as the objective fact on which justification rests, [Paul]
also places the resurrection of Christ (Rom. 4:25). . . . Death and

[89] At this point the emphasis in Baur's sermons seems to differ somewhat
from his treatment of the Pauline doctrine of atonement. Paul focuses almost exclusively on the death of Christ, not on the mediatorial and reveal-
ing function of his life. He interprets the significance of the death in terms
of satisfaction and substitution, which thereby frees men from the requirement of the law. Cf. *Neutestamentliche Theologie*, pp. 135–53, 157–60; and
Paulus, II, 148–60, 163, 166–71 (E.T., 137–47, 150, 153–57). Baur's understanding of atonement, as expressed in the sermons and also in *Versöhnung*,
is closer to the Johannine than the Pauline view, probably because, as we
have seen, he has been deeply influenced by Hegel's interpretation of the
doctrine of reconciliation, where the emphasis is on the actualization of the
implicit unity of God and man through the mediation of Christ (see above,
pp. 58–59.
[90] Cf. Sermon on Laetare Sunday, John 6:1–27 (U.B.T., Mh 969, 247–50);
and Sermon on Misericordia Domini Sunday, John 10:11–18 (U.B.T., Mh
969, 317–19).
[91] Cf. Sermon on the Sunday after New Year's, John 12:44–50* (U.B.T.,
Mh 969, 69–71); and Sermon on Rogate Sunday, John 16:23–33, Luke 11:
9–13 (U.B.T., Mh 969, 350–52). See below, p. 231.
[92] Sermon on the 22nd Sunday after Trinity, Matt. 18:21–35 (U.B.T., Mh
969, 651–53). Cf. also Sermon on Palm Sunday (U.B.T., Mh 969, 295–97);
and the passage from Sermon on the 18th Sunday after Trinity, Matt. 22:34–
46 (U.B.T., Mh 969, 626–29), quoted above, pp. 113.

resurrection belong so together that the *dikaiōsis* effected through the death is completed through the resurrection, in so far as God could not have raised Christ had he not intended to declare through the resurrection that *dikaiōsis* is accomplished through the death."[93]

The place of the death of the Lord in the transition from his earthly to eternal ministry, and in the establishment of a community of the faithful, is shown in a sermon based on John 12:24:

If it is necessary that a grain of wheat die in the earth in order to multiply and bear much fruit, then it is also necessary that the Lord die, if he is to become the founder of a community consecrating and sanctifying his name. At first glance, this appears unthinkable and contradictory, and to the natural man it will not be plausible that fullness of life can unfold only from death and the grave. Yet the same law which prescribes the eternal order of nature is valid also for the spiritual life. The corruptible must be put away if the incorruptible . . . is to emerge from it. . . . The bond of the community which binds him to his own can first develop only out of death and the grave. For it must be clear and certain that this bond is stronger and more powerful than death and the grave, just as the community with him ought not to be earthly and mortal, but immortal and eternal. For, as he himself said, no man has greater love than he who lays down his life for his own.[94]

The same sermon shows how, through his resurrection, the Lord continues to live in the community he founded.

We see here how the crucified and risen Lord cannot rightly remain alone, if, like the grain of wheat which falls into the earth and no longer remains a single grain but bears much fruit, he is risen in his community, continuing to work and live in it. . . . In the members of his community, . . . the Lord of the community again and again commemorates the victory of life over death and is glorified in them. . . . The more they bear his image in themselves and express it in the entire fullness and multiplicity of its forms, the more he, the Redeemer, lives in all his redeemed and fills and rules them as members of his spirit and body, in order to join them all to the holy building, pleasing to God, which rises up from earth to heaven. . . .[95]

Baur interprets the meaning and significance of the resurrection in this way because he is concerned to understand it in nonsupernatural, nonmiraculous terms, i.e., not as the physical resuscitation of a corpse but rather, as he puts it in a letter to Heyd, in a

---

[93] *Neutestamentliche Theologie*, pp. 162–63. Cf. also pp. 122–27, where Baur discusses the death and the resurrection as the point of transition from the teaching of Jesus to that of the apostles.

[94] Sermon on Judica Sunday, John 12:20–32* (U.B.T., Mh 969, 260–62).

[95] *Ibid.* Cf. Sermon on Misericordia Domini Sunday, John 10:11–18 (U.B.T., Mh 969, 317–19), where the same point is made by describing Jesus as the future shepherd of the one flock. It is important to note the identity between the future shepherd (the risen Lord) and the present shepherd (the historical Jesus).

"spiritual" sense.[96] The "victory of life over death" is indeed a reality, but it is a reality congruent with the natural and historical order. Therefore, Baur describes the resurrection as that event through which "the principle of life enters into humanity which is imparted to it through Christ and which overcomes the reign of death."[97] This principle of life is existence "according to the Spirit," which has been decisively actualized in the life of Christ. The glory of his authentic humanity already represents the victory of life over death: "The living, creative Spirit in him, the spiritual principle constituting his special nature, cannot be touched by death."[98] The resurrection, according to Paul, is in the first place proof or authentication of the fact that the Spirit was fully present to Christ as that divine relationship by which he was authentically human spirit. By virtue of this presence, he was the "spirit of holiness." But in the second place it is also the means by which Christ becomes the "life-giving spirit," through whom "all will be brought to life."[99] The resurrection is, consequently, both the proof of Christ's authentic spirituality and the means by which his spirituality becomes the life-giving spirituality of all men.[100] Viewed this way, there is no necessity for Paul, in Baur's view, to regard the resurrection as a miracle in the ordinary sense.[101]

At the same time, the resurrection is not to be understood as the dissolution of the identity of the self after death into the undifferentiated being of Eternal Spirit. Baur believes that this idea is specifically rejected by the resurrection faith. "Is our spirit anything other than the . . . fleeting thought of an Eternal Spirit, who allows everything living to proceed from his eternal fullness of life but which also, when its time has run its course, . . . returns into his eternal nature, from which everything finite must disappear? . . . Faith [in the resurrection] . . . knows nothing of such a description of the future life. . . . For why is there a resurrection, if the man who is risen from death to life is not the same person whose life here sinks into the night of death?"[102]

---

96 Baur to L. F. Heyd, 24 March 1840 (U.B.T., Md 619r, 25). The sense in which the resurrection can be considered an event open to historical knowledge will be discussed below, pp. 234–37.

97 *Paulus,* II, 269 (E.T., 247); cf. also p. 236 (E.T., 216).

98 *Ibid.,* p. 269 (E.T., 247).

99 *Ibid.,* pp. 270, 274–75 (E.T., 247, 251–52).

100 Cf. also Sermon on Easter Sunday, Mark 16:1–8 (U.B.T., Mh 969, 307–310). "The great fact of his resurrection from the dead alone gives for the first time firm certainty to our faith in him. It confirms him as the teacher of truth sent from the Father, as the true witness, as the redeemer from sin and death. . . . Also, his resurrection from the dead ought to be an obvious proof to us of the higher, immortal life in which he is to complete the entire spiritual life which he has here awakened in us."

101 *Paulus,* II, 270 (E.T., 247).

102 Sermon on the 22nd Sunday after Trinity, Matt. 22:23–33* (U.B.T., Mh 969, 645–47). Baur thinks that this is the point made by Jesus against the Sadducees in Matt. 22:31–32: "And as for the resurrection of the dead, have

The resurrection implies a continuity between life before and after death, a continuity in which the identity of the finite self is not dissolved into a Universal Soul but rather continues in the future as individual and personal life. This is what resurrection *of the body* means in contrast to immortality of the soul; this contrast is implied by Baur but is never specifically stated as such. It marks, however, the distinction between Christianity and the Greek and Indian religions. For Christianity, "the concept of personal individuality cannot be abandoned"; it is preserved even after death rather than being absorbed into the divine totality.[103] ". . . to be sure, God is All in all [for Christianity], but only through Christ, and as Christ is the eternal Mediator, the eternal unity of the divine and human, so also the human self-consciousness united with the Godhead is at the same time always separated as an individual consciousness, never equalized into a complete identity with the divine totality."[104]

The Relation Between the Work of Jesus and the Faith of the Community. We have seen from the preceding section that the death and especially the resurrection of Jesus make possible the connection between a past historical figure and a living community of faith: Jesus and his redemptive work are present to the community by virtue of his resurrection from the dead. If we ask more especially *how* he is present, the answer is, in the faith of the community. This is not to say that it is merely the faith of the community that he is risen from the dead, or that his resurrection is simply constituted by the faith of the community. He is really eternally at work in the community, by virtue of his victory over death, and the existence of the community's faith gives evidence of this fact. This is of course a dogmatic, not an historical, affirmation; for, when it comes to the resurrection, the historian is limited to the outward mark, faith, behind which he cannot penetrate to the actuality of the resurrection-event itself.[105]

Faith is the subjective completion of the divine reconciling process which has its objective locus in the earthly and eternal ministry of Jesus. Indeed, the reconciliation between God and man, which has its start in the objective gift of grace, is actualized only when it is completed in the subjective response of faith. Faith is subjectively what divine grace is objectively; faith and grace are subjective and objective sides of the same righteousness of

you not read what was said to you by God, 'I am the God of Abraham, and the God of Isaac, and the God of Jacob'? He is not God of the dead, but of the living." This implies that Abraham, Isaac, and Jacob are still living as distinct personal spirits, in continuity with their earthly identities.

[103] *Symbolik und Mythologie*, II/2, 450–52. Cf. also the passage from *Dreieinigkeit*, III, 996–99, quoted above, pp. 104–105.

[104] *Symbolik und Mythologie*, II/2, 454.

[105] See below, pp. 234–37.

God.[106] By virtue of this close connection between subjective condition and objective reality, faith is not only reckoned or imputed as righteousness but is in fact that righteousness itself subjectively realized. "One cannot believe in Christ without also knowing oneself one with him and without being aware, in this unity of consciousness with him, of that which is the proper object of faith in Christ as an immanent determination of one's own consciousness."[107]

Believing in Christ, we become one with him and thus become in him the righteousness of God. "Faith is [the] unity of man with Christ by means of which the deliverance from the law which the death of Christ has effected becomes man's own deliverance from it."[108] It is the means by which the Spirit of God, who constitutes the divine presence in Jesus Christ, is mediated to the spirit of men. Faith is a relation of divine Spirit to human spirit, or, more precisely, it is the subjective condition of this relation and thus corresponds to divine grace. It is in this relationship that the whole process of justification is completed.

. . . [Faith] is a relation of Spirit to spirit, in which the [human] spirit, as the principle of subjective consciousness, is drawn into union with the Spirit of God who, as the Spirit of Christ, is its objective basis. . . . The divine Spirit . . . has come to reside in man as the principle of his Christian consciousness and life. . . . It is thus in the Spirit that God and man are related to each other as Spirit to spirit and are one with each other in the unity of the Spirit. But this unity of man with God, in which the essence of justification consists, is only possible on the precondition of faith. The Spirit is indeed the true and living mediation of the unity of man with God; yet it must not be forgotten that since we only receive the Spirit on the ground of faith, justification has its essential element only in faith, and that the bond of unity, in which justification consists, is formed only through faith, which can be taken only as the unity of man with Christ.[109]

The relation of the divine Spirit to human spirit, as mediated subjectively by faith, is also understood by Baur as the divine act of revelation. Revelation and faith are correlates. This means, on the one hand, that revelation is congruent with human subjectivity; it does not consist of supernaturally communicated religious truths.[110] On the other hand, the content of faith is God in his self-revelation, not subjective human concepts. Indeed, the knowledge which

106 Cf. *Paulus*, II, 161–62, 164, 170–71, 173–74 (E.T., 149, 151, 157, 160); and *Neutestamentliche Theologie*, pp. 134, 160, 186.

107 *Paulus*, II, 173 (E.T., 159).

108 *Ibid.*, p. 163 (E.T., 150).

109 *Ibid.*, pp. 175–77 (E.T., 161–63).

110 Because of its supernaturalistic connotations, as, for example, in the work of the Confessionalist theologians, Baur rarely used the category of revelation. But the idea is by no means lacking from his theology; cf. below, pp. 266–67.

faith has of God corresponds to the knowledge God has of himself, since the Spirit of God, to whom man is related in faith, is the principle of divine self-consciousness, just as human spirit is the principle of human self-consciousness. Thus, through the mutual congruence of revelation and faith, God and man are *internally* present to each other.[111]

In conclusion, it is through faith that the unity of God and man achieved through the atoning work of Christ receives the "universal significance . . . subjectively for the consciousness of humanity" for which it is intended when "through his person and history it first enters into the consciousness of humanity."[112] Christ himself thereby becomes the principle of the Christian community which he founded; and the Church is nothing other than the historical continuation and development, through faith, of that Christian consciousness first decisively and definitively actualized in the life and death of Jesus of Nazareth.[113]

THE NATURE OF THE CHURCH: CONGRUENCE OF IDEA AND MANIFESTATION

The Congruence of Idea and Manifestation in the Historicity of the Church

What Baur says of Christianity in his central Christological affirmation, namely, that "it is everything that it is solely through the person of its founder,"[114] applies equally to the Church and its history: the Christian Church is everything that it is through the person of its founder. Jesus Christ is at the source and center of the history of the Church since he is the individual in whom the idea of reconciliation first appears definitively, decisively, normatively. He is the point of origin of that series of historical manifestations of the idea of reconciliation which constitutes the historicity of the Church. His history is the most essential moment in the historicity of the Church, and therefore one cannot speak of the history of the Church without speaking of him. On the other hand, however, the Church is the more inclusive historical reality. In expressing the connection between Christ and the Church, for Baur it would be more accurate to say that Jesus Christ is a part of the Church than that the Church is part of Jesus Christ. The total historical process takes precedence over the individual, no matter how important or crucial that individual may be for this process. If individuals are to be treated historically, they must be understood as part of the historical community to which they belong.

---

111 Cf. *Dogmengeschichte*, I/1, 50–51; and *Paulus*, II, 139 (E.T., 128). At this point Baur sounds remarkably Barthian.
112 *Dreieinigkeit*, III, 969. See above, pp. 108–109.
113 Cf. *Neutestamentliche Theologie*, p. 195.
114 *Das Christenthum*, p. 23 (E.T., I, 23). See above, p. 100.

The same is true of Jesus Christ, although he is the ground and source of his community. If he were not the founder *of a community,* he would be historically incomprehensible. Baur is a Christocentric theologian, but for this very reason his theology is driven to a conception of the historicity of the Church.

The historicity[115] of the Church is constituted by its existence at the point of congruence of an idea[116]—the idea of reconciliation— and the various historical manifestations (*Erscheinungen*)[117] by which this idea is actualized. This is a characteristic the Church shares with historical reality in general, for history itself transpires at the point of juncture of ideas and manifestations. It is content as well as form, meaning as well as occurrence. In history, these components are not actually separable; they are only considered separately in analysis. It is as much a part of an historical event to be the factual manifestation of an idea, which is its "content," as it is of an idea thus to manifest itself. In Baur's view there is no such thing as sheer, opaque facticity any more than there are abstract ideas. "Meaning" and "event" are inseparably related in history. The *congruence* of idea and manifestation marks the *essence* of the Church. The Church does not have a supernatural

---

[115] The term *Geschichtlichkeit* (usually translated "historicity") is not used by Baur. It apparently came into technical usage for the first time in the work of Dilthey, and it has been given a more specialized and rather different meaning in the vocabulary of existentialist philosophy. As used in this work, it simply means the quality of being historical in the full and complete sense. This is close to the meaning intended by Dilthey, who used it to refer to the full and vital historical reality of human existence, as against the confining perspectives of naturalism and positivism. It is not inappropriate to borrow one of Dilthey's categories, since his view of history was probably deeply influenced by Baur's. See below, p. 169.

[116] For Baur's use of "idea" as a category of historical interpretation, see above, pp. 92–93.

[117] There is a double meaning in this word, inherited from its root, *scheinen,* which can mean either "to shine forth" or "to seem." An *Erscheinung* on the one hand is a most concrete and visible occurrence, but on the other hand it is the outward appearance of an inward, hidden, unseen reality. The difficulty is in finding an English word which expresses this double meaning in the sense intended by Baur. "Manifestation" has been chosen since it suggests on the one hand that something *other* than sheer facticity is manifested in an historical event, namely, an idea, but on the other hand that this idea *does in fact* come to concrete, real manifestation (cf. *manifestus,* that which is struck by the hand, hence, palpable). There is nothing ephemeral, apparitional, or subreal about the historical world, as Plato suggests with his realm of "appearances"; and therefore "appearance" as a translation of *Erscheinung* could be misleading. The same is true of "phenomenon," because of its association with the Kantian epistemological distinction between noumena and phenomena. In his distinction between *Idee* and *Erscheinung,* Baur does not have in mind either a Platonic or a Kantian dualism. As synonyms for *Erscheinung* in this context, Baur also uses *Wirklichkeit* ("reality"), *Ereignis, Geschehene, Geschehnis* (all meaning "event" in one sense or another), *Tatsache* ("fact"), *Positivität* ("positivity" or "facticity"), *Form* ("form," in the sense not of a Platonic form but of the shape or structure of an event).

or suprahistorical essence, for its essence is precisely its historicity, which means its ideality-in-positivity and positivity-in-ideality. Its essence cannot be identified with either of these elements alone but only with both together.

The categories of idea (*Idee*) and manifestation (*Erscheinung*) are first used in this systematic way in *Die Epochen der kirchlichen Geschichtschreibung*, only eight years before Baur's death, which means that his "system" came to maturity late in life. These categories are anticipated in earlier works,[118] but they are not used systematically until the *Epochen*. They now replace language with a more Hegelian flavor, such as "the inner movement of the concept in history," used during the middle period in *Versöhnung* and *Dreieinigkeit und Menschwerdung Gottes*. This means that Baur's conception of history sharpened, matured, became more independent in his attempt to describe the historicity of the Church. To understand the Church, he fashioned a new vocabulary to understand history as a whole.

In the *Epochen*, Baur writes that if one can speak with justice of an idea of the Church then this idea, like every other, must contain in itself the living drive to go out from itself and to actualize itself in a series of manifestations, and that therefore the history of the Church is the movement of the idea of the Church.[119] The same point is made in his discussion of the Protestant doctrine of the visible and invisible Church. "If one starts with the idea of the Church, one must maintain that it belongs to the essence of the idea to actualize itself; an idea which does not possess in itself the drive or the principle to actualize itself in the sensible world is no idea. Likewise, one cannot think of a reality which does not have some sort of connection with an idea lying at its basis."[120] Here the mutual ingredience of idea and reality (manifestation) is so clearly expressed that it is impossible to think of either abstractly, apart from the relationship by which they are, respectively, idea and reality. Elsewhere, this relationship is described as that of soul to body: individual events and persons, which make up the contents of history, have their basis in a "guiding and determining thought" which is related to the "stuff of history" as the soul to the body.[121] Soul and body are, respectively, what they are by virtue of their relationship; disembodied souls are abstractions, and bodies without souls are lifeless corpses.

Baur thinks that even in the "most recent presentations of the

---

[118] E.g., *Symbolik und Mythologie* (see above, p. 92, n. 9), *Die christliche Gnosis, Dreieinigkeit und Menschwerdung Gottes*, and the lecture manuscript from the Blaubeuren period, "Geschichte des Alterthums" (U.B.T., Mh II 166, q), p. 13.

[119] *Epochen*, pp. 248–49.

[120] *Dogmengeschichte*, III, 283–84. Cf. also *Die Tübinger Schule* (1st ed.), p. 4.

[121] *An Hase*, p. 81; cf. also *Die Tübinger Schule* (1st ed.), p. 8.

history of the Christian Church"[122] there is something amiss, namely, "the wrong relationship of the idea to the manifestations in which the historical development thereof is to be presented." "The idea still hovers at a great distance and in indefinite form over the manifestations to which it must be related. It is not yet strong and vital enough to penetrate into and animate the historical material, as the soul the body, and to become in such an organic unity the moving principle of the whole series of manifestations in which the history of the Christian Church takes its course."[123] The reason for this failure is that the pragmatism and the abstract idealism of the Enlightenment have not yet been completely overcome in the modern striving for an "objective historical comprehension."[124] A similar abstract transcendence of the idea was found in medieval theory, although here the historical facticity of the Church was identified with the idea in such a way that the empirical Church itself was regarded as a transcendent, suprahistorical, infallible institution.[125] Augustine, however, realized that the idea of the Church (the City of God) is historically actualized without being identified with its temporal medium, since the empirical Church always remains a mixture of the two Cities.[126]

To conclude, the relationship between idea and manifestation is a dialectical one. They can be neither identified nor separated. The idea achieves its self-actualization by penetrating into and objectifying itself in outward manifestations, but at the same time it retains its autonomy by withdrawing from its objective forms so that no confusion between them will result. This dialectical process of penetration and withdrawal constitutes the historical process and is the mark of historical reality.[127] It characterizes especially the history of the Church, which, by virtue of the supreme divinity of its idea and the sustained historical power of its forms, is the most fully historical of all earthly phenomena.

The Historical Forms of the Church

Baur provides a convenient summary of his theology of the Church in the *Epochen:*

The Church is the real form in which Christianity comes to its manifestation. If one asks for the idea of the Church, one asks, therefore, for

[122] He has in mind here Marheineke, Neander, Gieseler, Hase, and others. See below, pp. 158–60.

[123] *Epochen,* pp. 247–48; cf. also pp. 200–201.

[124] *Ibid.,* p. 248. Baur here refers to Schelling's observation on this matter in *Vorlesungen über die Methode des academischen Studium* (Stuttgart and Tübingen: J. G. Gotta, 1803), pp. 213 ff. See below, pp. 153–54.

[125] *Geschichte der christlichen Kirche,* Vol. III: *Die christliche Kirche des Mittelalters in den Hauptmomenten ihrer Entwicklung,* F. F. Baur, ed. (Tübingen: L. F. Fues, 1861), p. 3. See below, pp. 150–51.

[126] *Kirchengeschichte,* II, 48–50. Baur here seems to recognize a certain similarity between Augustine's theology of history and his own theology of the Church.

[127] Cf. *An Hase,* pp. 90–91.

Christianity itself. . . . Christianity can be essentially nothing other than that which Christian consciousness of all times, in whatever form it may occur, has perceived in the person of Christ—the unity of God and man. However else one may conceive the essence of Christianity—as everything it ought to be to man according to various connections, such as the revelation of absolute truth, the establishment of redemption, reconciliation, blessedness—it has its absolute conception and expression in the unity of God and man, as it is perceived in the person of Christ and in this perception becomes a fact of Christian consciousness. Nothing other than this unity is, therefore, the substantial content of the historical development of the Christian Church. Everything can aim at realizing it for the Christian consciousness in the various forms in which it can be comprehended only in such fashion that it is itself only the form of this absolute content.[128]

"Christianity" itself is the idea of the Church; as such, it is nothing other than the unity of God and man perceived in the person of Jesus Christ. The unity of God and man, which can be otherwise expressed as the revelation of absolute truth or the establishment of redemption, reconciliation, and blessedness, is the substantial content of the historical development of the Church; and the Church is the basic form in which the idea of divine-human unity is manifested. Furthermore, there are a variety of secondary forms within the historical life of the Church by which the idea is differently manifested at different stages of its career. "Christianity has existed from the beginning as an historical manifestation in the form of the Christian Church," the history of which can "be divided into different major parts"; the idea of the Church "lives" in the various historical forms of the Church.[129] These forms are finite; they come into existence and pass away; but for this reason the infinitude of the idea is more clearly perceived.[130]

The relative primacy of the forms with respect to the actualization of the Christian idea marks the historical development of the Church and the different periods into which it is divided. Baur writes that "the major moments of the historical development of the Church" may be placed under the viewpont of "the different forms in which [the idea of divine-human unity] can be comprehended."[131] The major forms are dogma and institutional structure or government (and, although Baur does not mention it in this context, faith itself); the subordinate forms are worship, the ethical life of the community, and the secular power and relations of the Church. The major periods in the history of the Church—ancient, medieval, and modern (Reformation and post-Reforma-

[128] *Epochen*, p. 251.
[129] *Dogemengeschichte*, I/1, 1.
[130] Cf. "Über die geschichtlichte Bedeutung der fünfundzwanzig Jahre 1816–1841," p. 20.
[131] *Epochen*, p. 251. Cf. *An Hase*, pp. 82–83, 85.

tion)—are distinguished by the relative primacy of dogma, institutions, or faith as the basic forms of the life of the Church in each period.

From the development of the basic dogmatic symbols of the Church in the first six centuries, it can be seen that the underlying compulsion of the patristic period was to objectify its inner religious consciousness in the great Trinitarian and Christological dogmas and to construct other dogmas in relation to the Christological center of Christian thought. In no other period did the formation of dogma, i.e., the formulation of the truth of the Christian idea in objective, conceptual statements, possess such a weighty significance as in the first, during which the dogmatic systems of the Church received all the essential determinations which have remained with them since. The early part of the medieval period (from Gregory I to Gregory VII) represented the gradual formation of the hierarchical theological system and the gradual transition from emphasis on dogma to that on ecclesiastical hierarchy, which became the primary form in the high Middle Ages, impressing its systematizing tendency even on dogma. With the Reformation, the primary mark of the Church became the contrast between Protestant and Catholic understandings of the relation between idea and manifestation in the nature of the Church. Catholicism perpetuated and dogmatized the medieval solution, but with necessary modifications, while in Protestantism faith emerged as the primary form of the Christian idea. Dogma now tended to lose its objectivizing and systematizing tendency and to be expressed rather as "doctrines of faith" (*Glaubenslehren*). In each of the periods, of course, the other forms retained a subordinate although extremely important position.

This schematism provides the structure on which Baur's five-volume Church history is ordered. The bare summary given above does no justice to the richness and subtlety of Baur's employment of it, which becomes the primary concern in our subsequent analysis of his church history.[132] Let us only note here the significance of his approach: the structure by which the history of the Christian Church is made intelligible is itself a function of the nature of the Church as perceived theologically. The history of the Church is not ordered according to external criteria but according to the changing modes of its historicity. Any attempt to write a "naturalistic" or "functional" history of the Church can only fail to understand the history of the phenomenon it treats. One may want to quarrel with or modify Baur's theology of the Church, but his awareness of the intimate connection between the nature of the Church and its history, and his structuring of a history on the basis of this connection, is a fundamental achievement in Church historiography. In this internal congruence of theological and historical understanding, the historian seeks to penetrate to the very heart of the phenomenon

132 See below, pp. 251–56.

which he is describing and to draw forth *from it* the criteria by which he will order and elucidate its history. In his reply to Hase, Baur claims that if the Church in its historical development is considered as the self-realizing of the idea of the Church, and if its history is placed under the viewpoint of the varying relationships in which idea and reality stand to each other, then this represents a "speculative" comprehension of Church history. But "speculation" as used here means the attempt to penetrate *critically* to the objectivity of the matter itself, in so far as that is possible.[133] Hence the divisions of the history of the Church arise from the material itself as "speculatively" interpreted. No a priori schematism is imposed on the events. On the contrary, no interpretive pattern is more firmly rooted in the historical material itself than this one attempts to be.[134]

The Absoluteness and the Positivity of the Church

Baur expresses the congruence of the positive history of Christianity with the absolute and universal truth of reconciliation as follows: "In that it is wholly joined to the person of its founder and in no way can be separated from him, Christianity is an historical religion, resting on a definite, positive authority. But if this authority were *merely* external and positive, and not at the same time absolute, identical with the absolute authority of reason, Christianity as a positive religion could not at the same time be an absolute religion."[135] The universal and implicit truth of reconciliation as known to reason ought to be congruent with the positive actualization of this truth in history. This congruence is similarly expressed in two important passages written within a year of each other. The first is from the introduction to *Paulus*, the second from a *Streitschrift* in response to a critic.

Christianity is on the one hand the great spiritual power through which all faith and thought of the present are determined. It is the absolute principle through which the self-consciousness of spirit is supported and maintained, such that, if it were not essentially Christian, it would possess no consistency and duration. On the other hand, what Christianity essentially is, is a purely historical question, whose solution lies only in that past in which Christianity itself has taken its origin. It is for this reason a question which can be solved only by that critical posture which the consciousness of the present assumes toward the past.[136]

Christianity is and remains an historically given religion. However one may also think of its divine origin and of its absolute truth, it has in any case this human, finite side as a part of it, in that, like everything

133 See below, pp. 162–67.
134 *An Hase*, pp. 90, 93–97.
135 "Das christliche des Platonismus," *TZT*, X:3, 90–91. Italics mine.
136 *Paulus*, I, 4 (E.T., 2).

historical, it is subjected to the conditions of historical existence. It enters into the general continuity of historical events at a specific time, and can be known only from specific writings, as the documentary witnesses of its origin. Like everything which belongs to the source-literature of history, these writings must themselves first be critically examined and investigated if our knowledge of primitive Christianity is to be mediated through them in a certain and credible fashion.[137]

The essence of Christianity is to be perceived as both an "absolute principle" of truth and "a purely historical question." It is therefore incumbent upon the Church historian to take account of Christianity's absolute principle, just as it is upon the dogmatic theologian to take account of its historical character. Emanuel Hirsch believes that the passage from *Paulus* expresses the heart of the historical-critical task for theology, for it "includes the presupposition that Christianity requires to be comprehended and known as a power entering into the history of humanity"—that is, as the absolute spiritual "power" or principle of reconciliation—"according to all the rules of historical knowledge in the free movement of scientific research in connection with human-historical life."[138]

An early, important, and suggestive expression of the congruence of absoluteness and positivity in Christianity is found in *Symbolik und Mythologie,* where Baur's thought and language are still more directly under the influence of Schleiermacher, although even here the movement of his thought toward the precise statement quoted from *Paulus* is clearly evident:

The external revelation hangs inseparably together with the internal, with the immediate perception of the divine in his relation to the finite; and the history in which this revelation is given to us is only the historical beginning point of the excitation of self-consciousness, through which it is raised with spontaneous power to a new, indeed the highest, level of its development. This is the *ideal* significance of Christianity, which must necessarily be bound together with its *historical* significance, . . . if the essence of Christianity is not to be established in a system of fixed dogmatic determinations but . . . in a completely peculiar determination of self-consciousness. . . . Only on this presupposition are content and form most exactly congruous in Christianity. . . . In Chris-

137 *Der Kritiker und der Fanatiker, in der Person des Herrn Heinrich W. J. Thiersch. Zur Charakteristik des neuesten Theologie* (Stuttgart: Becher's Verlag, 1846), p. 3.

138 Hirsch, *op. cit.,* V, 526. He adds that this presupposition excludes the possibility that an absolute authority can be attributed to the New Testament, for then free scientific examination and historical judgment would be excluded; or that absolute miracle can occur, for then the inner connection of historical life opened up by the scientific spirit would be torn asunder. He believes that these denials and the presuppositions on which they are based must be accepted by contemporary historical-critical theology. (See pp. 526–27).

tianity alone is religious consciousness equally as independent of the external authority of revelation as it also is excited by and developed through it. . . . Therefore Christianity does not rest on any proper demonstration but on immediate feeling and self-consciousness. . . . That which distinguishes Christianity from . . . [the other two monotheistic] forms of religion in a most particular way is its not merely external and historical but also internal and essential connection with the person of its founder.[139]

The emphasis in this passage differs from that in later works, in so far as a certain precedence is given to religious consciousness and the immediate apprehension of the absoluteness of Christianity over the historical foundations of the same, although their internal congruence is also carefully expressed, whereas in later writings the precedence is reversed. Never, however, does Baur claim, as he warns against doing here, that faith can be "demonstrated" from historical study. The congruence of ideality and positivity is such that they can be grasped only together; one must start both with religious consciousness and the positivity of Christianity, since neither can be demonstrated from the other and both are essential for the full reality of the Church.

If Christianity itself is marked by the congruence of absoluteness and positivity, then it is to be expected that the Christian Church would express this congruence as it emerged into an autonomous historical phenomenon, distinct from Judaism on the one side and Gnosticism and Montanism on the other. The peculiar nature of the Church was defined by its opposition to alternative possibilities. "If from the standpoint of the question of salvation, Christianity stood in danger of being submerged in Jewish particularism," i.e., in the outward forms of a religious tradition for which the universal truth of salvation had lost its vitality, "then from the standpoint of Gnosticism, it was on the point of dissolving into a concept, into the generality of a transcendental world-view," for which historical form was renounced in favor of universal, speculatively grasped truth. "Both dangers had to be met by the catholicizing tendency of Christianity in the realization of the Church."[140] The danger to Christianity from Gnosticism was no less serious than that from Judaism, namely, that of "the generalization and evaporation of its content through ideas in which the Christian consciousness in its limitless expansion would entirely lose its specific historical character."[141] In view of these opposing and mutually exclusive tendencies,

a reaction was necessary, if Christianity was not to lose its peculiar and original nature. . . . The first necessity was to have a unifying point at which related and corresponding elements could be opposed to all

---

139 *Symbolik und Mythologie*, I, 156–57, 159–61. Italics mine.
140 *Das Christenthum*, p. 234 (E.T., I, 244).
141 *Ibid.*, p. 176 (E.T., I, 185). See above, pp. 66 ff.

heterogeneous and eccentric tendencies. This is the idea of the catholic[142] Church. Already this idea had united Jewish and pagan Christians in a common interest, as a higher power standing over the oppositions. And now, in opposition to the Gnostics and the Montanists, it developed into a more definite consciousness and realized itself in a more stable form in ever wider expanse.[143]

The "idea of the catholic Church," in relation to the two elements of universality and positivity which constitute it, is most clearly expressed in the following passage: "The catholic Church must, above all, in accord with its idea, seek to rise above everything particular and to merge it in the universality of the Christian principle; but on the other side it belongs equally strongly to its task to hold fast to the positive elements of Christianity. The Church is a catholic Church simply in that, as the reconciling mean of all tendencies, it holds the one extreme equally far from itself as the other."[144]

We might add in conclusion that since Christianity is both absolute and positive in character, it is necessary to start at two places smultaneously in our knowledge of it. We must start both with Jesus Christ and the Church and with the pious consciousness of the individual believer. Neither of these starting places can be collapsed into the other or made a function of the other; they exist only in a relationship of independence. Schleiermacher was right in making pious consciousness a locus of religion, but he was in danger of collapsing the historical Jesus and the Church into this locus and thus of losing the objective, historical foundation of Christian faith. This foundation must be discovered and tested historically-critically. Schleiermacher did move from pious consciousness to the historical Jesus, but he did not also make the opposite move by starting historically with the factual testimony of the Gospel. He was therefore in danger of dissolving the authoritative and positive aspect of religion into the autonomous and universal. What was a danger in Schleiermacher became an actuality in Hegel. It would be equally fatal to make the opposite error, which was the dilemma of Protestant scholasticism and modern Catholicism. The two extremes to be avoided are, in short,

142 As used here, "catholic" means "universal" and "orthodox," or "old catholic." In *Das Christenthum,* where Baur treats the patristic period, the term "catholic Church" is used synonymously and interchangeably with "Christian Church." When used in this sense, the adjective will not be capitalized in translation. When used in other works to refer to the medieval and modern (Roman) Catholic Church, it will be capitalized. Baur never uses the term "Roman Catholic." Therefore, whether he intends by use of the adjective *katholisch* to refer to the old catholic Church or to the Roman Catholic Church must be inferred from the context, which is usually not difficult.

143 *Das Christenthum,* pp. 246–47 (E.T., II, 1–2). Cf. also p. 305 (E.T., II, 62).

144 *Ibid.,* pp. 175–76 (E.T., I, 185).

"Gnostic universalism" and "Jewish particularism." The authentic tendency of the Church has always been to mediate between them, to temper each by the other.

Catholic and Protestant Views of the Church

The basic issue of the Reformation, as Baur sees it, is not justification by faith, or *sola gratia*, or *sola scriptura*, but the nature of the Church, i.e., the way in which the relationship between idea and manifestation in the historicity of the Church is understood. From the historian's point of view, the importance of the Reformation for the understanding of the history of the Church as a whole is that in it Catholic and Protestant perceptions of that history come into irreconcilable opposition, and that this opposition provides the structure for the development of Church history since the Reformation. Protestantism breaks with Catholicism because it becomes convinced "that the unity of God and man, which is the absolute content of Christianity and of the Church as the form of its manifestation, cannot be envisioned in such a form of the Church as that represented by the Papacy."[145]

For medieval Catholicism, the Christian idea is completely identified with the visible Church as its outward manifestation. The basic form of the Church is the hierarchical system culminating in the Pope as the absolute mediator of the unity of God and man; dogma, as a subordinate form, is represented by the scholastic systems which seek, by the power of their dialectic, to penetrate to the inner truth of this unity. The empirical Church, as represented by both hierarchy and dogma, thus shares in the very absolutism of the idea of which it is the completely adequate representation and assumes a suprahistorical, supratemporal purity. There is a twofold lack: the idea is not ingredient in an authentically historical form, and the empirical Church is supernaturalized by its identification with the divine idea.[146]

The change wrought by the Reformation is described by Baur as follows: "In the entire period of the Church up to the Reformation, the whole trend of the idea of the Church was to enter into the reality of the world of manifestations and to merge with it in an inseparable unity, while, on the other hand, after the Reformation the development of the Church strives just as much [*ebensosehr*] to retract the idea from the reality of the visible Church and to hold idea and manifestation apart from each other in the full extent of their distinction."[147] On the basis of this statement Karl Hase charged Baur with arguing that for Protestantism the idea soars far above the opaque factuality of the historical Church and that for it the only authentic Church is

[145] *Epochen*, p. 258; cf. also pp. 249, 250.
[146] *Ibid.*, pp. 253–55, 257; and *Kirchengeschichte*, III, 282.
[147] *Epochen*, p. 250.

the ideal or invisible one. Baur replies that his critic has over-looked the adverb "ebensosehr," which binds these two propositions together equally, "in such a way that Protestantism, in the same proportion that it seeks to introduce the idea into the reality, must also withdraw it, and such that it does this indeed as Catholicism does, but not one-sidedly, rather only so that in the relation of idea and reality these two sides, which belong together, may be well distinguished and set in the right relation to each other—the unity of idea and reality and the incongruence of both."[148]

The distinction between Catholic and Protestant views of the Church is most clearly expressed by Baur in the following passage:

[This distinction] can consist only in the difference of the relationship in which idea and reality are set to each other. The Catholics allow idea and reality completely to coincide; the idea penetrates completely into the reality; the Church as it is, is also as it ought to be; if it has defects, they are only a disappearing accident in the substance of the Church; one cannot distinguish between a visible and an invisible Church but only between a militant and a triumphant one. From the Protestant perspective, idea and reality are not so immediately one. . . . It is possible for the Church, as it exists in manifestation, to stand in such a wrong relationship to the idea of the Church that one does not at all know whether there still is an actually existing Church. . . . But it can never go so far that the connection of the real Church to the ideal is com-pletely sundered. . . . Just as Christ, at the most extreme point of his humiliation, still emanated a few rays of his divine majesty, so also the confession of a few martyrs shone forth from the deepest humiliation of the Church in order to give a clear witness to its permanency and truth. This must necessarily be assumed if one is not to make the Church into a bare ideal or a Platonic state, against which Melanchthon already protests in his Apology.[149]

The Protestant conception of the historicity of the Church is expressed in the doctrine of the visible and invisible Church, which enables the Reformers to understand the idea of the Church as that which "freely relates itself" to its manifestations "in the same proportion as it stands over them,"[150] and which is of fundamental importance for Baur's own theology of the Church. His theology of the Church is, in fact, nothing but a modern and critical development of this doctrine, inspired and guided, as we have noted, by Schleiermacher's interpretation of it.[151] The re-lation between invisible and visible Church becomes the most pressing problem in the Protestant doctrine, one which Luther

148 An Hase, pp. 83–84; quotation from p. 84.
149 Dogmengeschichte, III, 282–83.
150 Cf. Epochen, pp. 256–58.
151 See above, pp. 51–53.

himself leaves in a state of ambiguity, and which is not alleviated by the Lutheran symbols, such as the Augsburg Confession. The Catholics accuse the Protestants of teaching a doctrine of two Churches—an ideal and an empirical one. But this is clearly not the Protestant intention, as unambiguously stated by Quenstedt and Gerhard in their dogmatics. The conviction at which they arrived is that "the invisible Church exists within the visible; they are related to each other as inner and outer. One cannot look for the elect, who form the invisible Church, outside the community of the called; the elect are the called, but not vice versa."[152] The Protestant doctrine, therefore, does not claim that the visible Church is either identical with the actualized idea or totally different from it, but that the idea should be "regarded as the *principle* of the visible Church, immanent in itself and engaged in its steady actualization."[153]

In its doctrine of the Church, Protestantism especially reveals its *critical* character, in that it distinguishes in given reality between idea and manifestation, such that the real is not in itself true but is the visible manifestation of that which is true in itself. Baur insists that this critical principle does not entail a Platonic dualism of two worlds—a realm of ideas and a realm of appearances, in which appearances are only the shadows of reality and truth. There is only one realm, that marked by the intersection of these two principles. The divine idea, God in his outward relatedness, takes up his life in history, providing every created thing with substance, reality, truth. But the critical principle prevents one from absolutizing historical forms or from attributing to creation its own substantial ground. All things exist only in God, including the Church, and therefore the visible Church must not itself be divinized. On the other hand, the invisible Church—the divine idea of reconciliation—must exist historically, and the Reformers are therefore right when they join the existence of the Church to certain *notas externas,* which for Calvin are Word, Sacrament, Church discipline, and purity of doctrine. The more perfectly these marks exist in the visible Church, the more this Church is the true and universal Church. Baur concludes this description of the Protestant doctrine of the Church as follows:

If the outward manifestation of the Church is, in each case, never the adequate expression for the overarching ideality of its principle, it does not follow from this that the Church does not exist at all but only that every form of its outward existence is a merely finite one, beyond which the principle in its continual development always again precedes. *The consciousness of this inadequate relationship is the moving power of Protestantism,* the driving principle which leads it on from one level

---

152 *Dogmengeschichte,* III, 282.
153 *Ibid.,* p. 284. Italics mine.

of development to another. The more strongly Protestantism holds to the critical tendency which belongs to its nature, and the more exactly therefore it distinguishes between idea and manifestation in the visible Church, all the less can it regard a single, definite member of the visible Church as the proper and exclusive representative of the true Church.[154]

The precision with which the Reformers describe both the distinction and the unity between idea and manifestation soon breaks down into a number of Protestant distortions. Protestant scholasticism embraces a new authoritarianism in which idea and manifestation are too immediately identified, the basis of which is not, of course, the papal office but the normative exegesis of Scripture and the binding symbols of faith. The autonomy and priesthood of all believers is thus violated in the name of Scripture, which ought properly to be interpreted only in the freedom of faith. Similarly, the Anabaptists claim that the visible Church, as the community of the Spirit, is, in its empirical existence, already the completely pure and true Church and must therefore be severed in all its relations from the rest of the world. On the other hand, the Protestant mystics offer the greatest resistance to this notion. Frank insists that there is no visible Church at all, that the true Church is the invisible, spiritual body of the members of Christ existing in the Spirit, that it has no outward marks. Schwenkfeld allows that there was a single, true realization of the Church in the time of the apostles, but that none of the present Churches are the true Church.[155] Finally, as we have noted before, the Protestant rationalists have no interest in a doctrine of the Church because of their subjectivism and lack of concern for the positivity of Christianity and in this respect are anticipated by Socinianism. Baur regards Schleiermacher's *Glaubenslehre* as containing the first authentic restatement of the Protestant doctrine of the Church for modern times, returning to principles that have been obscured since the beginning of the seventeenth century; and his own theology of the Church is an attempt to further the important steps taken by Schleiermacher as well as to provide a theological foundation for historical-critical theology.

GOD AND HISTORY

If there is a fundamental dogmatic conviction which provides the dynamics and continuity for Baur's theological position as a whole, it can be described as follows: the story of reconciliation between God and man, which is told centrally in the history of the Christian Church, has its foundation and reality in the self-

154 *Ibid.*, pp. 284–85. Italics mine. For this and the preceding paragraph as a whole, see pp. 277–82, 284–85, 287.
155 *Ibid.*, pp. 285–90.

explication of the idea of God. Christianity, as the historical enactment of the divine idea of reconciliation, has as its foundation and presupposition God himself, who is the ground of the historical process in which Christianity participates, or of which (it would be more accurate to say) it is the prime exemplification. History exists because God, as the triune self-relatedness of the Absolute Spirit, explicates himself historically. God "lives" historically; history is God's triune life. Therefore Baur can say, in specifying Hegel's advance beyond Schleiermacher, that "historical Christianity is simply an element of the same course in which the process immanent to the nature of God explicates itself historically,"[156] that "Christianity is essentially . . . the life-process of God explicating itself in thought, as the nature of Spirit."[157]

If it is possible to say what God essentially is, then Baur agrees with Hegel that God is essentially Spirit, Spirit related to itself in the process of thought.[158] Therefore, with respect to a doctrine of God, Baur has little to offer beyond an Hegelian understanding of the Trinity.[159] But Baur insists, with a consistency not found in Hegel, that the process in which the Absolute Spirit mediates himself with himself in thought is historical. Baur's idealism remains concrete and historical; it never becomes abstract or "absolute." Spirit—divine Spirit—is the law of nature and history. History always points to God, and God to history.

This connection is affirmed by Baur's strong sense of providence, which is especially evident in sermons dealing with major events in the course of human life, such as marriage and death.[160] In these contexts, Baur expresses the conviction that all events in objective and personal history are closely yet mysteriously ordered by the guiding hand of God, a guidance which does not annul but rather enhances human freedom by providing the context of grace in which it can flourish. We become more immediately aware of divine providence at moments of great joy or sorrow. When death comes, we are not to complain that a fruitful life has been cut short before its proper end, but to be thankful that so much has been given an individual to accomplish in his short span and to realize that his life, like others, serves the larger purpose of God. It is from this perspective that we are able to appreciate the ultimate significance of marriage and to find some comfort when death strikes.

---

156 *Ibid.*, p. 353.

157 *Lehrbuch der Dogmengeschichte* (1st ed.), p. 257.

158 *Dogmengeschichte*, III, 350; *Lehrbuch der Dogmengeschichte* (1st ed.), p. 257.

159 See above, pp. 54–55.

160 Cf. Sermon at the Wedding of Emilie Caroline Baur and Eduard Zeller, 22 June 1847 (privately printed by Königlichen Hofbuchdruckerei, Stuttgart; U.B.T., Md 750, iv, 6); and *Worte der Erinnerung an Dr. Friedrich Heinrich Kern*, pp. 7–10. Cf. also "Geschichte des Alterthums" (U.B.T., Mh II 166, q), p. 21.

Baur's dogmatic understanding of the relation between God and history thrusts him almost inevitably into an historical-critical theology; for it is in history, critically examined and speculatively interpreted, that the theologian encounters the being and life of God. The inner congruence between dogmatic and historical theology, and between faith and historical knowledge, which we shall examine in the following chapters, has its ultimate foundation in the ontological connection Baur establishes between God and history.

But now we must ask whether these connections are not too tightly woven. Do they not tend to blur into identifications? Is there not the danger in Baur's thought that historical process be identified with God, that dogmatics be identified with historical theology and faith with historical knowledge? It is with the possibility of confusion or identification on the ontological level, in terms of the relation between God and history, that we are concerned in this section. For if there is confusion here, it is likely also to be reflected on the epistemological level, in terms of the relation between dogmatics and historical theology, which we shall have occasion to examine later.[161]

With Baur as with Hegel the danger is one not of atheism but of acosmism.[162] For the question is not whether God exists but whether the world and history exist other than as a subsistent mode of the divine being. We have already noted that for Baur Spinoza's view of "the immanence of God and the world" can "scarcely be avoided" in modern theism.[163] The question is whether Baur moves beyond an immanental theism or a panentheism entirely to Spinoza's acosmism, without, of course, sharing the latter's doctrine of absolute Substance. On the one hand, it would seem that such a move is made inevitable by his sharing with Hegel the view that God has no independent substantiality apart from his involvement in cosmic and historical process, whereby he becomes an other to himself in order to actualize himself. The historical process, as the arena in which God's mediation of himself with the other takes place, thus becomes a part of the divine process of life and possesses no independent substantiality of its own. On the other hand, it would seem that Baur's radically historical theology, and his strong emphasis on the positivity of the Christian Gospel, would mitigate against such a total merging or confusing of history with God. We must ask, therefore, whether Baur succeeded in avoiding the acosmism which he apparently recognized, late in life, as a danger in Hegel's thought.[164] In actualizing the positive and creative insights for an historical-critical theology of

---

161 See below, pp. 261–71.
162 On the use of these terms in this work, see above, p. 55, n. 73.
163 *Dogmengeschichte*, III, 346.
164 See above, pp. 55–58.

his vision of the internal congruence between God and history, and thus between dogmatics and historical theology, faith and historical knowledge, was he also able to avoid the dangers which accompanied this vision?

Despite the strongly immanental character of Baur's theism, he clearly emphasizes the mutual transcendence of both God and the world. With respect to the transcendence of God, Baur defends himself against the charge of a "pantheism which puts man in the place of God," brought against his notion that the essence of Christianity is the idea of the unity of God and man.

Is it not also a question of the unity of God and man when Christianity gives to man the consciousness of a peace offered to man by God himself, in which he is reconciled with God and in community with God knows himself to be one with him? What do the blessings of the Sermon on the Mount intend to express in the simplest form other than just the unity of man with God, which, as the blissful rest of a spirit raised above all the limits of finitude and gratified in thoughts about God and his kingdom, is the essence of all the blessings of the Gospel? This unity is indeed perceived in the person of Christ, but not at all speculatively. . . . Only the simple recognition is needed [to avoid calling this notion of unity "pantheistic"] that there is not merely a physical but also a moral unity and that man may know himself one with God when in his religious consciousness every limitation is removed which separates him from God.[165]

That is to say, when the unity of God and man is conceived in the context of the "moral" reconciliation mediated by Jesus Christ, there is no question of confusing the substantial reality of God with that of man in a pantheism of physical identity.

Similarly, Baur criticizes Plato and paganism for regarding the divine as

. . . only another form of the human. . . . The divine is not thought of as truly substantial being, which absolutely determines the human. . . . The whole of paganism moves only in the sphere of the human. . . . Where the distinction between the human and the divine has not yet been disclosed, the unity of this distinction cannot be disclosed either. . . . All this . . . takes shape completely differently for the first time from the standpoint of Judaism and Christianity. The subjectively divine becomes objectively divine, which alone is truly substantial being and absolutely real. Everything which appears in the sphere of the human as truly divine can therefore only be a revelation of the divine itself. . . .[166]

165 *An Hase*, pp. 85–90; quotation from pp. 86, 89.
166 "Das christliche des Platonismus," *TZT*, X:3, 150–51. On the transcendence of God, cf. also *Das Christenthum*, pp. 16–17 (E.T., I, 17–18), quoted below, p. 221.

This insistence on the transcendence of God recalls Schleiermacher's emphasis on the absolute dependence of man on "a higher divine causality."

Baur also stresses the transcendence of the world and of man from the divine. An example is his polemic against docetic Christologies, which repudiate the independent substantiality of the human because of their cosmic dualism. For the Gnostics, the opposition between spirit and matter is so fundamental that the spiritual element of man is taken up into the divine and the psychical and physical elements are sloughed off into the realm of nonbeing. Further and closely related evidence for this attitude is to be found in the way Baur treats the docetism of nature and history implied in the theory of transubstantiation first advanced by Paschasius Radbertus and Lanfrank. The basis of this theory is a transcendental supernaturalism which vitiates the intrinsic substantiality of created nature. In order to ground all reality in the divine, the finite world is set in a purely negative relation to God and in fact subsists "docetically." "The inner ground of being of finite things, the intrinsic substance of their nature, is only the divine will acting in them. In this connection the possibility is established that in every moment, at every point of finite being, the absolute causality of God replaces the natural causality of finite things."[167]

As we have seen already, Baur urges that the finite individual must not be absorbed or merged (*aufgegangen*) into the Infinite by the idea of reconciliation.[168] This insistence is what lies behind his modified Christology and his strong emphasis on moral autonomy and freedom; the key to his thought in both cases is the notion of a distinction within unity. We may also consider here Baur's insistence in *Symbolik und Mythologie* that for Christianity, as distinguished from the nature religions, "the concept of personal individuality cannot be abandoned [*aufgegeben*]," that the identity of the finite self is preserved even after death, rather than being absorbed into the divine totality.[169]

In attempting to express the mutual transcendence of God and the world, however, Baur encounters difficulties which blur the distinction he has drawn. In his reply to Hase, quoted above, he makes it clear that the unity between God and man is to be understood as moral rather than physical or substantial. It is unity in the moral sense which comes increasingly to be stressed in Baur's theology, as his historical study focuses more directly on the teaching of Jesus: man's unity with God is a function of his religious feeling or religious consciousness, specifically, of his awareness of moral reconciliation with God mediated through Christ. But in earlier works, there are hints that Baur has in mind unity in

[167] *Kirchengeschichte*, III, 72–73.
[168] Cf. the passage from *Dreieinigkeit*, III, 996–99, quoted above, pp. 104–105.
[169] See above, p. 119.

a substantial sense as well. In the *Versöhnung*, written during his most Hegelian period, there are some suggestions that the distinction between man and God is simply a matter of sin or temporal estrangement, which will be eliminated or overcome in an implicit substantial unity.[170] It is not certain that Baur ever completely repudiated this view, although he was clearly moving away from it in later years.

The same difficulty is involved in his use of the ambiguous term *Aufhebung*. From passages referred to above, we can see that among the verbs employed by Baur to describe that annihilation of the distinction between God and man which he rejects are *aufgehen* (to be merged or absorbed) and *aufgeben* (to abandon, relinquish, discontinue). In *Symbolik und Mythologie*, he uses *aufheben* and its derivatives in this same sense. For example, he describes the Indian notion "of a complete *Aufhebung* of all human individuality in the absolutely simple essence of the Godhead."[171] Later, however, he uses the same term quite differently, in a more technical and sophisticated sense, which he has learned from Hegel, to describe the unity-in-distinction of divine and human Spirit, as in the following passage from "Das christliche des Platonismus": "Where the divine and the human stand opposite each other in such a relationship, the distinction between them must stand out ever more clearly and appear as one which could absolutely never be equalized, were it not a distinction that is implicitly *aufgehoben* in the implicit unity of the divine and the human."[172]

The "true unity" of God and man "is not an abstract unity, excluding every distinction," but rather is "a concrete unity, mediated with itself through the *Aufhebung* of the distinction," which is provided by the "notion of the Christian Trinity."[173] *Aufhebung* is used in a similar sense in the *Versöhnung*, which dates from the same period, 1837–38. In other respects, also, this period seems to represent the high-water mark of Hegel's influence on Baur. His intention in using the term in this sense seems perfectly clear. He wants to say on the one hand that the distinction between God and man must not remain a raw and unmediated distinction, but that on the other hand it must not be erased by means of an "abstract unity." Rather it is to remain a distinction-in-unity; and this is to be achieved by "taking the distinction up into" the unity, by incorporating it in the unity, by making this a unity in which distinction is preserved, i.e., by regarding this unity as an internally mediated relationship of two substantially distinct components. This would seem to be the meaning of Baur's use of *Aufhebung*. The only difficulty is that this term had become rather

170 *Versöhnung*, p. 2.
171 *Symbolik und Mythologie*, II/2, 453–54.
172 "Das christliche des Platonismus," *TZT*, X:3, 152.
173 *Ibid.*, pp. 76–77.

heavily freighted by Hegel's systematic use of it, and there is a real question as to whether anything of a distinction is left after an Hegelian *Aufhebung*. Whether Baur was aware at that time of the ambiguity and difficulty in Hegel's use of it is not certain, although he was clearly aware of the danger of Hegel's *Aufhebung* of the historical Jesus into absolute knowledge. At first, his awareness of difficulties in Hegel's Christology does not seem to have carried over into a confrontation with the difficulties created by Hegel's panentheism. Later Baur does not use the term *Aufhebung* to express his own understanding of the unity of God and man, and he seems tentatively to have become aware of these difficulties. Even when he uses it positively and technically, however, it is to describe a relationship or unity in which distinction remains untranscended. To describe the relationship, Baur always uses the terms *Einheit* (unity) or *Verhältniss* (relationship), never *Identität* (identity).

Is it possible, however, to maintain such distinctions in the context of an Hegelian panentheism? Is not Baur's panentheism, like Hegel's, in danger ultimately of becoming an acosmism, which is after all a form of pantheism? For Baur shares with Hegel his notion of the diremption of the Absolute Spirit into human history as his other in order to enact his spiritual life, rather than insisting that God is first his own other totally apart from man and that in the freedom resulting from this absolute self-sufficiency he then elects man into eternal fellowship with himself. Hegel's view of the Trinity makes God dependent on man for his self-actualization and therefore tends to reduce man to a mere function or mode of the divine life. What is needed to avoid this danger, and what seems to be implied by Baur's conception of the radical historicity of the Christian Church and by his Christology, is a doctrine of creation which is actually found neither in Hegel nor in Baur. What is required is an understanding of the relationship between God and the world which is sustained, not by the necessity[174] of the divine diremption into an other than himself to actualize his own spirituality, but by the free grace of the one who is first his own other and then in the freedom of his love creates a world which he also adopts, analogically, as his other in Jesus Christ. What is needed as the basis for an adequate doctrine of creation is a conception of the triune God who is free, self-sufficient, and complete in his own right prior to and as the foundation of his eternal elective act, which posits creation as well as reconciliation and redemption.[175]

[174] This "necessity," however, is perfectly congruent with the freedom of the divine life. In Baur's terms, God would be subject to "necessity" only if it were a necessity not his own, namely, the necessity of nature, as is the case with Gnosticism. Cf. *Die christliche Gnosis*, pp. 66–67.

[175] Cf. Karl Barth, *Church Dogmatics*, Vol. I/1, G. T. Thomson, trans. (Edinburgh: T. & T. Clark, 1936), §§ 8–12; and Vol. II/1, G. W. Bromiley & T. F. Torrance, eds. (Edinburgh: T. & T. Clark, 1957), esp. § 28.

Would such a doctrine of creation destroy the internal congruence between God and history, dogmatics and historical theology, faith and historical knowledge, which Baur's theology is able to elucidate precisely because of its panentheism? On the contrary, such a doctrine could preserve the internal congruence and also avoid the tendency toward confusion or identification which is implicit in Baur's treatment of these relations. It could eliminate some of the ambiguities or difficulties in Baur's treatment of history, e.g., his view of the "necessity" of the historical life of God, the possible *Aufhebung* of human spirit into substantial identity with the divine, the lack of genuine contingency in finite freedom, and the tendency to view subjectivity as simply the relative and spatiotemporally conditioned reflex of an eternal and objective process.[176] It could provide a more adequate theological basis for Baur's understanding of history as constituted by the untranscended relation of divine Spirit to human spirit, or as occurring at the point of juncture of idea and manifestation. It could enable him to take more adequate account of the contingency and autonomy of historical events and persons and of the authentic subjectivity of historical knowledge. It could perhaps enable him to develop a more adequate understanding of the incarnation, for a truly transcendent God could relate himself completely, perfectly, archetypally to a single historical individual without exhausting his omnipotence. In short, a genuine doctrine of creation could provide a more adequate basis for the historical-critical task of theology which Baur so imaginatively envisioned and explicated.

[176] On the last two of these difficulties, see below, pp. 148–50, 172–74.

4 ∗ THE METHODOLOGY OF AN HISTORICAL THEOLOGY

Just as Baur wrote no *Glaubenslehre,* so also he wrote no single, systematic study in epistemology or hermeneutics. His historical method as well as his theological convictions were so much a part of his total work as an historical-critical theologian that they cannot be neatly separated out and distinguished as "presuppositions" and "method" from "results," despite such efforts at elucidation in these chapters. We already have noted that Baur is a thinker for whom unities are more vital than distinctions. What unifies his work is its subject matter. But for Baur the theological consciousness of the present age as well as the historian himself are included in the "subject matter." These factors interpenetrate and affect each other: theological presuppositions and historical method are shaped by the subject matter at the same time that they are shaping it. The subject matter is the common historical process which past and present share and by which each participate in the reality of the other. This is the basic hermeneutical presupposition which supports Baur's entire historical procedure. It is what enables the historian to penetrate conceptually and linguistically to the historical agent's intention, his "mind," and (to use Dilthey's famous aphorism) "to understand the author better than he understands himself." This presupposition is expressed by Baur in a variety of ways but never directly and as such. He did not develop it in terms of a theory of knowledge, a philosophy of history, or a hermeneutical system.

Since Baur is first and last an historical theologian, his discussion of hermeneutics is primarily historical, not systematic. Each of the great historical studies of his mature years is prefaced by an in some cases epoch-making study of the history of the discipline in question. The best known and most important of these is *Die Epochen der kirchlichen Geschichtschreibung,* which serves as an introduction to the five-volume Church history. This work comprises an extensive analysis of various types and periods of Church historiography and concludes with a section in which Baur presents his own principles as well as his theology of the Church. A similar and extensive introduction is provided in the first volume of *Vorlesungen über die christliche Dogmengeschichte*, where Baur considers the position of history of dogma in the theological disciplines, the object, methods, and periods of history of dogma, the relation of the history of dogma to the history of philosophy, and the history of the study of history of dogma—its origin and development into a science. This introduction, as important as the *Epochen*, is duplicated in shorter form in the *Lehrbuch der christlichen Dogmengeschichte*. A lengthy introduction to *Kritische Untersuchungen über die kanonischen Evangelien* surveys the history of Gospel criticism, dividing previous methods into three basic types, and presenting a seminal statement of the procedure of historical-critical theology. The conception, history, and development of the study of New Testament theology are discussed at length in the introduction to *Vorlesungen über neutestamentliche Theologie*.[1] In addition to these extensive historical introductions, Baur's earlier works are provided with prefaces where he discusses some of the methodological questions involved. The earliest of these is the preface to *Symbolik und Mythologie*. Of special interest are the prefaces to *Die christliche Lehre von der Versöhnung* and to *Die christliche Lehre von der Dreieinigkeit und Menschwerdung Gottes*. *Paulus* contains an introductory chapter of singular importance. Finally, Baur devotes himself to hermeneutical questions in his polemical writings, the most important for this purpose being "Abgenöthigte Erklärung gegen einen Artikel der *Evangelischen Kirchenzeitung*," *An Herrn Dr. Karl Hase*, and *Die Tübinger Schule und ihre Stellung zur Gegenwart*.[2]

Since Baur's hermeneutical material is not systematic in itself, this chapter makes no pretense of systematizing it. The materials collected here do not fit together into a "system" or a total theory. Yet they show the originality and penetration, the plasticity and coherence of Baur's mind as he sought to shape in practice a method by means of which he would investigate and interpret historically-critically the historicity of the Christian Church. This method is of importance in structuring a theological hermeneutics for our own day, not so much for the language and philosophical framework it embodies as for the way Baur envisioned the purpose and task of historical-critical theology. Since Christianity is by its very nature rooted in history, Baur believed it both possible and necessary that an appropriate historical discipline—one

[1] This introduction is anticipated by an important monograph, "Die Einleitung in das Neue Testament als theologische Wissenschaft. Ihr Begriff und ihre Aufgabe, ihr Entwicklungsgang und ihr innerer Organismus," *TJ*, IX:4 (1850), 463–566; X:1, 2, 3 (1851), 70–94, 222–52, 291–328.

[2] Except for "Abgenöthigte Erklärung" and the above-mentioned article, "Die Einleitung in das Neue Testament als theologische Wissenschaft," Baur did not write journal monographs on hermeneutics or historical method. His articles were almost exclusively occupied with historical investigations, the results of which were then usually incorporated into his books or lectures, or which brought earlier studies up to date. Therefore, for a study of this nature, it is not necessary to work extensively with the journal articles.

which is at once critical and speculative—should penetrate to the full reality of this historical phenomenon to discover its meaning and truth. To develop such a discipline was therefore an essential component in historical-critical theology.

The first section of this chapter is introductory in nature, since it examines Baur's understanding of "history" as a process and as a form of disciplined knowledge. His treatment of previous historical methods in the theological disciplines, as analyzed in the second section, contributes importantly to his own hermeneutics, which takes shape from the nature and direction of his criticism of these methods. The third section describes the congruence of critical objectivity and critical subjectivity, which for Baur constitutes the essence of historical knowledge and which is reflected, for example, in the way he understands the relation between faith and critical historical study in theology (section four). The topics of the fifth and sixth sections—past and present, the relation of parts and wholes, historical development, and the question of miracle—are not arranged or discussed systematically but are selected because each in its own way represents an important methodological problem for Baur and contributes to the total shape of his method. In the last section I shall discuss the method employed by Baur in his literary and historical criticism of the New Testament writings, a method which has not been substantially altered since his day.

THE NATURE OF HISTORY

Historical Event and Historical Knowledge

Baur notes that the word "history" has an objective as well as a subjective meaning and that in this double sense it expresses as an unmediated unity that which is separated by analysis: "history" is both the objective event and the critical knowledge of that event. Furthermore, just as all events are not historical events, so also not all knowledge of events is historical knowledge. "Historical knowledge first takes place where the event appears important enough to become known not just for the moment but also to be transmitted to the enduring knowledge of future generations."[3] In other words, an event becomes "historical" when it exists not just "for the moment" but endures through time in the memory and knowledge of future generations. An historical event or an historical process is one which is in principle *knowable*—not necessarily actually known—through historical knowledge.[4] Although it is quite probable that an historical event can *also* be known in non-

---

[3] *Epochen*, p. 1.

[4] The historical theologian is obliged to grant one exception to this rule: the resurrection is an historical event for which historical understanding assumes an entirely negative and secondary, though for that reason no less

historical ways, e.g., through faith, an event from which historical understanding is totally excluded in principle is not an historical event. Furthermore, there is no evidence in Baur's thought of a distinction between various modes of "historical" knowledge, just as he knows nothing of the later distinction between *Historie* (objective, empirical history) and *Geschichte* (internal, personal human existence). Baur uses these terms and their adjectival derivatives interchangeably. If an event is knowable historically, i.e., if it is an "historical" event, then it is knowable historically-critically, i.e., by a discipline which is at once critical and imaginative. The components which later become separated in an historical dualism are held together internally in Baur's view of historical knowledge.[5]

Furthermore, the knowledge of historical events ought ideally to be closely related to the events themselves. "Historical presentation [is] to be nothing other than the true, adequate reflex of the objective event." But the distance between the historian and his object in terms of time and point of view is often so great that it becomes questionable whether the historian has access to the "real factuality of the matter itself." "Thus, there is no historical presentation which must not first be critically tested in order to determine the relationship in which the writer presenting it stands to the pure objectivity of historical truth"; and even when the credibility of the historian, his sources, etc., have been established, "history itself . . . is something so infinitely large that its contents can never be exhausted by historical knowledge, through which what has objectively taken place is also to become subjectively known."[6] The relation between event and interpretation becomes the central problem in Baur's consideration of historical knowledge. Before we turn to this problem, however, we must first examine more closely what he means by historical occurrence or historical process —the subject matter of historical presentation.

Toward a Definition of Historical Process

As with his theory of religion, a certain evolution can be detected in Baur's definition of historical process. The earliest forms of the definition clearly show his indebtedness to Schleiermacher and Schelling. For example, in his Blaubeuren lecture manuscript, "Geschichte des Alterthums," he follows the distinction Schleiermacher establishes in his philosophical ethics between nature and history. Not everything generally, but only what happens to man, only the actions of men, constitute the proper content of history; natural occurrences are a part of history only in so far as they are

---

relevant, posture. The historical theologian has access only to faith in the resurrection, not to the event itself, although on this account he by no means denies the objective reality of the event. See below, pp. 234–37.

[5] I return to these questions in chap. VI; cf. esp. pp. 271–84.

[6] *Epochen*, pp. 1–2.

related to men. "Real history, and the object of history, therefore, is man in so far as he acts and presents in the course of time a manifold diversity of manifestations."[7] In the same work, Baur also shows the influence of Schelling when he suggests that history as a whole is the revelation of divine providence.[8] This suggestion is developed more fully in *Symbolik und Mythologie:* "If world history generally, in its widest and most worthy sense, is a revelation of Divinity, the most living expression of divine ideas and purposes, then, since generally, where spiritual life exists, consciousness exists also as the unity of such life, world history can be perceived only as the development of a consciousness, which is to be thought of analogously to the development of individual [human] consciousness, although it may not be measured by the limited standards of the latter."[9]

Historical process is the revelation of Divinity, but it is also the development of divine consciousness. Already this statement anticipates Baur's later definition of history, influenced by Hegel, as that which exists by virtue of God's self-realization. It is clear, however, that this understanding of historical process is not simply indebted to Hegel; it is first developed in Baur's pre-Hegelian period and employs different categories. Since history is a spiritual (*geistlich*) process, it is not simply the revelation of Divinity but also the manifestation of the consciousness of the divine Spirit, and, in a subordinate fashion, of human spirit as well. The Hegelian language appears for the first time in *Die christliche Gnosis,* where Baur suggests that the "most recent philosophies of religion" share with ancient Gnosticism the attempt "to understand nature and history, the whole course of the world with everything it comprises, as the series of moments in which the Absolute Spirit objectifies himself and mediates himself with himself."[10]

That Baur also shares with Gnosticism this understanding can be seen from his lectures on the history of dogma: "The historical process, in which Christianity comes to historical manifestation, is simply an element of the general process which is the life-process of God himself, in which the idea of God explicates itself in the distinction of its moments. . . . As triune, God is the Absolute Spirit mediating himself with himself in the process of thought. Historical Christianity is simply an element of the same course in which the process immanent to the nature of God explicates itself historically."[11] History exists because the inward process of the divine life also explicates itself outwardly. God "lives" in history; he mediates himself historically; therefore history exists. The ontological foundation of history is God. Since history is part of

---

7 "Geschichte des Alterthums" (U.B.T., Mh II 166, q), p. 2.
8 *Ibid.*, p. 21.
9 *Symbolik und Mythologie,* I, v.
10 *Die christliche Gnosis,* p. 24.
11 *Dogmengeschichte,* III, 352–53.

the very life of God, it cannot cease to exist unless or until God should cease to mediate himself outwardly; but the Christian Gospel declares that it is the nature and purpose of God thus to live. This is a dogmatic affirmation which undergirds Baur's historical-critical theology.

A similar and well-known definition is found in the preface to the *Dreieinigkeit* where Baur writes that the task of historical research is not only the reproducing in itself of what individuals have thought and done but also the rethinking in itself "of the eternal thoughts of the eternal Spirit, whose work history is."[12] This definition serves to confirm what was said earlier about Baur's use of "idea" as a category of historical interpretation.[13] An idea or concept is an expression, form, or actualization of thought, which in turn is the "life" or "nature" of Spirit, that whereby Spirit mediates itself with itself in order to become thinking, free, self-conscious Spirit. The reality of history is primarily constituted by those ideas which are the expressions of the thought of the eternal or divine Spirit, although the ideas of human individuals and communities also contribute to that reality but do not basically shape it. The foundation of history is ideas, divine and human.

But, in addition, as we have seen in discussing Baur's theology of the Church,[14] the historical process takes place at the point of congruence of ideas and manifestations, which is the mark of authentic "historicity." Although "idea" is by no means an abstract category for Baur, history does not consist merely of ideas, but rather takes place at the point where ideas become ingredient in outward manifestations. The relationship between idea and manifestation can be otherwise expressed as that between the universal and the particular, between concept and reality (or fact), between content and form, or between divine Spirit and human spirit (or human consciousness).

In some of his early writing, Baur describes the relation as that between divine being and human consciousness. The divine idea has its truth in itself, implicitly; but it becomes true for history, for human consciousness, by means of the "constant correlation of ideal and real." The real "mediates the *consciousness* of the idea."[15] Human consciousness, in other words, is the historical reality by which the divine idea is manifested. This consciousness can express itself in many ways, e.g., in dogma and faith. "If the idea is that which exists implicitly, it can actualize itself only in that its implicit being becomes one which is known. [Human] consciousness is the ground in which the idea actualizes itself; and idea and reality are related to each other as being and knowing, objective and subjective. In the knowing of the subject, reality

12 *Dreieinigkeit*, I, xix.
13 See above, pp. 92–93.
14 See above, pp. 121–24.
15 Cf. *Die christliche Gnosis*, p. 655. Italics mine.

and idea, finite and Infinite, are joined together in unity. The subject is infinite only as a knowing subject, and only in its consciousness does it have both at the same time—the unity as well as the distinction."[16]

In the preface to the *Versöhnung*, Baur employs Hegelian terminology to describe the relation between idea and manifestation as that between the "inner movement of the concept" and the "historical material" in which it moves:

> The material is only one side of the task of the historian of dogma. It is not only more important but also more difficult so to comprehend the form of the material, which lies before us as objectively given, that in the historical presentation the inner movement of the concept is portrayed. . . . If that history which makes external facts the object of its presentation is not worthy of its name when it ranges fact upon fact without penetrating to the inner connection of events, then the demand for a presentation which pursues inner unity is made with all the more justification of an historical discipline [history of dogma] which has as its immediate object not events but thoughts, not externals but internals, the thoughts expressed by Spirit. . . . Only when in the historical presentation the nature of Spirit itself, its inner movement and development, its self-consciousness progressing from moment to moment, is presented, is the true objectivity of history recognized and grasped.[17]

This notion of the "inner movement of the concept" in history serves as a speculative explication of Baur's empirical discovery that history develops to a certain extent through the opposition of opposing tendencies, although these tendencies are to be regarded as a general historical phenomenon, to be discovered anew by critical research in each instance that they occur, not to be imposed on the face of events as an a priori pattern. The inner movement of the concept explains why this phenomenon should exist, for this movement, as the expression of thoughts of Spirit—divine and human—is dialectical in character.[18]

The Question of Historical "Necessity"

The congruence of idea and manifestation, or of concept and fact, as the mark of historical process helps to account for the "necessity" which Baur attributes to the development and movement of historical events. "The historically given ought not to be comprehended merely externally, according to this or that arbitrary

16 *Dreieinigkeit*, III, 998. The bracketed qualifier seems required by the context. Cf. also *Versöhnung*, p. 726.

17 *Versöhnung*, pp. v–vi; cf. *Dreieinigkeit*, I, vi.

18 See below, pp. 188–90; cf. also *An Hase*, pp. 90–91. Emanuel Hirsch suggests (*Geschichte der neuern evangelischen Theologie*, V, 521) that this is one of two characteristics of an idealistic philosophy of history which Baur shares with Ranke. The other concerns the relation of individual historical agents to the "development and movement of an historically powerful idea" which shapes the connections of historical becoming and events.

relation in which the subject sets himself to it, but according to its inner essential continuity. The sole presupposition which is thereby made is that history is not merely an arbitrary aggregate but a connected whole. Where continuity exists, there also is reason, and that which is through reason must also be for reason, for the reasoning consideration of spirit."[19] The "necessity" of history is its continuity and rationality, which are functions of the fact that it exists by virtue of the divine life in it. The mysteries of history are ultimately rational, for they are the mysteries of God. History possesses patterns of fitness and wholeness and is thus not constituted by irrational, arbitrary, or fortuitous states, the products of sheer chance. It is the task of the historical theologian as well as of the metaphysician to describe these rational mysteries. But he does not impose rational or necessary patterns on history a priori, for he does not see things *sub specie aeternitatis*. He can discover the rationality of history, the patterns of fitness and wholeness, only a posteriori, through the painstaking analysis of data and events.

Formidable difficulties, however, plague Baur's discussion of historical necessity. Despite his suggestion that the particular form of historical events may result from the free and undetermined acts of individual human agents, these events are also entirely consequent upon the divinely ordained necessity of the historical process as a whole. In terms of "the great continuity of history," Baur writes, such "free self-determination" is seen to be "just as much necessity as freedom." If one historical agent had freely chosen not to do what he in fact did, then another would have done it, also freely, but "on the whole . . . with the same end result."[20] Although there is genuine human freedom in history, according to Baur's claim, there is no contingency, no novelty, no genuine possibility. Free acts are done *with* the will and as morally responsible acts. But such human freedom is entirely embraced by divine freedom; and from the human perspective, what happens in accordance with divine freedom happens with necessity. The congruence between divine and human freedom, between idea and manifestation, which Baur so wants to preserve, tends to evaporate into an identity in which only the necessity of the divine prevails. This dilemma can be seen as another result of Baur's tendency to identify history with the divine life itself. When such an identification is made, the introduction of contingency, novelty, and possibility into history creates acute problems. Under such circumstances, to the extent that one allows genuine autonomy and contingency to historical events, one diminishes the freedom of God by subjecting him to a process not his own as a necessity for his own self-realization. On the other hand, to the extent that one allows genuine freedom to

19 *Dreieinigkeit*, I, xix. Cf. also *Versöhnung*, p. 11; and *Paulus*, I, 4 (E.T., 2).
20 *Die Tübinger Schule*, pp. 8–9.

God, one diminishes the autonomy and contingency of the created world.

Only in terms of a genuine doctrine of creation would it be possible to understand how divine and human freedom can stand over against each other without canceling each other out. Such a doctrine need not embrace the other and equally objectionable alternative, namely, a view of the world and history as purely irrational, arbitrary, or fortuitous. One must believe, with Baur, that the mysteries of history are ultimately rational and meaningful, that these mysteries are not closed to all but the divine mind, but also that they are rational and meaningful because God providentially and intelligibly orders the genuine contingency and novelty of history for his own appropriate purposes. One can even talk of a "necessity" in history, when viewing events as past rather than present or future; but such necessity does not derive from God's necessary ingredient in the historical process. It derives rather from his lordship in and over the contingencies of history. It derives also from the historical theologian's ability to discover why and how things happen as they do, to penetrate, as Baur puts it, to the true objectivity of historical process, to unveil something of the mystery of historical causality, even perhaps to disclose, or to show forth the self-disclosure, of the divine purpose in history. With these modifications, the insights from Baur's discussion of historical necessity could be usefully applied to an understanding of the historical theologian's task.

SURVEY OF PREVIOUS HISTORICAL METHODS IN THE THEOLOGICAL DISCIPLINES[21]

Old Catholic Historiography: Abstract Supernaturalism

In the patristic and medieval periods, Church history and history of dogma are characterized by an abstract supernaturalism, according to which the idea of the Church is completely objectified in and made identical with the visible, institutional Church. The visible Church, accordingly, is distinguished as an eternal essence from the changing forms of history. By virtue of the total identification of idea and manifestation, the idea remains transcendent, not becoming ingredient in an authentically historical form, and the empirical Church is absolutized or divinized. This twofold weakness is described as follows: "Once the general lack of the

[21] This discussion is not limited to Baur's consideration of methods in Church historiography but also takes into account similar material relating to the historical study of dogma and the history of Gospel criticism. The sources for this section therefore include the introduction to Baur's lectures in history of dogma and to his study of the canonical Gospels, as well as the *Epochen*. When these materials are assembled, it is possible to classify Baur's treatment of the periods and types of theological historiography in five groups, as presented below.

system, i.e., the transcendence of the idea, which never accomplished the full concretion of the idea and which allowed the absolutism of the Church to appear as a merely abstract theory—once this lack had become clear at even one point, only a general dissolution of religious and ecclesiastical life could follow."[22]

This point of view, which comes to its completion in the hierarchical absolutism of the Church of the high Middle Ages, has its origin with the patristic and early medieval Church historians, from Eusebius to Gregory of Tours and the Venerable Bede. Following Bede, no significant Church histories are written, and the medieval historians merely produce external chronicles of events.[23] The distinction between the absolutism of the Church and the relativities of history is carried over into history of dogma, as first attempted by the Church Fathers. They regard the moving and changing aspects of history as merely docetic, as bare representations of the truly real, from which they sought to distinguish the unchanging and eternal dogmatic consciousness of the Church. Movement and variation become the mark of heresy.[24]

Finally, the patristic period marks the beginning of the "dogmatic comprehension" of the New Testament, which rests on the presupposition of a "spiritual inspiration" of Scripture. The Holy Spirit himself is regarded as the author of Scripture, and the subjectivity of the human authors becomes the organ of the Holy Spirit. The agreement between the four Gospels is attributed to the *auctor primarius,* and disagreement is relegated to unessentials which have crept in via the human organ. Irenaeus claims there are not four Gospels but a *quadriforme evangelium;* and Augustine, in *De consensus evangelistarum,* argues that each of the Gospels contributes different elements to the whole but that there are no contradictions. Already the elements for a harmonization of the Gospels are present in Augustine's work, which has a direct impact on the late medieval nominalist theologian, Jean de Gerson. Further attempts at a Gospel harmony following the Reformation represent only a development of Gerson's basic work.[25] Thus to Scripture, as to the Church and dogma, is attributed a position of abstract transcendence over the relativities and changes of history.

Reformation and Old Protestant Historiography: Dualism and Polemicism

The tendency of old Protestant Church historiography is the exact opposite of the identification of idea and manifestation in old catholic historiography. Now a sharp dualism is established between idea and manifestation, such that the idea of the Church

22 *Kirchengeschichte,* III, 3.
23 *Epochen,* pp. 7–38.
24 *Dogmengeschichte,* I/1, 102–108.
25 *Die kanonischen Evangelien,* pp. 2–5.

(the invisible Church) is totally separated from all historical manifestations. Historical study of the empirical Church thus becomes a polemical critique of it. This point of view is masterfully represented by the *Magdeburg Centuries,* a history of the first thirteen centuries of the Church, produced by Lutheran theologians at Magdeburg under the guidance of Matthew Flacius, a Gnesio-Lutheran, and published in thirteen folio volumes (one for each century) between 1559 and 1574. Baur suggests that with this work the Church rises for the first time to a "true historical consciousness of its entire past" and that no previous work in Church history is carried out with such "a clear consciousness of the task which Church history has generally to solve" and with such "a definite, methodically projected plan." It is epoch-making by virtue not so much of its exhaustive contents as of "the inclusive conception of Church history" from which it proceeds.[26] This conception, however, by virtue of its sharp dualism, represents a vitiation of the authentic Reformed view of the Church, according to which idea and manifestation, invisible and visible Church, are understood in their unity-in-distinction. The *Centuries* is important for its conception of what a Church history ought to attempt, not for what it actually accomplishes.

Early Protestant historians of dogma, such as Forbesius a Corse, Gerhard, and Quenstedt, share the polemicism of the *Magdeburg Centuries.* Their purpose is to show, against Catholic charges of heresy, that Protestant doctrine is in agreement with that of the early Fathers and represents an authentic development of Church dogma. They are not as skillful, however, as their Catholic counterparts and are largely precritical and dogmatically bound by their polemical function.[27]

The precritical attitude is also exhibited in the Protestant scholastic doctrine of the verbal inspiration and infallibility of Scripture, which represents a hardening of the earlier patristic notion of spiritual inspiration and the general belief of the earlier Reformed theologians that Scripture was written under the suggestion, inspiration, and witness of the Holy Spirit. But when *verbal infallibility* becomes a dogmatic principle, the relation of the writers to the Spirit becomes one of pure passivity, and the Protestants now possess a basis for absolute truth as authoritative as that of dogmatic tradition.[28] This attitude encourages the struc-

[26] *Epochen,* pp. 39–71, esp. pp. 43–44. Baur also considers Gottfried Arnold's response to this work from the point of view of Protestant pietism. Cf. *ibid.,* pp. 84–107, esp. pp. 85–86.

[27] *Dogmengeschichte,* I/1, 115–18.

[28] *Dogmengeschichte,* III, 59–64. The ancient doctrine of inspiration did not become important dogmatically until the seventeenth century, when Protestant orthodoxy was forced into a quasi-rational account of *verbal* inspiration (the hallmark of which is inerrancy) in order to strengthen its formal principle (*sola scriptura*) against Roman Catholic claims for the Church. As Strauss remarked, this formal attestation of Scripture became the "Achilles' Heel" of Protestantism.

turing of a tight Gospel harmony which could explain away contradictions and show the Gospels to be the infallible work of the
Holy Spirit. In the eighteenth century Gospel harmonization receives a semicritical and more scientific basis in the work of
G. C. Storr (leader of the old-Tübingen school) and J. A. Bengel.[29]

Protestant Rationalism: Abstract Empiricism

If the theological historiography of the ancient and medieval
periods is characterized by an abstract supernaturalism in which
ideas and manifestations are identified in a transcendent and absolute Church which loses its concrete, historical quality, and if
that of old Protestantism is marked by a dualism in which idea and
manifestation are separated from each other and by a precritical
polemicism designed to render absolutely authoritative the dogmatic principles of the Reformation, then the historiography of
Protestant rationalism is characterized by an abstract empiricism,
for which the focus of interest lies in the critical examination of
facts, details, and development, apart from interpretation and
meaning. It can readily be seen that this pragmatic or empirical
attitude is simply the reverse of old Protestant dualism. Whereas
earlier the interest had been in the idea of the Church isolated from
its manifestations, now it is in manifestations isolated from any
rational and transcendent structure. The dualistic separation of
idea and manifestation is in any case preserved.

One of the characteristics of rationalist historiography is its interest in historical development. Baur devotes an entire chapter in the
Epochen to "the gradual transition from the dualistic world-view
to the concept of historical development," which also marks the
transition from polemicism to criticism, such that source-research
is now undertaken in order to free the historian from dogma and
tradition and to enable him to confront the material on its own
terms.[30] The most important historian of this "epoch" is J. S. Semler, who bursts all the bonds by which ecclesiastical historiography
has previously been restricted, but who gains a merely capricious
and fortuitous freedom. He goes to the other extreme from the
Catholic vision of the stability of dogma by perceiving in history
only a moving, steadily changing element; the essence of dogma
is only restless change. History for him is governed by the arbitrary
powers of subjectivity. Accordingly, his historical work is characterized by an all-embracing formlessness; it consists only of raw
material which he has taken straight from the source studies of
his day. At the same time, his work represents the first critical
examination of primitive Christianity and the development of
dogma. It is based on the assumption that Christianity can be
regarded only as an historical phenomenon, to be studied histori-

[29] *Die kanonischen Evangelien*, pp. 5–11, 21, 24.

[30] *Epochen*, pp. 108–51. Baur here treats Weismann, Mosheim, Semler,
and Walch.

cally, free from dogmatic presuppositions, and that its historical manifestation must be analyzed in the context of its historical milieu; that milieu is Jewish, and everything "Christian" can be traced to it. Semler's criticism is negative; but, Baur adds, negative criticism is a necessary first stage in the movement toward a truly objective and positive mode of historical consideration.[31]

A second characteristic of rationalist theological historiography is its pragmatism or empiricism and its accompanying arbitrary subjectivism. Baur remarks that according to his critics, who accuse him of forcing the facts into a speculative system and of constructing history according to a "fertile schematism," the proper model for an authentic historiography is an objectivity which represents "a real surrender to the material." He replies that this attitude represents the continuation of rationalist empiricism and that, far from representing true objectivity, it substitutes for the objective its own abstract and subjective criteria of authenticity. "Only the rawest empiricism," he writes, "can intend that one should surrender oneself absolutely to the subject matter, that the objects of historical consideration can be taken only as they lie before us."[32]

The most important of the ecclesiastical historians who exemplify the empirical or pragmatic mode of historiography is G. J. Planck.[33] His extensive research accurately chronicles the doctrinal struggles of the Reformation period, but he views everything that happens as subjectively and arbitrarily motivated and seeks to know nothing of the objective course of history and its inner "necessity." In addition, post-Kantian rationalist theologians such as Stäudlin and Wegscheider demonstrate in their treatment of history of dogma that rationalism has no sense of history and that its interest in it is subjectively motivated. They use history only to furnish material for their rationalistic critique of supernatural beliefs and thus impose on the historical data arbitrary and subjective criteria and interpretations.[34] It should be recalled that it is also in this context that Baur mentions Strauss's *Glaubenslehre* as the "most striking example" of the lack of an "historical sense" in rationalism.[35]

It is in the context of rationalist historiography that Baur also examines one of the major trends in the scientific study of the Synoptic Gospels in the late eighteenth and early nineteenth centuries, the theory of a Proto-Gospel, first suggested by Lessing and further developed by Eichhorn, which explains the literary relationships between the Gospels in terms of a common *Urschrift*,

[31] *Dogmengeschichte*, III, 307–309.
[32] *Lehrbuch der Dogmengeschichte* (1st ed.), p. ix.
[33] *Epochen*, pp. 152–97. The others considered here are Schröckh, Spittler, and Henke.
[34] *Dogmengeschichte*, I/1, 123–25.
[35] Cf. *Lehrbuch der Dogmengeschichte* (1st ed.), pp. 42–43; *Dogmengeschichte*, I/1, 124–25; and above, pp. 81–82.

used independently by all three of the Evangelists. Baur criticizes this theory as representing an "abstract literary conception" of the Gospels.

In place of the previous dogmatic consideration there now steps a scientific, purely critical consideration—or rather, above all, since the Gospels are not yet taken as historical manifestations but only as products of a definite class of literature, a literary or abstract critical consideration. The criticism developing in this type of consideration is only a higher level of the word-criticism with which men had hitherto been engaged [i.e., the Gospel harmonizers]. Of concern in this new type of criticism, the so-called higher criticism, are also only sentences, smaller or larger fragments, various writings, composed sometimes in this and sometimes in that form.[36]

Baur regards Eichhorn's Proto-Gospel as a purely literary invention for which there is no defensible external evidence. It is based on the false supposition that materials which are so closely related and agree verbally must have sprung from a common, original, written source. As an eyewitness account written in Aramaic, it contains in skeleton fashion the important events of the life of Jesus, in so far as these events can be reconstructed from passages occurring in all three Synoptics. The Synoptic Gospels are not regarded as theological writings in their own right but merely as collections of data from later revisions of the Proto-Gospel. Where the details of the Gospels differ, the facts behind them remain the same. The Proto-Gospel thus comes to substitute for the verbal inspiration of the Holy Spirit, and the dogmatic interests of the older harmonizers are thereby glossed over with a critical, literary apparatus.[37]

The same weaknesses are carried over in various modifications of the Proto-Gospel theory, as developed by Hug, Gieseler, Credner, de Wette, Schleiermacher and others. Schleiermacher claims that a multiplicity of written sources lay behind the canonical Gospels and tries to isolate the literary rules which governed the collection of these materials by the Evangelists. His Gospel criticism, Baur asserts, "is arbitrary, artfully ingenious, petty, and on the whole dismembers and disintegrates" the Gospels.[38] Finally, sceptics such as Bruno Bauer have turned the theory of a Proto-Gospel on its head, claiming that the mythical traditions about Jesus originated solely with it and have no foundation in fact.[39] "The general deficiency of all these theories," Baur concludes, "is that

[36] *Die kanonischen Evangelien*, p. 23.
[37] *Ibid.*, pp. 23–27. Baur's rejection of early forms of the two-document hypothesis (which posits the existence of Q and the priority of Mark) is partially based on his clear perception of the weakness of all theories concerning a Proto-Gospel. His own solution of the Synoptic problem is discussed below, pp. 214–17.
[38] *Die kanonischen Evangelien*, pp. 28–40; quotation from p. 37.
[39] *Ibid.*, pp. 65–68.

they move only in the narrow circle of a self-made, abstract representation, and do not yet know how to transpose themselves into
the objective reality and truth of the concrete life of history."[40]

Baur continued to maintain that Griesbach had been correct in
holding that similarities between the Gospels can best be explained
by a theory of literary interdependence rather than by the notion
of a Proto-Gospel independent of and prior to all three of our
Synoptic Gospels; and he also believed him to be correct in defending the priority of Matthew, the dependence of Luke on Matthew,
and of Mark on both Luke and Matthew. But all attempts hitherto
made, including Griesbach's, to determine the order of the Gospels
(once the canonical order no longer was regarded as sacrosanct)
have been based on purely literary considerations—the phenomena
of agreement and disagreement in the order and content of the
various pericopes of the Gospels, the relative length of the Gospels, etc. These attempts do not take into account the historical
context and theological intentions of the writings as a whole. The
literary phenomena are such that it can be argued equally well
that Matthew is earliest (as Griesbach claimed) or that Mark is
earliest (as maintained by Storr). On this basis alone, it is impossible to settle the question of the priority of the Gospels.[41]

Post-Reformation Catholic Historiography:
Development Without Change

In the introduction to his lectures on the history of dogma, Baur
mentions only two Catholic historians of dogma,[42] not because he
desires to neglect the Catholics (so he claims) but because in fact
the history of dogma is largely a Protestant science. They are the
seventeenth century French historian Dionysius Petavius, and the
Bonn theologian Heinrich Klee, whose *Lehrbuch der Dogmengeschichte* was published in 1837–38. Petavius' *De theologicis dog-
matibus* is a "noble and skillful" work, rich in materials, which
argues that dogmas are the absolutely valid and unchanging doctrines of the Church, the substance to which the content of history
is related as mere accident.[43] His interpretation, in fact, establishes
the point of view from which later Catholic histories of dogma, such
as Klee's, are written.

The basic difficulty with this point of view, according to Baur,
is its failure to grasp the authentic meaning of historical development. When Klee discusses the "development" of dogma, he seeks
to distinguish the fortuitous, empirical, and finite manifestations

[40] *Ibid.*, p. 40.
[41] *Ibid.*, p. 36.
[42] The only Catholic historian of the Church considered in the *Epochen*
is Cardinal Cesare Baronius, whose *Annales Ecclesiastici* was published in
the late sixteenth century as a response to the Lutheran *Magdeburg Centuries*. See pp. 72–84.
[43] *Dogmengeschichte*, I/1, 112–14.

of dogma from that which is its true, substantial essence, unchanging through time and history. Thus he tries to show that in the entire period before the Reformation everything which was not congenial with the essence of dogma—i.e., heresy—*either* was eventually absorbed back into it and given the dogmatic stamp, *or* was stamped out or destroyed itself. In so far as this thesis is scientifically pursued, Protestant historiography has no quarrel with it. But then comes the rock upon which the Catholic theory of dogmatic development founders: the Reformation. For Protestantism, unlike all earlier heresies, was neither absorbed back into Catholic dogma nor stamped out. It is impossible to account for its existence on the thesis that in its development dogma remains absolutely identical with itself in its absolute truth. Thus Protestantism is the living contradiction of the Catholic theory of development; there are no categories or principles by which to comprehend it. Consequently, Catholic historians of dogma such as Petavius and Klee have no choice but fundamentally to ignore Protestantism. "How can one trace dogma in the course of its development," asks Baur, "if one cannot follow it the whole way but must come to a halt in the middle of the way, as if exhausted?"[44] The opposite failure is represented by certain Protestant historians, who see only the radical novelty of Protestantism and make no attempt to understand it in its historical continuity. The failure of both is a lack of understanding of the historical life and development of the Church as a whole.[45]

Finally, Baur claims that Catholic historiography lives in the *Anschauung* of miracle as the absolute beginning of Christianity: "The whole history [of Christianity] is only the continuation of the miracle established as the beginning; only that which existed directly from the beginning repeats itself in this history."[46] According to this theory there is "development" without real change or

[44] *Ibid.*, pp. 132–34; quotation from p. 134. Cf. also *Epochen*, pp. 249–50. Unfortunately, Baur was not familiar with John Henry Cardinal Newman's *Essay on the Development of Christian Doctrine* (1845), for his description and critique of Klee's theory could in many respects equally well have been applied to Newman. Newman's seven notes of genuine development of doctrine are unable to account for a real change which is not simply an organic unfolding of the seed of truth implanted in the ancient faith of the Church (in fact, they are designed precisely to exclude real change); and Newman, like Klee and Petavius, is unable to account for Protestantism as a continuing, vital religious phenomenon and thus fundamentally ignores it. Newman may, in fact, have been influenced by Klee and other liberal nineteenth-century German Catholics in his theory of development.

[45] *Epochen*, pp. 249–50.

[46] *Die Tübinger Schule*, pp. 45–46; quotation from p. 45. Baur claims that the criticism brought against the Tübingen School by Gerhard Uhlhorn reflects the Catholic mode of historical comprehension. Uhlhorn objected to Baur's thesis of opposition in primitive Christianity and proposed instead the harmonious development of the original, unchanged, and supernatural essence of the Church.

novelty; but authentically historical development always involves real change and opposition, and genuine novelty as well as continuity.

Protestant Post-Rationalist Strivings for an Objective Historical Comprehension

In the final chapter before the conclusion of the *Epochen*, Baur considers a number of Church historians contemporary to his own life and writing—P. K. Marheineke, J. A. W. Neander, J. K. L. Gieseler, and Karl August von Hase.[47] Each of these sought to free himself from the abstract empiricism and subjectivism of rationalist historiography and to comprehend in some fashion objectively the history of the Christian Church. But the progress they have made is far from complete. There is still something amiss in modern Church historiography, which consists, briefly, in "the wrong relationship of the idea to the manifestations in which the historical development thereof is to be presented." For these historians, "the idea still hovers at a great distance and in indefinite form over the manifestations to which it must be related."[48] Or, to view the weakness from another perspective: "The progress from the pragmatic standpoint of historiography to the universal is still lacking. Since Church history finally came down from the transcendent heights of its abstract dualism to the empirical ground of history, it has become pragmatic; but in essence it has not yet moved beyond the pragmatic mode of treatment."[49] That is to say, pragmatism and abstract idealism are opposite sides of the same coin. A pragmatic or empirical view of the facts excludes the possibility of perceiving them as the actualization of ideas and thus of penetrating to their objective meaning. Likewise, an abstract idealism is unable to understand the concretion of ideas and thus to treat the Church as an authentically historical phenomenon. In either case, idea and fact remain disjoined or are at best artificially, abstractly, or supernaturally related.

Marheineke, under the influence of Schelling, errs on the side of abstract idealism. In his *Universalkirchengeschichte*, there remains an "unfilled cleft" between the idea and "the historical life whose moving principle it ought to be."[50] Consequently, following Marheineke, it has been necessary for Church historiography to deepen itself in the materials of history and to engage in fresh and fruitful investigations of the sources, "in which historical life opens itself to us in its inner richness and in the clarity of its outward manifestation."[51]

[47] Cf. *Dogmengeschichte*, I/1, 127–30, for a brief treatment of contemporary historians of dogma.
[48] *Epochen*, pp. 247–48. See above, p. 124.
[49] *Ibid.*, p. 248.
[50] *Ibid.*, pp. 200–201.
[51] *Ibid.*, p. 201.

Neander, more than any other contemporary Church historian, has concerned himself with the task, method, and compass of source-study. He is also the historian with whom Baur is most continuously in dialogue in his own Church-historical studies, and his criticism of Neander is extremely important for the delineation of his own position.[52] If Marheineke errs on the side of abstract idealism, then Neander errs on that of empiricism. The peculiar excellence of his historiography is its capacity not to view things in the "deceiving reflex of its own subjectivity," but to transpose itself into the singularity of every different age, each possessing its own definite form of consciousness. Historical persons and events are given the "full right of their individuality" over against the historian. For him the substantial content of history consists of individual agents acting freely and separately.[53] In these respects it seems likely that he was influenced by his colleague at Berlin, Leopold von Ranke.

But at the same time Neander assumes, under the influence of Schleiermacher, that all religious manifestations can be judged only according to the immediate quality of religious consciousness. The historian can know only the subjective element of feeling, which alone is the true, inner source of history; no objective historical consideration is possible. Therefore, when Neander seeks to know what religious feeling and faith are objectively, in themselves—what Christianity is generally as the idea of reconciliation —as he must in order to present its historical development intelligibly, he falls into a dualism which separates idea from manifestation. This dualism is a consequence of his failure to attempt to penetrate historically and critically to the objectivity of Christianity instead of simply remaining with its subjective expressions.

Furthermore, it is evident from his major works that he holds to a strongly supernaturalistic conception of the origin and nature of Christianity. If Christianity is absolutely supernatural, a miracle splitting apart historical connections, then historical knowledge can have nothing further to do with it. As miraculous, the origin of Christianity is an absolutely unconceptualizable beginning, and Neander's historiography becomes apologetic, not critical. Yet he allows for miracle only in the first part of the history of the Church; for the remainder the divine principle takes the form of natural connections. But Neander provides no criterion for this inconsistent treatment, nor does he indicate when and why the miraculous origin ceases and the natural connections take over.[54] If

---

[52] Early in his Tübingen career Baur shows himself to have been quite favorably impressed by Neander and wishes there were an historian of his stature on the Tübingen faculty with whom he could work. Baur to L. F. Heyd, 1 Oct. 1832 (U.B.T., Md 619r, 11). Later, however, he has changed his mind. Cf. Baur to L. F. Heyd, 10 July 1840 (U.B.T., Md 619r, 26).

[53] *Epochen*, pp. 202–206.

[54] Baur discusses this inconsistent treatment of miracle in Neander's study of Acts and the conversion of Paul: some materials are omitted or softened

Christianity is in principle so different from human nature that its origin cannot be clarified in terms of it, then Christianity and human nature are two essentially different principles, opposites, working externally on each other, provoking and affecting one another, but never becoming internally one. Christianity is as a leaven cast into human dough; leaven and dough remain always separate despite their mixture. In terms of the humanity of the Church—the dough—Neander sees only an infinite multiplicity of appearances, not a unity of the whole and a principle of development. The supernatural character of Christianity remains always the same; historical alterations and development come only from the human, subjective side. From an historical-critical standpoint, in Neander's judgment, the historian can deal only with this human side and therefore must remain standing with his own subjectivity and that of the historical agent. But for this reason it is not so certain that he is really able to penetrate to the religious subjectivity of historical agents other than himself. Finally, the various forms of the Church and its periods of development are determined by factors external to its authentic historicity, and thus Neander's periodization, as well as his treatment of the starting point, is unconvincing.[55]

Gieseler and especially Hase have sought to correct Neander's subjectivism, but each has weaknesses of his own. Hase fails to clarify the nature of the Christian Church, and his periodization is determined by external factors. Nevertheless, his work is marked by impartiality, objectivity, and attention to the peculiarities of each age, and he is the only contemporary Church historian to continue his studies into the modern period, where he excels.[56]

It is in the context of the present state of ecclesiastical historiography that Baur fashions not only his theology of the Church, according to which its historicity exists at the juncture of divine idea and temporal manifestations, but also his conception of a critical and speculative historical method, by means of which historical knowledge is able to penetrate from the subjective stance of the historian to the objective reality of the Church. This method must be responsible to the theological situation of the present day. It must not represent a return to the perspective of either old catholic supernaturalism, old Protestant dualism, or eighteenth-century rationalism.[57] To this method we turn in the next section.

---

which do not fit the theory, others are both allowed and "partially naturalized" by a psychological explanation. Cf. *Paulus*, I, 24–27, 29–31, 87–88, 109–112 (E.T., 20–22, 25–26, 76–77, 96–98).

[55] *Epochen*, pp. 207–212, 221–32.

[56] *Ibid.*, pp. 236-44.

[57] *Ibid.*, pp. 4–5.

THE BASIC CHARACTER OF HISTORICAL KNOWLEDGE

Authentic Objectivity

The Task of Historical Knowledge: To Penetrate to the Objectivity of Historical Events. We already have observed from the introduction to the *Epochen* that "historical presentation [is] to be nothing other than the true, adequate reflex of the objective event."[58] Baur's most eloquent statement of this intention is found in the preface to the first volume of *Das Christenthum.*

My standpoint is in one word the purely historical one, the sole purpose of which is to comprehend the historically given in its pure objectivity, so far as is generally possible. In whatever fashion I may have succeeded in this, I am, in any case, conscious of no other aspiration. . . . Every attempt to investigate more exactly and deeply the foundation which above all must be laid, and which no one can lay other than as history itself has laid it in its unalterable truth; to bring continuity, harmony, and unity into the whole; to separate and trace in their interrelations the different elements which here work together and the moving powers and principles whose product is the result of the first three centuries; to unite, as far as possible, into one harmonious picture all the individual traits which belong to the character of an age engaged in such a momentous movement—every attempt to do all this can appear justified only through itself, in so far as it is not lacking too greatly in all the requirements needed for the solution of its task. It is from this viewpoint that I would wish to see the present work judged . . . and the significance of such a task evaluated.[59]

The task of the interpreter is to allow that which actually happened to be expressed through and in his interpretation; his task, in other words, is to discipline his subjectivity so that it may serve as the medium of the objectivity of history. The dawning awareness of this task marks the progressive history of Gospel criticism. ". . . the theological consciousness coming to an understanding with the phenomenon lying before it as its given object gradually purged and freed itself from the dogmatic and otherwise subjective presuppositions which stood more or less restrictively and opaquely in the way of the pure consideration of the subject matter. Thus theological consciousness learned so to place itself within the objectivity of the historical relations to which this phenomenon itself belonged that it could grasp this objectivity as something proceeding from itself."[60]

The demand that "unity and continuity" be "the soul of every historical presentation" cannot be satisfied by a "subjective prag-

[58] *Ibid.*, p. 1. Cf. also *Dogmengeschichte,* I/1, 29.
[59] *Das Christenthum,* pp. vi–viii (E.T., I, x–xii).
[60] *Die kanonischen Evangelien,* p. 2.

matism" which, "in place of the objectivity of history, sets the subjectivity of the individual portraying it."[61] "A true historical method can only be one which holds to the object itself, which pursues the movement of the subject matter itself, and transposes itself wholly into it in order to exclude everything merely subjective and arbitrary, everything which is not based on the subject matter itself but belongs only to the mode of representation [*Vorstellungsweise*] of the subject."[62] That "subject matter" which is the true object of historical knowledge is precisely that which constitutes the mark of historical process—the congruence of idea and manifestation, or, to use Baur's earlier, more Hegelian, categories, the "inner movement of the concept" in the historical materials.[63]

The historian's ability to grasp this phenomenon enables him to describe the inner unity and continuity of historical data. Historical presentation ought not merely to connect causes and effects externally but to penetrate into their inner relations, in order to "uncover the inner web of history before us." It ought to "show what has happened in its continuity, in its development and movement; but this movement ought to be immanent in the subject itself, not something first manufactured and merely represented."[64] Similarly, it is "the task of historical consideration to see in what has happened not merely a fortuitous aggregate of temporally and spatially bounded events but also to penetrate into the inner continuity and above all to hold in view the point at which the inner, moving powers, the universal which lies at the basis of the particular, the ideas ruling the whole, are given to be recognized by us in the outward happenings."[65] The *way* in which the historian penetrates to the inner continuity and objective meaning and reality of events becomes the subject of discussion in the next subsection.

"Speculation" as the Basis of Critical and Objective Historical Knowledge. In his Blaubeuren lecture manuscript, "Geschichte des Alterthums," Baur distinguishes between three methods of writing history: a "purely objective" method, appropriate to annals and chronicles, which treats events in their simple sequence, without developing connections or involving the reflection of the writer; a "pragmatic" method, which treats the connections between events according to the laws of causality; and a "philosophical" method, which shows that historical events are manifestations of a ruling idea, which serves as the basis of the inner continuity and meaning of the historical process.[66] This statement anticipates the well-

61 *Versöhnung*, p. vi.
62 *Dogmengeschichte*, I/1, 29.
63 Cf. *Versöhnung*, pp. v–vi; quoted above, p. 148.
64 *Dogmengeschichte*, I/1, 29.
65 *Die Tübinger Schule*, p. 7.
66 "Geschichte des Alterthums" (U.B.T., Mh II 166, q), pp. 12–14.

known words with which Baur's earliest published work, *Symbolik und Mythologie*, begins: "I do not fear the noted reproach concerning the mixture of philosophy with history: without philosophy, history remains for me eternally dead and dumb. Whether, however, in the reconstruction of a single myth or of a whole religious system [in this work] any sort of *subjective, arbitrarily limited* philosophical opinion be mixed in, can naturally only be established at that spot and place on historical grounds."[67]

The context in which this sentence appears makes clear its intention. To understand the relations between the various manifestations of religion, an idea of religion is required, and this already involves a philosophical or speculative perspective from which the data of history are ordered into a meaningful unity; conversely, this perspective must constantly be tested by the data which it is being used to interpret. The meaning of the historical process is not simply written on the face of events, to be read off uncritically by an unbiased observer. Rather, the categories by which this meaning is elicited are brought to the data by the historian as a part of the critical apparatus with which he views the past. Since the speculative or philosophical tools with which this task is executed change constantly, history must be written afresh from the perspective of each new generation. This is what Baur means by "speculation," by "the mixture of philosophy with history"; he had learned it before his introduction to the thought of Hegel.[68]

Later, in the preface to the *Lehrbuch der Dogmengeschichte*, Baur explains that an historical method based on a *critical* theory of knowledge must be *speculative* in nature; for the historian, like the philosopher, has learned that knowledge filters through categories of the mind and that there is never an immediate comprehension of things in themselves, as the empiricists imply by their insistence that the historian should simply surrender himself to "the facts." Only he who is aware of this epistemological procedure is able to penetrate through his own subjectivity to the objectivity of the thing itself, by not confusing his interpretive categories with that objectivity.

Only the rawest empiricism can intend that one should surrender oneself absolutely to the materials, that the objects of historical consideration can be taken only as they lie before us. Ever since there has been a critique of knowledge, a critical theory of knowledge (there is confessedly such in any case, at least since Kant), any one who comes to history not without philosophical education must know that one has to distinguish between things as they are in themselves and as they appear to us, and that they come to appearance for us in that we can reach them only through the medium of our consciousness. Herein lies the

[67] *Symbolik und Mythologie*, I, xi–xii. Italics mine.
[68] Most interpreters have regarded this sentence as the hallmark of Baur's "Hegelianism"; cf. Karl Barth, *Die protestantische Theologie im 19. Jahrhundert*, p. 454.

great distinction between the purely empirical and the critical modes of consideration; and the latter, which is called the critical because its task is sharply to distinguish and to hold apart what in the objects of historical knowledge is either objective or subjective, wants so little to set in the place of the objective something merely subjective that for it everything depends on the fact that it considers nothing which is only of subjective nature as the pure objectivity of the thing itself. It intends to see only with the sharpest eye the subject matter on the basis of its own nature. On such simple principles, . . . when one knows how to apply them to the historical material, rests the *critical*—or if one will, the *speculative*—method.[69]

Baur's most eloquent defense and explanation of speculative historical criticism is found in the preface to the *Dreieinigkeit,* where he is replying to the charge of "Hegelianism" brought against him by a critic.

. . . what [the critic] calls "Hegelianism" is nothing other than the direct opposite of everything that he has revealed in his judgment of my writing; it is the scientific consideration [*die wissenschaftliche Betrachtung*] of the subject matter, as contrasted with a thoroughly unscientific procedure which evidences a complete lack of philosophical thought. Whether one calls the speculative method "Hegelianism" or something else, the nature of speculation is and remains the reasoning consideration [*die denkende Betrachtung*] of the object with which one is concerned; it is the posture of the consciousness in relation to the object, in which the object appears as that which it really is; it is the striving to place oneself in [*sich hineinstellen*] the objective course of the subject matter itself and to follow it in all the moments in which it moves itself on. . . . Without speculation, every historical investigation . . . is a mere tarrying on the superfluous and external side of the subject matter. The more important and comprehensive the object is with which historical investigation is concerned, and the more directly it belongs to the element of thought, the more such investigation approaches not merely a reproducing in itself [*in sich zu reproduciren*] of what the individual thought and did but a rethinking in itself [*in sich nachzudenken*] of the eternal thoughts of the eternal Spirit, whose work history is.[70]

A number of important observations can be made about this passage. The "scientific" consideration of the subject, which Baur insists is all that can be implied by his "Hegelianism," is not construed on the model of the natural sciences. Instead of "explanation" or "demonstration," it is a question of "consideration" or "striving"; the task is not to "prove" or to "predict" but to "place oneself in" and to "follow." The "speculative" aspect of this method

69 *Lehrbuch der Dogmengeschichte* (1st ed.), pp. ix–x. Italics mine.
70 *Dreieinigkeit*, I, xviii–xix. The German original of some of Baur's technical vocabulary has been bracketed, since it will be referred to later in our discussion of the categories of historical knowledge.

is to posture the consciousness in such fashion that the historical object *appears* as it really *is* and so that the historian may comprehend, express, or describe (not "explain") the rational mystery which lies at the heart of the inner continuity and objective course of historical events, that mystery which is shaped by the congruence of ideas and manifestations. The ideas in question are the expressions of the thought of both human and divine Spirit, but especially the latter, "the more important and comprehensive" the objects under investigation are. Hirsch comments that Baur regarded the "rethinking . . . of the eternal thoughts of the eternal Spirit, whose work history is," as "speculation" only in the sense of meaning the "understanding of the spiritual continuity in a group of facts known to him through research."[71]

Another important observation on this passage is that Baur regards the speculative mode of historical consideration to be a peculiarly Protestant phenomenon and therefore history of dogma to be a peculiarly Protestant science. The truth in the Catholic view of dogma is that there is an objective unity in its history to which all subjective arbitrariness must be subordinated. The untruth is that Catholicism takes this objective unity as something bare and external, as the external, visible unity of Church dogmas, not as something to be penetrated critically and speculatively by subjective knowledge. The freedom by which Protestantism is released to this task of subjective penetration ought not, however, to become that of subjective arbitrariness, but to be a freedom which, through the inner necessity of its own immanent law, is determined by the objective concept of the matter. That there is an *absolute truth* in history, not merely fortuitous, subjective opinions and an infinite multiplicity and alteration of data, and that there is also a *consciousness* of the absolute, are the fundamental presuppositions of all speculative thought. Therefore, from the speculative standpoint, the history of dogma can be regarded only as the movement of absolute truth, which opens itself in this history to subjective consciousness, or as the movement of the thinking Spirit, who mediates himself with himself in this process. That there can really be a relationship between this absolute truth and subjective knowledge of it is the conviction of the speculative method—it is this which distinguishes an authentically Protestant conception of the history of dogma from Catholic abstract objectivism on the one hand and rationalistic arbitrary subjectivism on the other.[72]

Baur found it necessary to explain that his "speculative" method did not entail a priori historical construction. In reply to charges of this nature brought against him by Hengstenberg in the *Evangelische Kirchenzeitung,* he argues that he is not dependent upon

[71] Hirsch, *op. cit.,* V, 520. Cf. also Wilhelm Dilthey's comments on this passage in "Ferdinand Christian Baur," *Gesammelte Schriften,* IV, 422–23.
[72] *Dogmengeschichte,* I/1, 134–37.

philosophical presuppositions which control his conclusions in either *Die christliche Gnosis, Die sogenannten Pastoralbriefe des Apostels Paulus*, or his 1831 monograph on the opposition of Petrine and Pauline elements in the ancient Church. The conclusions presented in these writings are only the critical results of his research. "Above all, I proceed from definite, historically advanced facts and seek on this foundation for the first time to draw together the different threads of my critical combinations into a whole. This holding fast to the historically given is the characteristic mark of my criticism. . . . Whoever has read my writing with care must be convinced how much I strive not only to maintain nothing without a definite historical verification but also to obtain above all a total historical impression which governs the whole."[73] In letters to Heyd, Baur stresses the importance of basing historical interpretations on detailed source-studies, where the "true life" of history is to be encountered. "There is nothing," he writes, "more annoying than the abstractions of historians."[74]

Later Baur provides an example of what he means by "speculative" historical consideration. The notion of a universal Church history depends on a speculative comprehension of that history, in which a specific theological conception of the nature of the Church is brought to bear on the data in order to elicit from it its meaning. If the Church in its historical development is regarded as the self-realizing of the idea of the Church, and if its history is placed under the viewpoint of the varying relationships in which idea and reality stand to each other, then this already represents a "speculative" interpretation of Church history.[75] The theological categories by which Baur orders the history of the Church are "speculative" in nature; apart from such categories there could be no coherent history of the Church as a whole, only a rehearsing of arbitrarily selected facts. But these speculative categories are themselves drawn forth from and corrected by historical research; they are applied interpretively only on a foundation of "historically advanced facts." The historian seeks a "definite historical verification" for every interpretation. There ought to be a constant dialectic between fact and interpretation.

Baur comments that Karl Hase has objected to his "speculative" procedure but that he also is forced to acknowledge that if

---

73 "Abgenöthigte Erklärung," *TZT*, IX:3, 185–86, 206; quotation from p. 206. Baur claims that this point was already made in the Introduction to his *Pastoralbriefe*, written in the autumn of 1834. There he had insisted on the necessity for objective and honest historical research, without regard for the results.

74 Baur to L. F. Heyd, 7 Mar. 1828 and 16 June 1841 (U.B.T., Md 619r, 8 and 28). Cf. also his reply to the charge of apriorism in the preface to *Das Christenthum*, quoted above, p. 161. On this point, see also Zeller, *Vorträge und Abhandlungen*, pp. 407–408. We return to the question of Baur's apriorism below, pp. 200–201.

75 Cf. *Epochen*, p. 268, and *An Hase*, p. 90.

"thought" is not used to interpret history, it remains pure chaos. Are not questions about the beginning, end, movement, and direction of an historical process "speculative" in nature? Speculation as such cannot be avoided; the question is whether the idea by which history is interpreted "is so congruous with the objective content of history that one can see in it nothing of what intrudes upon history and is put into it, but rather the immanent principle of its movement, the adequate expression of its idea."[76] Furthermore, Baur's periodization of Church history, based on these speculative categories, is not intended to import an a priori theory into the historical process but to correspond to what actually happened in this process and to elicit from it its true objectivity. "These few remarks may at least give an indication of why it is not difficult for me to bring to bear through the entire content of history categories established for the determination of the major periods and to group particulars in conformity with these categories in such fashion that they come to stand under the viewpoint corresponding to the nature of the case without the pressure of an arbitrary schematism."[77]

The Categories of Objective Historical Knowledge. The categories by means of which Baur describes the effort of the historian to penetrate critically and speculatively to the objectivity of the historical process become important in later German historiography. As a whole, they reflect both the spontaneity and the passivity with which the historian stands before the data. A first group of categories makes clear that the historian's task is not that of measuring a phenomenon or explaining a process with generally agreed-upon criteria of great exactitude, as is usually the case with the natural sciences. It is rather the "comprehension" or "interpretation" (*Auffassung*[78]) of the historically given in its pure objectivity,[79] the "reasoning consideration" (*die denkende Betrachtung*[80]) of the object.[81] "Comprehension" and "consideration" involve both an ordering act of the intellect and an awareness that that which is beheld stands outside the mind, must be "held on to," and to a certain extent resists assimilation, measurement, and explanation.

A second group of categories stresses the recapitulative quality of historical understanding, whereby what has happened in the past is re-enacted or made present in the consciousness of the his-

[76] *An Hase,* pp. 91–93; quotation from p. 93.
[77] *Ibid.,* pp. 94–97; quotation from p. 97.
[78] *Auffassung* also means "conception," but in the contexts in which Baur uses it, it suggests more the root idea of grasping hold of, or apprehending (*fassen*), that which exists objectively. If Baur meant "conception" he would use *der Begriff* or *das Begreifen.*
[79] Cf. *Das Christenthum,* p. vi–vii (E.T., I, x).
[80] *Betrachtung* can also be rendered "viewing," "contemplation," "reflection."
[81] Cf. *Dreieinigkeit,* I, xix.

torian: his task is to "reproduce" (*reproduciren*) or "rethink" (*nachdenken*) past thoughts.[82] Similarly, "historical presentation" (*die geschichtliche Darstellung*) renders a past act objectively present and therefore knowable. Baur makes a systematic distinction between *Darstellung* and *Vorstellung*.[83] The latter term, translated as "representation," refers to a subjective and arbitrary imposition of meaning on the data, contrived and unreal in the sense that a performance or representation on the stage is contrived and unreal. The work of the true historian is that of presentation, not representation. A third group of categories, closely related to the second, shows that historical knowledge *follows* and is *consequent upon* that which it seeks to know. The historian is not primarily a creative artist but rather an investigator and interpreter of what is already there, what has already happened. He presents rather than invents (hence, again, the distinction between *Darstellung* and *Vorstellung*), although imagination, of course, is required for an authentic presentation. He should "follow" (*folgen*) or "pursue" (*nachgehen*) the objective course of the subject matter itself; he must "penetrate" (*eindringen, eingehen*) to the objectivity of the historical data.[84]

A fourth and final group of categories suggests the way in which the historian should come into a relationship of unity with the objects of investigation. On the one hand he should "take up" (*aufnehmen*) the objectively given in himself or allow it to "reflect itself" (*sich reflectiren*) in his subjective consciousness.[85] This is a relatively passive mood in historical consciousness. On the other hand there is a relatively active mood in which the historian should "place himself in" (*sich hineinstellen*)—or "transpose himself [*sich versetzen*] into"—"the objectivity of the subject matter itself, . . . in order that, instead of making history the reflex of his own subjectivity, he may simply be the mirror in which the historical manifestations are perceived in their true and real form."[86]

An example of the way several of these categories are used together is found in the following passage: "A true historical method can only be one which holds itself to the object itself, which pursues [*nachgehen*] the movement of the subject matter itself, and transposes itself [*sich versetzen*] wholly into it in order to exclude everything merely subjective and arbitrary, everything which is not based on the subject matter itself but belongs only to the mode of representation [*Vorstellungsweise*] of the subject. Historical presentation [*Darstellung*] ought not merely to connect causes and effects externally; it ought also to penetrate [*eingehen*] into their connec-

82 Cf. *Ibid.*, p. xix.
83 Cf. *Dogmengeschichte*, I/1, 29.
84 Cf. *Dreieingkeit*, I, xix; and *Dogmengeschichte*, I/1, 29.
85 *Dogmengeschichte*, I/1, 100.
86 *Epochen*, p. 247; cf. also *Dreieinigkeit*, I, xix.

tion, to uncover [*enthüllen*] the inner web of history before us."[87]

This special use of categories, although not developed into a hermeneutical system such as Dilthey's, shows that Baur regards historical knowledge as a relatively unique and *sui generis* method of knowing a particular sort of datum—events of the "spiritual" (*geistlich*) past. It cannot be construed on the model of other sorts of knowing—experiential, purely cognitive, scientific (in the more restricted, English sense of the word), aesthetic or poetical, moral, religious. There is, however, no evidence that Baur regards historical knowledge as an a priori and *qualitatively* distinct function of the mind; he does not talk of a unique "historical reason," as Dilthey did, but simply of "historical knowledge." The processes of thought in such knowledge are not unique; but the method by which and the object for which such processes are employed are unique. Thus, although Baur has not systematized the language which he uses to describe historical knowledge, it is clear that he has gone a long way toward developing a conception of a method by which the past might be critically understood. Perhaps even more important, the language or categories by which he describes this method are taken over and refined by some of the great representatives of the "Historical School" in the late nineteenth and early twentieth centuries—Dilthey, Troeltsch, Croce, Collingwood. Whether Baur is to be regarded as a source of this language is uncertain. It is clear that Collingwood and Troeltsch learned many of their categories from Dilthey, and that he in turn was a youthful admirer and disciple of Baur; but there were, of course, many other strains of influence—philosophical, sociological, and historical—on Dilthey. It is also uncertain whether Baur himself created the categories and conceptions by which he describes the task and method of the historian. It is perhaps significant that some of these categories and conceptions appear quite early in Baur's career.[88] But the extent to which he was influenced by the work of the great secular historians of his day, such as Niebuhr and Ranke, remains an unanswered question.[89]

[87] *Dogmengeschichte*, I/1, 29. A similarly compact use of categories is found in *Dreieinigkeit und Menschwerdung Gottes*, I, xviii–xix, quoted above, p. 164.

[88] Cf. the Introduction to the Blaubeuren lecture manuscript, "Geschichte des Alterthums" (U.B.T., Mh II 166, q).

[89] In the methodological introductions to his major works Baur never discloses the sources which lie behind his own method, except to refer generally to the "present state" of historical-critical study; and in his discussion of other historians, he always limits himself to Church historians, historians of dogma, and biblical historians. There is, however, evidence that he had read Ranke rather thoroughly at least toward the end of his life; and there are some striking similarities between Ranke's striving for objective historical understanding and Baur's. We also know that he read Niebuhr while a student in Tübingen. In addition, the influence of Schleiermacher, Schelling, Plato, and the classical historians is clearly seen in "Geschichte des Alter-

Authentic Subjectivity

Although Baur places major emphasis on the task of the historian to penetrate to the objective process of history and on the "speculative" method by which this task is to be accomplished and arbitrary subjectivism eschewed, at the same time he recognizes that the subjective perspective of the historian has an important and necessary place in the total structure of historical knowledge. It is precisely this perspective which provides the speculative categories through which the objectivity of the past is to be penetrated. Also, this perspective is a constantly changing one; hence Baur would agree with Joachim Wach's claim that history must always be written anew, from the most radically contemporaneous perspective available. ". . . [it] belongs to the nature of history itself that, from every standpoint from which we look anew back into the past, it presents a new image, through which we . . . obtain a truer, more vital and significant perception of what has happened."[90]

The shape of the past depends on the perspective from which one views it. The historian must not deceive himself into thinking that he does not have a perspective, that he sees things immediately, as they are in themselves. Furthermore, only a *present* perspective is suitable for the presentation of the past *to the present;* only thus is the work of the historian relevant and intelligible. The Church historiography of the nineteenth century cannot be written from the perspective of old catholic supernaturalism, or old Protestant dualism, or eighteenth-century rationalism. An *authentic* subjectivity is one which is critical, i.e., takes itself into account in the shaping of categories by which the past is interpreted, and contemporaneous.

The way in which the changing theological milieu shapes anew the writing of Church history is described in the introductory chapter of the *Epochen*.

If each of the various theological viewpoints which have been elevated to a higher degree of autonomy [in the history of theology] has disclosed and impressed itself in its own treatment of the history of the Christian Church, then there can be no comprehensive work in Church history whose historical perspective does not wholly bear in itself the character of the theological standpoint shared by its author. Thus there are as many different historical perspectives as there are different theological standpoints; and it is worth the trouble to consider them more closely in their relationship to each other and to place them under the viewpoint of an historical process taking its own definite course. If the

---

thums" and other early writings; and later of course there was the impact of Hegel. But none of these latter thinkers can account for the specific categories by which Baur delineates the procedure of objective historical comprehension.

[90] *Epochen*, pp. 2–3.

general task, that of raising the content of the objectively given into the clarity of subjective consciousness, remains always the same, nevertheless the attempts at its solution are very different. . . . All these attempts together, as they represent in particular historical presentations the various possible standpoints, form the epochs of Church historiography, in whose course the spirit working in the depths and struggling toward the solution of its task has raised itself, at first gradually, to the level on which it stands in the mode of perception of the present.[91]

Similarly, the dogmatic standpoint of the historian of dogma shapes his treatment of the subject. The following important passage from the introduction to *Vorlesungen über die christliche Dogmengeschichte* shows why penetration to the objective course of Christian dogma depends on an authentically contemporaneous subjectivity of the historian.

The historian of dogma can take his position only from the standpoint of the most recent dogmatic consciousness. His task is to follow Christian dogma from its first origins through all the periods and moments of its development up to the most recent point of its development. From where, however, can he obtain the precise conceptualization of the object, whose historical movement is the problem with which he ought to concern himself, other than from the consciousness of the present? The historian can move back into the past only from the present. His whole task is to move backward through the same course by which the subject matter [*die Sache*] has come down to him, in order to complete the movement, which the subject matter has completed only objectively, also in his consciousness of it. In order to make the subject matter, in its origin and progress, the object of historical consideration, he can comprehend it only from that point in its historical development at which it steps into the consciousness of the present. Herein lies the inner, essential connection of history of dogma with dogmatics. Only when the historian of dogma has before him the whole system of dogmas, as it has been explicated in the dogmatic consciousness of the present with respect to its entire content, can he follow the movement of dogma from its beginning in such fashion that he can transpose himself into the movement of the subject matter itself in order to follow it from moment to moment and to recognize already in its first beginnings the elements of its entire subsequent development, in which everything preceding can only be the necessary presupposition of what follows. Only when one knows what the subject matter is with respect to its nature, what it includes within itself, does one also know what one has to look for in history, in order to embrace everything which belongs to the subject matter itself and not to overlook anything which is a moment of its development.

The more the historian of dogma has assimiliated the entire content of the dogmatic consciousness of his time, and the more his own conscious-

91 *Ibid.*, pp. 5–6. Cf. also *Die kanonischen Evangelien*, pp. 1–2; and *Versöhnung*, pp. 738–42.

ness is filled by it, the more capable he becomes of comprehending and expressing for subjective consciousness the whole wealth [of material] which the historical development embraces in itself objectively.[92]

Baur continues this passage by suggesting that, since the historian must view the past from the standpoint of the present, and since history itself is a never-resting process, the entire content and expanse of the development under question, from its very beginning up to the present, must be embraced by historical study. In the case of history of dogma, this means the treatment must start with the New Testament and terminate only with the most recent works in theology. To stop a history of dogma sooner is arbitrary and not justified by the nature of the material, as is the case with Engelhardt's *Lehrbuch der Dogmengeschichte* (1839), which ends its treatment with the Formula of Concord in 1580. To stop at such an arbitrary point really fixes the perspective of the whole history of dogma from *this* standpoint, beyond which the dogmatic consciousness has long since moved; and it means that the historian has failed to penetrate to the objectivity of the material because he has lacked an authentically subjective stance of his own.[93]

The historian, then, orders the past from the perspective of the present. Indeed, it is the role past events play in relation to the present which helps to shape their meaning and significance. For example, the significance of medieval Catholicism is differently seen from a post-Reformation perspective. It no longer appears as the whole and complete truth, as Catholic histories of dogma still represent it, but as a vital and indispensable moment in the historical development of the Church, beyond which the dogmatic consciousness has now irrevocably moved.[94] Similarly, the present stage of dogmatic development must not be absolutized, for it is "only a newly achieved standpoint, from which the work of the Spirit, which even now never rests, takes a new start."[95] It is in this fashion that Baur describes the subjectivity of present theological and historical consciousness as it shapes the interpretation of the past. He realizes that it is from such a conditioned perspective that his own structuring of Church history and history of dogma is executed.

At the same time, however, there are some difficulties in Baur's understanding of subjectivity. Subjectivity in historical knowledge tends to be regarded by him chiefly as the relative and spatio-temporally conditioned reflex of the eternal and objective his-

92 *Dogmengeschichte*, I/1, 12–13.
93 *Ibid.*, pp. 13–14. This criticism could also be brought against Harnack and Seeberg; see below, p. 242, n. 152.
94 Cf. *Epochen*, pp. 259–60.
95 *Dogmengeschichte*, III, 359. Cf. *Lehrbuch der Dogmengeschichte* (1st ed.), p. 258.

torical process. However, does not the historian also bring to his knowledge of the past critical categories of interpretation, in terms of which he is in some sense a creator of meaning as well as an observer of it? Or does he simply view the past with the necessary perspective of his own place and time, which in turn is merely a temporal manifestation of the objective process itself? Does not the historian stand partially outside of or transcend history, as well as stand within it, in order to view it? Baur does not want to deny that the historian brings to his interpretive task the critical categories by which he elicits the objective meaning of the process. Only by means of a critical subjectivity in this sense is he able to penetrate to the true objectivity of events. This is the whole point of Baur's use of "speculation" in historical knowledge and of his polemic against the "absolute surrender to the materials" of a "raw empiricism," as well as against an arbitrary and uncritical subjectivism. But in so doing, it cannot really be said that for Baur the historian stands even partially outside the historical process. In his view, there is no nonhistorical knowledge, no knowledge left unconditioned by the relativity of time and place, no knowledge which is untinged by a perspective. Thus even the critical subjectivity of the historian is entirely the function of this relativism. In order to understand the past, the historian in his view does not attempt to transcend the relativity of his stance but rather to penetrate critically to the center and ground of his own subjectivity, for there he also encounters the true objectivity of the historical process.

What Baur has to say about historical relativism and about the congruence of subject and object is true, but it is not entirely true. Here again we may observe one of the dangers of his idealism: in probing the congruence of objectivity and subjectivity, he tends, ultimately, to identify them. In this case, the relativity and freedom of the historian become only a subjective reflex of what is in itself necessary, and no single historical interpretation is more or less adequate than any other, as long as the historian allows himself to serve as a faithful vehicle of this reflex. In practice, Baur does not embrace this extreme, for he introduces various criteria for measuring the truth of an historical interpretation, some of which have been discussed in the pages above. But in principle this is one of the dangers which besets his position and which is reflected in his tendency to regard subjectivity in historical knowledge more as the relative reflex of an objective process than as the interpretive power of a critical mind, although he does not ignore the latter aspect. For this reason, his tendency is to collapse dogmatics into historical theology. Likewise, faith tends to become fundamentally an historical form of knowledge or consciousness. Thus in faith the believer is at one with the historical truth of Christianity. Certainly this also is true, as we shall discover in the next section, but it is not entirely true. For a nonhistorical or normative element must be preserved in faith and dogmatics, as well as in the historian's vision of the past, if the truth of God and of man is not entirely a function of historical process.

FAITH AND HISTORICAL KNOWLEDGE

In historical theology as well as in dogmatics, the congruence between objectivity and subjectivity can be clearly seen in the reciprocal relationship between faith and historical knowledge. Baur rarely discusses this relationship as such,[96] but by drawing together materials from a wide range of sources, where it is both directly and indirectly at issue, it is possible to suggest, perhaps rather synthetically, that the reciprocal relationship can be stated as follows: On the one hand, historical-critical theology is dependent on authentically subjective faith, for it is only through the freedom thus achieved that the historical theologian is able to transpose himself critically into the objectivity of the historical data. On the other hand, faith is dependent on, or must be instructed by, historical knowledge, since the content of faith is mediated historically and knowable historically-critically, and because authentic faith requires the continual prodding and testing of historical criticism, for its certainty is of a different order than the empirical certainties of this world.

The first mode of dependence can be discussed briefly, since it receives less emphasis in Baur's thought. He believes that the rise of historical-critical study in theology was made possible by the Protestant conception of faith, which for the first time freed the historical theologian from the restraints of an externally and arbitrarily imposed authority of tradition and dogma and allowed him to transpose himself freely into the data, remaining open to the results, whatever they might be. Thus, as we have noted, Church history and especially history of dogma are peculiarly Protestant disciplines.

There was no longer an interest in always finding in the history [of dogma], as the content of one's own religious and dogmatic conviction, only the eternal uniformity of an unchanging tradition, and of not acknowledging differences between the doctrines and opinions of different periods and teachers. . . . In this fashion the possibility of a purely historical comprehension of dogma and of a history of the same was first established through the Reformation and Protestantism. And as the Reformation generally first awakened and enlivened the historical sense and instinct, so also it called forth the first historical investigations of the course and alterations of dogma.[97]

[96] He does, however, in "Abgenöthigte Erklärung," *TZT*, IX:3, 179–232, and in his academic opinion of 20 Dec. 1835. These two writings will be employed in the discussion which follows.

[97] *Dogmengeschichte*, I/1, 111; cf. I/1, 62–64, 111–12; III, 358–59.

Faith in the "authentically Protestant sense," Baur suggests, is "the most certain consciousness of that which one holds as true."[98] Therefore, in the following quotation, "self-certainty of consciousness" refers to that certainty achieved by the internal mediation—through faith—of the objective truth of the Gospel with the subjectivity of the believer. "The possibility of criticism is conditioned by the fact that the subject knows himself to be free. Only when the subject establishes himself in himself, has taken a firm standpoint in himself, in the self-certainty of his consciousness, does he have a definite point from which to orient himself, and is he able to set everything which has a relation to him in the proper relationship to himself."[99] Faith in the Protestant sense, Baur claims, "is the essential principle through which the subject frees himself from that outward objectivity which never lets him come to himself, and through which he raises himself to free, self-conscious subjecthood." The freedom of the subject is gained through the "certainty of faith." This freedom is the foundation of critical historical study.[100]

The second mode of dependence, that of faith on historical knowledge, to which we are devoting the greater share of our attention in this section, is not meant to imply that faith can be "proved" by historical investigation or that such investigation can be the "source" of faith.[101] Rather it is being proposed that, if and when authentic faith comes into existence, it must be honestly instructed and tested by historical study because its content is both *mediated* historically and *knowable* historically-critically.

From our earlier discussion we have seen that religion differs from philosophy in that its content is always mediated through historical forms.[102] Although the *locus* of faith is subjective consciousness or pious feeling, its *content* is not this feeling but rather the reconciling act of God, which is mediated to us historically and positively through Christ and the Church. Baur makes this clear in commenting on the centrality of the Holy Communion in Pauline theology.

The Holy Communion is the chief means of keeping alive the historical memory of Christ as the founder of Christianity. As an historical religion, Christianity depends wholly on the person of its founder. Therefore, an essential condition for the survival of the Christian community is to maintaitn the historical connection with him in a steady and vital

98 "Abgenöthigte Erklärung," *TZT*, IX:3, 209.

99 *Dogmengeschichte*, III, 306.

100 Cf. *Ibid.*, p. 5. A good discussion of Baur's argument concerning the connection of the Reformation and the Protestant conception of faith with critical research is found in Christoph Senft, *Wahrhaftigkeit und Wahrheit: Die Theologie des 19. Jahrhunderts zwischen Orthodoxie und Aufklärung*, pp. 60–64, 70.

101 This issue is discussed elsewhere and need not further concern us here; see above, pp. 102–103, 128–29, and below, pp. 177–78.

102 See above, pp. 93–94.

consciousness. The more closely and immediately, therefore, the Holy Communion joins the members of the Christian community together with Christ, the more it is itself the substantial midpoint of that community, that which distinguishes it from all other religious communities. The central point of a religion can only be where its members become most immediately conscious of the essential content of every religion, reconciliation with God. . . . The Holy Communion is the proclamation of the death of Jesus and thus also of the reconciliation effected through him. However, one can become conscious of this reconciliation only by historically remembering the death of Jesus on the cross.[103]

Faith itself might be described as an "historical remembering" of the event of reconciliation, which is another way of saying that its content is mediated historically. This passage also recalls to mind another point we have examined earlier, that the Church, as the historical community of the faithful possessing continuity of form and intentionality through time, is the means by which the content of faith is mediated to the pious consciousness of the believer. The central cultic act of this community, by which this mediation is accomplished, is the Holy Communion.[104]

Because Christianity is an "historically given religion," because the content of its faith is historically mediated reconcilation, it must subject its claims of truth to the scrutiny and verification of historical study, the results of which cannot be predetermined. The historicity of faith is not hidden and esoteric; it is the proper concern of the historical-critical theologian. "Where can this faith obtain a firmer foundation and richer nourishment than from the study of history?"[105] Faith, by its very nature, requires this sort of foundation. Whether there is in fact such a foundation is a question to be settled historically-critically. The "dependence" of faith on historical study thus becomes evident, although the results of such study do not "prove" or necessarily induce faith. Emanuel Hirsch suggests that Baur's view that Christian faith must have an historical foundation and verification took shape against Strauss's argument that at the center and basis of Christian faith there is nothing but a web of myth and miracle. Baur thus rightly sensed the scientific, spiritual, and religious situation of his time and ours: "A faith which intends to maintain itself in the maturing spiritual posture of European-American humanity, a posture which looks to the real and the given, needs a firm support in historical reality. That which is mythically transparent no longer has any binding power. Only that is historically real to us, however, which proves

103 *Paulus*, II, 197 (E.T., 180–81). Cf. also *Neutestamentliche Theologie*, pp. 200–202.

104 See above, pp. 52–53.

105 Cf. "Geschichte des Alterthums" (U.B.T., Mh II 166, q), p. 21; and "Über die geschichtliche Bedeutung der fünfundzwanzig Jahre 1816–1841," p. 20.

itself as historical to the most rigorous testing of historical research."[106]

The requirement that faith be instructed and tested by historical study arises not only from the nature of Christian faith and the spiritual situation of our time, but also from the development in the eighteenth and nineteenth centuries of scientific historical study, capable of probing in its own fashion the content and truth-claims of the Christian faith. Given the existence of this tool for knowing the past, theology had no choice other than to submit its historical claims to its scrutiny and to defend them by its use. Faith is dependent upon historical knowledge, not only because its content is mediated historically, but also because this content can be known historically-critically. This argument is advanced in the first of Baur's academic opinions and in his "Abgenöthigte Erklärung" against the criticism of Hengstenberg, who claims that because Baur has brought historical criticism to bear on the Pastoral Epistles, questioning their Pauline authorship, he will evaporate the Apostle Paul himself into myth.

In developing his response, Baur first shows the respect in which faith is *not* dependent on the scrutiny of petty and insignificant historical details. The fear that faith will be subverted by criticism displays a lack of faith: "I will now show my opponent that behind the fear expressed by him a very severe unfaith lies hidden, that he is lacking in true faith just as much as in true science."[107] The *immediate* ground and source of true faith in the authentically Protestant sense is not the mere "letter" of Scripture but the "spirit," which alone is the source of life. If faith hangs on every letter of Scripture, then it will be shaken and collapse every time one of these letters is critically tested. Faith is in the *first* instance a reality of subjective religious consciousness, and cannot be proved or disproved by historical criticism of Scripture. This assertion frees faith from slavery to the words of Scripture, which in a critical age would mean its sure death. Likewise, Hengstenberg is lacking in "true science," for what sort of historical criticism would extrapolate from a few cases of unauthenticity to the spuriousness of the entire Pauline canon?[108]

The same independence of faith from the "mere letter" is expressed in the academic opinion accompanying Baur's resignation from the Evangelische Verein in December 1835. "The question is none other than that of whether the whole content of the Christian faith depends on the mere letter, or whether one may elevate oneself from the letter to the spirit. However, as soon as one surrenders the spirit, one must also surrender the fact that the Christian faith is not merely purely empirical or purely historical, since the divine is certainly not an object of sensuous but only of

[106] Hirsch, *op. cit.*, V, 542–43; quotation from p. 543.
[107] "Abgenöthigte Erklärung," *TZT*, IX:3, 208.
[108] *Ibid.*, pp. 209–212.

spiritual perception. The spirit, however, does not come from the letter but from above or from what God-manhood is in itself according to its essential nature, of which we become conscious through historically given facts."[109] It is as fallacious to assume that everything contained in the Gospel story is of equal importance for faith as it is to assume that the laws of historical criticism, valid elsewhere, do not apply to Scripture.

What guidance does Scripture itself provide for the distinction between the essential and the nonessential with respect to the historical character of the Gosepl story? Who has more gloriously developed the depths and fulness of the Christian faith than the Apostle Paul in his Epistles? But does he also hold to the details of the life history of Jesus? Does he possibly deny[110] particular miracles and incidents? Does he actually always come back to the historical character of the life of Jesus? Is it not the most general facts of the Gospel story, which no one can deny, which basically remain standing without the Gospels, which he alone presupposes and from which he alone proceeds?[111]

It is by no means being suggested in these passages that a non-historical essence of Christianity can be distilled from its outward trappings, but that the Christian must learn to base his faith, which has its locus in subjective consciousness, on the central, crucial, and critically sustained realities of the historical past, which must always be freed from mere letter and tradition. He must learn to discriminate between the essential and unessential aspects of the Gospel tradition. Later, Baur never suggests, as he does here, that the central facts of this tradition can remain standing without the Gospels themselves.

In what sense, then, *is* faith dependent upon historical knowledge? Baur continues in "Abgenöthigte Erklärung" by explaining that the Protestant is distinguished from the Catholic in that he not only believes in nothing other than the Word of God (i.e., Scripture) but also "gives account of the grounds of his faith." Such an account can be given not by faith itself, but by "science" (*Wissenschaft*)—the knowledge (*Wissen*) of faith. This "science" (and Baur has in mind here historical science in particular) entails a "never resting investigation, which has no definite limits and which does not allow itself to predetermine its results." It is precisely the demand of faith that the critical investigation of Scripture lead where it will, "because faith in a purely human word of Scripture is a false faith, because the more highly faith esteems the Word of Scripture the more it is incumbent upon it to hold nothing for the Word of God which does not allow itself to be authenticated as such, and because faith, if it knows how to dis-

---

109 Gutachten of 20 Dec. 1835 (U.B.T., Md 750, v, 1).
110 Reading of the manuscript as *verneinen* is uncertain.
111 See n. 109, above.

tinguish the authentic from the unauthentic with the help of science, thereby gives a proof of its power and enlightenment, its penetration into the inner spirit of Scripture."[112]

This passage is eloquently anticipated by the academic opinion of December 1835, in which Baur responds to the question raised by the president of the Evangelische Verein as to whether the new works in scientific theology endanger the faith of the evangelical Christian.

The question is not whether Christianity on the whole is still to be regarded as truth or not, but . . . whether the origin of Christianity is to be understood thus or otherwise. . . . With the question concerning [its] origin, however, we are referred to the written documents of Christianity. Faith regards them as Holy Scripture, the Word of God. However, faith can succeed to this certainty only by means of investigation and knowledge, if it is or ought not to be merely an authoritarian faith. . . . The more highly faith esteems these writings, the more it is incumbent upon it *that it hold nothing as the Word of God which does not allow itself to be established historically as the Word of God.* . . . The Protestant distinguishes himself thereby from the Catholic in that he not only believes in nothing other than the Word of God but also gives account of the grounds of his faith. However, only knowledge, the knowledge of faith, . . . can give this account; and this is a never resting investigation, which, in so far as it is not conditioned through certain general, self-established truths of religious and Christian life, has no definite boundary and does not allow its results to be determined in advance.[113]

Protestantism replaced the authority of tradition with that of Scripture. But this Protestant principle, in order not simply to re-embody the Catholic principle of authority, is fully warranted only with the establishment of the critical method, which must be applied to Scripture in order to distinguish its authentic, divinely given content from merely human traditions. Historical-critical investigation of Scripture has never ceased in the Protestant Church since its origin; and the Protestant theologian therefore acts wholly in accord with his right and duty even when his investigations lead to radical results, such as questioning the authenticity of some of the New Testament writings. This is not an impairment but the demand of faith, for, as we have seen, faith in a purely human word of Scripture is a false faith. Baur concludes that monotony and deathly silence would rule if the desires of the supernaturalistic systems were satisfied, if everything furnished by Schleiermacher and Hegel, by the philosophy and criticism of the day, were eliminated, and if the sole scientific operation consisted in transposing the simple Word of Scripture into other words. "Who would want

[112] "Abgenöthigte Erklärung," TZT, IX:3, 216–217.
[113] Gutachten of 20 Dec. 1835 (U.B.T., Md 750, v, 1). Italics mine.

to live in such a world," he asks, "and what cause would we have
to thank God for allowing us to live in a world into which he has
sent the fulness of his Spirit, and in a Church which he has built
up through the splendid harmony of the gifts of his Spirit?"[114]

The reciprocal relationship between faith and scientific historical
knowledge is summarized in the following passage from "Abgenöthigte Erklärung."

Both [true faith and true science] nourish and refresh each other, and as
science can only gain from faith, so also faith from science. Only from
faith does science learn to purify itself of everything foreign and impure, and to surrender itself undividedly and unconditionally to the holy
affair of truth; and on the other hand faith has science to thank for
the fact that it is not delivered over to an indolent rest but is maintained in a fresh, vital movement, in order to become always more
clearly and immediately conscious of its divine content. No matter how
inimically science appears to position itself with respect to faith, . . .
it proves thereby of the greatest service to faith. For the question is not
how much one believes but only what and how one believes, whether
one believes in such fashion as to know to distinguish in one's faith the
true from the false, the certain from the uncertain, the essential from
the less essential. True faith is satisfied with a little, so long as what
it has remains a firm and certain possession. . . . A single place in
Scripture was sufficient for the greatest Church Father of ancient times
to serve as a basis of his faith and to convert him to a pillar of the
Church. All the doubts which the newer criticism has awakened are for
faith healthy and fruitful in the highest order; they are to be viewed
as a powerful means of its education and formation. Faith ought never
to be idle and secure but always to grow and become stronger.[115]

In this passage, Baur suggests that authentic faith requires the
continual prodding and testing of historical criticism, for faith's
certainty is to be secured only in the context of uncertainty, doubt,
and striving. Its certainty is of a different order than the certainties
of this world. Historical study, by disclosing the contingency and
relativity of all historical events and of our knowledge of the past,
renders faith possible. For faith is the acceptance as authoritatively
true for oneself of that which is precisely always only probably
certain in the historical mode. Faith is the living with and from
that probable certainty. Faith becomes both possible and necessary
because of the contingency of historical knowledge. Faith and historical-critical study complement rather than oppose each other;
here is another respect in which they are to be seen as internally
congruent modes of knowing, subjective and objective components
in the work of the historical theologian. Faith provides the inner
certainty which frees the historian from dependence on outward
authorities, so that he may "surrender himself to the holy affair of

114 *Ibid.*
115 "Abgenöthigte Erklärung," TZT, IX:3, 213.

truth" and pursue his investigations unrestrictedly. On the other hand, historical study reminds faith that its certainty becomes authentic only through the inward appropriation of doubt. For doubt has a necessary place in both faith and historical criticism.[116]

OTHER CONSIDERATIONS IN HISTORICAL KNOWLEDGE

Past and Present

We turn now to some additional elements in Baur's quest for an historical method which follow upon but are not systematically related to his central conception of the character of historical knowledge. The first and perhaps most important of these is the relation between past and present. We already have seen that the shape of the past is determined by the present perspective from which the historian views it. But at the same time the past exercises a reciprocal influence on the self-understanding of the present; the relationship between past and present is a dialectical one. For this to be the case, Baur must insist on the objective reality and meaning of the past over against the present; he must insist that the "meaning" of the past cannot be artificially disjoined from its "brute factuality" and made simply a function of the ever present dialectic of self-conscious human spirit. In discussing Baur's relation to Hegel, I have sought to make clear that Baur rejects this notion of the past.[117] The tremendous weight he places on the positivity of the Church, its origin with Jesus of Nazareth and its subsequent development through historical forms, and the inseparability of its universality from its positivity, show that Baur regards the historical past as an independent reality of intrinsic importance in shaping the historical present. The critical task through which "the consciousness of the present must be mediated with the past" is nowhere of greater significance than "where the present is connected with the past most closely and immediately, and where this connection is established in the innermost interests of our spiritual nature"—namely, in the Christian Church.[118] The past possesses a primacy in its relation to the present; the present follows from the past, not the reverse.

In the introduction to the *Versöhnung*, Baur writes that history or historical study[119] consists of "the process of the present making itself understood to itself from the past [*die Selbstverständigung der Gegenwart aus der Vergangenheit*]."[120] *Selbstverständigung* is

[116] On this latter point, cf. *Die kanonischen Evangelien*, p. 51; *Dogmengeschichte*, I/I, 63–64; III, 309; and Gutachten of 20 Dec. 1835 (U.B.T., Md 750, v, I).

[117] See above, pp. 64–65.

[118] *Paulus*, I, 4 (E.T., 2).

[119] The term used here is *Geschichte*, but in this context it seems more nearly to suggest "critical knowledge of the past" than "events of the past."

[120] *Versöhnung*, p. vii.

a difficult term both to understand and to translate. Its meaning is not quite that of *Selbstverständnis,* "self-understanding." *Verständigung* means "understanding" in the sense of "agreement"; but an understanding issuing in an agreement is always the result of a dialectical or at least a dialogical process. *Selbst-verständigung* would involve a rational process by which self-understanding is achieved or self-estrangement overcome. Hence it could be translated as "the process of coming to terms with oneself," or "the process of making oneself understood to oneself." The term appears to be Baur's own; according to the glossary of terms in the Hegel *Jubiläumsausgabe,* it is not used by Hegel himself. And the meaning is also Baur's own: historical knowledge is the process by which the present achieves self-understanding or self-reconciliation from its knowledge of the past.

Why the past? Because it is in the past historical process that those divine acts of reconciliation occur which shape the existence of the present if and when the present relates itself to the past critically and renders the past "present" by means of "historical presentation." The present thus participates in the process of the past, and its process of self-reconciliation is a re-enactment of the whole historical process itself, of the whole story of the relation of God and man. If there were no past, or if the past were simply a moment in the present dialectic of self-consciousness, then there would be no *history* of reconciliation, no historical mediation of the relation between God and man, and consequently no real, positive, objective ground for authentic existence in the present. A similar point is made, in a nontheological framework, by R. G. Collingwood, who writes that history is studied for the sake of "human self-knowledge." The value of historical study, he suggests, is that it teaches us "what man has done and thus what man is."[121] For Baur, history teaches us what God and man have done together, and thus what the concrete basis for the process of authentic self-understanding is.

The same idea is quite possibly intended in an enigmatic and well-known passage from the *Lehrbuch der Dogmengeschichte.*

What history is generally—as the eternally clear mirror in which spirit perceives itself, views its own image, in order to be what it is in itself also for itself, for its own consciousness, and to know itself as the moving power of historical becoming—is concentrated in an all the more intensive significance in the restricted field of history of dogma. As in history as a whole, so especially in history of dogma, this general spiritual interest can be modified in two ways, according to whether it is directed chiefly to the universal, substantial content of historical movement, which remains always the same, or to the never resting

121 R. G. Collingwood, *The Idea of History* (Oxford: Clarendon Press, 1946), p. 10.

succession of historical forms, in which everything universal seems to be completely submerged. It is the task of historical consideration always to place the one interest in a relationship to the other which corresponds to the nature of the case.[122]

The interpretation of this passage hinges on the meaning of the terms "history" (*Geschichte*) and "spirit" (*Geist*). It has been generally assumed that Baur here means "history" in the sense of historical process rather than historical study. As we have seen, Baur uses this term in both senses.[123] In addition, Karl Barth assumes that Baur is here referring to the divine Spirit or the eternal Spirit.[124] On his reading, then, the passage means that the historical process is the eternally clear mirror in which the divine Spirit objectifies himself and views his own image. History in general, and Church history in particular, are thus not understood as divine self-revelation in which God speaks to man, but as divine self-contemplation, in which God reflects himself. Baur therefore lacks a doctrine of revelation and reduces the autonomy of the historical process to a function of the divine life.

However, from the context it seems more plausible that Baur is here referring not to the divine Spirit but to finite human spirit, to empirical self-consciousness. He talks of spirit becoming conscious of itself and of "the highest interests which condition the spiritual life"; his concern is with the "general spiritual interest" in "history." At any rate, this is the way Rudolf Bultmann, Christoph Senft, and Ernst Wolf read the passage.[125] At the same time, they assume that by the term "history" Baur means the historical process. Therefore, he seems to be saying that history as a whole is simply the outward mirroring of *human* spirit as it comes to consciousness of itself, that history is the work of man, not of God. Thus Bultmann writes: "By reducing faith's self-understanding to a consciousness which arises in historical development *out of man himself*, so that in him spirit comes to consciousness of itself, [Baur] eliminates the kerygma."[126] Similarly, Senft claims that for Baur the historical past is ultimately "bare" and "empty" because it is only a moment in the ever present dialectical process of *human* thought, only a step to the present. This understanding of the historical process, however, is entirely foreign to Baur. As we have seen earlier in this chapter, the ontological foundation of history

---

[122] *Lehrbuch der Dogmengeschichte* (3d ed.), p. 59. This passage differs slightly from the 1st ed., pp. 55–56.

[123] Cf. *Epochen*, p. 1, and above, pp. 144–45.

[124] Barth, *Die protestantische Theologie*, p. 458. See below, pp. 262–66.

[125] Cf. Rudolf Bultmann, *Theology of the New Testament*, Vol. II, Kendrick Grobel, trans. (New York: Charles Scribner's Sons, 1955), p. 244; Senft, *op. cit.*, pp. 75–78; and Ernst Wolf, "Einführung" to Vol. II of F. C. Baur, *Ausgewählte Werke in Einzelausgaben*, pp. viii, xx, xxiii.

[126] Bultmann, *op. cit.*, p. 244. Italics mine.

is God, not man; it exists by virtue of God's self-realization. "The historical process . . . is simply an element of the general process which is the life-process of God himself."[127]

Is it possible, then, that in this passage "history" means "historical study" rather than "the historical process"? This is in fact suggested by the context. The passage is found toward the beginning of the final section in the Introduction to the Lehrbuch der Dogmengeschichte, the announced purpose of which is to explore the "value and uses," not of the history of dogma as such, but of "*studies* in the history of dogma [*dogmengeschichtliche Studien*]."[128] The question is: Of what purpose and value is the *historical study* of dogma? Furthermore, in the quoted passage, Baur appears to use "history" and "historical *consideration*" as parallel or synonymous terms. Most important, however, is a striking parallel in language between the Lehrbuch and a passage found in the Introduction to the Blaubeuren lecture manuscript, "Geschichte des Alterthums": "For this purpose [the practical determination of man, his moral life in community] a thorough study of history [*ein gründliches Studium der Geschichte*] is indispensable. This [the study of history] is the inexhaustible source out of which the foundations . . .[129] of moral action can be created; *it is the eternally clear mirror in which human life* in its manifold forms, the moral acts of men in all their connections, *can be glimpsed.*"[130] In this passage, "the study of history" is the "eternally clear mirror" in which the moral life of man can be glimpsed. If the passage in the Lehrbuch can be regarded as parallel to it, history—the study of history—is there described as the "eternally clear mirror" in which human spirit perceives itself, comes to self-consciousness. The earlier passage reflects the influence of Schleiermacher, the later, of Hegel. But the meaning in both cases is the same: the study of history, i.e., of the historical past, is the clue to human moral life and self-understanding in the present. The past is by no means merely a moment in the present dialectic of human thought, as Senft claims. The study of the past is rather the "inexhaustible source" from which the present obtains its moral and spiritual foundations.

The Relation of Universal and Particular

The relation of the particularities of history to their context and foundation, whether it be a specific institution, a nation, a culture, an idea, or the total historical process, is one of the basic factors in historical understanding. The singularities of history derive their significance from their relationship to an appropriate totality,

127 See above, pp. 145–47, especially Dogmengeschichte, III, 352–53, quoted above, p. 146.
128 Lehrbuch der Dogmengeschichte (3d ed.), p. 58. Italics mine.
129 Manuscript unreadable.
130 "Geschichte des Alterthums" (U.B.T., Mh II 166, q), p. 18. Italics mine.

and the totalities are shaped by the composite of singularities out of which they are formed. Although the relation of parts and wholes was developed into a specific hermeneutical tool by Dilthey, Baur was fully aware of its importance. He insists that the historian must concern himself both with the details which "make up the concrete life of history" and with the unity, the continuity, the universal, the ideas, which bind the multiplicity of details to-together. The one is the clue to the other; neither can be understood without the other. The universal is the clue to an *historical* interpretation of the particular. "The task of historical consideration is . . . to see in the occurrences of the past not merely a fortuitous aggregate of temporally and spatially bounded events but also to penetrate into the inner continuity of events and above all to hold in view the point at which the inner, moving powers, the universal which lies at the basis of the particular, the ideas ruling the whole, are to be recognized by us in the outward occurrences."[131]

What is required of the historian is not that he should avoid attention to details but that, at the same time as he deepens himself in the research of particulars, he should also gain the perspective by which his data can be properly interpreted. He must first view the material from close at hand, in order to become familiar with its details, and then at a greater distance, from which he can see events in their "true light" and wider context.[132] This perspective also furnishes the criterion of selectivity by which the historian judges which materials to include in his study and which to exclude. Baur exercises this criterion freely: although displaying a mastery of the concrete materials, his historical studies are not crammed with data irrelevant to his argument and presentation. Obviously such a criterion is needed and valid, so long as it is not used arbitrarily to exclude materials which prove an embarrassment to the thesis being argued. Baur has sometimes been accused of this latter excess; but there is no proof that he ever deliberately excluded data which he could not account for or explain in terms of his interpretive hypotheses. It must be realized that his major works are artfully produced totalities, not source books of historical data. If he has selected the "wrong" data, then it is not the principle of selectivity itself which is at fault but the interpretive categories and perspectives he has brought to the data. This is a risk every historian must take if he is to create studies that truly illuminate the past.

The reciprocity between the universal and the particular in historical consideration is summed up in the concluding paragraph of the *Epochen:*

[131] *Die Tübinger Schule,* p. 7. Cf. also *Epochen,* p. v; *An Hase,* p. 98; *Das Christenthum,* pp. v, vii (E.T., I, ix, xi); *Versöhnung,* pp. v–vi; and *Paulus,* I, ix (not translated in the English edition).

[132] Cf. *Epochen,* p. 2.

A history of the Christian Church can rightly be called "universal" only if the historical material, which it must accept as given, is so penetrated by the idea as the moving principle . . . that the universal shines through in the particular as determinative. The concept of the universal also establishes the double task, based on the reciprocal relationship of universal and particular, of comprehending and perceiving the universal in the particular as well as the particular in the universal. . . . In proportion as the historian must, on the one hand, become absorbed as deeply as possible in the particular, individual, and concrete aspects of historical manifestations, in order to succeed to the complete reality of historical life, so also must he on the other hand raise himself to the heights of the universal idea, in order to understand the particular from the universal and to see in it only the particularity of the universal. The task of historiography is completed only in the unity of these two mutually complementary procedures, forming the two sides of the same process, moving from the particular to the universal and from the universal to the particular.[133]

On the basis of such explanations as this, as well as his actual procedure in his historical writing, especially his study of Jesus, Hirsch suggests that "Baur had taught himself the capacity, through lengthy work in history of dogma, to see the interpenetration of the eternal and the historical-individual."[134]

It is in the context of the hermeneutical problem of the relation of parts and wholes that Baur's treatment of historical individuals must be considered. Critics contemporary to Baur as well as more recent ones have accused him of submerging individuals in the general historical process and making them mere pawns of the idea. To these charges Baur replied that he does not neglect individuals and their role in history, and that he regards the universal and the particular as essentially connected factors, neither of which can be known without the other. If the empirical course of historical manifestations is lost, then the idea evaporates.[135] His treatment of historical individuals

is in no way a purely abstract historical perception, a one-sided emphasis on the universal, in which the single and particular, the individual and personal, would be completely without significance. Neither of these two factors belonging together may be separated from the other. Just as, without a universal as its enlivening idea, the single and particular would be a body without a soul, so also the universal and ideal first obtains the ground of its real existence, the concrete life of historical existence, in the single and particular, in the individuality of historical subjects. Therefore, what gives historical subjects their historical significance is the energy with which, as the representatives of their age, as

133 *Ibid.*, pp. 268–69. Cf. *Lehrbuch der Dogmengeschichte* (1st ed.), pp. 56–57.
134 Hirsch, *op cit.*, V, 551.
135 *Die Tübinger Schule*, pp. 4–5.

the living expression of the consciousness of the age, they lay hold of the ideas moving their time, forming and developing them in themselves and representing in themselves their real manifestation.[136]

The *historical* significance of individuals, then, is a function of the success with which they lay hold of and express the ideas shaping the age in which they live—the success with which they become the medium and instrument of the course of history. The historian is not interested in personality as such or for its own sake. Nevertheless, the *historical* treatment of personal agents enhances rather than diminishes their significance and individuality, for all historical persons would be for us "mere names if what each thought and did and made the task of his life and striving were not also a thought grounded in the essence of Spirit itself." If this "general spiritual context" were removed, it would be indifferent to us whether an individual were named Athanasius or Arius, Nestorius or Cyril.[137] Similarly, Baur asks: "What empty names would all persons significant in any way in history be, if they did not first possess their highest interest for us in that we perceive in them the reflex of an idea standing over them and enlivening them, in which they have the firm support of their historical existence?"[138]

In the light of these statements, it is clear that Baur does not dismiss the importance of historical persons but rather sought to discover the true ground for the significance of their respective individualities. As Dilthey puts it, he realizes that all historical lives—including that of Jesus—may be represented historically only in terms of their world-historical connections.[139] His high estimate of the importance and role of individuals in the historical process is nowhere more clearly seen than in his treatment of Jesus and Paul as historical agents. Indeed, his entire study of first-century Christianity focuses on these two figures, as he himself acknowledges in the Introduction to *Paulus*: "Here also, as in the Gospel history, the unity of an individual life is the real object of historical-critical consideration."[140] His analysis of Paul's character shows clearly how the true individuality of an historical agent consists in his serving as the medium of an objective power and process, such that his own subjectivity merges with it. At the same time, his distinctive personality gives shape and direction to that process.[141] The same is true of other great figures in the

---

136 *Ibid.*, pp. 7–8.
137 *Dreieinigkeit*, I, xx.
138 *Die Tübinger Schule*, p. 8.
139 Cf. Dilthey, *op. cit.*, p. 429. In this respect generally, Baur seems to have anticipated Dilthey, who argues that great men are determined by and dependent on the "meaning system" of which they are a part.
140 *Paulus*, I, 6 (E.T., 3).
141 *Ibid.*, II, 294–99 (E.T., 270–74). For his treatment of Jesus, see below, pp. 221–37.

history of the Church, such as Constantine, Charlemagne, and Luther.[142] In short, Baur acknowledges great men but rejects a great-man theory of history.

Historical Development

In discussing Baur's argument for the historical "necessity" of a specific and individual founder of the Christian Church, I suggested that a specific understanding of the nature of historical development and of hermeneutical procedure connected with it lies at the basis of the argument.[143] This understanding may now be stated as follows: "It is not permissible simply to abstract the end toward which every individual thing strives from an indefinitely flowing sphere of manifestations. Rather everything proceeds from a beginning point in which the idea which is to be realized through its entire temporal manifestation is clearly and definitely expressed; and the development, once begun, proceeds from one point to another in a continuity in which it cannot be difficult to relate everything individual to the idea which lies at the basis of the whole and to determine the relationship in which the one stands to the other."[144]

The nature and *telos* of any historical process is ingredient in it from its specific point of inception, which therefore is of decisive importance in shaping the process as a whole. To understand a community, institution, or culture, historical consideration must concern itself first and foremost with the circumstances and character of its origin. This is especially the case with the Church: "The more everything in the history of the Christian Church depends on the beginning from which it proceeds, and is conditioned by that through the whole continuity of its development, the more depends on the way one comprehends this beginning itself, which is so significant, from the fundamental perception of which the whole historical presentation is born."[145] Without a clear and definite understanding of the historical Jesus, who is the founder and source of the entire subsequent development of the Church with its manifold tendencies, an "historical perception of the way in which Christianity was formed into the Church" is not possible.[146]

---

[142] On Constantine, see *Das Christenthum*, pp. 464–66 (E.T., II, 226–27); on Charlemagne, *An Hase*, pp. 99–101, *Die Tübinger Schule*, pp. 3, 5–6; on Luther, *Kirchengeschichte*, IV, 4–5, *Epochen*, p. 256, *Die Tübinger Schule*, p. 10. A number of interpreters have defended Baur's treatment of historical personality against unjust criticism: Barth, *Die protestantische Theologie*, pp. 456–57; Hirsch, *op. cit.*, V, 520–21; Otto Pfleiderer, "Zu Ferdinand Christian Baur's Gedächtnis," *PK*, XXXIX:25, 571; and Eduard Zeller, "Ferdinand Christian Baur," *Vorträge und Abhandlungen*, pp. 409–411.

[143] See above, p. 102.

[144] *Epochen*, p. 3.

[145] *Ibid.*, pp. 3–4.

[146] *Das Christenthum*, p. vii (E.T., I, xi).

The beginning point of an historical development also contains its *telos* or goal. In the case of Christianity, the *telos* of God-man unity is envisioned in the person of Jesus Christ. Historical development is constituted precisely by the movement toward this *telos;* it is teleological.[147] But this assertion does not involve Baur in either of two untenable options: that teleology means progress in the sense of continual improvement or betterment, or that real novelty is excluded from historical development. With respect to the first, Baur never suggests that succeeding stages in Church history are "better" than preceding ones. They are different, to be sure, but there is no absolute criterion by which to judge whether one mode of realization of the idea of the Church is "better" than another, nor any basis on which to prophesy what the historical future will bring. Furthermore, as we have seen, the *perfect* realization of God-manhood remains only a transhistorical possibility; every epoch in the historical life of the Church is relative and imperfect. On the other hand, however, historical development does involve real novelty and change. Although the goal of a development proceeds from its beginning point, this does not mean that the "beginning already contains in itself the full consciousness of what follows from it," in the sense intended by Catholic historiography, so that it can be claimed that the bishops of the Church have taught nothing other than the apostles and Paul nothing other than Christ.[148] Baur's objection to the conception of development embraced in Catholic historiography has been explained above.[149] Authentic development involves change and novelty as well as continuity, opposition and conflict as well as harmony.[150]

Opposition and conflict serve, in fact, as vehicles of historical development. Development through opposition is a phenomenon of historical reality generally; since the Church also is an historical phenomenon, it exemplifies this general pattern of development. The opposition of forces and tendencies in history is not an ultimately destructive process, however, but a unifying one.[151] Baur insists that these observations are empirically based, not derived from philosophical dialectic. His earliest description of opposing tendencies in primitive Christianity is based on purely critical studies and antedates his acquaintance with Hegel. His later description, clearly influenced by Hegel, of the inner, dialectical movement of the thoughts of Spirit in the historical process, serves as a speculative explication of what he had originally discovered

---

[147] Cf. *Die Tübinger Schule*, pp. 9–10.

[148] *Ibid.*, pp. 45–46; quotation from p. 46.

[149] See above, pp. 156–58.

[150] Baur's notion of historical "necessity," however, would seem to exclude the possibility of that novelty which he here demands. See above, pp. 149–50.

[151] Cf *Die Tübinger Schule*, pp. 78–80.

and continued to observe independently and critically as a phenomenon of historical reality generally.[152]

THE QUESTION OF MIRACLE

"Miracle," in the absolute or classic sense, was defined in the controversy between rationalism and supernaturalism.[153] It means, according to Baur, "an interruption of the natural continuity, dependent on an immanent law, of cause and effect, which is not further explicable by natural causes and which results from an external, intermittently operating causality."[154] It involves an absolute distinction between a miraculous event and a natural one, as well as a mechanical view of nature, according to which nature is regarded not as a living organism but as a machine, set in motion by an external force and embracing purely external relations between cause and effect. It is impossible, therefore, to speak of miracle in the absolute sense as though it were a *tertium quid*, both supernatural and natural, but without the offense of being either. The partial naturalizing and psychologizing of miracles, as attempted by Olshausen and especially by Neander in his critical studies of Acts, will not do, since miracle, by its classic definition, is absolutely supernatural. If supernatural causality is present, then the event is miraculous, no matter how much it may also yield to a natural explanation.[155]

Baur's basic objection to miracle is that it destroys the historicity of a phenomenon and removes it from historical-critical consideration. Furthermore, once an exception has been granted, there is no reason miracles cannot recur at other points in the historical continuum. "Miracle is an absolute beginning; and the more such a beginning conditions everything which follows, the more the entire series of manifestations which belong within the sphere of Christianity must bear the same miraculous character. Historical connection having once been severed at the outset, the same interruption of the historical process is equally possible at any further point."[156]

Every event, of course, involves a new beginning in the sense that it is a discrete and unique occurrence, but at the same time it cannot be severed from its historical context. It is conditioned by the sequence of causes and effects of which it is a part, and consequently its new beginning cannot be regarded as *absolute*. However, this is precisely the claim of miracle, which is why this claim cannot be countenanced by a critical-historical interpreta-

---

152 We return to this question below, pp. 200–201; see also above, pp. 148, 165–67.

153 On Baur's use of the term "supernatural," see above, p. 5, n. 13.

154 *Paulus*, I, 110 (E.T., 97).

155 For Baur's criticism of Neander on this point, cf. *ibid.*, pp. 25–26, 30–33, 87, 110–12 (E.T., 21–22, 25–27, 76, 97–98).

156 *Das Christenthum*, p. 1 (E.T., I, 1).

tion of the past. The task of historical consideration is "to investigate what has happened in the context of causes and effects; however, miracle in the absolute sense annuls the natural context." If the beginning of Christianity were regarded as a miracle, then there would be no historical analogies by which to understand it, and its subsequent development would bear the same miraculous character. It is not possible, as some Protestant Church historians have attempted, to combine a supernatural origin with a subsequent natural development. The Catholic supernatural historical perception of the entire Church is more consistent. One has to make a choice: either Christianity as a whole is historical in its inception and course of development, or it is not; there is no third possibility.[157]

A further objection to absolute miracle is that it reduces human agents to the status of passive instruments of an external and totally transcendent power. In Acts, the apostles' "human individuality stands in such a secondary relation to the divine principle acting in them that they seem to be only the organs and bearers of it, and everything they do bears in itself an immediate divine character."[158] Baur suggests that the proponents of miracle argue on the basis of "the very worst modification of the doctrine of irresistible grace" and that what is believed to be gained on the one hand by "a theory of miracle which completely destroys the continuity of the spiritual life" "is irretrievably lost on the other by the sacrifice of the moral dignity" of the apostles.[159]

What is the role of historical criticism with respect to accounts which contain descriptions of miracles in the absolute sense? "In an historical-critical investigation of the miracle stories in Acts, I regard it as completely superfluous to go into the general dogmatic question as to whether miracles are actually possible, for in such an investigation it is a question not of the possibility but simply of the recognizability of miracle, to which all questions belong with which criticism should occupy itself."[160] The task of criticism is to ask whether there is any historical evidence which would allow us to conclude that a miracle in the absolute sense actually happened. Baur judges that such evidence is lacking in Acts, that its miracle stories cannot be regarded as authentic but rather purely as the product of a literary intention. But this conclusion is based, not on a dogmatic judgment about the possibility of miracles, but on an historical judgment concerning the implausibility of the accounts and the lack of all historical analogies

---

[157] Cf. *ibid.*, pp. 21–22 (E.T., I, 22–23); and *Die Tübinger Schule*, pp. 14–15.
[158] *Paulus*, I, 29 (E.T., 24); cf. also pp. 90–92 (E.T., 79–80). In Baur's judgment, this external, absolute, and arbitrary notion of miracle discredits the historical authenticity of the miracle stories in Acts and discloses the literary and theological tendency of the work as a whole. Cf. *ibid.*, pp. 33–34 (E.T., 28).
[159] *Ibid.*, p. 88 (E.T., 77).
[160] *Ibid.*, p. 109 (E.T., 96).

by which to explicate them. Because of this distinction, there is some justice in Zeller's claim that Baur did not argue that scientific historiography itself directly rules out the *possibility* of miracle, as Ritschl and A. B. Bruce claimed he did, and that he clearly delineated the limits within which the historian must treat miracle.[161] Nevertheless, on Baur's principles, miraculous claims are clearly *incompatible* with historical consideration. Furthermore, he specifically states that it is the task of historical criticism to examine "whether what is implicitly possible also takes place in reality, according to the documents in question, without the interposition of an actual miracle."[162] "Historical consideration has therefore very naturally the concern to draw the miracle of the absolute beginning into the continuity of history and to resolve it, so far as is generally possible, into its natural elements."[163] The force and meaning of the "so far as is generally possible" will be examined shortly.

Miracle in the absolute sense refers to events in which divine power or action disrupts, abrogates, severs the natural connections between causes and effects which characterize the order of nature and history. As Bultmann suggests, in a miraculous *Weltanschauung* divine action is thought of as happening *between* worldly actions or events, not *within* or as part of them.[164] For this reason Baur claims that miracle embraces a "mechanical" view of nature, according to which the relations between cause and effect are external and not vital, so that an additional, divine cause must be unnaturally or supernaturally inserted between existing causes and effects. But it is possible to conceive of a relation between God and the world in which divine action can be mediated naturally and historically, like any other action. In such a conception, the notion of the "supernatural" or the "suprahistorical" disappears. The distinction between God and the world is not thereby necessarily destroyed; rather, the reality of nature and history is conceived such that it is constituted by the action and interaction of divine and human Spirit as well as by a substratum of nonspiritual forces or energies. If natural and historical *life* is conceived as a complex of energies or activities rather than as the mechanical combination of static substances, then the basis for making a distinction between the "natural" and the "supernatural" disappears. Although Baur knew nothing of the life-philosophy of a Bergson or the process philosophy of a Whitehead, he did have available the immanental theism of Spinoza, a conception of the relation of God and the world which he remarked is "scarcely to be avoided in the modern view of the world," and

161 Eduard Zeller, "Die historische Kritik und das Wunder," *SHZ*, VI, 364.
162 *Paulus*, I, 87 (E.T., 76).
163 *Das Christenthum*, p. 1 (E.T., I, 1–2).
164 Rudolf Bultmann, *Jesus Christ and Mythology* (New York: Charles Scribner's Sons, 1958), p. 61.

which he judged to serve as the speculative foundation of Schleier-macher's *Glaubenslehre*. Baur's historical-critical theology clearly shares this foundation in what was for his day a revisionary theism; it is also informed by the vision of an internal relation between God and the world, and of the presence of the divine Spirit to human spirit, as achieved by Hegel's system.

Although Baur himself never explicitly develops a metaphysical foundation for historical reality which would exclude the necessity and possibility of absolute miracle and lay the foundation for a purely historical conception of the divine presence in historical occurrence, his suggestion of a congruence between nature, history, and Spirit presupposes it. "What Schleiermacher, in the well-known proposition in his *Glaubenslehre*, has said in regard to the divine omnipotence, that we no longer consider that the divine om-nipotence shows itself greater in the interruption of the continuity of nature than in its orderly course, is valid in the same way for the power of Spirit over nature. Spirit shows its power over nature, not through the interruption and dismembering of the continuity of nature, but, since its essence is conformity with law, through the fact that it is the immanent law of nature."[165] What Baur says about the relation between nature and Spirit in this passage holds equally well for the relation between history and Spirit. He also quotes the proposition with which Schleiermacher introduces his discussion of miracle in the *Glaubenslehre*: "It can never be nec-essary in the interest of religion so to interpret a fact that its dependence on God absolutely excludes its being conditioned by the system of nature."[166]

Baur does not allow the one exception to this rule—the absolute God-consciousness of Jesus Christ—which Schleiermacher does. If Spirit—presumably both divine and human—is indeed the im-manent law of nature and history, then the divinely grounded relation by which human spirit authentically exists must be re-garded not as the disruption but as the foundation of nature and history. Far from being miraculous, the "most complete possible" God-consciousness of Jesus is the most intensely historical of all human acts of consciousness, for history itself is constituted by the fellowship of God and man, by the presence of the divine Spirit to human spirit. Only if this act of consciousness is regarded as absolute or perfect in the sense of being "primal" or "archetypal," is it in Baur's judgment miraculous in the absolute sense, for then it cannot be regarded as the act of an authentically historical individual. But neither Schleiermacher nor Baur explains why this should be the case, i.e., why a perfect or absolute God-consciousness should have to be miraculous in the sense of being supernatural;

---

[165] *Paulus*, I, 110–11 (E.T., 97).
[166] *Die Tübinger Schule*, p. 15. The translation is from Friedrich Schleier-macher, *The Christian Faith*, § 47, p. 178.

this does not seem to be required by the immanental theism in the context of which they are working.

Baur's position is that nature and history on the one hand and Spirit on the other are internally congruent realities such that the presence of divine action in history does not interrupt the historical process miraculously but rather can be understood itself as an historical action or event. This is evident from his treatment of the conversion of Paul as fully historical in character but as also witnessing to the power of God.[167] Baur's position is most clearly stated, however, as follows:

The accusation that he who does not believe a miracle in Acts like the one in question [the healing by Paul of a man lame from birth, Acts 14:8 ff.] does not also acknowledge the divine vital powers [*die göttlichen Lebenskräfte*] which have entered into humanity through Christ, establishes a very unworthy view of Christianity, since it must follow that miracle belongs so essentially to Christianity that, wherever Christianity is not accompanied by miracle, it does not manifest its divine vital powers. Since it is now acknowledged that miracles no longer take place, at least of the sort with which we are here concerned, . . . Christianity must long since have been dead. It is therefore only just to concede that Christianity possesses divine vital powers apart from miracles which one is completely able to acknowledge, even when one does not consider every one of the miracles recounted in the New Testament as an actual miracle, because the letter of the narrative so reads.[168]

It is this conviction of the immanence of divine action in historical reality, specifically in the reality of the Church, that leads Baur to grant a certain credence and justification to *some* of the language of miracle in the New Testament. For example, he distinguishes between the miracle stories in Acts and the Gospels: the "hardness" of miracle in the former does not "correspond with the character of miracle otherwise in the New Testament"; the complicated and calculated series of miraculous occurrences found in Acts in connection with the conversion of Paul has but little in common with "the miraculous character of the Gospel history."[169] As we have seen, the concern of historical consideration is "to draw the miracle of the absolute beginning into the continuity of history and to resolve it, *so far as is generally possible*, into its natural elements." The qualification suggests that Christianity is by no means to be regarded *simply* as a natural phenomenon, devoid of a divine foundation. The passage in which these words are contained continues by suggesting that the task of the historical theologian is to ask "why *the miracle* with which the history of Christianity begins meshes into the continuity of world history at

---

167 Cf. *Paulus*, I, 70–88, (E.T., 61–76).
168 *Ibid.*, p. 110 (E.T., 96–97).
169 *Ibid.*, pp. 33, 92 (E.T., 27–28, 80).

just this point," and that this raises a series of questions "which can be answered only from the standpoint of historical consideration."[170] It is not true, Baur writes in answer to Uhlhorn, that the Tübingen School excludes a divine causality from the origin of Christianity; its position rather has been that the origin of Christianity cannot be explained so long as its miraculous character is not also established as an historically given fact.[171] Similarly, he writes in a letter to Tholuck: "From none of my writings can it be proved that I reject the entire history of miracle."[172]

"The miraculous character of the Gospel history" is its foundation in a divine causality, in the divine gift of reconciliation between God and man, in the salvific reality which is one dimension of the Church's historicity. But this miraculous character is not an "absolute" miracle, miracle in the classic sense, for at the same time that Christianity is the *absolute* truth it is also a *positive* reality, an historically given fact; these two dimensions of its historicity are completely congruent. If the language of miracle in the Gospels is intended to express the divine foundation of Christianity, without implying that the acts of God are supernatural or suprahistorical in the ordinary sense—if this is what the word "miracle" means—then it is not incompatible with a "purely historical" comprehension of Christianity. Obviously, this is not what miracle in the classic sense means, "absolute" miracle as understood in the controversy between rationalism and supernaturalism. Nor is it the *tertium quid* invented by those attempting a partial naturalization of miracle, an event which is both natural and supernatural. What Baur has in mind is not miraculous in the ordinary sense at all. Yet the authentically biblical and Christian belief in miracle points to a dimension of historical reality which he does not want to deny but rather to elucidate. Hence Baur's treatment of miracle, unlike that of his student Eduard Zeller, is not entirely rationalistic by any means.[173] He did not simply reject miracle point-blank, as most of his critics claimed, but was seeking for a broader conception of historical reality and historical knowledge than that permitted by a thoroughgoing rationalism. Nevertheless, he did not fashion a clearly defined alternative conception to miracle. After two early articles devoted to a critical investigation of the reference to "speaking in tongues" in the story of Pentecost, he never directly addressed himself to the question of miracle,

---

[170] *Das Christenthum*, pp. 1–2 (E.T., I, 1–2). Italics mine.

[171] This is the probable meaning of an obscure passage in *Die Tübinger Schule*, p. 16.

[172] Baur to F. A. G. Tholuck, early summer 1836, rough draft (U.B.T., Md 750, ii, 9, 1).

[173] Cf. Zeller's dispute with Ritschl over miracle, which continued for some years after Baur's death in the pages of *Sybels historische Zeitschrift* and the *Jahrbücher für deutsche Theologie*. The rationalism of his treatment of miracle is especially evident in "Die historische Kritik und das Wunder," *SHZ*, VI, 364 ff.

except for occasional footnotes and comments in *Paulus* and *Das Christenthum*. This question had become so polemically explosive after 1835 that Baur perhaps decided it was futile to try to explain that his position was neither rationalistic nor supernaturalistic in the sense defined by the old controversy. This fact, however, is already apparent from the first of the articles on "speaking in tongues," which clearly anticipates Baur's position on miracle described in the pages above.[174]

TENDENCY CRITICISM

We turn now from more general considerations of historical method in the theological disciplines to a look at the principles behind Baur's literary-historical criticism or "tendency criticism" of the New Testament writings. He first used the term "tendency criticism" to describe his procedure in the 1831 article which explored the opposition between Petrine and Pauline elements in the history of primitive Christianity.[175] His fullest explanation of tendency criticism is found in the introduction to *Kritische Untersuchungen über die kanonischen Evangelien*. This work, together with *Paulus* and some of the journal articles, is of seminal importance in the development and application of a critical method for treating the New Testament documents. These works, Emanuel Hirsch suggests, "introduce the procedure of source criticism, as developed by German historical science in the first half of the nineteenth century, into biblical science, since they treat the New Testament writings straightforwardly and self-evidently as themselves historical documents belonging to history."[176] Similarly, Ernst Käsemann writes that, with some of Baur's early articles in which tendency criticism is first used, "the truly historical investigation of primitive Christianity and of the New Testament is first established," and that both the fundamental and (for the most part)

---

174 "Über den wahren Begriff des *glōssais lalein*, mit Rücksicht auf die neuesten Untersuchungen hierüber," *TZT*, IV:2 (1830), pp. 99–104, 117–19, 128–29, 132. In this article, Baur makes it clear that he differs from the rationalistic explanations of Acts 2:4 by insisting that "tongues" refers not simply to ordinary human organs but to "higher" organs filled by the Spirit of God, and from the supernaturalistic by arguing that "other tongues" does not mean a simply miraculous ability to speak foreign languages, or an incomprehensible, magical, unconscious mode of discourse. It rather means the "spiritualizing" of intelligible human discourse so that men now speak, as it were, a "new language." "Speaking with tongues" is an outward manifestation of the inner working of the Spirit, congruent with human nature.

175 Cf. "Die Christuspartei in der korinthischen Gemeinde, der Gegensatz des petrinischen und paulinischen Christenthums in der ältesten Kirche, der Apostel Petrus in Rom," *TZT*, V:4 (1831), pp. 75, 114. Preparation for the article began as early as 1826; see above, p. 22, n. 85. These dates prove that Baur was not indebted to either Strauss or Hegel for the basic direction of his New Testament studies.

176 Hirsch, *op. cit.*, V, 524.

the concrete problems raised in them are still very much alive and still unsolved.[177]

"Tendency criticism" is Baur's term for literary-historical criticism of the New Testament writings. He proposes that this method, which is generally recognized in scientific historiography, should also be applied to the Gospels, which are historical documents like any others.

Why ought not this [procedure], with which in general no one can quarrel, also find its application with respect to our canonical Gospels? That they offer themselves as historical presentations of the life of Jesus in no way excludes the supposition that their authors were guided in their presentations by definite motives and interests. Indeed, it cannot be otherwise thought than that they are literary products of the time in which their authors lived. The first question which every criticism of these Gospels has to ask must be concerned with the will and intention of each of the authors. With this question we first come to the firm ground of concrete historical truth.[178]

Baur calls this procedure the "historical" comprehension of the Gospels, as distinct from the "dogmatic," the "abstract critical," and the "negative critical or dialectical," because it regards its most essential task to be that of "placing itself within the whole context of temporal circumstances from which these writings have proceeded."[179] The failure of the abstract critical approach, as we have seen, is that it bases its study of the Gospels on purely literary phenomena and does not take into account the historical context and theological intentions of the writings in which these phenomena are found. It is therefore unable to achieve convincing conclusions on certain pressing questions, such as the priority and sources of the Gospels.[180]

The procedure of tendency criticism is marked by two fundamental rules. First, every New Testament *writing* must be placed in its context in the history of primitive Christianity, thus being set in relation to definite directions or tendencies realized in this history and associated with a definite theological posture which has developed in it. Second, the *stories* about anything factual contained in these writings must be judged on the basis of the historical position and theological tendencies of the writings; they should never be directly compared with similar stories in other writings in order to test their historical authenticity.[181] These rules concern, respectively, writings or literary units and the stories or pericopes contained in the writings. Baur's insistence that the latter must not be considered separately and abstractly but as a part of the

[177] Ernst Käsemann, "Einführung" to Vol. I of F. C. Baur, *Ausgewählte Kerke in Einzelausgaben*, pp. viii, xiv.

[178] *Die kanonischen Evangelien*, p. 74.

[179] *Ibid.*, p. 76.

[180] See above, pp. 154–56.

[181] Cf. *Die kanonische Evangelien*, pp. 71–76; and Hirsch, *op. cit.*, V, 524.

literary context in which they are found, in order to reach a sound judgment concerning their historical authenticity, is a direct product of his criticism of Strauss's "dialectical" historical procedure, whereby Strauss was able to reduce the entire Gospel story to a web of myth and miracle by playing one report off against another.[182] Thus the prior task is to discover the general tendency or point of view, the theological orientation, the historical milieu, of the writings. As Baur puts it, a Gospel has not only an historical bearing; it is also a "tendency-writing,"[183] i.e., a writing exhibiting a theological or religious point of view, one in which a particular understanding of faith unfolds. It is necessary to understand it as both an historical document and an expression of faith at one and the same time. Only when the theological intention of the author with respect to the stories contained in his Gospel has been determined is it possible to consider critically the authenticity of the factual reports contained in the stories.

In this connection, Klaus Scholder has suggested that Baur made a distinction between two sorts of New Testament study: an interpretation, *in* faith, of the New Testament writings as witnesses *of* faith, i.e., as theological or kerygmatic writings; and a "factual criticism" which seeks as much as possible to establish "the real Gospel history," and which therefore treats the New Testament writings "scientifically" as historical sources. Scholder sees contemporary New Testament theology as pursuing primarily the first course, and suggests that Baur provides a necessary corrective or balance by pursuing primarily the second course.[184] To be sure, this distinction is characteristic of contemporary New Testament theology. But Baur more nearly pursues both sorts of study simultaneously: an analysis of the Gospels as historical sources can be achieved only by considering them also as theological or "tendency" writings; and the validity of their claim in faith is inextricably related to the "firm ground of concrete historical truth" on which they rest. Theological and historical-critical considerations are inextricably intertwined in the study of the New Testament: this is the character of tendency criticism.

The results of tendency criticism are immediately concerned with a body of theological literature *about* certain events, not with the events themselves. We know the events only as they are mediated to us through theological documents; we do not have immediate access to them. Thus Baur writes that "the teaching of Jesus stands at an historical distance from us, in which it eludes the sharpness of historical consideration, and one can lay one's eyes more on the totality than on the details."[185] Of Matthew, which he

---

182 See above, pp. 79–80.
183 *Die kanonischen Evangelien*, p. 76.
184 Klaus Scholder, "Ferdinand Christian Baur als Historiker," *ETh*, XXI:10 (1961), 453–58.
185 *Neutestamentliche Theologie*, p. 122; cf. pp. 45, 297–98.

regards as the earliest and most historically reliable of the Gospels, he writes: "Even this Gospel is already a secondary report, whose relation to the objective facts can be only approximately determined."[186] It is extremely difficult to distinguish the actual teaching of Jesus from the literary context in which it is reported.[187] Yet this difficult distinction can and must be attempted, and the approximate determinations undertaken, for the ultimate interest and goal of the biblical historian and theologian is not writings themselves but the facts they present and interpret.[188] The procedure Baur uses to isolate the authentically historical substratum in the Gospels is familiar to modern biblical students. In his lectures on New Testament theology, he distinguishes the authentic teaching of Jesus from the literary context in which it is presented by taking the most Jewish of the Gospels, Matthew, and then designating as authentic in it precisely those elements which transcend Judaism radically, which represent a break with Jewish messianic expectations: this is the authentic teaching of Jesus, in broad outline.[189] Those materials have the greatest claim to historical truth in which the subjective intentions and interests of the author are, for whatever reason, suppressed.[190]

It certainly cannot be regarded as a weakness in Baur's procedure that he knew nothing of form criticism. Yet the lack of a method by which critically to elucidate the period of oral tradition between the events of Jesus' ministry and the written Gospels means that his treatment of the sources and relations of the Gospels, as well as the authenticity of their stories, could not be fully convincing. As we shall see, Baur believed that the Gospel traditions were transmitted in literary rather than oral form. The earliest Gospel, Matthew, which received its present form sometime during the second century, was related, through a series of recensions and modifications, to a first-century Gospel of the Hebrews, possibly an eyewitness account written by the Apostle Matthew.[191] At the same time, Baur found no evidence for the existence of a Proto-Gospel —an eyewitness source used independently by all three Evangelists. The development of form criticism in the twentieth century replaced the weakest link in Baur's approach to the Synoptic Problem and eliminated the need for all hypotheses concerning the Proto-Gospel and the Hebrew Gospel.

[186] *Die kanonischen Evangelien*, p. 621.

[187] *Neutestamentliche Theologie*, p. 86.

[188] Cf. Hirsch, *op. cit.*, V, 543: *"There exists a true and rich knowledge of the origin of the Christian religion and of its founder and mid-point. The objective of Baur's Gospel criticism is to prove this against Strauss."* (Italics his.)

[189] Cf. *Neutestamentliche Theologie*, Pt. I, pp. 45–121. The same procedure is used, although less extensively and with less attention to a systematic exegesis of the texts, in Baur's treatment of the teaching of Jesus in the first part of *Das Christenthum*.

[190] Cf. *Paulus*, I, 8 (E.T., 5).

[191] See below, pp. 217-20.

The term "tendency criticism" was taken up by Baur's opponents and used as a polemical device either to ridicule his procedure or to suggest that he imposed dialectical and a priori patterns on the New Testament writings. These attacks were usually motivated by fear that his New Testament studies would destroy the traditional foundations of the faith. Baur replied to such criticism in his own day by claiming that a critical method cannot be demolished simply by the use of slogans and party labels. In any case, this method is not an invention of the Tübingen School but rather the application and continuation on its part of a general critical tradition. Furthermore, the term "tendency criticism" ought not to be abandoned to polemical usage, for it is an accurate way of indicating an essential element in the task of the New Testament theology, that of determining the literary and theological intentions of the canonical writings and the stance of their authors in relation to their intellectual environment. It is in the interest of authentic historical research, not a priori speculation, to search for the "tendencies" of an author's literature.[192]

Nevertheless, it is in connection with his tendency criticism, especially his delineation of Judaizing and Paulinizing tendencies in primitive Christianity, that Baur has usually been accused of an a priori procedure. It would be well, then, at the conclusion of this section and of this chapter as a whole, to summarize the arguments advanced elsewhere that this accusation is groundless. In the first place, we have Baur's unequivocal testimony that his historical investigations are in no sense a priori or predisposed by philosophical considerations to arrive at certain results.[193] Second, his original discovery of theological opposition and controversy in primitive Christianity, and his description of the method of tendency criticism, preceded by several years his acquaintance with Hegel's philosophy, and details of his thesis only gradually emerged and were sometimes modified.[194] Third, for Baur, "speculation" in historical knowledge means the critical attempt to elicit meaning and rationality *from* history rather than to impose it on history. It provides, for example, a theoretical explication of the empirical discovery that history develops to a certain extent through the opposition of antithetical tendencies; but the shape and character of this development in every instance is something to be determined only by painstaking research. The meaning is ingredient in the historical process; but it must be elicited and interpreted by an imaginative mind. Baur was enough of a master of his own discipline to be able to affirm with confidence that the speculative explication did not create the illusion in his mind of dialectical patterns which were not really there.[195] Finally, the "speculative" or

---

192 *Die Tübinger Schule*, pp. 17–21.
193 See above, pp. 161, 165–67.
194 See above, p. 22, and below, p. 209.
195 See above, pp. 148, 161–65, 189–90.

theological categories used by Baur to interpret and order the history of the Church are distinctively his own, and they produce a vision of that history far too rich, complex, and imaginative to be attributed to an a priori procedure. The motif of the dialectical resolution of opposition plays only a small part in this total vision. We shall see in the next chapter that his treatment of early Christian literature in the context of the Jewish-Pauline opposition is too complex to be fitted neatly into a thesis-antithesis-synthesis pattern. For example, Baur understood Paul to be as strongly opposed to what later developed into Gnosticism as he was to the particularism of the Judaizers. Furthermore, his treatment of the early period cannot be appreciated until it is placed in the context of his total interpretation of the development of the Church through its historical forms, of which it is only a small part. Baur's work as an historian is more compelling when the entire canvas on which he painted can be seen. One of the tasks of the next chapter is to provide this perspective.[196]

[196] See below, pp. 207–212, 251–56. It is instructive at this point to note the criticism Baur brings against the dualism of the Magdeburg Centuries, according to which the entire preceding history of the Church is rigidly ordered according to the a priori notion of a cosmic struggle between God and the Devil, light and darkness: "The abstract dualism from which the authors of the Centuries proceed, and from which they detect the conflict in Church history between two mutually exclusive tendencies, is shown to be completely untenable as soon as one draws closer to historical reality and looks more deeply into the concrete content of the manifestations of individual life. The rigid, monotonous antithesis of the abstract theory is dissolved into the infinite multiplicity of purely relative antitheses by the subjects whose individuality fits into neither the one nor the other of the categories. There is no chasm in history which absolutely separates the one from the other; the whole movement of history is a flowing transition, a steady mediation of the one with the other; and thus every individual thing first comes into its own as an historical reality when one permits it to be considered for what it is in the immediacy of its individual existence." *Epochen*, p. 66.

5 ✱ SOME CONTENTS AND
RESULTS OF AN
HISTORICAL THEOLOGY

The scope of Baur's historical investigations was immense. It included lectures and studies in the history and philosophy of religion and non-Christian religions as well as in New Testament and in the whole of Church history and history of dogma. In addition to his major books in these fields, which have been mentioned in the first chapter, he published extensive journal articles on various subjects in New Testament, patristics, Reformation studies, and other areas. It would be impossible in the space of a single chapter to survey this entire literature. Rather, I shall concentrate on two topics of central concern to Baur's historical-critical theology: first and primarily, his study of the historical Jesus as the founder, origin, and center of meaning of the Christian Church; and second, his determination of the major motifs and periods in the development of the Church and of Church dogma, as well as his conception of the historical disciplines engaged in the study of this development. The first topic is given priority because of the conviction, argued elsewhere,[1] that Baur's Christology serves as the focus of his theology, both dogmatically and historically. Here we take up the historical-critical explication of the Christology whose dogmatic foundations were described in Chapter III. This topic also entails a look at Baur's study of New Testament history and literature, which provides the necessary context in which the historical Jesus can be critically approached.

NEW TESTAMENT HISTORY AND LITERATURE

Paul, the Apostle of Jesus Christ

Baur began to unravel the mysteries of the New Testament with his Pauline studies. From this starting point, he gradually pieced together the historical and theological framework of the first two

1 See above, pp. 100–121.

centuries, which made a critical study of the Synoptic Gospels and ultimately of Jesus possible. One can trace a steady progression from 1831, when the first of his Pauline studies appeared, through a series of monographs on various facets of primitive Christianity, to his solution of the Johannine question and the Synoptic problem, and finally, in 1853, to his treatment of the teaching and ministry of Jesus. He remarks that his work on the Pauline Epistles served as the "foundation and firm support" for his later investigations.[2] Paul represented, in fact, Baur's first love and lifelong interest.[3] His first source-critical study in New Testament literature (1831) was concerned with Paul, and much of the last year of his life was devoted to a revision of the first edition of *Paulus* and of his lectures on Paul's theology for his course in New Testament theology, following upon a series of articles published in the 1850's dealing with Corinthians, Philippians, Thessalonians, and Romans.[4]

In the introduction to *Paulus*, Baur claims that the major historical importance of the life and work of Paul is that by means of him Christianity, "instead of remaining a mere form of Judaism and being ultimately lost in it, lay hold of itself in its own independent principle, broke loose from Judaism and set itself against it as a new, essentially different form of religious consciousness and life, freed from its national particularity."[5] Baur concludes that it is an "undeniable historical fact" that "Christianity achieved its universal historical significance for the first time through the Apostle Paul."[6] He was "the receptive soil in which the principle of Christian consciousness, which through him for the first time obtained its living features, developed into a concrete consciousness."[7]

But at the same time, "the Pauline universalism contains nothing which must not be regarded as already orginally an essential element of the self-consciousness of Jesus and which is contained implicitly in the purely moral tendency of his teaching."[8] Paul, therefore, did not invent a new Gospel but rather made explicit what already was implicit in the life and work of Jesus.[9] The relation as well as the distinction between the teaching of Jesus and the theology of Paul was mediated by the death of Jesus. Paul regarded the reconciliation of God and man to have been decisively accomplished in certain "positive historical facts, and above all [in]

---

[2] *Kirchengeschichte*, V, 398.

[3] Cf. Zeller's remark to this effect in his Foreword to the second edition (1866) of *Paulus*, which he edited (I, iii; not translated in the English edition).

[4] For reasons presented above, p. 101, the *content* of Paul's theology has been considered for the most part in Chapter III, in connection with Baur's dogmatic understanding of the person and work of Jesus. Here we shall limit ourself primarily to Baur's study of the Pauline Epistles.

[5] *Paulus*, I, 5–6 (E.T., 3).

[6] *Ibid.*, p. 6 (E.T., 3).

[7] *Paulus*, II, 302–303 (E.T., 277).

[8] *Die Tübinger Schule*, p. 36.

[9] Cf. *Neutestamentliche Theologie*, p. 128.

the great fact of the death of Jesus on the cross."[10] He saw this death, rather than the fulfilling of Jewish nationalistic expectations, to be the true meaning of Jesus' messiahship. According to Baur, there are intimations that Jesus also was aware of this uniquely redemptive aspect of his messianic role; but the distinctive quality of Paul's theology is that it focuses on the *person* of Christ, while the teaching of Jesus never makes his person its *direct* object[11] but rather the truth of the kingdom of God and its reception among men. It was because of Paul that the doctrine of the person of Christ became the fundamental dogma of the Christian Church.[12]

It is Paul's role as the theological exponent of the universal significance of the life and death of Christ against a Judaizing party in the Corinthian Church (the "Christ party" mentioned in I Cor. 1:12) which comes to Baur's attention in his first source-critical study in New Testament literature, "Die Christuspartei in der korinthischen Gemeinde, der Gegensatz des petrinischen und paulinischen Christenthums in der ältesten Kirche, der Apostel Petrus in Rom" (1831).[13] In this essay and in the second of his Pauline studies, "Über Zweck and Veranlassung des Römerbriefs" (1836),[14] he provides a summary statement of Pauline theology as defined by and in this conflict which agrees in essential respects with his later interpretation of Paul's thought in the 1845 and 1866 editions of *Paulus*.[15]

10 "Die Christuspartei in der korinthischen Gemeinde," *TZT*, V:4, 69.

11 Despite the fact, Baur adds, that the definite significance of what Jesus taught resided in the fact that he himself was what his teaching proclaimed and that there was an oblique indication of this in his teaching. See below, pp. 231–34.

12 *Neutestamentliche Theologie*, pp. 123–24, 127, 129–32.

13 Cf. "Die Christuspartei in der korinthischen Gemeinde," *TZT*, V:4, especially pp. 69–70, 134–35. The adequacy of Baur's thesis that the opponents of Paul in Corinth were Judaizers will be considered below, pp. 211–12.

14 "Über Zweck und Veranlassung des Römerbriefs und die damit zusammenhängenden Verhältnisse der römischen Gemeinde. Eine historisch-kritische Untersuchung," *TZT*, IX:3 (1836), 59–178.

15 These two articles were incorporated with relatively minor revisions into the first edition of *Paulus* (Stuttgart: Becher und Müller, 1845), the rest of which dates from 1845. They were thoroughly revised in 1860, while Baur was in the process of preparing a second edition of this work. He had only half completed this task, however, when he was kept from further work by his first stroke. The revised material was published as Volume I of the second edition by Zeller in 1866. Volume II of this edition represents the unrevised, second half of the first edition. It includes the whole of the third section of the work, the discussion of Paul's theology. However, Baur managed in 1860 to rework the section on Pauline theology for his New Testament lectures, and the new material is included in the posthumous publication of these lectures in 1864. The new organization which he gave to this section of his lectures might well have provided the pattern for his treatment of Paul's theology in the new edition of *Paulus*. The presentation in the lectures is somewhat more Christocentric and on the whole more refined and better structured than in *Paulus*. Albert Schweitzer, in *Paul and His Interpreters: A Critical History*, W. Montgomery, trans. (London: Adam & Charles Black, 1912), pp. 14–21, professes to see a great contrast between the "Hegelian

The mark of authenticity of what according to Baur are the four indisputably Pauline Epistles—Galatians, I and II Corinthians, and Romans—is in each case their affirmation of the universality of the Gospel of the grace of Christ against various expressions of Jewish or Jewish-Christian particularism and legalism. The earliest of these Epistles is Galatians, where the opposition between Paul and his Judaizing opponents is most clearly and simply drawn: the issue is the external symbol of bondage, the rite of circumcision, which the Jewish Christians sought to impose on the Gentiles as the necessary condition of salvation. "What appears in Romans as the complete development of Pauline doctrine . . . we can see in Galatians in its first outlines, yet already traced with precision. One can thus start from this Epistle to pursue the development of the Pauline system through the various major moments in which it is presented to us in the four major letters of the Apostle."[16] The distinctive content and quality of Paul's theology, then, first develops out of his conflict with Jewish Christians; it is this struggle which propels him to an articulation of a new theological understanding which is brought to its fullest expression in Romans.

It is precisely because these four Epistles honestly reflect the struggle of Paul against the Jewish Christians that they, rather than Acts, must be used as historical sources for the life of Paul. This is especially the case with Galatians, the earliest of the four. Baur was one of the first to question the historical value of Acts for an understanding of Paul. As with the relation between the Synoptic Gospels and the Gospel of John, so also with that between the Pauline Epistles and Acts, "historical truth can only be either on one side or on the other." In general, the authentic Pauline Epistles must be very highly regarded as historical sources among the New Testament writings, because of their early date and certain authorship. But in addition, Acts displays a definite theological intention to minimize as much as possible the differences between the two chief apostles, Peter and Paul. To this end, the factual material is modified whenever necessary. Another mark of literary invention in Acts is its use of miracle stories to convey a generally idealized account of events and to stress the supernatural guidance of their course. At the same time, Baur grants that there is undoubtedly an historical residuum to much of what is narrated in Acts and that despite its apologetic character it still remains "a highly important

---

intellectualism" of Baur's interpretation of Paul's theology in 1845 and the "historical and empirical" approach of 1860, which, by virtue of its greater loyalty to historical fact, no longer possesses the "bold effectiveness of the speculatively constructed system of the year 1845." Although there is some truth to this statement, in my judgment the differences between these two works in point of view and interpretation are relatively minor. In discussing some aspects of Baur's interpretation of Pauline theology in Chapter III, I have tried to show the essential agreement of these two texts by drawing citations from each of them on common points so far as possible.

[16] *Paulus*, I, 287 (E.T., 257); cf. also pp. 286, 344 (E.T., 256, 309).

source for the history of the Apostolic age," but one which must be used only in a highly critical fashion.[17]

In Baur's judgment, only Galatians, I and II Corinthians, and Romans can be regarded as unquestionably authentic among the Pauline Epistles. Objections of one sort or another can be raised against all the others from the standpoint of the four chief Epistles. With respect to Colossians and Ephesians, the Christian universalism of these Epistles reflects a post-Pauline, semi-ecclesiastical ethos. In addition, the peculiarly Pauline conception of faith as an inward process of consciousness based on trust in God and the experience of the impossibility of justification through the law is not found in these Epistles. Finally, they display traces of Gnostic influence.[18]

Baur regards as probably unauthentic three other Epistles which are ordinarily considered as genuinely Pauline today: I Thessalonians,[19] Philippians, and Philemon. With respect to I Thessalonians, Baur bases his argument on its lack of originality, independence, and significant content. The chief doubt about Philemon is the unlikelihood of our having any Pauline Epistles from the period of Roman imprisonment. Philippians lacks some of the distinctively Pauline elements, but more important, it employs Gnostic ideas and expressions for its own purposes, but with necessary modifications, in 2:6–9 (a passage now shown, by Lohmeyer and others, to be a pre-Pauline Christ hymn, incorporated into the text by Paul).[20]

Baur does not believe that the unauthenticity of any of these Epistles has been proved beyond question. Rather, enough doubts about them have been raised to place them in a "second class" of Pauline Epistles, the antilegomena, to distinguish them from the four great Epistles of the "first class," the homologoumena, whose genuineness has never been seriously questioned. But an "overwhelming probability of actual unauthenticity" applies to a "third class," the so-called Pastoral Epistles, doubts about which were first raised by Schleiermacher.[21] Baur bases his argument on grounds first stated in his *Die sogenannten Pastoralbriefe des Apostels Paulus* (1835), namely, that the heretics mentioned in the Pastorals were Gnostics, probably Marcionites, and therefore that these Epistles must date from a post-Pauline era, around the middle of the second century.[22] He concludes his treatment of the deutero-Pauline Epistles by suggesting that, while we may regret that they are not

17 *Ibid.*, pp. 7–9, 11, 17, 39–40 (E.T., 5–6, 8, 13, 32–33).
18 *Ibid.*, II, 21–25, 39–47 (E.T., 18–21, 35–42).
19 The authenticity of II Thessalonians had already been effectively questioned before Baur's time, and he does not add anything new to the argument. Today, scholars are divided on the question, although all acknowledge the difficulties in regarding it as Pauline.
20 *Paulus*, II, 50–51, 89, 94 (E.T., 45–46, 81, 85).
21 *Ibid.*, I, 276–77 (E.T., 246–47).
22 *Ibid.*, II, 109–10 (E.T., 99–100).

authentic products of the Apostle's spirit, at the same time they are immensely valuable as sources for a period which is of great importance in the history of the development of Christianity and about which we know so little. "It is out of place to speak of any real loss where what belonged to the truth of history from the beginning is merely given back to it."[23]

Antithesis and Reconciliation Between Jewish and Pauline Tendencies in Primitive Christianity

The "moments" or "motifs" into which Baur divides the history of the Christian Church are not primarily functions of chronology but of the different ways in which the idea of the Church is historically defined and realized. Accordingly, the first moment is that of the life and work of its founder, Jesus of Nazareth. The second moment, that represented by the writings of the New Testament canon, is concerned with the establishment of the idea of a Christian Church as a universal principle of salvation against a return to Judaism. This moment, which terminates somewhat past the middle of the second century, partially overlaps chronologically with a third moment, which represents the struggle in the second century between the *historical manifestation* in the catholic Church of the idea thus realized and the notion of Christianity as a *pure* idea or as universal *cosmological* principle, as distinct from a principle of *salvation*. Thus the second and third moments are defined, respectively, by the struggles between Jewish and Pauline Christianity and between the catholic Church on the one hand and Gnosticism and Montanism on the other. Both of these moments are, in turn, encompassed chronologically by a fourth motif in the history of the Church, that in which the primary manifestation of the idea of the Church is found in the form of dogma, i.e., in the formation of a body of Christian thought with its focus on the person of Jesus Christ, a process which begins with the New Testament writings and continues down to the end of the patristic period, with the termination of the papacy of Gregory the Great.[24]

In the New Testament period, the establishment of the idea of the Church as a universal principle of salvation is realized by a process of antithesis and accommodation between Jewish and Pauline elements, a process which reaches its completion when the two chief apostles, Peter and Paul, are reconciled in the tradition and thought of the Church. This accommodation is first openly proclaimed by Irenaeus and then by Tertullian, although it is anticipated much earler and is reflected in some of the New Testament writings.[25] Furthermore, "mediating factors" must lie between these two extremes, "and there is nothing more probable than that the mediation proceeded, not from one side alone but

---

23 *Ibid.*, p. 122 (E.T., 111).
24 See below, pp. 251–56.
25 *Das Christenthum*, pp. 141–42 (E.T., I, 148).

from both, in different ways," since each is more or less aware that they belong together. "Without such a process, the factual result, the emergence of a Christian catholic Church, could never have come to pass. . . ."[26] By means of this process both the institutional forms of the Church and the universal significance of its Gospel are firmly established.[27]

We can see, then, that the second period—that comprising the New Testament writings—consists of three moments: an initial period of antithesis and open conflict, a process of gradual reconciliation, and a period of final accommodation. It is worth noting that this is not exactly the dialectical process of thesis, antithesis, and synthesis which Baur has been accused of imposing on history. To be sure, in the course of this development a synthesis is effected between two initially antithetical interpretations of the meaning of the Christ-event; but the moments of the historical process—conflict, gradual reconciliation, accommodation—do not correspond to a statement of the terms of the dialectic: thesis, antithesis, synthesis. It is worth noting, too, that the process of the second period is not simply repeated in the third; for in the latter it is a question not of accommodation between the catholic Church and Gnosticism but of ultimate victory of the former over the latter (with, however, an appropriation of some of its speculative tools).

The writings of the New Testament are to be understood *historically* in terms of the tendency of the subperiod in which they were written, whether of open conflict, or of partial reconciliation, or of final accommodation. The period of conflict includes only the authentic Pauline Epistles and Revelation. It terminates with the destruction of Jerusalem in A.D. 70, an event which provides the immediate context for the writing of Revelation. The period of reconciliation, by contrast, is the most productive of New Testament literature. It runs from about A.D. 70 through "the first decades of the second century," and includes Hebrews, James, I Peter, the Synoptic Gospels, Acts, and the entire Pauline antilegomena with the exception of the Pastoral Epistles. Baur stresses the difficulty of providing more precise dating for any of these writings, and he does not display the compulsion of some contemporary New Testament scholars to tie everything down with as precise a date as possible. His dating is cautious and conservative: unless there is compelling reason for dating a document early, it is safer to assume that it is not as early as it would like to appear. For example, the period during which the Synoptic Gospels were written can be designated "in general only as the first decades of the second century," although Baur never rules out the possibility that they might have come earlier in the period of reconcilia-

---

26 *Ibid.*, p. 100 (E.T., I, 105).
27 *Ibid.*, pp. 101–109 (E.T., I, 106–114); and *Die Tübinger Schule*, pp. 75–76.

tion, as early perhaps as the last decades of the first century.[28] However, he sees no convincing evidence to this effect.[29] It is worth noting, too, that all three of the Synoptic Gospels are found in the period of gradual reconciliation, and thus display different aspects of the *same* tendency. There is no simple triadic movement from Matthew (thesis) to Luke (antithesis) to Mark (synthesis). Finally, Baur provides no exact chronological termini for the last of the New Testament periods, that of final accommodation. It has its focus around the middle of the second century, and includes the Gospel of John, the Johannine Epistles, the Pastoral Epistles, and II Peter.[30]

The New Testament writings, then, cannot be understood in terms of the dogmatic representations and viewpoint of early Christian literature, which for the most part sought to convey the impression of perfect unity in primitive Christianity.[31] Only when, on the basis of clues first provided in the authentically Pauline Epistles, the actual historical conflicts and developments of this period were discovered, did it become possible to treat the New Testament material both critically and constructively as products of literary-theological tendencies. It is thus clearly evident how Baur's Pauline research was the foundation and support for his subsequent investigation of the Gospels.[32] As Hirsch suggests, Baur was able to write an *interpretive* and *critical* history of this period when its diverse materials had been ordered into this general framework—a framework not imposed on it a priori out of philosophical dialectic but which rather gradually emerged and was clarified from many years of careful study.[33]

We turn now to three further characteristics of the Jewish-Pauline antithesis. The first is that the two tendencies in primitive Christianity have their point of origin and unity in two factors in the person of Jesus, a universal or divinely exalted and a particular or human.

As soon as it is established that, in his person as it appears to us in the Gospel history, those two sides are to be distinguished which are related

[28] Cf. *Das Christenthum*, p. 73 (E.T., I, 77).

[29] Cf. "Rückblick auf die neuesten Untersuchungen über das Markusevangelium," *TJ*, XII:1 (1853), 86.

[30] This periodization of the New Testament writings is based on *Neutestamentliche Theologie*, pp. 38–42; see also the Table of Contents. It represents a considerably more refined treatment of the problem than that found in *Das Christenthum*, Part II, which covers the same ground. There, for example, Luke is considered in the period of antithesis and the Pastorals in the period of reconciliation. This proves that Baur remained flexible and open, sometimes modified his results, and did not force them into rigid patterns.

[31] *Die Tübinger Schule*, p. 77.

[32] Cf. *Kirchengeschichte*, V, 398.

[33] Emanuel Hirsch, *Geschichte der neuern evangelischen Theologie*, V, 528.

to each other as content and form, idea and reality, universally human and Judaistically national, divinely exalted and humanly limited, there can be no doubt that the same antithesis of the two elements, which in our perception of the person of Jesus we must think of as joined together in the personal unity of his self-consciousness, is also the moving principle for the historical development joined to him. This development is to be understood in terms of a series of manifestations in which the original unity [in Jesus] dissolves and falls apart into the whole expanse of the distinction between the two moments, which belong together but are essentially different.[34]

The existence of the two tendencies in primitive Christianity is legitimized by their correspondence to the perfect copresence of the divine and the human, the universal and the particular, in the person of "the true historical Christ," who is "not merely the Jewish but also the Gentile Christ." The tendencies are related as content and form, idea and reality. Jewish Christianity, in placing the emphasis on form, does not, however, completely lose grasp of the content; nor does Paul possess the content of the Gospel of Christ apart from its historical form. Nevertheless, the one-sided emphasis of each is completed by the other in the process of the historical development of the Church, and thus the full historicity of Jesus Christ is faithfully re-enacted.[35] Both tendencies are necessary in the history of Christianity. "If Paulinism, through its mission to the Gentiles, won the basis for catholic Christianity in the great mass of those who came into the primitive community of the sealed (Revelation 6:9) out of all peoples and races, all nations and tongues, so it was Jewish Christianity which erected the hierarchical structure on this foundation with its organizing forms. No matter how heavy an influence Jewish Christianity had, in this respect, on the development of Christianity into the catholic Church, the part due to Paulinism in the history of the development of the Christian Church is by no means foreshortened."[36]

The need of each tendency for the other, and the mutual completion of each in their process of interaction, is a second important characteristic of the antithesis. The life of the Church and its for-

---

[34] *Die Tübinger Schule*, pp. 32–33. This passage can be seen as corroborating the interpretation of Baur's understanding of the person of Christ given above, pp. 110–15. Here two dimensions of the human life of Jesus are delineated—the divinely exalted and the humanly limited. The first refers to Jesus' existence according to the Spirit of God; it is that dimension of Jesus' authentic human spirituality which corresponds to and is a function of the divinely grounded relationship, the idea of reconciliation, by which man is truly spirit. The second dimension refers to Jesus' existence as a particular, empirical man in a specific human community; it is his existence *in* the flesh (but not *according* to the flesh). Baur here insists that these two dimensions are held together in perfect unity in the person of Jesus, and that they can be "perceived" as such.

[35] Cf. *ibid.*, pp. 35–37.

[36] *Ibid.*, p. 76.

ward movement are constituted by the interpenetration of idea and reality.[37] Baur's special interest and preference lies with the Pauline tendency; without it, the purely hierarchical and dogmatic would result in a "wounding of the faith." Paulinism embodies and expresses the *fundamental* thought from which Christianity originally proceeded and which is the *moving* principle of its entire historical development.[38] But at the same time Baur stresses that Paul's lack of interest in structural forms by which the Church could endure through history needed to be supplemented by another tendency.

The third point is that Paul himself did not possess the universality of the Gospel of Christ apart from its historical form, and consequently that Paul was as far from a Gnostic position as he was from that of the Jewish Christians. Baur makes this point clearly in his argument that Colossians, Ephesians, and Philippians are *non*-Pauline precisely because they contain, in his judgment, Gnostic ideas and expressions.[39] He does not believe that Paul himself engaged in controversy against Gnosticism, because "such an early existence of Gnostic conceptions cannot be proved."[40] Had Paul been familiar with Gnosticism, however, there is every reason to believe that he would have opposed it, since the universalism of the Gospel was irrevocably wedded to its positivity in his thought, which accordingly became the backbone of the authentically catholic conception of Christianity in its second-century struggle against the pure idealizing of Christian Gnosticism.[41] Baur acknowledges that in Paul's Christology there are some elements of a view that regards Christ as a universal cosmic principle (one of the characteristics of Christian Gnosticism) rather than as the agent of salvation.[42] But on the other hand he emphatically insists on the authentic humanity of Christ and therefore must be distinguished from every form of Gnostic docetism.[43] For example, Baur distinguishes the "born in the likeness of *men*" of Philippians 2:7, which he regards as Gnostic, from the "in the likeness of *sinful flesh*" of Romans 8:3, which he regards as authentically Pauline.[44]

In light of Baur's recognition of Paul's anti-Gnostic posture, it is relevant at this point to ask whether the adherents of the "Christ party" mentioned in I Corinthians 1:12 as the opponents of Paul in Corinth were in fact Judaizers. Ernst Käsemann sug-

---

[37] *Ibid.*, pp. 75–76.
[38] *Ibid.*, pp. 77–78.
[39] *Paulus*, II, 21–25, 50–59 (E.T., 18–21, 45–53).
[40] *Ibid.*, p. 25 (E.T., 21).
[41] One may recall Baur's claim that Marcion was not an authentic exponent of the Pauline tradition, although he was a fanatical Paulinist. See above, p. 67, n. 112.
[42] *Das Christenthum*, p. 189 (E.T., 198–99).
[43] Cf. *Neutestamentliche Theologie*, pp. 189–91; and above, pp. 110–12.
[44] *Paulus*, II, 58 (E.T., 52).

gests that Baur arrived at this conclusion because he could not have realized, writing as he did before the discovery of the significance of primitive Christian eschatology, that there were spiritualistic as well as Jewish aberrations of the Gospel in the first century, and that therefore, as many scholars now maintain, the "Christ party" was more likely a group of Hellenistic-Jewish enthusiasts led by Apollos, proto-Gnostics who claimed to possess special knowledge and spiritual gifts, rather than Petrine fanatics claiming a direct contact with the Lord himself.[45] This modification is not a rejection of Baur's basic point: that primitive Christianity developed through internal oppositions. Rather it suggests that the oppositions were different and more complex than Baur had recognized: there was not simply a struggle between Paul and Judaizing Christians in the first century; there were Hellenistic spiritualists and Gnostics as well (which means that his dating of Gnosticism would have to be modified). But Baur's basic point would seem to be strengthened rather than diminished by the recognition of greater complexity in this internal development, and he would have been the first to recognize that his reconstruction could be rendered "too simple" by the discovery of fresh data. Furthermore, as we have seen, he would have been amenable to the suggestion that Paul opposed himself to Gnostics or proto-Gnostics as well as to Judaizers.

The Fourth Gospel

In his 1837 article, "Das christliche des Platonismus," Baur gives indication that he uses the Fourth Gospel, with the Synoptics, as a relatively reliable historical source for information about the life of Jesus. The Synoptics are concerned more with the outward side of the appearance of Christ, while John represents his higher nature and immediate divinity. The distinction between these two portrayals is seen as analogous to that between the Xenophonic and the Platonic Socrates, but there is nothing to suggest that one is basically more historically authentic than the other, although an idealizing tendency is as clearly evident in the Johannine Christ as in the Platonic Socrates.[46] But the next year, in a letter to Strauss, Baur remarks that he has recently made the Gospel of John an object of special study in preparation of lectures, and that he has already gained the very decided impression, even from the first chapter, "that historical truth, relatively speaking, can be sought only on the side of the Synoptics."[47] This position is stated publicly for the first time in 1844, after several years of intensive

---

[45] Ernst Käsemann, "Einführung" to Vol. I of F. C. Baur, *Ausgewählte Werke in Einzelausgaben*, pp. ix–xi.

[46] Cf. "Das christliche des Platonismus," *TZT*, X:3, 116, 123–26. At this point Baur still follows Schleiermacher's interpretation of John.

[47] Baur to D. F. Strauss, 29 May 1838 (U.B.T., Md 750, ii, 7, 2).

research, in a monograph in the *Theologische Jahrbücher*, reprinted with minor modifications in 1847 in *Kritische Untersuchungen über die kanonischen Evangelien*. Baur refined and further clarified his position in a series of monographs which continued to the end of his life. The basic point is that the narratives and speeches in the Fourth Gospel are controlled throughout by an idealizing *Weltanschauung* which renders them historically unauthentic; they are all made to serve the basic Johannine thesis of the incarnation of the divine Logos.[48]

In John's Gospel the substance of the person of Christ is not his humanity but his divinity, the Logos of God, with whom he is identified in aboslute fashion.[49] The Logos is the divine principle of life and light, revealed in a world of darkness. The categories for the Johannine dualism have been borrowed from Gnosticism, although it is primarily an ethical rather than a cosmological dualism. The Logos becomes incarnate, to be sure—in this fashion the light of God shines forth in the world of darkness—but the Logos itself is not substantially affected by the incarnation. It remains the absolute subject of the incarnate Lord, never permitting a truly human subject to take its place.[50] The proximity of Johannine Christology to Gnostic docetism is thus readily apparent: "The flesh has no absolute significance for the person of Christ. Its relation to his person is not implicitly necessary and inseparable, from which the conclusion can only be drawn that, according to the representation of our Evangelist, Christ has really divested himself of the earthly husk of his flesh in the moment of his resurrection and ascension to the Father."[51]

Baur is by no means suggesting that the author of the Fourth Gospel was a Gnostic. Although appropriating some of the Gnostic categories and sharing some of its tendencies, in a higher sense this Gospel is a polemic against Gnosticism; it is Gnostic only in so far as the latter can be a "moving element of the general Christian consciousness."[52] As we have seen from his sermons, Baur believes that the focus in the Fourth Gospel is on the historicity of the Logos, on the historical mediation of salvation through the earthly ministry and death of Jesus, and that therefore it is distinct from Christian Gnosticism properly so-called, for which reconciliation remains a pure idea and a universal cosmological principle.[53] In John, Christianity is established as a universal principle of salvation; in this sense the Gospel represents the fruition of the development of the idea of the Church in the New Testament period. By

[48] *Die kanonischen Evangelien*, pp. 238, 292–304.
[49] *Ibid.*, pp. 312–13. See above, pp. 109–110.
[50] *Ibid.*, pp. 88, 93–97, 233.
[51] *Ibid.*, p. 233. Other examples of docetism are found in the "mysterious appearances of Jesus," e.g., John 10:39, 12:36 (see p. 286).
[52] *Ibid.*, pp. 373–74.
[53] See above, p. 110.

virtue of the universality with which it regards the Christian Gospel, it is free from the milieu of party conflict and Jewish particularism. But it does not lose sight of the practical tasks involved in the historical realization of the idea of the catholic Church.[54]

Baur suggests that if the Fourth Gospel is regarded as the product of a highly refined theological position, which employs narratives in a nonhistorical fashion to express its own distinctive conceptions, then it is a contradiction to regard John, the Beloved Disciple, as its author.[55] He believes that the Apostle John was the successor to Paul at Ephesus, that he was the author of the Revelation and subsequently the highest authority for the Church in Asia Minor. The Evangelist, on the other hand, could not have written before the middle of the second century, because of the Gnostic influence in his work and its freedom from party conflict. Yet he conceived himself as an heir of the tradition founded by the Apostle John, which he sought to preserve and to spiritualize in his Gospel.[56]

The Synoptic Problem

The determination of the historical unauthenticity of the Fourth Gospel is the clue to the relative historical credibility of the Synoptic Gospels. As Baur puts it, "In the same proportion in which the historical value of John sinks, that of the Synoptics rises."[57] This judgment puts an end to Strauss's tactic of showing contradictions between the Fourth Gospel and the Synoptics in order to question the historical authenticity of both.[58] It is therefore clear why and how Baur was able to turn to the Synoptic problem with a fresh perspective only after he had settled the Johannine question.[59]

54 *Das Christenthum*, pp. 172–73 (E.T., I, 180–81).

55 Heinrich Ewald's attempt to combine the unhistorical character of the stories in the Gospel with the apostolic authorship prompts this remark by Baur in *Die Tübinger Schule*, p. 166. The "critical dilemma" in the Johannine question is that one must hold either to its historical unauthenticity and later authorship, or to its historical authenticity and apostolic authorship, but not to a combination.

56 *Das Christenthum*, pp. 146–48 (E.T., I, 153–55).

57 *Kirchengeschichte*, V, 397.

58 *Ibid.*, p. 397.

59 Cf. *Die kanonischen Evangelien*, p. 617; and *Das Christenthum*, p. 24 (E.T., I, 25). Cf. also Hirsch, *op. cit.*, V, 531, 534–36; and Otto Pfleiderer, *The Development of Theology in Germany*, p. 231. Baur adds in *Die Tübinger Schule*, p. 33, that the presupposition of an absolutely miraculous beginning to Christianity and of the identity of the Johannine Logos with the Synoptic Jesus excludes the proper viewpoint for the comprehension of primitive Christianity: "The question whether the origin of Christianity is to be comprehended purely historically or as miracle is in fact wholly identical with the critical question concerning the relation of the Johannine Gospel to the Synoptics; and it is therefore chiefly to be attributed to the one-sided preference which Schleiermacher's theology awakened and disseminated for the Johannine Gospel that the response to that question still has to struggle with such a great prejudice."

Once the Gospel of John has been eliminated as an historical source, the question concerning the relation of the Synoptic Gospels to each other and to the historical facts which they present and interpret focuses on the position of Mark with respect to Matthew and Luke. In addressing ourselves to this question, we must first recall that Baur rejects the theory of a Proto-Gospel, used independently by all three of the Evangelists, on the grounds that it is a purely literary invention, sustained by no defensible external evidence.[60] Furthermore, without the prior assumption of a Proto-Gospel, Markan priority would never have been seriously proposed in New Testament scholarship. Since Mark would be closest to the hypothetical contents of a Proto-Gospel, the latter being identified with material common to all three Gospels, the existence of such a Gospel would lead to the presumption of an early date for Mark.[61] As we have seen, Baur follows Griesbach in defending the literary interdependence of the three Gospels and the dependence of Mark on Luke and Matthew; but he does not believe that the question of the order of the Gospels can be settled by a purely literary consideration of the phenomena of agreement and disagreement between them. On this basis alone, it can be argued equally well that Mark is the earliest or the latest of the Synoptic Gospels.[62] What is needed, in addition to comparative literary analysis, is a study of the theological tendencies of the Gospels in order to determine the fundamental characteristics of each and the approximate milieu and context in which each was composed. These two methods are interdependent. The peculiar characteristics of each Gospel must be investigated in order to obtain the criteria for determining the relationships between them. But at the same time, these peculiarities cannot be established without comparing the Gospels with each other.[63]

These two types of analysis are applied to Mark in *Die kanonischen Evangelien* and more extensively in *Das Markusevangelium nach seinem Ursprung und Charakter* (1851). In the latter work, on the basis of an extensive redactional analysis of the contents of Mark,[64] Baur concludes that this work reveals a double dependence on Matthew and Luke. It is primarily dependent on Matthew and varies only occasionally from the Matthean order. By comparison with Matthew and Luke, it can be seen that Mark's basic tendency is "to round off the Gospel story into a harmoniously ordered, clearly arranged whole." This helps to explain the author's eclectic procedure: he excludes anything which is abnormal, repetitious, or

---

[60] See above, pp. 154–56.

[61] Cf. William R. Farmer, *The Synoptic Problem*, pp. 11–14, 40–41, 43.

[62] See above, p. 156; and *Die kanonischen Evangelien*, pp. 36, 68–71.

[63] Cf. "Rückblick auf die neuesten Untersuchungen über das Markusevangelium," *TJ*, XII:1, 91–92.

[64] *Das Markusevangelium nach seinem Ursprung und Charakter. Nebst einem Anhang über das Evangelium Marcion's* (Tübingen: L. F. Fues, 1851), pp. 4–110.

adventitious, as well as most of the teaching material, especially the parables; his fundamental idea is to present "the objective facts of the Gospel story," freed from the special interests of Matthew and Luke. Evidence that he is a purely secondary writer can be seen by the fact that whenever he expands his given sources, he clearly does so from his own imagination, providing the narratives with color and detail and the apparent vividness of an eyewitness account. Although he is not guided by any special dogmatic interests, the author intends to give his Gospel the appearance of an original document, of equal if not greater importance than the other two. In this respect, Baur comments, he was remarkably successful, if one is to judge from the great variety of critical opinion respecting the relation of the Gospels to each other. Baur concludes that Mark was written by an unknown author sometime after the completion of Matthew and Luke, probably during or just after the first half of the second century. He rejects the theory of a Proto-Mark as well as the Papias tradition concerning Mark; nor is there any evidence of favoritism toward the Apostle Peter in this work.[65]

With respect to Luke, Baur's basic thesis is that an original form of the Gospel, no longer extant, was written in Greek by a Paulinist sometime after the completion of Matthew, which he deliberately revised in order to soften its Judaizing tendency, before Marcion's edition of the Gospel. Thus the *terminus ad quem* for the original Gospel would be about A.D. 139, the earliest date usually given for the Marcionite edition of Luke. The *terminus a quo* would depend on the date established for Matthew, which we shall discuss shortly. The only indication given by Baur is that it must have been later than A.D. 70, because of its reference to the destruction of Jerusalem.[66] With respect to Marcion, there is no evidence to sustain the "mutilation hypothesis," according to which he deliberately expurgated canonical Luke in order to bring it into line with his anti-Jewish and docetic tendencies. Rather he worked with an original form of the Gospel, which he modified in ways characteristic of the development of the Synoptic tradition as a whole. For just this reason the hypothesis of a Proto-Luke is required. In some instances Marcion preserved the original more faithfully than canonical Luke. The latter was the product of an editor who worked sometime shortly after Marcion's Gospel and just after the middle of the second century. On the one hand, he attempted to correct the Marcionite interpretation of the Gospel, and hence there is an anti-Gnostic polemic in canonical Luke.

---

[65] *Ibid.*, pp. 138–52. These conclusions are defended two years later in a thorough analysis of Hilgenfeld's thesis that the proper order of the Gospels is Matthew—Mark—Luke, and Ritschl's, that the order is Mark—Matthew—Luke. Cf. "Rückblick auf die neuesten Untersuchungen über das Markusevangelium," *TJ*, XII:1 (1853), 54–93.

[66] Cf. *Das Christenthum*, p. 73 (E.T., I, 77).

On the other hand, he attempted to mediate between the Paulinism of the original author and the Judaizing spirit of Matthew. He worked in an irenic spirit; he was especially responsible for introducing the birth and infancy narratives (not found in the original), which bring Jesus into line with Old Testament expectations of the Messiah; and he restored some of Jesus' teaching concerning the validity of the law as found in Matthew. The Prologue to the Gospel shows that he was working at a late stage in the development of the Synoptic tradition; and he had access to some sources of that tradition independently of Matthew (e.g., Lk. 1–2, 13:1–9, 15:11–32).[67]

The "Historical Character" of Matthew

The quest for "a firm historical basis" for the Gospel story has led successively, says Baur, from John through Mark and Luke. "If, in the series of our canonical Gospels, there is a Gospel in which we have before us the substantial content of the Gospel story in an original, authentically historical source, it can only be the Gospel of Matthew."[68] He believes that this possibility is indeed sustained by critical research.

In order to appreciate Baur's solution of the Matthean problem, we must call to mind certain factors. On the one hand, he found no evidence for the existence of a Proto-Gospel, used independently as a common source by all three Evangelists. Luke and Mark were rather dependent on Matthew. On the other hand, it had been clearly demonstrated by Sieffert, Strauss, and others that canonical Matthew must have been written after the eyewitness period. Finally, Baur knew nothing of the possibility of an oral transmission of the primitive traditions and in any case possessed no critical tools by which to analyze oral forms. Where, then, was there a reliable point of contact with the historical foundations of Christianity?

Baur finds this point of contact in the ancient witness of Papias and Hegesippus[69] to a Gospel of the Hebrews, i.e., a Gospel intended primarily for use by the Palestinian Jewish Christians, the "Hebrews." This same Gospel is also referred to as the Gospel of Peter or the Gospel of the Apostles by Justin Martyr and the Pseudo-Clementine Homilies. At the same time, both Papias and St. Jerome indicate that this Gospel was written by the Apostle Matthew. Baur finds no compelling reason to deny that the Hebrew Gospel was written by Matthew, although it is surprising in this case that it would be referred to by other names in the ancient tradition. This Gospel was at an early date translated into Greek, as Papias also indicates. This translation went through various recensions

[67] Cf. *Die kanonischen Evangelien*, pp. 424–523; cf. also *Das Christenthum*, pp. 73–77 (E.T., I, 77–82).
[68] *Die kanonischen Evangelien*, p. 571.
[69] Eusebius, *Historia Ecclesiastica*, III, 39; IV, 22.

and modifications, until finally it was given its present form by an unknown author writing in Greek sometime in the second century. It can clearly be shown that canonical Matthew is not identical with the Hebrew Gospel: doubts of this nature were already raised by St. Jerome; citations from "Matthew" in the Pseudo-Clementine Homilies and Justin Martyr differ significantly from our Matthew; some of the citations from the Old Testament in canonical Matthew are drawn from the Septuagint, others, with a messianic reference, are translated directly from the Hebrew text; there are theological inconsistencies in our Matthew which indicate a composite origin. However, it is not simply to be assumed that the more universal, less legalistic elements in the teaching of Jesus are introduced by the later author, if the Hebrew Gospel is indeed "the oldest documentary source for our knowledge of the teaching of Jesus"; these more universal elements are found in the teaching of Jesus itself and are faithfully preserved in the earliest source. The Hebrew Gospel is essentially a collection of *logia* (sayings) of Jesus, as Papias indicates, while canonical Matthew includes a great deal more narrative material, derived presumably from other sources.[70]

In his New Testament lectures, Baur indicates that the date for the Synoptic Gospels can be given "only as the first decades of the second century."[71] However, in *Die kanonischen Evangelien,* he hazards a more specific date for the final composition of canonical Matthew. The clue is found in the little apocalypse of Matthew 24. Baur claims that the details of this chapter refer not to the destruction of Jerusalem in A.D. 70 but to the Jewish rebellion which broke out in A.D. 132 under the leadership of the Messiah-prophet Bar-Kokhba (Simon ben Kosibah). Specifically, the warning against "false Christs" (24:5, 24) refers to the messianic claims of Bar-Kokhba; the reference to continuous war and the persecution of Christians (24:6-9) suggests the persecutions suffered under both Bar-Kokhba and the Emperor Hadrian upon his conquest of Jerusalem; and, most striking, "the desolating sacrilege . . . standing in the holy place" (24:15), refers to the temple to Jupiter erected by Hadrian upon the ruins of Herod's temple in Jerusalem. Hence the years 130-134 can be designated as the period for the final composition of Matthew, followed shortly by the original version of Luke.[72]

70 *Die kanonischen Evangelien*, pp. 571-82.

71 *Neutestamentliche Theologie*, p. 42.

72 *Die kanonischen Evangelien*, pp. 605-609. Luke, on the other hand, makes his version of the apocalypse refer to the destruction of Jerusalem in 70. *Ibid.*, p. 608. Further evidence of this date for canonical Matthew is to be seen in the fact that Papias, whose "Expositions" was written about A.D. 140, does not yet have much respect for the Greek version of Matthew, whereas by the time of the Easter Controversy (A.D. 154-67), its authority is clearly established. *Ibid.*, p. 582. Cf. also *Neutestamentliche Theologie*, p. 109.

With this sort of foundation, it is not implausible to suggest that canonical Matthew preserves the traditions about Jesus' teaching and ministry in relatively credible fashion. Baur argues that the chronological framework of the ministry is authentic, although many of the details within the framework are not. Furthermore, the contents of the sayings and teachings of Jesus in Matthew are for the most part authentic; but the form in which the speeches are presented—the five great discourses—reflects the special intention and viewpoint of the Evangelist (i.e., the author of canonical Matthew), who handles the material in this respect with the freedom of literary prerogative. This is especially the case, as we have seen, with the last of the discourses, the little apocalypse of Matthew 24. Finally, the stories of Jesus' birth, baptism, and temptation are not authentic, having been introduced into the Gospel at a later date, nor are the miracle stories, which point to the presence of certain more or less mythical elements in the Gospel.[73]

Despite its generally historical character, canonical Matthew is not an eyewitness account[74] and reflects a theological tendency, like the other Gospels; thus there can be no question of its *absolute* credibility. "Even this Gospel is already a secondary report, whose relation to the objective facts can be only approximately determined."[75]

We cannot regard the Gospel of Matthew as a purely historical account of the original facts of the Gospel story. It has, likewise, a definite, individual, literary character. In its distinction from the other Gospels, one can call it only the most Judaizing of the Gospels, as is already shown by its peculiar pragmatism. If the free, literary composition which is not to be denied even here is based on a definite principle, an interest guiding the author by preference, it is the striving to understand the Gospel story from the viewpoint of the Old Testament idea of the Messiah and to prove its actualization in the person of Jesus, to prove the identity of the Messiah who has appeared with the prophetically envisioned Messiah, according to definite criteria.[76]

Marks of this Judaizing tendency are found, not only in Matthew's proofs from prophecy, but also in expressions concerning the eternal significance of the Mosaic law, in Jesus' words of 15:24 ("I was sent to the lost sheep of the house of Israel and to them alone"), in his self-references as the Son of David, in the establish-

---

[73] *Die kanonischen Evangelien*, pp. 600–605. This material is from the last section in Baur's discussion of Matthew, entitled, "Historical Character."
[74] Baur summarizes the arguments against its eyewitness character, as developed by Schleiermacher, Sieffert, Schneckenburger, Strauss, and others, *ibid.*, pp. 617–18.
[75] *Ibid.*, p. 621; cf. also pp. 619–20.
[76] *Ibid.*, pp. 606–609.

ment of the Davidic descent of Jesus in the first two chapters, and in a general predilection for the Old Testament.[77]

This Judaizing tendency, however, is not necessarily a mark of the Gospel's historical unauthenticity; rather, it reflects Christianity's immanent origin out of Judaism. Nothing is more important for the original character of Christianity than Jesus' claim in the Sermon on the Mount that he had come not to abolish but to fulfill the law and the prophets. That Matthew presents Jesus as saying this is a clue to its precise place in the history of Christianity—a place very close to the religious consciousness of Jesus himself. For Jesus' teaching calls for the fulfillment and transcendence of Judaism, the fulfillment of the law in the true surrender to God, which marks the authentically moral quality of the divine-human relation. Jesus himself marks the juncture and transition between Judaism and Christianity; Matthew is relatively the most credible of our Gospels because it stands closest to that juncture, by virtue of its relation to the Hebrew Gospel. The Sermon on the Mount is an authentic expression of the kernel of the messianic significance of Jesus.[78]

Baur isolated, then, through the process of historical criticism retraced in the preceding pages (a process which took some twenty-two years, 1831–53, to complete), that stratum of New Testament literature which probably stands nearest to the original consciousness of Jesus himself. But what we have is still a writing, not the immediate words and actions of Jesus. We are able to penetrate through the writing to its content by focusing at those points in the writing where it permits material to stand that is not entirely congruent with its tendency. Matthew, the most Jewish of the Gospels, reports that Jesus claimed that he had come to *fulfill* the law—in a way quite unanticipated by the law itself, that the kingdom of God is not a theocratic institution, that righteousness is a gift of God mediated by the One sent from God, not the result of obedience to the law. Precisely at this juncture, where the radical originality and universality of the teaching of Jesus is found in Matthew and its source, the Hebrew Gospel, do we encounter the authentic content of that teaching.[79]

---

[77] *Ibid.*, pp. 609–611.
[78] *Ibid.*, pp. 613–15.
[79] See above, pp. 198–99. I am not competent to judge whether in its broad outlines Baur's solution of the Synoptic Problem is right or wrong. However, I find his arguments for the priority of Matthew and the literary interdependence of the Gospels intriguing and am convinced that the alternative—the priority of Mark and the two-document hypothesis—has never really been proved. There is, of course, much that is dated in his approach to the problem. Most important is the fact that form criticism has now provided a means of critically elucidating the period of oral transmission of the Gospel traditions and thus eliminates the need for Baur's theory of a literary rather than an oral transmission of the traditions and his hypothesis of a Hebrew Gospel. But by replacing the weakest link in Baur's approach to the Gospels, form criticism would seem to substantiate that

THE HISTORICAL JESUS AND THE FOUNDATION OF CHRISTIANITY[80]

The Founder of Christianity

If it is not to be regarded as an absolute miracle, then the origin of Christianity must be understood in its historical context. "If it lies in the religious interest to hold fast to the peculiar content of Christianity, to set Christianity as the one true, absolute religion in absolute opposition to everything non-Christian, then on the other hand science must not surrender the right to consider Christianity in its historical point of origin not merely as a manifestation secluded and isolated in itself, negatively related to its entire historical environment, called into existence only through a miracle."[81] Consequently, Baur devotes the first twenty-two pages of *Das Christenthum* to a discussion of the relation of Christianity to the Roman Empire, to Greek philosophy, and to Judaism. It shares the universalism of the Empire, the sense of moral consciousness of pagan philosophy, and the monotheism of the Jewish belief in God.[82] Baur stresses the latter connection especially against any form of Marcionite dualism: "Christianity itself emerged from Jewish soil, and it stands in a much closer and more immediate relationship to Judaism" than to Greek philosophy. "In its consciousness of God, Christianity knows itself above all one with Judaism. The God of the Old Testament is also the God of the New, and everything taught by the Old Testament with respect to the essential distinction of God from the world, and the absolute majesty and holiness of his nature, is also an essential part of Christian doctrine."[83] Baur suggests that Christianity emerges at the point where these various anticipatory factors converge, producing an environment which renders historically plausible the appear-

---

approach as a whole and thus render unnecessary the theory of a Proto-Gospel and its later modification, the two-document hypothesis. Finally, I see no convincing reasons for dating the Gospels as late as Baur does. But he himself makes it clear that all dates are hypothetical and that the Gospels could have fallen anywhere in the period between A.D. 70 and 150. As he reads the evidence, it points to the latter portion of this period.

[80] For the relation of this section to the discussion of Baur's dogmatic Christology in chap. III, see above, pp. 100–101.

[81] "Das christliche des Platonismus," *TZT*, X:3, 1–2. Cf. also *Die Tübinger Schule*, pp. 13–14: "Christianity is once and for all an historical manifestation; as such it must allow itself to be historically considered and investigated. It appears in an historical context which it can in no way deny, which only dualists and docetists, like Marcion, can boldly tear apart in the most powerful fashion. Therefore, how can one know what it is, how it originates and enters into the world, if one does not also return to the historical relationships in which it has appeared, the ways in which it was introduced and prepared, and the causes which worked together in its emergence, and if one does not seek to clarify the origin and nature of Christianity from all these elements together . . . ?"

[82] Cf. *Das Christenthum*, pp. 1–22 (E.T., I, 1–23).

[83] *Ibid.*, pp. 16–17 (E.T., I, 17–18).

ance of Christianity at a specific point in space and time.[84]

But by no means is the origin of Christianity to be explained simply in terms of its historical context.

The question arises as to whether what has been said is valid for Christianity in its entire extent, or only for one specific side of it, and whether it applies directly to that which we must consider as the true kernel and substantial mid-point of Christianity. When one considers Christianity from the viewpoint previously discussed, then it is self-evident that one has in mind above all those aspects where all those points of contact are to be found which bring it into such a close and inner relation to the entire preceding history of the development of humanity. However, does this aspect of Christianity consist of its original and substantial essence, or rather merely of what is secondary and subordinate? Can one speak actually of the essence and content of Christianity without making the person of its founder above all the major object of consideration, *and without recognizing the peculiar character of Christianity as consisting in the fact that it is everything it is solely through the person of its founder?* If this is the case, it is of no importance to understand Christianity, with respect to its essence and content, from the viewpoint of its world-historical connections. For its entire significance is so conditioned through the personality of its founder that historical consideration can start only from this point.[85]

"These questions," Baur suggests, "lead us back to the sources of the Gospel history and to the distinction which the most recent critical investigations have made among them."[86] We are led primarily, that is, to the Gospel of Matthew, where, on the basis of critical study, we can indeed affirm that Jesus is the founder, and thus the "original and substantial essence," of Christianity, as the Church has claimed in faith.

Many of Baur's contemporary critics—Uhlhorn, Hase, Ritschl—asserted that he was never willing or able to make this affirmation. In response to these criticisms, Baur writes: "Where have I ever maintained that Christianity did not have its origin with the appearance of Jesus of Nazareth? Where have I ever proposed that Socrates, the Alexandrines, or the Essenes are the authors of Christianity, or that its origin is only to be dated for the first time from Paul or the author of the Fourth Gospel?"[87] For example, in his lectures on New Testament theology, he writes: "The teaching of Jesus is the principle to which everything else which constitutes the peculiar content of New Testament theology is related in derived and secondary fashion. It is the foundation and presupposition of

---

[84] Cf. *ibid.*, pp. 21–22 (E.T., I, 22–23).

[85] *Das Christenthum*, pp. 22–23 (E.T., I, 23–24). Italics mine. Cf. Hirsch, *op. cit.*, V, 544; and above, p. 100.

[86] *Das Christenthum*, p. 23 (E.T., I, 24).

[87] *Die Tübinger Schule*, pp. 12–13.

everything that belongs in the history of the development of the Christian consciousness. Just for this reason it is that which lies beyond all temporal development, that which precedes it, that which is immediate and original. . . ."[88] Baur suggests that what his critics really have in mind is that he does not permit the beginning of Christianity to be understood as an absolute miracle. But at the same time he by no means denies that Jesus of Nazareth is that beginning.[89] As is the case with other historical manifestations, there is both continuity and discontinuity in the origin of Christianity. Because of the radical and definitive significance of Jesus for the emergence of the Christian consciousness, Baur stresses the discontinuity more strongly than the continuity, but never to the point where Jesus and the origins of Christianity step out of the continuity of history entirely.

Jesus' work as founder consists primarily of the originality and radicalism of his teaching—that teaching which is the foundation and presupposition of the entire subsequent development of the Christian consciousness. This is his unique and essential role in the redemption of humanity. At the same time, this work is integrally related to his person, which, by virtue of the intensity and original-ity of his God-manhood, exemplifies and actualizes the content of his teaching: "The substance of the historical significance of the life of Jesus as it confronts us in the Gospel story is the conscious-ness of the idea of Christianity and its principle which Jesus first expressed and manifested through the devotion of his entire per-sonality."[90] His indirect awareness of the significance of his person can be seen in the way he modifies and appropriates the Jewish messianic expectations. These two factors—his teaching and his enactment of the messianic destiny—are both marks of the "glory" of his authentic manhood.[91] They are mentioned in *Die Tübinger Schule* as the two chief factors in the historical-critical investiga-tion of the life of Jesus.[92] We turn our attention to them in the next two sections.[93]

[88] *Neutestamentliche Theologie*, p. 45. Cf. also "Das christliche des Platon-ismus," *TZT*, X:3, 90.

[89] Cf. *Die Tübinger Schule*, pp. 13–16.

[90] *Paulus*, I, 5 (E.T., 3).

[91] Cf. the discussion in chap. III of Baur's dogmatic Christology, especially pp. 107–115.

[92] *Die Tübinger Schule*, pp. 30–32. Cf. also Hirsch, *op. cit.*, V, 544.

[93] In *Das Christenthum*, Baur devotes primary emphasis to the teaching of Jesus, while in *Vorlesungen über neutestamentliche Theologie* the greater emphasis is on Jesus' conception of his person. It seems clear that during the last two years or so of his life Baur became increasingly interested in Jesus' messianic self-awareness, as evidenced, for example, by his article, "Die Bedeutung des Ausdrucks: *ho huios tou anthrōpou*," *ZWT*, III:3 (1860), 274–92. In the discussion which follows, we shall rely on both *Das Chris-tenthum* and the *Vorlesungen* for the teaching of Jesus and primarily on the latter for his messianic consciousness.

The Teaching of Jesus: Its Originality and Radicalism

The radically original and underived element in Jesus' teaching can be summarized as follows: it is the expression of a religious consciousness penetrated by the deepest sense of both the antithesis and the unity between earth and heaven; it demands a radical moral inwardness, obedience, and universality of intention; and it calls for an absolute relation to God, corresponding to the righteousness of God, as the foundation of the religious consciousness. In each of these respects Jesus transcends his environmental context —especially that of Judaism—in a radical and unexpected way. His teaching might be summarized as the spiritualizing, inwardizing, universalizing, and radicalizing of the idea of the kingdom of heaven.

In the first place, Baur suggests that Jesus' religious consciousness, as evidenced from its clearest expression in the Matthean account of the Sermon on the Mount and especially the Beatitudes, is penetrated by the deepest sense of both antithesis and unity between earth and heaven, finite and infinite, present and future, time and eternity, visible and invisible, humiliation and exaltation, sin and grace, poverty and riches, need and fulfillment. The Beatitudes all express in different ways the idea that lies at the foundation of the Christian consciousness: the awareness of the anxiety, estrangement, sinfulness, and incompleteness of this present, finite existence, and the striving for a new, perfect, reconciled, and enduring relation with God.[94] This new relationship is described in the parables of Jesus, especially as they are contained in Matthew, as the kingdom of heaven or the kingdom of God. In his teaching, the kingdom has been freed from the theocratic and nationalistic expectations of Judaism. It consists rather of the perfect manifestation and realization of the will of God. The extent to which the will of God is fulfilled on earth marks also the actualization of the kingdom on earth. It is not, however, an imminent, this-worldly reality, progressively unfolding in history; it rather consists of a qualitatively different mode of relationship—a fundamentally moral relationship—between God and man, which stands in absolute contrast to everything earthly and temporal and can be established only through repentance and the forgiveness of sins. At the same time, the kingdom is not merely an eternal or heavenly reality; it represents the fulfillment of all authentic earthly longings and strivings.[95]

The second element in Jesus' teaching is its emphasis on a *radical* moral inwardness, obedience, and universality of intention.

---

[94] Cf. *Das Christenthum*, pp. 26–27 (E.T., I, 27–29); and *Neutestamentliche Theologie*, pp. 63–64. Also, see above, pp. 114–15.

[95] *Neutestamentliche Theologie*, pp. 69–75. Cf. also *Das Christenthum*, pp. 33–34.

The original and fundamental element of Christianity is set forth in the form of the absolute moral "ought" in the . . . Sermon on the Mount, where Jesus insists emphatically on the purity and sincerity of intention, on a morality which consists not merely in the outward act but in the inner intention. . . . The question is asked, nevertheless, how far Christianity here establishes a new principle. If Jesus himself came forth with the declaration that he had come not to abolish but to fulfill the law and the prophets, then he appears to have set himself in a purely affirmative relationship to the Old Testament, and one can say[96] that the entire distinction between the teaching of Jesus and the law of the Old Testament is to be regarded only as quantitative, not qualitative. . . . But when we consider what is said to be the fulfilling of the law in each separate instance, . . . we cannot but recognize in this a new principle, essentially different from the Mosaic law. What the law contained only implicitly is now explicitly made the major factor and expressed as the principle of morality. The quantitative expansion of the law amounts to a qualitative difference. The inner is opposed to the outer, the intention to the act, the letter to the spirit. This is the essential, fundamental principle of Christianity; and in its insistence on the intention as the sole factor wherein the absolute moral value of man consists, it is an essentially new principle.[97]

Not only does Jesus' teaching call for a radical inwardness and obedience in the intentionality of human behavior but also for a universality of action in which the individual ego is transcended and action is directed from and toward "the universal ego, the ego of humanity as a whole, identical with itself in all separate individuals."[98] Finally, the element of moral freedom, autonomy, and self-determination is stressed in the ethics of Jesus. It is only as a free, moral agent that man encounters God; the moral self is the essential locus of the religious relationship. In this sense, Christianity is a "purely moral religion."[99]

The similarity of Bultmann's description of Jesus' ethic of radical obedience in *Jesus and the Word* and elsewhere with this exegesis of the Matthean texts and especially of the Sermon on the Mount is perhaps not accidental—not in the sense that there is any direct dependence of Bultmann on Baur, but that both discovered, historically-critically, the original teaching of Jesus precisely in its transcendence of the ethics of Jewish legalism. Nor

[96] Baur here refers to Ritschl's *Die Entstehung der altkatholischen Kirche* (1st ed.; Bonn: Adolph Marcus, 1850), pp. 27 ff. He notes that Ritschl changed his views in the second edition (1857), but that this fact does not invalidate the accuracy of his description of this position as one which has been and may be held.

[97] *Das Christenthum*, pp. 28–29 (E.T., I, 29–30). Cf. also the discussion of the relation of Jesus to the Old Testament and the law in *Neutestamentliche Theologie*, pp. 46–60.

[98] *Das Christenthum*, p. 31 (E.T., I, 33).

[99] *Ibid.*, p. 35 (E.T., I, 37); and *Neutestamentliche Theologie*, p. 64.

is it accidental that their respective descriptions of this original element suggest the language of Kantian morality, for in different ways the ethical categories and conceptions with which both Baur and Bultmann are operating derive ultimately from Kant. As Kantians they are both deontologists. This is not to suggest that they have imposed a Kantian ethics on the teaching of Jesus but that they have interpreted his teaching through a Kantian filter. (It is of course undoubtedly also true that Kant's ethics was informed by his reading of the Gospels.) Baur acknowledges this dependence by suggesting that Jesus' ethics "is a formal principle of action which in its essentials coincides with the Kantian imperative: so act that the maxim of your action can be the universal law of action."[100]

With respect to the original and seminal quality of this element in the teaching of Jesus, as the only authentic source and norm for later dogmatic development, Baur writes:

This moral element, as it is made known in the simplest tenets of the Sermon on the Mount as the purest and clearest content of the teaching of Jesus, is the proper, substantial kernel of Christianity, to which everything else, no matter how great a significance it may have, stands in a more or less secondary and contingent relationship. It is the foundation on which for the first time everything else can be built. No matter how little it yet has the form and color of historically developed Christianity, it is still in itself already the whole of Christianity. . . . It remains the firm, unchanging point to which one must always return from all errors in dogma and life; it is that wherein the true Christian consciousness expresses itself in its most immediate originality and in its simplest truth, infinitely elevated above all the self-deceptions of dogmatism.[101]

This explains why, although the locus of religious faith is the free moral self, such faith must at the same time have its concrete source and content in the teaching of Jesus.

The second of the original elements in the teaching of Jesus is primarily ethical in character, while the first is both ethical and religious. The third, however—the call to righteousness—is purely religious, since it is fundamentally concerned with the relationship of man to God. "Dikaiosunē stands in the most immediate connection to the basileia tou theou. It concerns not merely the relationship of man to himself, as is the case in the moral self-consciousness, but the relationship of man to God, without which there is no religious consciousness. It is essentially identical with that perfection in which the highest task for man is set forth in the

---

100 Neutestamentliche Theologie, pp. 61–62. At the same time, we should recall Baur's criticism of the abstractness of Kant's Christology; see above pp. 42–43.

101 Ibid., pp. 64–65; cf. also Das Christenthum, p. 35 (E.T., I, 37).

demand to be perfect as the Father in heaven is perfect."[102] "In this demand, the absoluteness of the Christian principle is most immediately expressed."[103]

But how is the demand for righteousnes in the relationship to God to be satisfied? This raises again the question of the relation of Jesus to the law. According to the Old Testament, righteousness consists in the fulfillment of the law; without righteousness one cannot enter into the kingdom of God. Christianity is not the denial "but the immanent perfection, the complete actualization, of the Old Covenant." For it overcomes, through a perfect realization and internalization of the law, the state of separation between the individual and God which always rendered the subjective possibility of righteousness impossible under the Old Covenant. The separation between God and man is overcome and the law is perfectly realized by means of the "power of redemption and reconciliation which has come through Jesus." This is never explicitly expressed as such in the teaching of Jesus, but it is implied in the promise of satisfaction for those who hunger and thirst after righteousness (Matt. 5:6) and of rest for those who labor and are heavy-laden (Matt. 11:28–30), as well as in the parables of the kingdom. Paul simply made explicit in a general principle of Christian consciousness what already was implicit in the teaching of Jesus. Jesus' teaching was still expressed in the language and concepts of the Old Testament. But its content was radically different. Paul found a new vocabulary to express the new content—that the relationship of righteousness between God and man is established through the perfect righteousness of the One sent from God. "Paulinism did nothing other than to express for consciousness what was established, implicitly and factually, in original Christianity" (i.e., in the teaching of Jesus).[104]

This last point has already raised the question of the relation of the person of Jesus to his message. In Matthew, according to Baur, and also in the teaching of Jesus, his person is not the object of direct attention. But on the other hand, his person is inextricably related to his message: "It is not so much the person which gives the discourse [the Sermon on the Mount] its significance as it is much more the momentous content of the discourse which allows the person itself first to appear in its true light."[105] In addition, apart from their relation to his person, Jesus' words would have

---

[102] *Neutestamentliche Theologie*, p. 65.

[103] *Das Christenthum*, p. 32 (E.T., I, 33).

[104] *Neutestamentliche Theologie*, pp. 65–69. The equation between "original Christianity" (*das Urchristenthum*) and "the teaching of Jesus" is specifically stated in the long paragraph on which the above material is based. Also, see above, p. 113.

[105] *Das Christenthum*, p. 25 (E.T., I, 26–27). Cf. also *Die kanonischen Evangelien*, p. 614.

lost their special meaning and significance for the redemption of humanity:

> . . . what would Christianity have been, and what would have come of it, had it been nothing more than a doctrine of religion and morality in the previously discussed sense? Even though it were, as such, the substance of the purest and most immediate truths that have been expressed by the moral-religious consciousness, . . . a form still was lacking for the concrete formation of the religious life. . . . When one considers the course of development of Christianity, it is still only the person of its founder on which its entire historical significance depends. How soon everything that Christianity taught as true and full of significance would have been put back merely among the series of expressions of noble friends of humanity and philosophic sages of antiquity, which long since have died away, had not its teaching become words of eternal life in the mouth of its founder?[106]

This connection, and Jesus' own awareness of it, is required by the very nature of his message. As Hirsch puts it, according to Baur "the proclamation of Jesus is unthinkable without a consciousness of his personal mission."[107] This consciousness becomes the subject of the next section.

The Person of Jesus: His Messianic Self-Consciousness

In the passage quoted above, we find Baur arguing that "a form still was lacking for the concrete formation of the religious life." This form was provided by the messianic idea, "with which the person of Jesus was so identified that men perceived in him the fulfillment of the ancient promise, the Messiah who appeared for the salvation of the people. . . . Through the messianic idea, the spiritual content of Christianity obtained for the first time the concrete form by means of which it could enter on the path of its historical development. . . ."[108]

The important question—the "most difficult" in New Testament theology[109]—is whether the association of the messianic idea with the person of Jesus derives from the post-Easter faith of the earliest Christians, or in some sense from Jesus himself (and, if the latter, whether Jesus employs the idea in a different form from that of Jewish eschatology). In answer to this question, we must turn to the Synoptic Gospels, above all to Matthew, rather than to John, where the self-references of Jesus are clearly the product of the author's theological imagination. But even in the Synoptic Gospels the allegedly self-designating expressions of Jesus are so intertwined with factual and theological assertions about him on the part of the Evangelists that it is difficult to separate

---

106 *Das Christenthum*, pp. 35–36 (E.T., I, 37–38).
107 Hirsch, *op. cit.*, V, 547.
108 *Das Christenthum*, p. 36 (E.T., I, 38–39).
109 *Neutestamentliche Theologie*, p. 75.

the one from the other and to free his own self-references from the doubt that adheres to the descriptions of the miraculous circumstances under which these references are sometimes made (e.g., the healing of the paralytic, Matthew 9:1–8).[110]

The procedure by which Baur sought to unravel this question is strikingly modern. In the Synoptic Gospels, "Son of Man" is the most common messianic title (occurring some sixty-eight times), and it always appears on Jesus' own lips. This leads to the presumption that at least some of the Son of Man sayings are authentic expressions of Jesus. Modern scholarship sometimes divides the sayings into three groups, by type: a first group, known as the apocalyptic or Danielic Son of Man sayings, in which the exaltation of the Son of Man at the right hand of God is affirmed or his coming on the clouds of heaven is predicted; a second group, concerned with the suffering and Passion of the Son of Man; and a third group, the earthly Son of Man sayings, so designated because of the earthly locus of the activity of the Son of Man as described in these sayings, e.g., "the Son of Man has authority on earth to forgive sins" (Matt. 9:6), "the Son of Man has nowhere to lay his head" (Matt. 8:20). The apocalyptic sayings are scattered throughout all the strata of the Synoptic tradition, while the suffering sayings are those especially copied by Mark from Matthew (following Baur's ordering of the Gospels), and the earthly sayings are found especially in the material common to Matthew and Luke. The suffering sayings, which predict the Passion of the Son of Man, are today generally regarded as having originated from a post-Easter perspective, with the result that the quest for authenticity focuses on the apocalyptic sayings versus the earthly sayings. Baur structured the problem in a similar fashion. The prevailing critical opinion today is that the apocalyptic sayings, or at least the majority of them, are authentic: Jesus predicted the coming of a heavenly Son of Man in the context of an apocalyptic upheaval, to whom he was somehow mysteriously related, perhaps as a prophet or forerunner; the Evangelists assumed that these sayings were self-references and therefore placed the title on Jesus' lips in other instances as well.[111] Baur, however, questions whether in the time of Jesus the apocalyptic, Danielic Son of Man was such a customary designation for the Messiah that Jesus could have been expected to use it in this literal sense. He does not deny that there is an authentic substratum to many of the apocalyptic sayings, such as Matthew 13:37–43, 16:27, 19:28, 25:31–46, where Jesus refers to the Son of Man as the future judge of the world. But "it is impossible that such sayings can . . . be taken in the

110 *Ibid.*, pp. 85, 87.
111 This is the position taken, with varying modifications, by Bultmann, John Knox, and Heinz Eduard Tödt. Cf. my article, "The Son of Man and the Problem of Historical Knowledge," *The Journal of Religion*, XLI:2 (April 1961), pp. 91–108.

mouth of Jesus as other than figurative or even regarded solely as authentic expressions of Jesus. We can rather see precisely from such passages how much in this eschatological sphere of representation can, on the whole, be taken only figuratively." The tradition has clothed Jesus' expression of a fundamentally moral reality with apocalyptic imagery, or, if Jesus used the imagery himself, he filled it with a radically new content. Jesus' true meaning is to be seen much more clearly in Matthew 20:20–24, where, in answer to the request of the mother of the sons of Zebedee that her sons be permitted to sit at his right and left hand in his kingdom, he says that it is not his to grant who should sit at his right and left hand but the Father's. As we shall see, Jesus presents himself as judge of the world in another sense. Furthermore, Baur argues that the criteria for determining the authenticity of the Son of Man sayings must be the teaching of Jesus concerning the coming of the kingdom of God and the picture of his earthly ministry and person, as these are found especially in Matthew.[112]

These arguments are similar to ones advanced by Eduard Schweizer in a recent article.[113] They lead both Baur and Schweizer to a consideration of the earthly sayings rather than the apocalyptic sayings as the clue to the sense in which Jesus uses this title. What does Jesus intend to signify by referring to himself as "the Son of Man" in this context—a context in which customary Jewish messianic expectation does not apply and in which Jesus seems to use the expression in a new, different, and even mysterious sense? At this point, both Baur and Schweizer are forced to conjecture, and again their conjectures are similar (they are also based, to a considerable degree, on exegesis of similar texts). The conjecture is that Jesus appropriates an expression, "Son of Man," which at the time possesses an uncertain or ambiguous meaning, to *indicate without explicitly expressing* his divinely sent mission to preach the good news of the kingdom of God and in some sense to effect the reconciliation between God and man thus preached through his own person—specifically through his earthly ministry and eventually through his suffering and death. For Baur, "Son of Man" thus used does not refer to Jesus' divinity as such but to his authentic humanity—that humanity constituted by his special and redemptive relationship to God. He writes as follows: "What if Jesus, in order to counter such [messianic] expectations of his person from the very beginning, had, in contrast to the title, *huios tou theou*, intentionally called himself *huios tou anthrōpou*? He would have chosen a title which, no matter how understood, would have had no common messianic significance but would have included in itself the silent proviso to take the messianic idea into

---

112 Cf. "Die Bedeutung des Ausdrucks: *ho huios tou anthrōpou*," ZWT, III:3, 274–81; and *Neutestamentliche Theologie*, pp. 110–12; quotation from pp. 111–12.
113 "Der Menschensohn," ZNTW, L:3/4 (1959), 185–209.

claim for himself and to step forth with it as soon as it was sufficiently prepared and grounded in its higher significance."[114]

The "higher significance" of the messianic concept which Jesus indirectly expresses and relates to himself by his use of the Son of Man title is connected with the actualization of the idea of reconciliation in his ministry, in his suffering and death, and in his future judgment of the world. With respect, first, to his ministry, Baur writes: Jesus "can perceive his messianic calling only in this, *to actualize* the idea of the *basileia tōn ouranōn* in the sense of all those moral demands which he made on his followers."[115] Jesus regards himself as the Messiah in the sense that through him the kingdom of heaven is historically actualized, its moral demands stated and satisfied. He himself enacts the Gospel which he proclaims. Baur argues that this is evident from the exegesis of such passages as Matthew 7:21, 9:1–8, 10:5–42, 11:2–15; 12:1–8, 16:13–15. With respect to Matthew 11:2–15, Jesus indicates his messianic role vis-à-vis John the Baptist as that of preaching the coming and presence of the kingdom of heaven; "the essential task of his messianic designation" is "the ethical reform of the intentional virtue of the people"—this by means of his divinely given power and authority.[116]

This same idea is expressed in Jesus' reference to himself as the "Son of God." As with the much more common self-reference, "Son of Man," this title is not used by Jesus in its customary messianic sense. Rather, as in Matthew 11:25–30, he describes himself as "the Son" in terms of his realization of the kingdom of heaven through his ministry. He is the one sent from God through whom a new revelation of the will of God is mediated. He is "the Son" of God because, between the Sender and the One sent, a unity of consciousness exists such that the Sender knows only the One sent as the revealer of his will and only the One sent knows from whom he is sent. This passage is congruent with the Sermon on the Mount where, although the person of Jesus is not directly the object of attention, a new source of divine revelation is implied. Whoever could claim that the true meaning of the Old Testament law is disclosed in his teaching, or that those who hunger and thirst after righteousness will be satisfied, "must possess the consciousness that he can speak thus only as the One sent from God."[117]

[114] "Die Bedeutung des Ausdrucks: *ho huios tou anthrōpou*," ZWT, III:3, 279–80; cf. pp. 274–81. The same interpretation is suggested, less clearly and concisely, in *Neutestamentliche Theologie*, pp. 75-95, especially pp. 81, 83, 93. The article, which is Baur's last published work before he died, seems to be a further refinement of the position developed in the New Testament lectures. In the lectures, Baur claims that Jesus also used the title, "Son of God," to a limited degree and in a very specialized sense. See below.

[115] *Neutestamentliche Theologie*, p. 93. Italics mine.

[116] *Ibid.*, pp. 86–93; quotation from p. 90.

[117] *Ibid.*, pp. 113–14. See above, p. 227. This description of Jesus' consciousness as the Son sent to reveal the will of the Father is congruent with some of Baur's sermons based on Johannine texts; see above, pp. 115–16. In

Jesus also enacts the Gospel which he proclaims in the sense
that he regards himself as the instrument by which the satisfaction of the moral requirement of the kingdom is to be effected
and judged. "That Jesus regarded and announced himself as the
future judge cannot be doubted, according to the Gospel of
Matthew."[118] The Sermon on the Mount and the parables of Jesus
serve as the absolute standard for judging the moral value of the
actions and conduct of men. But if these are the standard for
judgment, then Jesus himself, in his own words, is the judge. "What
is valid first of all with respect to his teaching is also valid with
respect to his person, in so far as he is the originator and pro-
claimer of this teaching.[119] His person belongs essentially and inseparably together with his teaching; he is himself the concrete
perception [*Anschauung*] of the significance, extending itself into
all eternity, of the absolute truth of his teaching. If it is according
to his teaching that the moral value of man is to be judged for all
eternity, then he is himself the one who speaks this judgment, as
the future judge of men."[120]

Hirsch interprets this argument to mean that, according to Baur,
Jesus himself reinterprets the Jewish nationalistic-theocratic expectation of the Messiah and applies it to himself to show that
in his moral-religious consciousness and through his lowly human
suffering and death, by virtue of which he would be at one with
all men, he himself is to become the absolute moral-religious
standard according to which all men are to be determined in their
eternal relationship to God.[121] *In this sense*, and not as a suprahistorical heavenly king with external authority, his person is the
moral judge, as his word is the moral judgment, of the world. This
is what is meant by Jesus in the parables of the future judgment,
such as Matthew 13:37–43, 16:27, and 25:31–46, which are to be
interpreted figuratively, not literally.[122] Baur's moral interpretation

Die kanonischen Evangelien, pp. 614–15, Baur remarks that Matt. 11:25–30
is not characteristic of the rest of the Gospel but defends its authenticity,
and suggests that "even the original Gospel of Matthew possessed a point
of contact for a form of Christology which, if it had not been grounded in
the original nature of Christianity itself, certainly could not have achieved
such an independent significance in its further development, either in the
Apostle Paul or in the Johannine Gospel."

118 *Neutestamentliche Theologie*, p. 109. Baur does not regard Jesus to
have predicted a literal second coming as judge of the world in the words
contained in the little apocalypse of Matt. 24, which, as we have seen, reflects a perspective *post eventum*. Here the original content of the teaching
of Jesus with respect to his person has been modified to fit the hopes of
Jewish Christianity in a time of desperation. Jesus in actuality speaks of
himself as "future judge" in a different sense, as we shall see.

119 The German of this sentence is ambiguous: "Was aber zunächst von
seiner Lehre gilt, gilt auch wieder von seiner Person, sofern er der Urheber
und Verkündiger derselben ist."

120 *Neutestamentliche Theologie*, p. 110.

121 Hirsch, *op. cit.*, V, 548–49.

122 Cf. *Neutestamentliche Theologie*, pp. 110–11. See above, pp. 229–30.

of Jesus' eschatological language anticipates Bultmann's existentialist interpretation, except that Baur believes that Jesus himself already had "moralized" the apocalyptic imagery, if indeed he used
it at all.

With respect to Baur's important statement that Jesus "is himself
the concrete *Anschauung* of the significance, extending itself into
all eternity, of the absolute truth of his teaching," Hirsch claims
that this is for Baur the kernel and the authority of Jesus' messianic
self-consciousness and also one of the Christological foundations
of historical-critical theology.[123] By this statement Baur does not
mean to say that the person of Jesus is in actuality only a perception or intuition, possessed by the community of faith, of the
significance of a certain body of religious teaching, i.e., that the
faith of the community is the ground and source of his religiously-
significant "person" rather than vice versa. It is precisely this to
which Baur objects in Hegel.[124] Rather, this sentence is intended
as an explication of the significance which Jesus *himself* attaches
to his person, namely, that his person is the perception—the concrete perception or intuition—of the eternal significance of his
teaching. This would be its service *to* the community of faith; for
this reason it is the presupposition of the community of faith. In
this sense and by this means his person can continue to have
eternal significance for, and be present to, the faith of Christians
in all ages. In this way a past event—his person—will also be a
present reality. This is what he means when he speaks of himself
as the "future judge"—he himself, his person, will be the concrete perception or intuition for faith of the significance of his
teaching. His personal history will also be the history of faith, but
the former will always be the irreversible basis of the latter. If
his person is not in itself religiously significant, then it cannot be
made so by faith. Past and present are internally related for Baur
as for Hegel, but for Baur the reality of the historical past is always
prior to, and the foundation of, the reality of the present.[125]

According to Baur, Jesus was also aware that his imminent suffering and death were somehow connected with the realization of
the idea of reconciliation through his person. Jesus probably gave
some *general* indications of his impending death and eventual victory over death, but the definite predictions found on his lips in the
Synoptics cannot be historical. He also indicated a general awareness of the necessity of his suffering and death to fulfill his
messianic role. As he encountered increasing opposition to his

[123] Hirsch, *op. cit.*, V, 549.
[124] See above, pp. 61–62.
[125] See above, pp. 181–84. The connection here suggested between Jesus' historical existence and his future work in the community of the faithful is
also described in the Sermon on Judica Sunday, John 12:20–32* (U.B.T., Mh
969, 260–62), as quoted above, p. 117. On Baur's use of *Anschauung* ("perception") in connection with the person of Christ, see *Epochen*, p. 251, quoted
above, pp. 124–25.

messianic plan, he became aware that he himself would be "the sacrifice to his messianic designation." In direct contradiction to the Jewish expectation of their Messiah, he must suffer and die.[126] However, from the Synoptic evidence it is not likely that Jesus specifically predicted his Passion or was aware of an atoning significance to his death, as suggested by Matthew 20:28, which in its present form Baur does not regard as authentic ("the Son of Man came not to be served but to serve, and to give his life as a ransom for many"). Jesus may well have said, in Baur's view, that the Son of Man came not to be served but to serve (with this content the saying could belong to the earthly Son of Man group); but the notion of ransom reflects a later dogmatic consciousness.[127] Furthermore, he never made the entrance into the kingdom of God and the possibility of the fulfillment of its moral demands depend upon faith in the reconciling power of his death.[128] Finally, he probably regarded the Last Supper as an occasion for the remembrance of his death, but the words of institution as they appear in Matthew 26:26–29 are not authentic because of the atoning significance which they attach to his death.[129]

In short, the argument of this section can be summarized and concluded as follows: although Paul is the author of the theology of atonement and John of the absolute significance of the person of the God-man, the doctrine of the person of Christ, which is the fundamental dogma of the Christian Church, has its real origin with the teaching and self-consciousness of Jesus himself, not with Paul or John. In this respect, because of his confidence in the relative historicity of Matthew, Baur provides a more positive and even more orthodox picture of Jesus' self-awareness than most contemporary form-critical scholars.

The Resurrection and Historical Knowledge

In Chapter III we examined, from a dogmatic perspective, Baur's theology of resurrection.[130] In a general sense, the resurrection is an objective process or reality, congruent with but not the product of the natural-historical order (i.e., nonmiraculous in the absolute sense), by which individual life is sustained after death—both physical and spiritual—in an eternal fellowship with God. More specifically, the resurrection of Christ is the proof of the fact that the Spirit

---

126 *Neutestamentliche Theologie*, pp. 94–95. It was Paul, according to Baur, who saw the full significance of the messiahship of Jesus as lying in his death: through his atoning death Christianity was able to accomplish what the Old Covenant had never been able to accomplish—the reconciliation of man and God. Cf. *ibid.*, pp. 131, 157; and *Paulus*, II, 135–36 (E.T., 125–26). But in this respect, as in every other, Paul's theology is anticipated by Jesus himself.

127 *Neutestamentliche Theologie*, pp. 99–101.

128 *Ibid.*, p. 125.

129 *Ibid.*, pp. 101–105.

130 See above, pp. 116–19.

of God was fully present to him as the agent of that divinely grounded relationship by which he was authentically human spirit, and it is the means by which his spirituality becomes the life-giving spirituality of all men. Through the resurrection of Christ, that which is an implicit possibility for all men is historically actualized. The apostles argue from the former to the latter. Paul, for example, starts with what he regards as "an outward historical fact"—the death and resurrection of Jesus—"from which Christianity obtains its positive historical character." As such it must be properly authenticated, for which purpose Paul appeals to the appearances of Jesus both to the older apostles and to himself.[131]

The resurrection is an historical event in the sense that it is a spiritual process—a process constituted by the death-destroying, life-giving relationship of the divine Spirit to human spirit. But can this event also be known or described in historical-critical fashion? A clue is already provided by the fact that, in order to authenticate the resurrection, Paul does not describe the event itself but rather appeals to certain faith experiences of the apostles, himself included. In *Das Christenthum*, Baur answers the question as follows:

What the resurrection is in itself lies outside the sphere of historical investigation. Historical consideration has only to hold to the fact that for the faith of the disciples the resurrection of Jesus became the strongest and most incontestable certainty. In this faith Christianity first acquired the firm foundation of its historical development. For history [i.e., for historical consideration], the necessary presupposition of everything that follows is not so much the factuality of the resurrection of Jesus itself, but much more the belief in the same. No matter how one regards the resurrection of Jesus—as an objectively occurring miracle or as a subjective, psychological miracle, in so far as one assumes the possibility of such—yet no psychological analysis can penetrate into the inner spiritual process through which, in the consciousness of the disciples, their unfaith occasioned by the death of Jesus became faith in his resurrection. It is only through the consciousness of the disciples that we can attain to what was for them the object of their faith; and thus we can only remain with the fact that, whatever may have interceded, for them the resurrection of Jesus became a fact of their consciousness and had for them all the reality of an historical fact.[132]

A similar point is argued in the *Neutestamentliche Theologie*: it is difficult to draw the distinction between what is "objectively factual" and that which is "merely subjectively represented" in the resurrection of Jesus. Those who do not believe that the resurrection was a miracle in the absolute sense—the physical resuscitation of a corpse—"can only suppose that the faith in the resurrection proceeded from the entire spiritual process which took place in the

131 *Paulus*, II, 237 (E.T., 216–17).
132 *Das Christenthum*, pp. 39–40 (E.T., I, 42–43).

minds of the disciples following the death of Jesus." Given the vitality of their faith that Jesus was indeed alive, not dead, it is not difficult to understand how this faith assumed the form of visions which they regarded as appearances of the Resurrected One. Even if one says that Christ was not "bodily resurrected"— for this would require acceptance of the resurrection as an absolute miracle—but rather "spiritually resurrected in the faith of the disciples," nevertheless this faith was brought to "the certainty of the factual reality of his resurrection through the inner necessity of the thing itself."[133]

According to Baur, it is evident that the historian can know nothing of the nature and reality of the resurrection apart from its subjective appropriation in faith. In this respect the resurrection—as an objective event, something happening to Jesus—differs from every other event of constitutive significance for the history of the Christian Church, and it represents the one exception to the rule that an historical event or process is one which is in principle knowable through historical knowledge.[134] As I have indicated earlier, the resurrection is an historical event for which historical understanding assumes an entirely negative and secondary, though for that reason no less relevant, posture. The historical theologian has access only to faith in the resurrection, not to the event itself, although on this account he by no means denies the objective reality of the event. Baur never implies that the reality of the resurrection is constituted simply by the faith in it. Faith is the subjective acceptance and completion of an objectively realized, historically mediated process of reconciliation. The presence of faith points to the reality of something outside faith. With respect to faith in Jesus, historical theology can determine whether in fact he corresponds to what faith has claimed for him as the mediator of reconciliation. (Such a determination is not a "proof" of faith.) But in the case of the resurrection, there is nothing outwardly observable which corresponds to and is the mark of this event except the faith in it. In this epistemological sense the resurrection is not an historical event, although its effects are historical. The resurrection is "a fact of [the disciples'] consciousness," but this is not to say that it is a mere product of their consciousness. The very nature of this consciousness suggests that it is the product of an objective power and reality working upon it; through an "inner necessity," consciousness comes to "the certainty of the factual reality" of the resurrection. Both *Das Christenthum* and the *Neutestamentliche Theologie* imply that a "spiritual process" is at work in the creation of the resurrection faith, to which the historical theologian does not have immediate access and which he therefore cannot describe except by means of its effects. As Hirsch suggests, in commenting on these passages,

133 *Neutestamentliche Theologie*, pp. 126–27.
134 See above, p. 144.

". . . what we today are accustomed to call the hypothesis of the subjective (i.e., not miraculously grounded) visions suffices completely, according to Baur, for the historian and contains nothing injurious for the Christian religion, if it is bound together with an understanding of the necessity and the truth-content of the resurrection faith for the disciples. The subjectivity concerns only the form, not the meaning and significance, of the event."[135]

CHURCH HISTORY AND THE HISTORY OF DOGMA

As we move from the foundation of Christianity to its subsequent historical development, we enter upon a much broader and more extensive field of study. Rather than attempt to survey Baur's findings in Church history and history of dogma, I shall concentrate instead on his conception of the nature, structure, and range of these disciplines. This is not a return to the more general discussion of methodology in historical theology as found in Chapter IV, but rather a study of the procedure and contents in two specific disciplines. After examining the relation between Church history and history of dogma, we shall take a closer look at Baur's conception of dogma, and of the study of the history of dogma which takes shape from this conception. A similar look at Baur's conception of the Church is not required, since his theology of the Church was considered among the dogmatic principles of Chapter III. Finally, we shall study Baur's determination of the major motifs and periods in the history of dogma and Church history, which is the clue to his treatment of these two fields as a whole.

The Relation Between Church History and the History of Dogma

In the introduction to his lectures on the history of dogma, Baur establishes that, since Christianity "belongs in the succession of historical manifestations," what it is essentially can be known "only in historical fashion," and that as an historical manifestation it existed from the beginning "in the form of the Christian Church." Furthermore, everything that is connected with Christianity as an historical manifestation is included within the history of the Christian Church, which can be divided into different major "moments" according to the different "sides" (or "forms") in which the "life" of the Church exhibits itself. One of these "sides" or "forms" has as its object the "doctrine" on which the Church rests in its historical development, or the "dogma" of the Church in the widest sense of the word. Consequently, the discipline of history of dogma "is . . . properly a part of general Church history." If one removes the history of dogma from the general content of Church history and treats it as the subject matter of a separate theological discipline, this is done partially because of the importance which attaches to dogma in comparison with the remaining content of

[135] Hirsch, *op. cit.*, V, 550–51.

Church history, and partially because of the special difficulties which are ingredient in its historical treatment. Thus history of dogma as a discipline is related to Church history as a part to the whole. It is a discipline within a discipline and must never be abstracted from this relationship.

If dogma is removed from direct treatment by Church history, then the latter discipline directs itself especially to those manifestations or forms in which the factuality of the life of the Church expresses itself outwardly, i.e., to its institutional features, cultic life, missionary activities, and political relationships. Consequently, while Church history concerns itself with the external side of the life of the Church, history of dogma turns itself toward the internal side; and from this point of view, since everything external has its ground in the internal from which it proceeds, history of dogma occupies a higher level than Church history. The "condition of the Church generally" in its different periods is determined by "the inner process of development" of its self-consciousness as expressed in its various dogmatic forms. "It is therefore history of dogma which allows us to see into this inner aspect of the life of the Church and which acquaints us with the course of this spiritual movement, to which the outward manifestations are led back as to their ultimate foundation."[136]

This distinction, however, as is always the case with Baur, is only a distinction within unity. Having made the distinction, he then modifies it. For history of dogma *is* Church history; the life *of the Church* (on its internal, reflective side) is its object of investigation. Furthermore, Baur *includes* a treatment of dogma, as well as of the other historical forms of the Church, in his multi-volumed *Kirchengeschichte;* this is especially the case in the first, second, and fifth volumes of this history.[137] When he actually came to write a history of the Church, he did not limit it to a consideration of the "outward side" of the life of the Church. Church history is both internal and external history. In addition, while dogma is primarily an internal form, and Church institutions and outward relationships primarily external forms, there are other Church-historical forms which would appear to be both internal and external—for example, the cultic and ethical life of the Christian community. Also, in the preface to *Das Christenthum,* Baur moderates the primacy which he attributes to dogma as the internal form of the Church; other forms in the life of the Church must be given careful consideration as well.[138] Finally, despite what he says in the introduction to the *Dogmengeschichte,* Baur does not allow his periodization of Church history to be determined by his earlier periodization of the history of dogma. There are parallels

---

136 For these two paragraphs, cf. *Dogmengeschichte,* I/1, 1–3; and *Kirchengeschichte,* V, 2.
137 Cf. *Epochen,* p. 252.
138 Cf. *Das Christenthum,* pp. v–vi (E.T., I, ix–x).

and relations between these two sets of periodization, but it is not a question of "the inner [dogmatic] process of development" determining "the condition of the Church generally," at least with respect to the moments or motifs into which general Church history is divided.

Dogma and the History of Dogma

Baur claims that no important distinction in meaning has traditionally existed between the terms "doctrine" (*Lehre*) and "dogma" (*Dogma*). On the basis of general usage in early Christian thought (e.g., Chrysostom, Theodoret, Ignatius, Cyril of Jerusalem, Gregory of Nyssa, Socrates), "the *doctrines* of the Christian faith are understood as *dogmas*, in so far as they contain the absolute Christian truth."[139] Since that which concerns absolute truth ought to be defined as exactly as possible, dogmas can be described as "the doctrines of the Christian faith, in so far as they exist in propositions in which they have preserved as much as possible their definite ecclesiastical doctrinal form, as, for example, one cannot talk of a dogma of the Trinity without at the same time also thinking of a definite form of this doctrine. If dogma is Christian doctrine generally, then dogmas are the more exact determinations of the same, the contents of dogma explicated in its entire extent."[140]

Dogma is fundamentally a conceptual phenomenon. The "concept" of dogma is the outward expression or actualization of the thoughts of Spirit—both the divine Spirit and human spirits. Dogma therefore represents the outward patterning of the inward, dialectical movement of Spirit, as it mediates itself with itself and with other Spirits in thought. *Christian* dogma reflects primarily the relational life in thought of the Absolute Spirit, God. "Christian dogma has as its presupposition Christian revelation. Revelation is an act of the Spirit in which an Object as an immediate given stands over against the subjective consciousness and becomes for the subject the object of a faith filled with the content of the Absolute Idea."[141] The movement immanent to the concept of dogma, then, can be recognized only from the nature of Spirit. This movement, which constitutes the history of dogma, "is nothing other than the concept of dogma dividing itself into and proceeding from its moments, explicating itself to an ever further extent"; and the method of the discipline which treats the history of dogma "can only be the movement of dogma itself."[142] In this highly abstruse and Hegelian language, Baur attempts to explain the relation between Christian dogma and the fundamental historical and theological reality on which it is based. The historian of dogma

---

[139] *Dogmengeschichte*, I/1, 11. Italics mine.
[140] *Ibid.*, p. 12.
[141] *Ibid.*, pp. 49–50; quotation from p. 50. See above, pp. 92–93.
[142] *Ibid.*, pp. 29–30; quotations from p. 29.

is not dealing with mere abstract notions or concepts. In his work he is rather encountering the very substance of the life of the Church—the conceptual actualization of the divine idea of reconciliation, whereby the divine Spirit mediates himself with himself and reveals himself to human spirits.[143]

"Dogmatics" is "the system of dogmas" which determines and expresses the content of the Christian faith for a particular age;[144] or, as Baur defines it in one of his academic opinions, "dogmatics is the science of faith."[145] We already have seen that the historical study of dogma is necessarily dependent upon dogmatics: the historian of dogma can return to the past only from the perspective of the present dogmatic consciousness, as it is defined in contemporary dogmatic systems; he cannot adopt an earlier perspective in ecclesiastical historiography from which to interpret the past.[146] But at the same time dogmatics is part of the larger process of the history of dogma, and therefore the reverse dependence also holds, that of dogmatics on the history of dogma.

Dogmatics is the system of dogmas determining the content of Christian faith, ensuing as the result of the entire preceding historical development of dogma. Dogmatics is thus itself only the result of the history of dogma, or the point at which the dogmatic-historical movement stops and fixes itself in the consciousness of the time, in order firmly to establish as an enduring truth for the present that which has turned out to be the pinnacle of the development from the past. However, this is for a present which will itself become a past and which cannot prevent that enduring truth also from being engulfed in the continually moving flux of history, in which every result exists only in order to become itself a moment of a newly beginning sequence of development. From this is immediately clear the importance which history of dogma holds for dogmatics. If history of dogma is in its starting point only a part of Church history, so in its final point dogmatics itself is only a part of it, a part which is distinguished from the whole to which it belongs in that the movement which is the element of the history of dogma appears to make a cessation in it for the subjective consciousness, as if everything preceding had taken its course in order to come to an end in just this result.[147]

Baur continues by suggesting that the task of dogmatics is to clarify for the present, out of the flux of historical change, "the immanent substantial content of true Christian consciousness." The task of dogmatics is not to assemble a mere aggregate of his-

143 See above, p. 165.
144 *Dogmengeschichte*, I/1, 3.
145 Gutachten of 12 Apr. 1841 (U.B.T., Md 750, v, 4). See above, pp. 95–96.
146 See above, pp. 170–72.
147 *Dogmengeschichte*, *loc. cit.*

torical materials but to bring to definite conceptualization and expression that which has obtained a certain consistency in the dogmatic consciousness of the time.[148] Its task is to extract the steady and enduring from the constantly changing and moving. This can be done only when the dogmatician understands the entire process of dogmatic development which lies behind him. "The whole consciousness of dogmatics rests on the foundation of the history of dogma. Only he who has followed the entire course of the development of dogma and has rightly comprehended the moments of the inner process of its movement can take a firm standpoint in the present, in order to distinguish the periodic from what ought to be of more general value, and that which determines the fundamental character of the consciousness of an age from that which swiftly passes away and disappears insignificantly."[149] On the other hand, history of dogma points out that everything steady and enduring is actually only periodic, that what for the present appears to have such a strong "consistency" must once again return to the general flux of history. The destiny of dogmatics is that it always falls eventually into the grasp of history of dogma.[150]

That dogmatics is part of the history of dogma means that the latter includes the study, not simply of the formal promulgation of dogmatic truth in various doctrinal symbols and creeds, but also of dogmatic-theological reflection and formulation of all types in all ages. History of dogma includes, in other words, the history of theology or the "history of dogmatics." The history of dogmatics is close to one of the central concerns of history of dogma, namely, to explicate the unifying dogmatic principle of a particular ecclesiastical-theological period and the various attempts at a systematic connection of dogmas into a theology or a dogmatics. History of dogma is not simply a history of dogmas, or of creeds and symbols.[151] This conviction that history of dogma includes the consideration of theology or dogmatics helps to explain why Baur has a much broader conception of the *expanse* and *task* of history of dogma than most of his contemporaries (e.g., Engelhardt) or successors (e.g., Harnack and Seeberg).

With respect to the *expanse* of history of dogma, since history itself is a never-resting movement, historical consideration and presentation must trace the development of Christian dogma and Christian theology down to the present. To stop a history of dogma at an earlier, arbitrarily selected date is not justified by the nature of the material and results in establishing the perspective of the whole of the history of dogma from *this* standpoint, beyond which

---

[148] *Ibid.*, p. 4. Baur here contrasts Schleiermacher's *Glaubenslehre* as a true dogmatics with Hase's *Lehrbuch der Dogmatik.*

[149] *Ibid.*, p. 7.

[150] *Ibid.*, pp. 5–7.

[151] *Ibid.*, pp. 25–28.

the dogmatic consciousness has long since moved.[152]

Concerning the point at which history of dogma should begin, it has been argued that the New Testament (including the theology of Paul and the Gospels and the teaching of Jesus) should not be considered part of the proper content of history of dogma, which ought, accordingly, to begin with the termination of the apostolic era. This argument attempts to distinguish the changing, alterable, relative character of Church dogmas from their unchanging biblical content. The teaching of Jesus and Paul and the apostolic interpretation of Christianity are regarded as unchanging, authentic, absolutely true; the transition is located at the end of the first century, when the first alterations and conflicts within Christian doctrines can be detected. Baur replies that this distinction would be valid only if the New Testament writings were in fact a perfectly harmonious whole, displaying no historical movement, development, and conflict. But if they are historically conditioned writings, then they also must be considered a part of the history of the Church and its thought, and history of Christian dogma must begin with Jesus, Paul, and the Gospels. Generally speaking, then, New Testament theology is a part of history of dogma, which in turn is a part of Church history. The New Testament is not merely the presupposition of the history of dogma; it is itself already the beginning of its historical development. But since this beginning is so important for what follows, it is justifiably made the subject of a separate discipline. And, strictly speaking, the teaching of Jesus is not a part of the dogmatic development which is based

152 *Ibid.*, pp. 13–14. We have already noted above, p. 172, that Baur here refers to Engelhardt's *Lehrbuch der Dogmengeschichte* (1839), which ends its treatment with the Formula of Concord in 1580, and that the same criticism could be brought against Adolf Harnack and Reinhold Seeberg. With respect to Harnack, it may be that his more limited conception of dogma by comparison with Baur's—basically a product of Greek culture and mind, fashioned for an apologetic-philosophical function, antibiblical, distinct from theology of which it is a product but whose creativity in turn stultifies, defined as doctrines "logically formulated and expressed for scientific and apologetic purposes"—is directly a product of the dogmatic point of view with which he ends his treatment and which establishes the perspective from which he evaluates the whole history of dogma, namely the Reformation and Luther (and, by immediate association, the "simple gospel"). For example, he writes, "The Reformation is *the end of dogma* in a sense similar to that in which the gospel is the end of the law." See his *History of Dogma*, trans. from the 3d German ed. (1893) by Neil Buchanan (New York: Dover Publications, 1961), VII, 30; italics mine. See also pp. 27–34. For his definition of dogma, see I, 6–13. Seeberg follows Harnack, except that he argues that history of dogma ceases with the last dogmatic symbols formulated by the various divisions of the Church. Cf. his *Textbook of the History of Doctrines*, Charles E. Hay, trans. (Grand Rapids, Mich.: Baker Book House, 1952), pp. 22–23. Friedrich Loofs, on the other hand, associates himself with Baur against Harnack's literal definition of dogma and against the consequent narrowing of the task of history of dogma, although he believes that the latter must be distinguished from the history of theology. Cf. his *Leitfaden zum Studium der Dogmengeschichte* (4th ed.; Halle: Verlag von Max Niemeyer, 1906), I, 5–11.

on and related to it; it is the immediate and original foundation of the Christian consciousness, standing beyond all temporal development of that consciousness by virtue of its completeness and normative character. This is its position vis-à-vis the historical community of which it is the point of origin and center of meaning. Hence both the *Lehrbuch der Dogmengeschichte* and the *Vorlesungen über die christliche Dogmengeschichte* begin with the conflict between Judaism and Paulinism and with the post-Easter faith of the earliest Christians, rather than with the teaching of Jesus. Church history, on the other hand, begins precisely with his life and work as its most important single datum.[153]

In passing, it is interesting to note what important theological issues are raised by the seemingly simple question as to where history of dogma begins and where it ends! This fact demonstrates that one cannot study the history of the Church and its thought without having to make all sorts of theological judgments—if not consciously and by intention, then accidentally and by default.

We turn next to Baur's consideration of the *task* of history of dogma. In his judgment, it has a twofold task: to trace the unity, development, and movement of the central dogmas of the Church and of dogma itself; and to examine the peculiar dogmatic consciousness of each theological age in terms of the representative dogma of that age and the works in dogmatics or systematic theology in which this consciousness is most clearly expressed.

With respect to the first task, Baur's fundamental conviction is that the history of dogma is, "as closer consideration makes ever more evident, a self-connected process of development, specified through its inner moments, in which everything preceding is the necessary presupposition of what follows, and everything that follows only the result of what precedes, so that all special forms of dogma may be conceived as simply the moments of a unity penetrating through the whole." If this is the case, then the "true historical presentation" of the history of dogma must be one which "allows this process of development to appear entirely as it is in itself"; and this presentation errs when it can detect in the course of dogmatic development *only* the "singular, fortuitous, arbitrary, unconnected," or when it cannot penetrate from the "outward appearances" to "the inner concept of the thing itself," to "the inner, moving principle, which can only be thinking Spirit itself."[154] This

---

[153] *Dogmengeschichte*, I/1, 15–19. Cf. also *Neutestamentliche Theologie*, p. 45 (quoted above, pp. 222–23). Karl Barth desires to preserve just the distinction between the New Testament and Church history/history of dogma which Baur insists must be abolished. According to Barth, the Bible constitutes a qualitatively distinct stretch of history, which must be treated differently not just from secular history but also from Church history. Cf. his criticism of Baur on this point in *Die protestantische Theologie*, pp. 457–58; quoted below, pp. 262–63, and commented on, pp. 270–71.

[154] *Dogmengeschichte*, I/1, 60–61; cf. also p. 30, and *Versöhnung*, pp. vi, 11.

process of development is not imposed on the history of dogma as a logical dialectic but is rather discovered by means of a critical as well as speculative consideration of the data. With respect to the continuity in dogmatic development, Baur suggests that, while every period has its own representative dogmas and while the position of consciousness with respect to dogma is different in every period, Christian dogma in itself remains always the same. Thus, for example, the doctrines of justification, faith, repentance, and Scripture are not in themselves new to the Reformation, although the posture of consciousness with respect to these doctrines is different, and some of these dogmas here become historically important for the first time.[155]

The first step in understanding the unity of the history of dogma as a whole is to be found in monographs treating the history of single dogmas from beginning to end. In the preface to *Die christliche Lehre von der Versöhnung*, which represents such an approach, Baur writes that "there are not yet fundamentally any proper monographs in history of dogma in which the history of a single dogma is traced in its entire extent, through a continuous development, as complete as possible, and through all ages. This is to be regretted, since only on the foundation of such preparations is a basic work over the whole of dogma to be expected."[156] Each of the major dogmas—the Trinity, the person of Christ, atonement, sin and grace, the sacraments—contains the whole of Christian dogma, but each also constitutes a different, essential, basic article of the Christian faith. The object of history of dogma is dogma "in the multiplicity of its elements" as well as "in the unity of its concept."[157]

The second task of history of dogma is to examine the dogmatic consciousness of a particular age in terms of the major dogma or dogmas which become characteristic of it and expressive of its peculiar contents. The more completely a specific dogma exercises a controlling influence over a theological period, thus determining the configuration of Christian dogma for that period, the more a common Christian consciousness for that period is made explicit on the basis of a dogmatic "mid-point" to which all Christian thought adheres. This mid-point may provide the basic form for a whole system of dogmas, i.e., for systematic or dogmatic theology. An example of a dogma serving this function for an age is Augustine's doctrine of sin and grace. Since history of dogma includes within its bounds the history of dogmatics, its second task is to isolate and describe the historical function of the various dogmas as they become, respectively, the mid-points or determining centers of different theological periods.[158]

155 *Dreieinigkeit*, I, 107.
156 *Versöhnung*, p. iv.
157 *Dogmengeschichte*, I/1, 21–22, 28.
158 *Ibid.*, pp. 22–28.

Motifs in the Development of Dogma

As indicated above, Baur believes that the first step in understanding the history of dogma as a whole is to study the development of some of the major individual dogmas of the Church. Accordingly, his dogmatic-historical work opens in 1838 with a study of the Christian doctrine of reconciliation, where his first attempt at determining the development of dogma is to be found. He suggests in this work that there are three moments or motifs in the development, both historically and dogmatically, of the concept of atonement. In the first moment, that of unmediated objectivity, atonement is understood as a purely objective divine act, a process through which God mediates himself with himself in order to realize the concept of his nature. Viewed from this perspective, the reconciliation of man with God occurs not for the sake of man but purely for the sake of God. In the second moment, that of unmediated subjectivity, it is man who enacts reconciliation between himself and God, but only within his own self-consciousness, by means of achieving a subjective certainty in faith which expels doubt and alienation. Finally, "between these two moments, each of which holds fast to an equally one-sided concept, a third moment is to be found which emphasizes above all else in the notion of reconciliation the concept of mediation and which places the entire significance of the act of reconciliation in an historical fact, which is considered in its outward, historical objectivity as the necessary condition of the act of reconciliation ensuing between God and man."[159] This is the moment in which the objectivity of the act of reconciliation is historically mediated with or through the subjectivity of human consciousness. Although in the first two moments the relation of the death of Jesus to atonement is not denied, it remains a fact of merely external significance and has only a subordinate meaning in connection with the inner truth of the concept of atonement. It is only in the third moment that the death of Christ becomes of essential importance for the historical mediation of reconciliation.[160]

These moments are not necessarily related to each other serially and in simple progression. At any one time or in any one thinker (and a thinker is not necessarily bound to the perspective of his period) the doctrine of atonement is understood primarily in one of these three ways, but the other perspectives are also implied and present in greater or lesser degree. One is reminded of Karl Barth's development of the doctrine of reconciliation in the three parts of Volume IV of his *Church Dogmatics:* first, from the side of God; second, from the side of man; and third, from the stance of the Mediator as the God-man. The two theologians would agree that these three moments express the various dimensions of the

159 *Versöhnung*, pp. 9–10.
160 *Ibid.*, p. 10.

theological meaning of reconciliation. In addition, Baur claims that they also correspond to a certain extent to various phases in the *historical* development of the doctrine, although, as we shall see, he does not simply equate the theological motifs in the doctrine with the historical periods that mark its development.

In an obscure and abstruse statement at the beginning of the *Versöhnung*, Baur suggests that the divine Spirit himself, God in his triune being, is the ground for the event of reconciliation and for the various moments of the development of the corresponding dogma (in this sense both event and dogma are "necessary"), and that the movement of the latter is toward an ever more complete historical mediation of the objectivity of atonement (its divine foundation and reality) by its subjectivity (its human appropriation), and of its subjectivity by its objectivity, so that the event of atonement itself will be understood as existing at the juncture of objectivity and subjectivity, i.e., "as an objective historical fact . . . based on the absolute nature of God."[161]

On the basis of this general understanding of the development of the dogma, Baur divides the history of the doctrine of reconciliation into three periods. The first, most clearly represented by Anselm's theory of satisfaction, runs from primitive Christianity to the Reformation and is characterized as the period of "unmediated objectivity" in the comprehension of the dogma. The second period, that of the "transition from the standpoint of unmediated objectivity to subjectivity," runs from the Reformation to Kant. The awareness of the subjective aspect of atonement, which already was anticipated by scholastic dialectic, comes to fruition for the first time in the Reformation. With this fruition, however, a new danger emerges, that of a thoroughgoing subjectivism in which the self becomes the criterion of all knowledge and truth. The completion and transcendence of this subjectivism is found with the beginning of the third period, which runs from Kant to the present. In Kant both the strengths and weaknesses of Protestant rationalism are represented and to a certain degree transcended by virtue of the objective foundation of his moral philosophy. Schleiermacher and Hegel return to the objectivity of reconciliation, except that now its objective character is mediated by an authentically subjective consciousness of it. For just this reason, it is an historical rather than an abstract objectivity, and the historical mediation of atonement in the death of Jesus is for the first time fully and concretely understood. Consequently, this third period is termed "objectivity mediated through subjectivity." Baur suggests that this approach shows how all the forms which the dogma possesses in the different periods of its historical existence have their relative truth; absolute truth, however, is possessed only by the conception of reconciliation free from all finite determinations, absolutely

161 *Ibid.*, p. 12

related to itself, i.e., by God alone in his self-enactment of reconciliation.[162]

It is interesting to note from this survey that the moment of
"unmediated subjectivity" is not represented by a distinct and
autonomous historical period. Rather it is found as a part of the
conclusion of the second period and at the beginning of the third.
This indicates that Baur did not directly translate the *theological
moments* or *motifs* in the understanding of the doctrine into
historical or *chronological periods,* but that he used these moments
to help interpret, organize, and unify his historical treatment.
It is also undoubtedly true that the wide range of historical investigations which he undertook in preparation of this monograph
helped to shape his understanding of the theological motifs in
the doctrine.

The periodization which Baur worked out in the *Versöhnung*
suggests the rough pattern for his treatment of the development
of dogma generally. This treatment sees three basic moments,
motifs, or elements in the development of Christian dogma. In
the first, dogma serves as an external, objective, authoritative formulation of equally objective and external truths, to be believed
on authority rather than understood reflectively. The second is a
transition period, which might be described as "the penetration of
piety by dialectic."[163] The third realizes an internal unity, in faith
and knowledge, of the knowing subject with the content of dogma
as divine truth. For this period, in which historical consciousness
and study is first fully awakened, the historical mediation of the
objective truth of dogma with subjective consciousness becomes
concretely important.

A basic transition to Baur's mature periodization of history of
dogma is found in the second of his great dogmatic-historical
monographs, *Die christliche Lehre von der Dreieinigkeit und
Menschwerdung Gottes* (1841–43). The three periods are no longer
represented as the patristic-scholastic, the Reformation and post-
Reformation, and the Kantian and post-Kantian. There were
several defects in this arrangement. It diminished the importance
and ignored the tremendous internal variety of the dogmatic development of the first sixteen centuries; it elevated the fifty years
or so of the post-Kantian period to a level of significance, in comparison with the other periods, way out of proportion to its
actual theological contribution, great as that had been; and it failed
to take account of the inner continuity, if any, between the Reformation and modern Protestantism. The *Versöhnung* was, in
short, a work clearly—and brilliantly—reflecting the perspectives
and prejudices of a nineteenth-century German Protestant theologian steeped in Hegel, Schleiermacher, Schelling, and Kant.

The periodization in the *Dreieinigkeit,* however, is much more

---

[162] For this survey, see *ibid.,* pp. 12–15; also the Table of Contents.
[163] This phrase was suggested by Hans W. Frei.

judicious. The first period, that of unmediated objectivity, represents the creative formulation of the doctrines of God and Christ, for the most part in the abstract, objectivizing categories of Greek philosophical thought, from the Apostolic Fathers through the Council of Chalcedon. This period is further divided into three parts, concerned respectively with defining the relation of the Son to the Father (Nicea), of the Spirit to the Son and the Father (I Constantinople), and of the Son to humanity (Chalcedon). The second period, that of the gradual penetration of piety by dialectic, reaches from Chalcedon to the Reformation. It in turn is divided into two parts. The first is a transition period barren of fresh dogmatic formulation, comprising in a first subsection the Christological controversies following Chalcedon and dogmatic developments down through the last of the Greek theologians, John of Damascus; and in a second subsection the transition represented in John Scotus Erigena from a Greek to a Western European dogmatics. The second part of the "medieval" period is that of scholasticism proper, divided into three subsections: Anselm to Peter Lombard, the "great scholastic theologians" (Alexander of Hales, Albertus Magnus, Thomas Aquinas, Bonaventura, Duns Scotus), and the "breakdown" of scholasticism, from Scotus to the Reformation. Finally, the Reformation and post-Reformation era, up to the present, comprises the third period, the mediation of objectivity and subjectivity. In the first part of this period, through the middle of the eighteenth century, theological and philosophical developments are treated separately. In the second part, comprising "modern Protestantism," the "mutual interpenetration" of philosophy and theology in the formulation of the doctrines of the Trinity and incarnation is examined.[164]

It could be argued that the differences in periodization between the *Versöhnung* and the *Dreieinigkeit* simply reflect a different subject matter. This is undoubtedly true to some extent, but the change seems too basic to be accounted for just on this ground. It also involves further study of the data and more mature interpretive judgments. For example, Baur acknowledges to Heyd that his study of the scholastic theologians in preparation for the second volume of the *Dreieinigkeit* has led him to a much greater appreciation of their theological significance.[165] This may be one reason why the Middle Ages are treated as an autonomous period in the *Dreieinigkeit* and occupy a much larger proportion of the text than in the *Versöhnung*. In addition, the periodization in the *Dreieinigkeit* is adapted, with minor changes, to Baur's treatment of the history of dogma as a whole. As we have seen earlier, the structure of this treatment apparently took shape between 1842 and 1847,

164 For this survey, see *Dreieinigkeit*, I, 102–107, 131, 826; II, 3–4, 345–47, 354–55, 575–77, 867; III, 11–15; and the Tables of Contents at the beginning of each of these volumes.

165 Baur to L. F. Heyd, 16 Jan. 1842 (U.B.T., Md 750, ii, 6, 30).

when it assumed final form in the first edition of the *Lehrbuch der christlichen Dogmengeschichte*.[166] It may be safe to assume, then, that it was Baur's work on the doctrines of the Trinity and incarnation which opened the way to a periodization of the entire history of dogma.

The most important single difference between the *Dreieinigkeit* and the *Lehrbuch* is found in the first period. In the latter work, this period comprises dogma from the apostolic age to the end of the sixth century, rather than simply through Chalcedon, terminating with the end of the papacy of Gregory the Great in 604. This period, characterized as "the dogma of the ancient Church, or the substantiality of dogma," is divided into two parts at the Council of Nicea, with the dogmatic development preceding this council largely devoted to the doctrine of God, and the development following it to the doctrines of Christ, sin and grace, and the Church.[167]

Thereafter, however, the periodization in the *Lehrbuch* and in the history of dogma lectures follows the *Dreieinigkeit* rather closely. The second period runs from the seventh through the fifteenth century and comprises "the dogma of the middle ages, or the dogma of self-reflective consciousness." The first part of this period, to the beginning of the papacy of Gregory VII in 1073, represents a transition era to scholasticism proper, which begins with Anselm. The first theological motif in dogmatic development, that of unmediated objectivity, reaches a purely abstract and sterile expression here. The genuine richness of dogmatic formulation in the first period is now exhausted and dissipated in useless controversy and uncreative restatement. The second motif, the penetration of piety by dialectic, does not begin until the second half of the second period, which runs from Anselm through Scotus and Ockham. Finally, the third period comprises dogma from the Reformation to the present, and is characterized as "dogma of the recent period, or dogma and free self-consciousness." This period is divided into two parts at the beginning of the eighteenth century, distinguishing old and modern Protestantism from each other. The period comprises a number of subordinate motifs in dogmatic development, all of which are parts of the third basic dogmatic motif, the mediation of objectivity by subjectivity. The first, represented by the Reformation itself and old Protestantism, constitutes a completion and transformation of the medieval development from Anselm, by virtue of the achievement of an authentically free subjectivity in the comprehension of the objective truth of dogma. The delicate balance between objectivity and subjectivity envisioned

[166] See above, p. 32, n. 128.

[167] This basic arrangement is found as early as 1842–43 in a set of student notes taken from Baur's lectures on the history of dogma, which indicates that it had been arrived at while Baur was still working on the *Dreieinigkeit*. Cf. U.B.T., Mh II 154. In all probability, the difference in arrangement at this point reflects a difference in subject matter.

by the Reformers is, however, in danger of breaking down in a
return to a pure objectivism (the neo-scholasticism of the Protestant dogmaticians of the seventeenth century) or in a pure subjectivism (anticipated by Socinianism and Arminianism and always
present as both a potential and an actual danger in Protestant
rationalism). Finally, in the period from 1815 through the early
decades of the nineteenth century (which comprises the second
period in modern Protestantism[168]), the mediation of objectivity by
subjectivity first envisioned by the Reformers is more fully actualized than in either Protestant scholasticism or rationalism.[169]

As is the case in the *Versöhnung*, the *theological moments* or
motifs in dogmatic development do not simply correspond to the
three *historical periods* which Baur traces in these later works.
He uses the theological motifs to help interpret, organize, and
unify his historical treatment, not, as he explains in the introduction to the lectures on history of dogma, to impose arbitrary
divisions on the historical materials. The motifs, like the periods,
arise from the "objective process of history itself." He also points
out that, since each of the major periods is divided into two parts,
his treatment of the history of dogma as a whole structures it in
six divisions. If there are too many divisions, the total vision of
dogmatic development is obscured; when there are too few (or,
one might add, when they are too unequally distributed, as is the
case with the *Versöhnung*), then the richness and complexity of
dogmatic development are diminished.[170]

There is a final problem in the study of the development of
dogma, namely, the distinction between a systematic-dogmatic-
synthetic and a chronological-historical method of division. The
first method is easier and clearer in that it treats the development
of each dogma separately, but at the same time it ignores the connection between parts and wholes and separates what in the nature
of the case is joined together. The chronological-historical method,
on the other hand, discusses the historical development of dogma
as a whole in each of several historically determined periods. "It
shows how in the individual periods one dogma after the other
becomes the object of theological investigations and ecclesiastical
deliberations, and it can set forth the doctrines and systems which
especially distinguish themselves in their inner continuity without
interruption."[171]

---

[168] In these works, Baur had not yet arrived at the interpretation represented in *Kirchengeschichte*, V, wherein modern Protestantism is divided into
three parts; see above, p. 37.

[169] For this summary, see the Table of Contents of *Lehrbuch der Dogmengeschichte* (1st ed.), and especially pp. 198–200; and *Vorlesungen über die
christliche Dogmengeschichte*, I/1, 51–69.

[170] *Dogmengeschichte*, I/1, 65, 69.

[171] *Ibid.*, pp. 73–74; quotation from p. 74.

Since each of these methods has its respective virtues and weaknesses, the best procedure attempts to combine them, not externally, one after the other, but internally, by weaving them together as much as possible into a single fabric. This is achieved by dividing the entire history of dogma into periods which reflect its development in terms of the nature of dogma itself, and then by handling the given material in each period according to the sequence of the individual dogmas. Then, in order to bind together more closely the general nature of each period with the particular facts and data of individual doctrines in that period, an introduction is provided to each of the six periods which traces the historical development of that period in general and attempts to characterize its distinctive theological nature.[172] These introductions, which in themselves are quite extensive, are the richest and most suggestive and creative aspect of a very impressive work.[173]

Motifs in the History of the Church

When Baur turns to the question of the ecclesiastical moments or motifs through which the history of the Church as a whole developed, he does not attempt to impose on this broader phenomenon the pattern of development associated with one of its parts, namely, dogmatic or doctrinal reflection and formulation. Rather, as we observed in Chapter III, the motifs in Church history are functions of the changing modes of the Church's historicity, i.e., of the relative primacy of dogma, institutional forms, the cultic and moral life, and outward relationships as basic forms of the historical life of the Church.[174] There are, as would be expected, certain fundamental parallels between the periodizations of the history of dogma and of the Church. For example, the three basic chronological periods—ancient, medieval, and modern—are identical in each. But beyond that, the further division in the history of dogma of each major period into two subperiods, resulting in six *chronological* periods as a whole, is not found in Baur's organization of Church history.[175] In that organization there are only

173 This comment applies to the *Vorlesungen*. The *Lehrbuch* is structured in the same way, but it is so compact that it can really serve only as just that, a textbook or manual rather than an historical study. Harnack criticizes the "meager" and "abstract" nature of the *Lehrbuch* (*op. cit.*, I, 34), but this is precisely its intention, to provide a 284-page survey and outline (lengthened to 396 pages in the second edition) of the entire subject. Harnack evidently had not examined the four-volume, 2,353-page *Vorlesungen* (which is about the same length as his own many-volumed work), since he nowhere mentions it in his introduction.
174 See above, pp. 124–27.
175 Student notes taken from Baur's lectures in 1843–44 and 1844–45 show that at this time the Church history lectures were divided into six periods, identical with those in the history of dogma. The more distinctive treatment of these respective disciplines emerged somewhat later. Cf. U.B.T., Mh II 156.

three *chronological* periods; the further divisions, which are in a
sense imposed on the chronological periods, are the moments or
motifs in the changing modes of the Church's historicity. They
indicate theological or Church-historical distinctions rather than
chronological; as such they parallel in function, but are by no
means identical with, the dogmatic motifs imposed on and forma-
tive of the chronological periods in the history of dogma.

Baur did not live long enough to bring his work in Church
history to completion. Consequently, he was unable to work out
fully the details of his division of the history of the Church
into theological motifs as well as chronological periods, to explore
the interrelations between these two types of division, or to carry
the former forward into the last two volumes of lectures on Church
history, which were published posthumously. The structure of what
follows is the result of extrapolation from material[176] in which
Baur makes clear how he intended to organize the motifs of
Church history, and especially from the structure of the first three
volumes of the *Kirchengeschichte*, where these moments are most
clearly reflected in the organization and presentation. The contents
of this survey are based primarily on the *Kirchengeschichte*, but
they are supplemented in some instances with material from
Baur's various works in the history of dogma.

The ancient period of the Church, concluding with the papacy
of Gregory the Great in 604, encompasses four Church-historical
motifs. The first of these consists of the life and work of the founder
of Christianity, Jesus of Nazareth, who embodies the original,
most complete and normative actualization of the idea of reconciliation. The second motif, the establishment of the idea of a
Christian Church as a universal principle of salvation against a
return to Judaism, is represented by the struggle between Jewish
and Pauline Christianity through the middle of the second century.
These first two motifs have been examined earlier in this chapter.
With respect to the third moment, the struggle between the historical manifestation of the idea of reconciliation in the Christian
Church and the notion of Christianity as a pure idea or as a universal cosmological principle, I have summarized above Baur's
argument that the Church emerges as a distinct historical phenomenon, characterized by the congruence of absoluteness and positivity, in its struggle against Gnosticism and Montanism as well as
against Judaism.[177] The struggle against Gnosticism, which marks
the third moment, is carried forth both dogmatically, by Irenaeus,
Tertullian, and even the Alexandrine theologians, and institution-

---

176 Cf. *Epochen*, pp. 251–52; and *An Hase*, pp. 82–83, 85.

177 See above, pp. 66–70, 129–30. Although in themselves quite different,
Baur treats Gnosticism and Montanism together as posing a common threat to
the historicity of the Church. For example, Montanism's "chiliastic fanaticism"
precludes "every possibility of an historical development" of the Church. Cf.
Das Christenthum, p. 247 (E.T., II, 1).

ally, by the development of an episcopal form of government which enables the Church to achieve a viable historical structure.[178]

The struggle again Judaism and Gnosticism is encompassed chronologically by a fourth moment in the history of the Church, that in which the *primary* manifestation of the idea of the Church is found in dogma, understood as the doctrines of the Christian faith in which the content or object of faith is rationally formulated and expressed. From the rich and creative development of the great dogmatic symbols of the Church in the first six centuries, it can be seen that the fundamental achievement of the Church in the ancient period, that which shapes and defines its very historical nature, is to objectify its faith and to actualize the ideality of reconciliation in the historical form of dogma. Beginning with the Council of Nicea, this is done primarily by means of the abstract, objectivizing categories of Greek philosophical thought, with the result that dogma functions as an external, objective, authoritarian formulation of equally objective and external truths, to be believed on authority rather than understood reflectively. With the important exception of Augustine, this objectivism and authoritarianism characterizes the nature of both dogma and faith in the ancient period; it impresses itself also on the development of the Church hierarchy, which, however, remains of secondary importance. This motif begins with the New Testament writings and ends only with the termination of creative doctrinal formulation on the part of the ancient Church. The papacy of Gregory the Great, 590–604, is symbolic of this termination and of the transition to a new motif and period, since on the one hand he is the last of the "Church Fathers" and on the other hand is a prototype of the medieval popes; Baur regards him as a "Janus type" of figure.[179]

The medieval period encompasses some nine centuries and, like the patristic period, a number of different Church-historical motifs. The first of these is transitional in character, comprising the gradual formation of the hierarchical and theological systems of the Middle Ages. In this motif, whose chronological limits are the termination of the papacy of Gregory I in 604 and the beginning of the papacy of Gregory VII in 1073, dogma is still the primary mode of manifestation of the idea of the Church. But the period of creative dogmatic formulation has terminated, and this is a time of sterile and barren controversy and of abstract supernaturalism in dogmatic understanding (e.g., the controversies over Monotheletism, adoptionism, predestination, and the Eucharist). There are also early attempts at dogmatic systematization in the *Ekdosis* of John of Damascus and the *Sentences* of Isidore of

---

[178] Cf. *Das Christenthum*, pp. 248–56, 260, 272–74, 289, 299–304, 467 (E.T., II, 3–11, 15, 27–30, 56–61, 229); *Lehrbuch der Dogmengeschichte* (3d ed.), p. 75.

[179] Cf. *Kirchengeschichte*, II, 228; III, 1; *Epochen*, p. 252; *Dogmengeschichte*, I/1, 51–53; III, 114; *Dreieinigkeit*, 1, 827.

Spain, and also the transition to Western dogmatics in the system of John Scotus Erigena. This period also witnesses the formation of the Western conception of the papacy and the creation of an hierarchical organism.[180]

The second motif in the medieval period represents the fruition of the system of papal monarchy, characterized by Baur as "the ruling absolutism of the Church." The primary manifestation of the idea of the Church is no longer dogma but its hierarchical institutional structure, which becomes an end in itself. From the beginning, this structure is flawed by its absolute identification of a single individual with the universal idea and by the inherent conflict between papal absolutism and the conciliar system, a conflict which eventually leads to the breakdown of the medieval synthesis.[181] The systematizing and absolutizing tendency imposes itself also on dogma, which issues in the great scholastic systems, although at the same time another tendency begins to express itself in these works, namely, the gradual penetration of objective dogmatic statements by self-reflective consciousness, i.e., by rational dialectic. The contradiction between the absolutist and reflective tendencies in the dogma of this period leads eventually to the collapse of the scholastic systems. The great concern of scholastic theology is to mediate, philosophically, between the being and knowledge of God, and, epistemologically, between faith and reason. But the mediation is achieved only externally and artificially, not internally and dynamically.[182] A third and final moment in the medieval period appears in the fourteenth and fifteenth centuries, when the inherent instability in the hierarchical and dogmatic systems emerges into a process of dissolution or breakdown, which is most apparent in the ethical realm, where the impetus to reform first makes itself felt, but can also be seen theologically in figures like Duns Scotus and William of Ockham.[183]

Beginning with the Reformation, which marks the transition to the third period in the history of the Church, it is only possible to surmise how Baur would have structured the Church-historical motifs, since the last two volumes of his work in Church history consist of posthumously published lecture manuscripts which apparently had not yet been brought into full structural continuity with the preceding, published work. It is clear, however, from Volume IV, which carries the history of the Church from the Reformation to the end of the eighteenth century, that this history can no longer be characterized simply according to the relative primacy of dogma, institutions, or other Church-historical forms in the his-

---

[180] Cf. *Kirchengeschichte*, III, 1–6, 69–73; *Epochen*, pp. 253–54.

[181] Cf. *Kirchengeschichte*, III, 171–73, 254–56, 282; *Epochen*, pp. 254–55.

[182] Cf. *Kirchengeschichte*, III, 3, 281–82; *Dogmengeschichte*, I/1, 53–56; III, 3, 4; *Dreieinigkeit*, II, 345–69, 578–713, 866–80.

[183] Cf. *Kirchengeschichte*, III, 354–93, 516–37; *Dreieinigkeit*, II, 867, 871–79.

toricity of the Church. The new, fundamental, and characteristic fact in the life of the Church is the contrast and opposition between Catholicism and Protestantism. Consequently, the last two volumes of the Church history are organized so as to provide a continuing comparison of Catholic, Lutheran, Reformed (including Anglican), and other Protestant (chiefly sectarian) Churches, through several different chronological periods. (In the lectures covering the nineteenth century, Protestantism is treated as a whole rather than according to the different major Protestant Churches, and the scope of coverage is limited almost entirely to Germany.) In treating the histories of each of the respective Churches, Baur covers the familiar ground of dogma or theology, Church organization, worship, ethics, and outward relations, both ecclesiastical and political.[184]

For Catholicism, the hierarchy continues to function, with important and continuing modifications, as the paradigmatic form for the historical actualization of the Christian idea. In Protestantism, however, the locus of authority is no longer found in hierarchy and tradition but in Scripture, which accordingly serves as the formal principle of the Reformation. (This is another way of expressing the fact that Catholicism and Protestantism are distinguished according to fundamentally different conceptions of the nature of the Church.) The authority of Scripture, however, has as its presupposition the higher principle of the freedom of faith, since the objective and divine content of Scripture becomes authoritative only when it is accepted freely and as congruent with one's authentic subjectivity. The formal principle of the Reformation, then, requires for its completion the material principle, the doctrine of justification by faith. Faith is understood by the Reformation as an act of religious consciousness which mediates authentically between the objective truth of the Gospel and the

---

[184] There is much that is incomplete in this presentation, and it does not bear the form of a polished product. For example, in *Kirchengeschichte*, IV, there is almost no treatment of Protestant theology, which on the other hand is the almost exclusive concern of *Dogmengeschichte*, III. The sections devoted to Protestantism in *Kirchengeschichte*, IV are largely concerned with ecclesiastical controversies, institutional and political matters, worship and ethics. On the other hand, since there is no mention of Catholic dogma in *Dogmengeschichte*, III, this is considered at some length in *Kirchengeschichte*, IV. This would seem to mark a division of labor in Baur's lectures which might have been corrected and balanced had these volumes been prepared by him for publication. *Kirchengeschichte*, V is more heavily theological than ecclesiastical in its treatment of both Protestantism and Catholicism, apparently because of the lack of a corresponding set of lectures in dogma. Further, the scope of coverage in this volume is narrower than in the preceding one. Important material, however, is omitted from both. There is no consideration, for example, of Eastern Orthodoxy or of American Protestantism (although the latter is very briefly covered in short sections on the "dissemination" of Christianity in *Kirchengeschichte*, IV). The omission of Orthodoxy is also a conspicuous fault of Vol. III. Baur's focus of interest is Germany, and to a lesser extent the Continent and England.

subjectivity of human spirit. As such, although Baur never expresses it this way, faith is the characteristic mode or primary form of the Church's historicity in Protestantism. For it is in faith thus understood that the mediation between objectivity and subjectivity, which is the distinguishing mark of Protestantism when compared with the ancient and medieval periods, is achieved. By virtue of the distinction between the invisible and the visible Church, the institutional structure of the Church is no longer absolutized. The relationship between faith and knowledge is now understood differently than in scholastic theology: the content of faith is no longer given as something alien to thought, authoritatively demanding the consent of the intellect; rather, in faith the objective truth of Christianity stands internally related to the thinking subject, who thereby discovers that it is the truth of his own being, not a truth imposed on him externally and authoritatively.[185]

Finally, as we have seen in discussing Baur's periodization of dogma, the delicate balance between objectivity and subjectivity achieved for the first time by the Reformers has been in constant danger in the history of Protestantism of breaking down into a pure objectivism (orthodox dogmatics) or a pure subjectivism (Socinianism, Arminianism, rationalism).[186] Another way of putting it is to say that the task of Protestantism has been to work out a proper understanding of the relation of the objective content of faith to critical thought, both philosophical and historical. This task is by no means completed, and as we have seen earlier it has, according to the last volume of the Church history, gone through three phases in the modern period of Protestantism, from the middle of the eighteenth century to the middle of the nineteenth. This topic was taken up at some length at the beginning of Chapter II, in discussing the need for an historical-critical theology.[187] We have thus brought this survey to the point where Baur's study of the Church's historical past merges into his shaping of a new theological discipline.

A Look Backward

At the end of the last chapter, in defending Baur against the charge of apriorism, I suggested that it is more in terms of his universal vision than in his treatment of particular persons and facts that his power as an historian and imagination as a theologian become most apparent and compelling, and that the "fitness" of his interpretations might be more fully appreciated. Something

---

185 Cf. *Kirchengeschichte*, IV, 1–7; *Epochen*, pp. 257–58; *Dogmengeschichte*, I/1, 57–58; III, 4–7, 12, 19, 48–50, 59–64, 70–71, 114; *Lehrbuch der Dogmengeschichte* (1st ed.), p. 198; *Versöhnung*, p. 287.

186 Cf. *Dogmengeschichte*, III, 13–17, 81, 100–105; *Lehrbuch der Dogmengeschichte* (1st ed.), p. 205.

187 See above, pp. 37–39.

of that vision has now been presented—a vision of Christianity as a fundamentally historical phenomenon, possessing a point of origin constitutive of its very historical life and a sequence of historical forms which render its endurance and development through time a concrete possibility and reality. As we look backward from this broader perspective, our attention rests again on Christianity's point of origin in its relation to the larger totality of which it is a part. Here most of the methodological problems we considered in Chapter IV come into clearest focus: the historian's use of speculation in achieving critical objectivity and the concomitant question of apriorism, the place of the historical theologian's dogmatic perspective in shaping his interpretation of the past, the significance of historical study for faith, the relevance of the past for man's present self-understanding, the relation between the whole and its parts and between the universal process and individual agents, the problem of historical development, and the phenomenon of continuity and discontinuity as an historical equivalent to miracle.

These problems prompt a number of questions. Does Baur's historical-critical interpretation of Jesus possess the power and substance required by his own understanding of the central position of Jesus in the history of Christianity generally? Does a person, this person, really stand before us as the one in whom and through whom the universal idea of Christianity is concretely actualized? Does the essential originality or *discontinuity* of Jesus' self-awareness and message, as Baur shows them to us—a messianic consciousness which breaks through all previous expectation, and a radical insistence on the contrast between the kingdom of heaven and this world, on the inwardness and universality of moral intention, and on the establishment of a relationship of righteousness between God and man through the reconciling work of the One sent from God—does this historically explicated discontinuity provide sufficient basis on which to stake out an historical alternative to a miraculous and therefore totally nonhistorical conception of God-manhood? In a way, everything in Baur's historical-critical theology comes to rest at this point; for the promise of this theology has been that, since it is a "purely historical question" whether the person of Jesus of Nazareth "really possesses the attributes which belong to the established concept of the Redeemer,"[188] an historical investigation of the Gospels can at least help to disclose to us whether Jesus was in fact what Christian faith has claimed for him. Baur believes that historical study can provide an affirmative disclosure at this point.

But it might be objected that just at this point Baur's theology is a failure, that his historically explicated Christology lacks the imagination and brilliance of the Christologies of Schleiermacher

[188] "Anzeige der beiden academischen Schriften," *TZT*, I, 242. See above, p. 103.

and Kierkegaard, that his Jesus does not "live" in the way that history as a whole "lives" for Baur. His concern, it might be said, is too heavily weighted toward the rational content of Jesus' moral teaching and self-understanding, and not enough toward his proclamation of the Gospel of salvation or toward the shape of his *life* as the man-for-God and the man-for-other-men. In other words, it could be argued that Baur fails to deliver in a satisfactory way what has been promised in his envisioning of the need for an historical-critical theology, and what is required both by his treatment of the history of Church as a whole and by his dogmatic Christology, namely, that Jesus is to be understood as the most complete embodiment of God-manhood and as the one in whom Christianity is first clearly, definitely, and definitively expressed, the founder to whom every subsequent development in the history of the Church must be related as a subordinate effect. Baur fails, it could be said, because ultimately his vision of Jesus does not move beyond that typical of liberal theology and of Kant. There is certainly some truth in this criticism. Baur himself acknowledged his indebtedness to Kant in interpreting Jesus' morality of intention; and Baur's Jesus may indeed by the real, unacknowledged source of the Jesus of Ritschl and Harnack and the other great liberal theologians at the end of the century.

And yet, in my interpretation of Baur on this point, I have tried to see more in his Jesus than one can find either in Kant on the one hand or in Ritschl and Harnack on the other. Something vital has been lost in the transition from Baur to his successors. For Christology really is the unifying, vital center of Baur's work as an historical theologian. What evidence can we adduce? In the first place, I have described earlier Baur's clear rejection of Kant's Christology and of the Christology of rationalism generally—specifically, the notion of Christ as an abstract ideal in the moral consciousness of mankind which could never come to decisive historical actualization in a single individual; we have likewise examined his dissociation from the Christology not only of Hegel but also of left- and right-wing Hegelianism.[189] In the second place, Baur's historical treatment of Jesus must be interpreted in the light of his dogmatic stance on the Christological question; i.e., we can give him credit for envisioning what is needed in an historical approach to Jesus, even if his own approach is not entirely satisfying.[190] Third, Jesus' teaching, according to Baur, includes more than a Kantian ethic of intentionality, more than the Beatitudes of the Sermon on the Mount. There is a purely "religious" as well as ethical element in his teaching, namely, the call to perfect righteousness in the relationship to God, a righteousness made

189 See above, pp. 42–43, 58–64, 71–73.
190 I have, however, raised some questions about Baur's dogmatic Christology too, namely, its refusal to allow the total and perfect union of divine idea and human form in Jesus. See above, pp. 106–107.

possible through the "power of redemption and reconciliation which has come through Jesus." In addition there is the teaching concerning the kingdom of heaven contained especially in the parables, the kingdom which comes as a gift and stands in complete contrast to the anxieties and estrangement of finite existence. Although Baur finds the clearest expression and criterion of Jesus' teaching in the Sermon on the Mount, this teaching implies what is found elsewhere more clearly, for example in Matthew 11:29–30 and in the parables of the kingdom: that Jesus also proclaimed the Gospel of grace and connected himself with this Gospel.[191] This fact suggests the final and most important point, that during the last decade of his life Baur was moving increasingly toward the discovery of an essential link between the teaching of Jesus and his person, a link drawn not only by the primitive faith in Jesus but by Jesus himself. This movement is to be seen in the lectures on New Testament theology, where Baur argues that Jesus referred to himself as the "Son of God" (Matt. 11:25–30) in the sense of possessing a unity of consciousness with the Father such that he knew himself to be the mediator of a new divine revelation. Or, more specifically, Jesus' person "belongs essentially and inseparably together with his teaching; he is himself the concrete *Anschauung* of the significance, extending itself into all eternity, of the absolute truth of his teaching."[192] In these posthumously published lectures, Baur comes closest to satisfying in his critical exegesis the dogmatic requirement which he himself placed on the historical Jesus by virtue of his total conception of the historicity of the Christian Church. It is fair to suggest that his historical study of Jesus moved carefully in this direction from the beginning.

Consequently, Baur does say more about Jesus than his apparently liberal portrait would otherwise have seemed to allow. His difficulty at this point reflects the immensity of problems facing the historian as he seeks to understand and interpret, not only this particular man, but every individual historical agent in his specific place in the totality of the historical process. Dilthey suggests that the understanding of individuals is the most peculiarly difficult and at the same time the most ultimately rewarding task in historical study. What is difficult and rewarding for the historian with respect to individual men generally becomes agonizingly so with respect to the man Jesus. For the normal categories by which the historian elucidates historical personality—e.g., the relation of the individual to the idea or meaning-system he embodies or expresses —are applicable but not adequate; Jesus not only expresses the idea of God-manhood, he *is* this idea; in him the divine and the human, the universal and the particular, merge into a total yet differentiated unity. This unity need not be understood as a non-historical or miraculous phenomenon, for it is the fulfillment of

191 See above, pp. 113, 226–27.
192 See above, pp. 231–34.

manhood, of the historicity of man; but nevertheless it transcends historical understanding. Here, indeed, every historical interpretation must break down and point beyond itself. Yet at the same time the historical approach to this man, like every other, must be made. Thus we may applaud Baur for making the approach, but also for making it cautiously, hesitantly, and sparingly (our attention to the problem has overemphasized the amount of space, but not the *significance* it occupies in his historical study). And we need not be too surprised that his vision of Jesus *from a distance*, in the context of the historicity of the Church as a whole, which he so imaginatively interpreted through its development, is more compelling and satisfying.

6 * THE SIGNIFICANCE OF BAUR
FOR THE QUESTION OF
HISTORICAL KNOWLEDGE IN
CONTEMPORARY THEOLOGY

SOME PROBLEMS IN BAUR'S CONCEPTION
OF HISTORICAL THEOLOGY

At the beginning of this study, we reviewed some of the most common criticisms which have been brought against Baur's work as an historical theologian. It has been claimed that he was a disciple of Hegel's philosophy of Spirit, that he imposed a priori dialectical patterns on the historical facts, that he submerged individuals in the general historical process, that he denied any special significance to Jesus of Nazareth, and that he reduced Christianity to a purely natural and historical phenomenon. In the ensuing chapters, we have had occasion to examine each of these charges at some length. We explored the nature of Baur's relation to Hegel, noting that while he appropriated Hegel's view of the relation between God and history, he modified the latter's tendency toward acosmism and specifically criticized his Christology. I have claimed that the charge of apriorism must be rejected when Baur's historical methodology and results are rightly understood. I have pointed out that he saw the *historical* significance of individual agents in terms of their participation in the historical process as a whole, but that he by no means ignored the details and particularity of specific events and persons. I have argued that his historically explicated Christology, with its focus on the person and teaching of Jesus of Nazareth, forms the vital center of his work as an historical theologian. And I have suggested that his historical theology attempted to render the absolute truth and divine foundation of Christianity intelligible in a new way, without the interposition of supernatural or miraculous categories.

At the same time, however, I have raised some rather different questions about Baur's procedure in historical theology, which have at their basis his idealist vision of the historical process as a function of the divine life and his related tendency to collapse dogmatics into historical theology.[1] These questions can be made explicit by referring now to Karl Barth's important discussion of Baur in *Die protestantische Theologie im 19. Jahrhundert*. Barth suggests that effective opposition to Baur can be raised from only two sides. The first is represented by Franz Overbeck's rejection of any Church historiography, Baur's included, which attempts to treat the history of the Church in positive terms—i.e., which assumes that Christianity is indeed an historical possibility and attempts to describe its essential reality in terms of dogmas, institutions, forms of development, etc. Baur had "by no means described Christian history but rather with a stiff neck his own present."[2]

This is the sort of criticism which the Barth of the *Römerbrief* might have been expected to advance (and others, too, e.g., Kierkegaard, Schweitzer, Werner, and Nietzsche). But Barth no longer regards it as providing a viable alternative to Baur.

The other effective opposition could not come from such a supernaturalism but only from the sort of historical theology which would be fundamentally determined not to be a party to the step in which the old and the new supernaturalism are fundamentally at one with Baur: the identification of the Spirit indeed knowing and ruling history with one's own human spirit viewing history. This would be a theology which would intend to *believe* this Spirit as the Spirit of God and therefore just for this reason not to *have* it. Such a theology, as the proof of its faith and of its spirituality, would in no way subsume *Church history* under a concept of *history generally*. It would not put itself in a place above the Church but now really in the matter, i.e., not on the throne of God or in the idea of humanity but in concrete obedience in the Church. Furthermore, it would not abolish the distinction between history of dogma and biblical theology, as Baur did, and as has been done in approximately the whole of the more recent theology, just that being the substance of its method. It would, without having at its disposal another tool than that of historical criticism, and without renouncing this tool, know that the Bible must be read under all conditions, always as historical-critical, in *faith*, and the documents of Church history and history of dogma, however, in *love*. It would know that there, in the prophets and apostles, *God* speaks to us in the neighbor; here, however, in the voices of the Fathers, God speaks to us in *the neighbor*. It would know that history there, in the Bible, is to be understood as *answer*; here, in Church history, history of dogma, and history of theology, as *question*. It would know to seek the *criterion* of all instruction there;

---

1 See above, pp. 134–42, 172–74.
2 Karl Barth, *Die protestantische Theologie im 19. Jahrhundert*, p. 457. The reference is to Franz Overbeck, *Christentum und Kultur* (Basel: Verlag Benno Schwabe, 1919), pp. 180–82.

here, however, to seek the positive or negative instruction *itself*. In both places it would have to go between a pragmatism which wants too little and a dualism which wants too much. It has, in faith and in love, to watch over the boundaries which irreversibly distinguish man, who understands history, from God, who is the judge and director of history.

From here, then, without a know-it-all attitude but also without pussyfooting, the question may be directed to Baur, how the concept of the idea of history may perchance, according to the attributes specified by him, be related to the concept of God. What is history? Baur answers: History is "the eternally clear mirror in which spirit perceives itself, views its own image, in order to be what it is in itself also for itself, for its own consciousness, and to know itself as the moving power of historical becoming."[3] "Really?" might be the rejoinder. If then, at any rate, the history of the Church were to be such a history in which *God* in the neighbor and God in *the neighbor* speaks to us—ought then the history of the Church also to be understood and presented as such self-contemplation?[4]

The points raised in this important passage might be restated as follows: (1) By virtue of his German philosophical idealism, and as an heir of the all-too-Lutheran anthropocentrism which pervaded German liberal theology of the nineteenth century, Baur failed to watch over the boundaries which irreversible distinguish man, who understands history, from God, who is the judge and director of history. Consequently, he tended to identify the divine Spirit, who knows and rules history, with the finite human spirits who view history. (2) By understanding history primarily as the process in which the divine Spirit realizes himself or comes to self-consciousness in thought or in self-contemplation, Baur did not understand Church history as properly the process of *dialogue* between God and man but as an intradivine and possibly also intrahuman monologue (or as an intradivine monologue in which human spirit is understood as one of the modes of the divine being-in-thought); he did not understand Church history and the Bible as the realm in which God *reveals* himself to us. (3) A corrective theology, as proof of its faith in the Spirit knowing and ruling history as the Spirit *of God* and of its willingness not to "possess" this Spirit, or to encompass him by historical understanding, or to confuse him with the all-too-human spirits which also shape, for better or for worse, the course of history, would not subsume Church history under the general categories of history (and of historical knowledge?). (4) A corrective historical-critical theology would also make a distinction between its treatment of the Bible, which must be read in faith and understood as testifying to that prior

---

[3] *Lehrbuch der Dogmengeschichte* (3d ed.), p. 59.

[4] Karl Barth, *Die protestantische Theologie im 19. Jahrhundert* (3d ed., Zürich: Evangelischer Verlag AG., 1960), pp. 457–58. Italics his own. Copyright 1946. Quoted by permission.

and special stretch of history in which *God* speaks, and Church history, history of dogma, and history of theology, which must be read in love and understood as that "subsequent" history in which it is primarily the voice of *the neighbor*, in and through whom God speaks to us, that is heard. In either case, the historical-critical theologian must treat his data in faith and/or in love to perceive the presence and work and word of God in it.

I am substantially in agreement with the first of these points but not with the last two; in other words, I agree by and large with Barth's diagnosis but not with his prescription. The second point probably represents a misinterpretation of the passage quoted from the *Lehrbuch der Dogmengeschichte* to substantiate it, but it nevertheless raises an important question about Baur's theology which must be examined.

The first point indicates the inherent limitations which restrict the usefulness of German idealism in providing the conceptual tools by which to understand the relation between God and the world, history, and man. The inner congruence and mutual presence to each other of God and man are understood suggestively and profoundly by this philosophical tradition, but the distinction which, as Baur also recognized, is the presupposition of the relation is not clearly understood. More specifically, Baur fails to develop the doctrine of creation which would seem to be implied by his own historical treatment of Christianity and his Christology.[5] The reason would seem to be the defect his doctrine of God shares with Hegel, namely that God necessarily dirempts himself into an other than himself (the world, chiefly man, the human spirit, human consciousness) in order to actualize his own spirituality as free Spirit, concrete Spirit, thinking Spirit. God cannot fully exist apart from the world for Hegel and Baur, and therefore the world and man become, implicitly, a necessary mode of the Godhead. History is understood as the process of the divine self-actualization in thought. At the same time, Baur's conception and study of history, his continued insistence on the positivity of the Church and its Gospel, his various descriptions of the mutual transcendence of God and the world, and his apparent later criticism of Hegel's doctrine of God, mitigate against the acosmism or identity implicit in this view of the Trinity.[6]

Another symptom of the theological deficiency Baur shares with idealism is his disconcertingly ambiguous use of the term "Spirit" in certain contexts, for example, in describing the inner dynamic foundation of the historical process. Is this the divine Spirit or human spirit, or that quality of spirituality which God and man share in common? Are the ideas which constitute the life of history the actualizations of the thought of the divine or of human Spirit?

---

[5] See above, pp. 140–41.
[6] See above, pp. 134–42.

Obviously of both, since history is the work of God and man together. But in what sense is the historical work of man meaningfully independent of the divine life in thought? Wherein can the work of God and of man in history be distinguished from each other?

There are indications that, toward the end of his career, Baur had become provisionally aware of some of the difficulties involved in using the categories of Hegel's panentheistic idealism as the foundation for his own radically historical theology,[7] a theology in which the historical mediation, and thus the unity-in-distinction, of God and man remains the central factor. There is, for example, a curiously perceptive remark that Strauss's antihistorical Christology is already implied in the simple Hegelian propositions that finite spirit is man and that man is spirit implicitly.[8] There is the awareness that the "aberration" represented by Feuerbach's subjective egoism is "connected" with Hegel's doctrine of Spirit.[9] There is the fact that in Baur's *Kirchengeschichte des neunzehnten Jahrhunderts*, which represents his last study of his theological contemporaries, Hegel is given a very cursory treatment.[10] Also, in this work, Baur indicates that he views favorably the efforts by Rothe, I. H. Fichte, and Weisse to fashion a genuine theism in which the transcendence as well as the immanence of God would be preserved, in opposition to the tendency toward a pantheistic *Weltanschauung* on the part of Schleiermacher and Hegel.[11] But despite these factors, Baur never attempts to work out an alternative theological foundation—an adequate doctrine of creation— for his own historical theology; and the same Hegelian propositions which lie behind Strauss represent, at least for a while, some of the presuppositions of his own thought. Although Baur was partially aware of the danger in an implicit confusion of God and man, the theology of our century has become acutely aware of it, and there can be no return, therefore, to Baur's idealism as such or to some of the particular forms and categories of his theology.

Barth's second point against Baur is based on an enigmatic passage from the *Lehrbuch der Dogmengeschichte* which we already have discussed at some length, namely, that history is "the eternally clear mirror in which spirit perceives itself. . . ." In this passage, "history" apparently refers to historical study rather than the historical process, and "spirit" to finite human spirit rather than the divine Spirit.[12] Therefore, this particular passage does not imply, as Barth seems to suggest, that God does not *reveal* himself to man in history but merely engages in "self-contempla-

---

7 See above, pp. 56–58.
8 *Dogmengeschichte*, III, 536.
9 *Kirchengeschichte*, V, 393–94.
10 See above, p. 38, n. 3.
11 *Kirchengeschichte*, V, pp. 407–409.
12 See above, pp. 182–84.

tion." Nevertheless, on Barth's reading of the passage, it does correspond to others in which the autonomy and contingency of history are called into question, as we have seen from the paragraphs just preceding. And if history is understood primarily as the divine self-mirroring, how can it also serve as the medium of divine self-*revelation*? Can there be an authentic doctrine of revelation without a corresponding doctrine of creation?

Baur avoided for the most part the category of revelation because of its supernaturalistic connotations in the polemical situation of his time. But the notion of revelation is not entirely excluded from his theology. He describes the relation of the divine Spirit to human spirit as the divine act of revelation, to which faith corresponds subjectively.[13] The entire process of reconciliation between God and man, as mediated historically by the Church, is revelatory in character in the sense that communication between God and man is thereby established, and the knowledge given to faith corresponds to the knowledge God has of himself. Indeed, precisely because history is the process of divine self-mediation, it is also the medium of divine revelation: in history God unfolds his nature and redemptive purpose. With Schelling, as we have seen, Baur affirms that "history is revelation."[14] Ernst Käsemann has clearly recognized the sense in which this is true for Baur, and what its implications are for historical theology:

History is . . . understood as the process of the objectively unfolding revelation of the Spirit. In its objectivity it is as such and as a whole the object of research, indeed of an historical-critical nature. "Historical-critical" means that no single moment is to be absolutized or negated, but that each moment is to be understood as a member of the whole in the continuity of immanent historical progress and of the self-realizing revelation of the Spirit or of the idea in its totality. Historical-critical work is therefore for Baur obviously something more than a tool of the trade; rather, it has a deeply religious task and is the medium for attaining religious certainty. For it is the relevant counterpart to historical revelation as an address to the man called in faith; it is, namely, the adequate hearing and understanding of revelation, in so far as it has been handed down in the past. Historical criticism is the function of living faith on its way from a past which has consciously become such, into its own present and future, a present and future which just this past places within the comprehensive continuity of the totality of history.[15]

History as a whole is the revelation of God, and therefore historical theology as a whole is the "relevant counterpart" to revelation, the proper response of faith in the presence of revelation. But more specifically, divine revelation has its focus for Baur in the unique-

13 *Dogmengeschichte*, I/1, 50. See above, pp. 120–21.
14 See above, pp. 145–46.
15 Ernst Käsemann, "Einführung" to Vol. I of F. C. Baur, *Ausgewählte Werke in Einzelausgaben*, p. xix.

ness and particularity of Jesus Christ. It is more accurate to say that Church history is the contingent, reduced, derived perpetuation of Jesus' uniqueness, than that Jesus is simply the nonunique, accidental starting point of general Church history. Likewise, it is more accurate to say that Church history is unique within universal history, by virtue of the uniqueness of its founder, than that Church history is simply an instance of universal history. Thus, in saying that "history is revelation" for Baur, we must understand that he moves *from* Jesus Christ *to* the Church *to* history as a whole.[16] Although the theoretical foundation for a doctrine of revelation would seem to be lacking in Baur's thought—namely, a conception of creation such as would permit an authentic dialogue between God and man—nevertheless his theology does preserve a strong emphasis on revelation by virtue of its Christology. It is in the person and teaching of Jesus of Nazareth that the reconciliation of God and man is revealed in such fundamentally decisive fashion that the entire *telos* of Christianity and of history as a whole is contained therein. In some of his sermons based on Johannine texts, as well as in his critical exegesis of Matthew, Baur describes Jesus as the "revealer."[17] Thus, in saying that history is revelation, Baur does not, as has been claimed, eliminate the hermeneutical principle of the Reformation (its "gospel of justification by faith") or destroy the Christian kerygma.[18] Indeed, historical theology, as the relevant counterpart to revelation, is riveted to the uniqueness and particularity of Jesus of Nazareth as its most important single datum.

I have said that I agree by and large with Barth's diagnosis of the weakness in Baur's theology—his lack of a doctrine of creation—but not with his prescription. For if Baur was in danger of confusing the human spirit and human history with God, by virtue of his panentheism, then the solution is not to be found by separating God (and the knowledge of God—faith and dogmatic theology) from history (and the study of history—historical knowledge and historical theology), and by destroying all internal connections between them. God and history, faith and historical knowledge, dogmatic theology and historical theology, must be internally related precisely because, as we have seen, history is the medium of divine revelation, because historical theology is one important element in the theological response to this revelation, and because the Christian Church and its founding events are fundamentally historical in character. Baur discovered and explicated these internal relationships. He probed them more intensively and creatively than any other major theologian. This is the mark of his greatness and importance for theology. We have examined his conception of

---

16 I am indebted to Hans W. Frei for this observation.
17 See above, p. 231.
18 Cf. Käsemann, *op. cit.*, p. xxiv; and Ernst Wolf, "Einführung" to Vol. II of F. C. Baur, *Ausgewählte Werke in Einzelausgaben*, pp. viii, xx, xxiii.

the relation between God and history and between faith and historical knowledge at some length in the pages above.[19] We shall turn to the final relation, that between dogmatics and historical theology, in the concluding section of this chapter.

But my task first is to suggest that the *internal relationships* which Baur so imaginatively explicated tend to merge into *identity* because of the structural or systematic deficiency his theology inherited from German idealism. For example, all dogmatic theology tends to become historical theology in Baur's view. The dogmatic theologian possesses no normative or unconditioned truth; he is not in a position to make normative assertions. For in Baur's view there is no nonhistorical knowledge, no knowledge left unconditioned by the relativity of time and place, no knowledge which is untinged by a perspective. The subjectivity of the dogmatician as well as of the historian is regarded more as the relative reflex of an objective process than as the interpretive and creative power of a critical mind. Despite his effort to distinguish dogmatics from the history of dogma, the former tends to be regarded as simply a stroboscopic picture in which the relentless movement of the latter appears for a moment to stand still.[20] Hence there is some justification in Troeltsch's designation of Baur's position as "historicism"; for Baur, as for Troeltsch himself, there is no theological or philosophical knowledge which is not fundamentally and in principle historical.[21]

Hermann Diem fears that Troeltsch's resolution of dogmatics into "historicism" renders impossible the dogmatic task of the verification of the truth-claims of faith, since all truth becomes relatively conditioned.[22] Diem has accurately specified the danger attendant on any attempt, such as those made by Baur and Troeltsch, to develop an internal and reciprocally essential connection between dogmatics and historical theology. But this danger need not become an actuality, in light of the following considerations. First, it should be possible to explore the internal connection between dogmatics and historical theology without dissolving the former into the latter, as Baur tended to do, despite his intentions to the contrary, and as Troeltsch did in fact, or without surrendering the task of verification to a complete relativism. There are other forms of dogmatic verification than the historical, even if the latter is considered as an intrinsic and essential part of dogmatics.[23] Second, historical verification need not be surrendered as an impossible task even though it is inescapably

19 See above, pp. 134–42, 174–81.
20 See above, pp. 172–74, 240–41.
21 Ernst Troeltsch, "Adolf v. Harnack und Ferd. Christ. v. Baur," *Harnack Festgabe*, p. 284.
22 Hermann Diem, *Dogmatics*, Harold Knight, trans. (Edinburgh: Oliver & Boyd, 1959), pp. 4–9.
23 See below, pp. 283–84.

relativistic. For relative historical certainty is clearly a possibility, and this is all that dogmatics can require of an historical datum. Finally, both Baur and Troeltsch have shown that it is possible to know the Absolute relatively in history, that there can be a relative knowledge of the Absolute, and that therefore absolute truth can be the concern of historical-critical theology. Baur especially attempted to engage in the historical analysis of an event with absolute or primal or authoritative significance for a religious community. In other words, he attempted to examine a religious absolute in terms of its "historical absoluteness," or in terms of its historical function as an absolute. This is a legitimate and essential, but not the only, part of theological verification.

At the root of this implicit confusion between dogmatics and historical theology is the danger that for Baur, as we have seen, the historical process in which God actualizes himself and lives will be identified with God himself. On the ontological level, the tendency toward identification takes this form, since Baur (with Hegel) is a panentheist, for whom the root reality is the divine Spirit or Subject, not cosmic substance or process. His position is not atheistic, although his panentheism could of course be inverted into an atheism. But on the epistemological level, it is not historical theology that is absorbed into dogmatics, as is the tendency with Karl Barth, and which might be expected as the more logical implication of the idealist tradition they share in common; but dogmatics that becomes a function of historical theology. Baur thus combines an historicism with a panentheistic monism.

In this respect, it must be acknowledged that he represents a clear break with traditional theism, a break which is dangerous on the one hand but provides fruitful possibilities for constructive theology on the other. For it seems clear that we cannot simply return to a traditional theism, that we must affirm that in some sense God exists in process, that he "lives" in history, that he is enriched by and subjects himself to historical and cosmic experience, and that he can be known historically (i.e., historically-critically) as well as dogmatically. But we must affirm this without at the same time denying that God is first and primarily free and concrete in himself and that he then creates and adopts to himself analogically that historical process outside himself in which he *also* lives by grace but from which he remains radically distinct. If God is understood as radically distinct or transcendent, then he can also be understood (as, for example, in biblical faith) as radically immanent in *particular* historical events or persons in a way which even Baur was unable to affirm, for fear of supernaturalizing history or of relativizing God. Baur's refusal to identify totally the idea of God-manhood with the historical Jesus, which is the most critical deficiency of his Christology, is thus seen to be related to the most critical deficiency in his doctrine of God. In both cases, he weakened or diminished certain fundamental Christian affirmations. Any responsible use of his theology must attempt to correct these deficiencies. Therefore it is suggested that the relation of God and history (and thus also of faith and historical knowledge and of dogmatics and historical theology) should be understood as internal, not because God *needs* this relation but because he freely *wills* and *creates* it. In this way we can richly benefit from Baur's exploration of these internal relations without necessarily sharing or falling into his theological impasse.

Recent theology is sorely in need of such exploration. For the overriding tendency in Protestant theology since Kierkegaard has been to *separate* God and history, faith and historical knowledge, dogmatic theology and historical-critical theology, and to relate them only externally or paradoxically if at all. Barth's third and fourth criticisms of Baur are symptomatic of this tendency, at least as it applies to the separation of dogmatics from historical-critical theology. Although retaining for it in some unspecified sense a critical procedure, Barth would remove Church history from the concept of history generally, and also, presumably, from the categories of historical knowledge. In so far as the history of the Church can be regarded as an authentically *theological* discipline, it can be of interest and concern only to the theologian, not to the historian. There can be no critical, scientific, and *at the same time* theological historiography; critical historical science is not part of an authentically *theological* discipline. History can be rightly understood only from within the framework of dogmatics. It is not clear in what sense Barth can meaningfully talk in the quoted passage of an "historical" theology or a "Church history" and intend by these terms anything other than "Church dogmatics." And Church dogmatics, while not opposing itself to critical method (so it claims), is not an historical discipline as Barth exemplifies it.[24] If "Church history" is a theological discipline for Barth, then it is really Church dogmatics; if not, then it is simply a branch of secular historiography concerned with a particular range of historical phenomena to be empirically described, as Overbeck claimed it should be.

This separation is further exacerbated or compounded by Barth's qualitative distinction between biblical theology on the one hand and Church history and history of dogma on the other. If Barth really does intend to read the Bible historically-critically, then the insistence that it should be read in faith rather than in love would seem to make no difference for the *historical-critical* treatment of it. Baur permits a *relative* distinction between these disciplines,

24 In an early letter to Thurneysen, Barth remarks with respect to his sermons "how frightfully indifferent I have become about the purely historical questions." Barth to Eduard Thurneysen, 1 Jan. 1916, *Revolutionary Theology in the Making: Barth-Thurneysen Correspondence, 1914–1925*, James D. Smart, trans. (Richmond, Va.: John Knox Press, 1964), p. 36. This admission clearly reveals an attitude which, while later modified, has never been essentially abandoned by Barth.

by virtue of his special treatment of the New Testament writings as the foundation and presupposition of what follows in the history of dogma but also as a part of the total historical life of the Church.[25] But Barth demands more than this. Biblical theology is in some sense a qualitatively distinct stretch of history, distinct even from Church history, which in itself is qualitatively distinct from ordinary secular history. This means it is twice removed from the categories of the historical theologian and is properly the object only of purely dogmatic investigation. Without, supposedly, repudiating or ignoring the relatively assured findings of historical criticism of the Bible, although it is not at all clear how he uses these findings in his biblical exegesis, biblical theology would for Barth be much more than and quite different from historical-critical theology.

The separation of theology and historical knowledge in Protestant thought of the past century, of which this aspect of Barth's criticism of Baur is symptomatic, will be explored in the next section. In the final section, we shall return to some of the enduring possibilities in Baur's vision.

THE SEPARATION OF THEOLOGY AND HISTORICAL KNOWLEDGE IN THE MAIN STREAM OF PROTESTANT THEOLOGY SINCE KIERKEGAARD

The Protestant response to the challenge posed to faith by critical historical study, beginning in the eighteenth century, was envisioned for the first time in almost paradigmatic form by Gotthold Ephraim Lessing's famous aphorism that "accidental truths of history can never become the proof of necessary truths of reason."[26] This is the "ugly, broad ditch" which Lessing found it impossible to leap across.[27] If the phrase "eternal truths of faith" is substituted for "necessary truths of reason," then we have almost precisely the form in which Lessing's ditch was posed as a theological problem by Kant in *Religion Within the Limits of Reason Alone*, and above all by Søren Kierkegaard.

The question with which Kierkegaard introduces his *Philosophical Fragments*, indeed, the question posed on its title page, is stated thus: "Is it possible to base an eternal happiness upon historical knowledge?" Kierkegaard answers that it is possible only if the "historical point of departure" for an eternal happiness (or salvation) is distinguished from every other mode of historical occurrence and if knowledge of it is distinguished from every other form of historical knowledge. To be precise, he distinguishes between three modes of historical occurrence and three forms of

[25] See above, pp. 242–43.
[26] G. E. Lessing, "On the Proof of the Spirit and of Power," in *Lessing's Theological Writings*, Henry Chadwick, ed. and trans. (Stanford, Calif.: Stanford University Press, 1957), p. 53.
[27] *Ibid.*, p. 55.

historical knowledge. The three modes of historical occurrence are, first, the objective data of an event, second, existential transition or becoming (which is the mark of an event's "historicity" or existential quality), and third, the unique case of the paradoxical Moment of God's historicity (in which Eternal Truth "exists" under the conditions of becoming). The three corresponding forms of historical knowledge are scientific research (the work of the critical historian), "ordinary" faith (by which a past existential event is "reduplicated"), and "eminent" faith (the "happy passion" which does not take offense at the paradox).[28] Kierkegaard thus twice removes the historical point of departure for eternal happiness from the mode of historical event open to the critical investigation of scientific historians.

There are implied connections between these modes, but they are only implied, never made explicit. There is a connection between the first and second modes, for example, since it is impossible to have an existential transition without something objectively describable happening. Otherwise, it would be a merely private and esoteric—i.e., nonhistorical—happening. The objectivity of an event is implied in its existential subjectivity, but neither of these modes is known from or in terms of the other. Likewise, there is a connection between the paradoxical Moment of God-in-Christ and other existential moments which constitute the "becoming" of events. The paradoxical Moment is a peculiar and unique type of existential moment, but it is still a species which belongs to the genus "existential moment." Presumably, therefore, since there are connections between the first and second and the second and third modes, there must be some sort of connection between the first and third—between the paradoxical fact that God was in Christ and the limited objective data we can obtain about the life and teaching of Jesus from a critical study of the Gospels. The "merely historical" remains an "incommensurable" occasion, but that is all; as such it is not essential. Kierkegaard never denies this connection in principle. But he tends to deny it in fact. For example, at the end of the *Fragments*, he writes:

If the fact [of God in Christ] . . . were a simple historical fact, the accuracy of the historical sources would be of great importance. Here this is not the case, for faith [the happy passion] cannot be distilled from even the nicest accuracy of detail. The historical fact that God has existed in human form is the essence of the matter; the rest of the historical detail is not even as important as if we had to do with a human being instead of God. . . . [Faith's] absurdity makes all petty difficulties vanish. Inconsistencies which would otherwise be disconcerting do not count for anything here; they make no difference whatsoever. . . . If the contemporary generation had left nothing behind them but these words:

28 Cf. Søren Kierkegaard, *Philosophical Fragments*, David F. Swenson, trans. (Princeton, N. J.: Princeton University Press, 1936), chaps. III, IV, V, and "Interlude."

"We have believed that in such and such a year God appeared among us in the humble figure of a servant, that he lived and taught in our community, and finally died," it would be more than enough.[29]

Yet there are other passages in Kierkegaard's literature, especially in the devotional literature and in the Christology of later works such as *Training in Christianity,* where he bases his argument on the shape of the earthly life of Jesus, and which therefore show that he has not let go of the connection in principle and even in fact. These passages imply a correlation, although an external, disjunctive one, between the three modes of historical facticity Kierkegaard has so emphatically torn apart.

The argument in the paragraphs that follow is that Protestant theology since Kierkegaard has tended to accept his distinctions as normative, although usually it has seen them less radically than he. It has also assumed the connections which even he could not completely deny, and it has generally based more on them than he was willing to allow.

That is to say, Protestant theology has tended, by and large, to respond to the challenge posed to it by historical study by establishing a "correlation" between theology and historical knowledge in which the imaginative vision of faith and the critical categories of historical science are understood as *externally* related to each other, a relationship in which critical and exegetical historical knowledge is understood to be *more or less* relevant to dogmatics but not intrinsically proper or necessary to it. In being thus externally-correlatively related, history and theology are *separated* from each other. The critical historical study of Christianity, and especially of Jesus Christ, is not understood as a properly *theological* discipline, and theology is not understood to be *intrinsically* related to such historical study. Although God reveals himself in history, centrally in Jesus Christ, knowledge of this revelation is not "historical" in the exegetical-critical sense but, if at all, in some internal, existential, or similarly specialized sense. Nor can it properly be said that God "lives" historically, i.e., in the process of human events known and interpreted by the historical theologian. But Baur is correct in suggesting that an historical event or an historical process is one which is in principle *knowable*—not necessarily actually known—through historical understanding, i.e., by a discipline which is at once critical and imaginative. Although it is quite probable that an historical event can *also* be known in non-historical ways, e.g., through faith, an event from which historical understanding is totally excluded in principle is not an historical event.[30] Therefore, the Protestant tendency to say that God reveals himself in history, but not in the sort of history knowable by historical study, implies an incipient docetism.

29 *Ibid.,* p. 87.
30 See above, pp. 144–45.

This separation of God and history, of faith and historical knowledge, and of dogmatics and historical theology is unsatisfactory for a number of reasons. First, it tends to diminish or vitiate the radically historical quality (in the sense just described) of the Christian Church, its faith, and its Gospel. Second, it leaves unspecified the place of historical study in Christian theology. Third, it tends to embrace or imply a deficient conception of the historian's method and task—one construed on the model of an empirical investigation of factual data (the first mode of historical knowledge suggested by Kierkegaard). Finally, it means that the ideal or existential (*geschichtlich*) Christ—the archetypal Christ of faith —and the earthly, historical (*historisch*) Jesus are, as Baur claimed was the case with Schleiermacher and Hegel, separated from each other and at best only externally or artificially or supernaturally correlated. This means that Protestant theology finds itself, for the most part, in the difficult situation of trying to move from an existential analysis of universal guilt, or from the present redemptive encounter of God with the existing self, to a particular historical Christ-figure of the past who is not a myth but yet the ground of our salvation. It is unable to start with the historical Jesus and render manifest his identity as the Christ of faith, because it separates faith from historical knowledge, because it lacks the historical tools requisite for the task, and because it has denied to historical theology its proper place among the theological disciplines.

I have said that, for recent Protestant theology, historical knowledge is understood to be *more or less* relevant to dogmatics but not intrinsically proper or necessary to it. A great deal depends, however, on the "more or less." For some theologians, the correlation of faith and history tends to be *disjunctive*, and theirs is a movement in the direction of complete denial of the historical study of Christianity as a proper *theological* datum. For others, however, this correlation tends to be *conjunctive*, and their movement is in the direction of an affirmation of historical study of Christianity as a proper theological datum. It is characteristic of the external-correlative response to the problem of faith and history, however, that the movement in one direction or the other never arrives at an actual denial or affirmation of history (understood as both a process and a mode of understanding) as a proper theological datum. Its characteristic deficiency has been that it oscillates between two positions, neither of which it has been willing to affirm completely and unambiguously. This response has thus produced a *modus vivendi* but not a real settlement of the problem. It can and indeed has been forcefully argued that a "real settlement" is, in the nature of the case, both undesirable and impossible. To assert otherwise, the argument continues, would be to fail to recognize that there are indeed "two histories" (e.g., internal and external history), or two modes of knowing by which man is

conditioned, and that to attempt to resolve this situation by "synthesis" rather than by correlation would be to presuppose a transcendent metaphysical or metahistorical ground of identity between knower and known.[31] From this point of view, we are forced to settle for precisely nothing more than a *modus vivendi*.

Turning first to the *disjunctive* mode of correlation, of which Kierkegaard himself is a prime example, its answer to the question of the relevance of historical study for theology would be negative, but not completely so. It would argue that the certainty of faith is intrinsically independent of historical study, but not that such study is totally irrelevant to the task of theology.

It is true that a minority of Protestant theologians would want to make this latter claim. They would solve the "problem" of faith and history in a quite definite way, by denying that such a problem exists; by arguing that historical study represents a totally different order of knowledge from that of faith, and that God is not related to history in the ordinary sense at all. They would interpret Kierkegaard differently from the position taken in the preceding pages, claiming that he solved rather than stated or exemplified a theological problem precisely by effecting a total separation of faith and historical knowledge. Kierkegaard made it clear, they would argue, that the "problem" of faith and history is only a pseudo problem, invented by academic theologians, which can be cleared up by a proper understanding of the nature of religious language.[32] This would seem to represent, however, a strained interpretation of Kierkegaard. If this is all that the *Philosophical Fragments* is intended to say, then it says it in extraordinarily involuted fashion, and its rich analysis is only a dialectical joke, not a serious "project of thought." This interpretation seems to ignore Kierkegaard's movement from "Religiousness A" (where the total separation would be in order) to "Religiousness B."

To return to the main stream of the disjunctive approach: it would not attempt to broaden its understanding of the categories of historical study beyond a rather undefined empiricism; but it would want to affirm that even this study grasps a part—if only an insignificant part—of the irreducible datum of theology: that God has revealed himself or made himself manifest in an historical figure of the past; or it would affirm that in some sense the "historical" is an "adequate symbol" for the "ultimate." It would mark a sharp distinction—a dualism—between an internal, personal, or existential mode of "historical" understanding (congruent with or even constitutive of faith) and an external, factual, scientific historiography, construed on the model of positivism (the proper arena for the work of the critical historian). The Christ known or experienced in terms of the first mode would somehow be related to the empirical Jesus of past history, although this connection could never be elucidated. After Kierkegaard, this posture is anticipated by Wilhelm Herrmann alone among the Ritschlian theologians, and by Martin Kähler. In contemporary theology, there are, broadly speaking, two strands in the disjunctive posture: a neo-Kantian and an existentialist strand. As representative of the neo-Kantian strand one might name Emil Brunner, Karl Löwith, and Karl Heim; and of the existentialist strand, Rudolf Bultmann, Friedrich Gogarten, Paul Tillich, and Ernst Fuchs (who extends Bultmann's existentialist interpretation to a conception of the Word of God as an ever-contemporary "speech event" while seeming to diminish the theological significance of form criticism and historical criticism, since past historical facts can never really be determinative for the present act of faith but are absorbed into it).

Albert Schweitzer's radical distinction between the ideal, spiritual Christ and the mysterious, world-condemning fanatic who believed himself to be the Messiah (the "historical Jesus" whom Schweitzer believed he had "found" in the Gospel of Mark) belongs neither to the neo-Kantian nor to the existentialist strands. It is more reminiscent of Strauss and abstract idealism than of Kant's epistemological dualism. The disjunction is not complete for Schweitzer, however, since there is some mysterious, unspecifiable, even appropriate connection between this frightful historical figure, who will always remain a stranger to us, and the spiritual Christ who belongs to the religion of "eternal love."[33]

The answer offered by a *conjunctive* correlation to the question of the relevance of historical study for theology and faith would be positive, but not entirely positive. It would argue that in some never clearly specified sense the nature and content of faith are historical, but would deny that the certainty of faith is intrinsically related to the work of the historical-critical theologian. It would affirm that historical study is an important part of theology, but would deny that it is intrinsically proper and necessary to it. It would argue that internal, personal, or existential history and external, factual history are connected with each other, yet clearly distinguishable and therefore not confusable. Like the disjunctive correlation, it would tend not to broaden its categories of historical knowledge beyond those of a positivistic posture, and therefore it would be unable to explore the *internal* connections between faith and history which might otherwise be implied by the direction of its emphasis. Among contemporary theologians, one could include as representative of this tendency Karl Barth, H. Richard Niebuhr, Hermann Diem, D. M. Baillie, Paul Althaus, and a group of post-Bultmannian New Testament theologians—Ernst Käsemann, Günther Bornkamm, Hans Conzelmann, Nils Dahl—who drop

33 Cf. Albert Schweitzer, *The Quest of the Historical Jesus*, W. Montgomery, trans. (3d ed.; London: Adam & Charles Black, 1954), chaps. XIX, XX.

Bultmann's specifically existentialist categories of interpretation but strengthen in various ways the hermeneutical and historical-critical tasks. The conjunctive posture is also fully anticipated by the Ritschlian theologians other than Herrmann—by Ritschl himself, and by Adolf Harnack, Theodor Haering, and Julius Kaftan.[34]

[34] An example of Ritschl's conjunctive correlation is found in *The Christian Doctrine of Justification and Reconciliation*, Vol. III, trans. by H. R. Mackintosh and A. B. Macauley from the 3d German ed. (2nd ed.; Edinburgh: T. & T. Clark, 1902), p. 405: "Every form of [present] influence exerted by Christ must find its criterion in the historical figure presented by His life. Therefore the Godhead or universal lordship of Christ must be apprehended in definite features of His historical life, as an attribute of His existence in time." But Ritschl was never able to explain satisfactorily what might be implied in this passage for the place of critical historical knowledge in theology. At the same time he stressed, but without elucidating the dialectic, that it is only through faith derived from and directed toward the presently exalted and ruling Lord (the Christ of faith) that we can know the historical Jesus.

With respect to Ritschl's conception of the theological use of historical knowledge and his work as an historical theologian, in his essay, "Über geschichtliche Methode in der Erforschung des Urchristenthums," *JDT*, VI, 429–59, he maintains against Baur a distinction between the sort of historical research pursued by theologians and the "purely historical" or "scientific" method developed by secular historiography (see pp. 440–42). For example, the theologian, as a man of faith, has access to a peculiar sort of religious knowledge which is able to affirm that miracles occur and that they are objective, but on the other hand that they are not "empirically objective" and therefore not observable by "scientific" knowledge. Zeller criticizes this argument in "Die historische Kritik und das Wunder," *SHZ*, VI, 359, 366–69. This distinction between two types of "historical" knowledge perhaps marks the essence of Ritschl's methodological break with Baur, a break motivated by Ritschl's conviction that Baur had failed to take account of the supernatural causality involved in the origin of Christianity.

Ritschl's distinction is characteristic of later Protestant thought. It is also taken up in modified form by Harnack in some of his essays on historical methodology. He distinguishes between external, "factual" history and internal, personal, "legendary" history. The latter, which alone is essential to faith, comprises history by and about persons, in which "legends" become the prime medium for representing historical personality. Consequently, Harnack distinguishes between the "historical" Christ (the Jesus of history) and the "legendary" Christ (the Christ known to faith), neither of whom is complete or intelligible without the other.

The correlation between faith and historical knowledge is conjunctive or positive for Harnack, more so even than with Ritschl. In this connection, and with respect especially to his conception of historical development and of history fundamentally as *Geistesgeschichte*, the story of the progressive objectification of Spirit, Harnack shows himself, as Troeltsch suggests, to be more deeply indebted to Baur and the idealist tradition than is usually recognized and than would be apparent from his comments about Baur in the introduction to his *Dogmengeschichte*. (Cf. Troeltsch, *op. cit.*, pp. 283, 288–90. See above, p. 251, n. 173). His historical portrait of Jesus (which does seem colored by the "legendary" *Erlöserpersönlichkeit* supposedly known only to faith) and his conception of the Christian community as the prime medium of historical knowledge about Jesus also seem indebted to Baur, especially to *Das Christenthum*. A similar indebtedness can be seen in Ritschl's Christology, especially his fundamental understanding of the work of Christ as that of "founder." Baur is an essential link between Schleier-

Thus, in terms of the broad types of response to the problem of faith and history, twentieth-century theology has not yet for the most part developed any options not already anticipated by the nineteenth century. Despite the intense interest in the problem, a certain degree of stagnancy in its treatment has become apparent. Since Baur presents an alternative to the whole approach typified by Protestant theology since Kierkegaard, he may provide a means of moving beyond the impasse at which this tradition has arrived.[35]

Before concluding the discussion, two qualifications are in order. The first is that for the main stream of the Protestant tradition the problem is not simply the relation between faith and historical knowledge but also that between two components within historical understanding itself: what it has regarded as a "pre-critical" or imaginative grasp of the meaning and significance of events of the historical past, and the critical and scientific study of these events. This tradition holds firmly for the most part to the historical foundation of the Christian Gospel, meaning thereby that the Gospel is enacted in and through certain past events, which have a continuing meaning and power for the present. But on the

---

macher at one end of the nineteenth century and Ritschl and Harnack at the other; but his historical theology belongs neither to Schleiermacher on the one hand nor to the Protestant liberalism of which Ritschl was the father on the other. It represents a third, independent and autonomous theological position, yet one which links the other two together.

[35] In my judgment, there is one recent Protestant theologian who has succeeded in moving beyond the external-correlative posture to a genuine attempt at understanding the internal continuities between historical and dogmatic theology: Gerhard Ebeling. Indeed, for Ebeling, the hermeneutical problem in theology comes to focus at the point where historical investigation and dogmatic reflection are to be seen merely as different aspects of one single process of understanding. The way in which Ebeling relates historical-critical theology to the larger task of theological hermeneutic is extremely suggestive. In some of his recent essays he attempts to demonstrate the internal connection between Christianity's historical past, critically investigated, and the present situation and language of the believer. Thus far, Ebeling's proposals have been developed only in relatively brief programmatic essays and short monographs, and many details and problems require further elucidation and reflection. For example, the exclusive focus on a linguistic realism at the expense of other modes of manifestation of historical reality seems unduly restrictive of the work of the historical theologian. Also, given the internal congruence of the two disciplines, Ebeling must, as he himself recognizes, guard against the temptation of absorbing historical-critical theology into dogmatic reflection without remainder (the opposite temptation to that faced by Baur, and one to which Ernst Fuchs has apparently succumbed). Despite these dangers, however, Ebeling has pointed to a way beyond the impasse at which most Protestant theologians have arrived on the question of theology and history; whether this way can be fruitfully pursued to the end remains to be seen. Finally, the question as to the possible connections between Baur's approach to the problem and Ebeling's must be reserved for treatment at another time. On Ebeling, cf. his *Word and Faith* (Philadelphia: Fortress Press, 1963), especially Chaps. I, VII, X, XI; his *Theologie und Verkündigung* (2d ed.; Tübingen: J. C. B. Mohr, 1963), especially Chaps. II and III; and James M. Robinson and John B. Cobb, Jr. (eds.), *The New Hermeneutic* (New York: Harper & Row, 1964).

other hand, this tradition has usually seen a sharp distinction between the precritical or imaginative and the critical or scientific
modes of understanding events of the historical past; and it has
usually insisted that only the first mode is intrinsically relevant
to faith, i.e., to an interpretation of the events of the Gospel story.
Consequently, as I have suggested is especially the case with Kierkegaard, faith's knowledge of the Gospel events is "twice removed"
from critical or scientific historiography. But as Baur emphatically
maintained, authentic historical understanding embraces both imaginative and scientific elements; it is both speculative and empirical. This disjunction represents a false split in what must always
remain inseparably joined in the historian's work; therefore, Protestant theology has for the most part appropriated a deficient
conception of the historian's method and task. If this disjunction
can ever be healed, then it may be possible to deal more adequately
with the question of the relation of faith to historical understanding, in the broad sense envisioned by Baur.

The second qualification is that there is nothing intrinsically
wrong with the fact that the main stream of Protestant theology
has started primarily with the separation of faith and historical
knowledge and has then sought to move dialectically to a comprehension of their unity. Baur, on the other hand, in the context of
his idealistic understanding of the internal relations of Spirit,
started with the unity of faith and historical understanding (based
on the unity of God and historical process) and sought to move
dialectically to a statement of their distinction. I do not wish to
argue that Baur's metaphysics necessarily provides the better
starting point. I suggest rather, on the one hand, that none of
the theologians in the tradition since Kierkegaard has in fact satisfactorily moved from separation to a comprehension of internal
unity, and on the other that Baur, having started with the unity,
does provide us with a vision of that unity—a vision which can
instruct us no matter whether we adopt his metaphysics or not.
If the antimetaphysical Protestant tradition could surmount the
barrier erected by its separation of the precritical and the critical
in historical understanding, it might be a long way forward toward
a dialectical positing of the unity of faith and historical knowledge.
In other words, the problem is one of historical methodology as
well as of dogmatics.

THE ENDURING POSSIBILITIES IN BAUR'S VISION

I have suggested that since Baur presents a whole alternative
approach to the problem of faith and historical knowledge typified
by Protestant theology since Kierkegaard, he may provide a means
of moving beyond the impasse at which this tradition has arrived.
He presents this alternative through the formation of a new theological discipline, one understood to be intrinsically proper and

necessary to the task of Christian dogmatics as a whole, and one in which faith and historical study, as its two central components, are internally mediated. He called this discipline "historical-critical theology." The justification for its existence, and a description of its character, can be summarized as follows.

Christianity is both an "absolute principle" of truth and an "historically given religion." It is both idea and manifestation, both divine content and human form. Neither of these components can be divorced from the other; both are essential to an understanding of what Christianity essentially is. The dogmatic theologian must take account of its historical character as well as its normative claim; the historical theologian, of its absolute principle as well as its historical givenness. Consequently, historical theology is not only a *critical* discipline, sharing the methods and presuppositions of disciplined historical study generally, but also a *theological* discipline, embracing a specific understanding of the nature of God, man, Jesus Christ, history, and the Church.

As an "historically given" religion, Christianity is knowable historically-critically. I have already argued that Baur was correct in suggesting that an historical phenomenon is one which is in principle *knowable* through historical study, i.e., by a discipline which is at once critical and imaginative. An event from which historical study is totally excluded in principle is not an historical event. Baur wanted to avoid all forms of dualism with respect to both the content and the form of historical knowledge. He knew nothing of the later distinction between the terms *Historie* (objective, empirical history) and *Geschichte* (internal, personal human existence), and between two distinctive modes of "historical" knowledge associated with them—scientific, empirical historiography on the one hand, and an imaginative reduplication of events of the human past on the other. This distinction splits apart what in the nature of the case is a unity in history both as a process and as a form of knowledge.

The historical character of Christianity is in itself nothing new. It became a theological problem for the first time with the rise of critical historical study in the eighteenth century. The question had now to be confronted whether this study is appropriate to an examination of the historical claims and the historical contents of the Christian faith. Baur is significant because he affirmed unambiguously that the historical character of Christianity is open to examination and study by critical historiography—when this latter discipline is properly understood. The historicity of Christianity is not of a special or esoteric nature, hidden from the scrutiny of the critical historian.

If this is the case, then it can be seen that historical theology is intrinsically proper and necessary to the task of Christian dogmatics as a whole. It is necessary in the sense that, with the development of historical "science" as a critical and imaginative tool in the eighteenth and nineteenth centuries, Christian theology had no choice other than to submit its historical claims to the scrutiny of this tool and to defend them by its use. It is proper because it is in history, understood as the changing process of "spiritual" events through time, that God manifests and reveals himself; and therefore, as Käsemann puts it, historical-critical theology is the "relevant counterpart" to revelation, the proper response of faith in the presence of historical revelation. It is necessary for the vitality of theology that it should not acquiesce in that negative obligation; and it is proper that it engage in this positive response.

I have said that, because the historical theologian must take account of the absolute truth of Christianity as well as its historical positivity (these two elements being essential to an understanding of its nature, its historicity), historical theology is both a critical and a theological discipline. It embraces, therefore, an internal mediation of faith and historical knowledge. These two components in its method are intrinsically appropriate to each other; each requires the other.

In the first place, historical knowledge, properly understood, represents a congruence of the imaginative and the "scientific," the speculative and the empirical, the subjective and the objective. For example, Baur claims that the very means of obtaining critical objectivity in historical study is by the use of speculative categories shaped by the historian's philosophical and theological imagination. History is not a science of "explanation" but a discipline for "understanding"—or, to use Baur's favorite terms, "comprehension" and "consideration." It is thus more closely related to metaphysics than to empirical science, although its method (but not its use of reason) is relatively *sui generis*. To put it in Austin Farrer's terms, its concern is more nearly with mysteries to be described (always inadequately) than with problems to be solved.[36] Historical understanding is an "art," requiring imagination, empathy, re-enactment, subjective passion—albeit a passion to discover the objective, to transpose oneself into it, in a sense to become one with it. For at the most intense pitch of knowing, the objectivity of the process and the subjectivity of the historian tend to merge into a single differentiated unity (the threat to idealism was always that such a unity might become an identity). The historian encounters the true objectivity of the historical process by penetrating critically to the center of his own subjectivity. This unity of objective and subjective elements in historical understanding requires what might be called a hermeneutical "pre-understanding," which constitutes the hidden metaphysics of this approach to historical process and historical knowledge:

36 Cf. Austin Farrer's distinction between metaphysics and natural science in *The Glass of Vision* (London: Dacre Press, 1948), pp. 63–67.

"humanity" or "man" for Herder and Collingwood, "historical life" for Dilthey, the ethical a priori for Troeltsch, the mutual historicity of divine and human Spirit for Baur.

The congruence of subjectivity and objectivity in authentic historical understanding means that every historical theologian's interpretive perspective is shaped by his "theological standpoint" or his "faith." This is why there have been a number of different epochs of Church historiography, each reflecting a fundamentally different theological viewpoint—old catholic, scholastic, old Protestant, rationalistic, modern Catholic. This is why the historian of dogma can interpret the past only from the perspective of "the most recent dogmatic consciousness." It is as wrong for the historical theologian to attempt to deny his stance in faith as it is for him to surrender the striving for objective and critical understanding. For if he attempts to deny this stance, he will only become the captive of another perspective of which he is not aware and over which he possesses no control; Baur argues that authentic faith frees the historical theologian from the restraints of an externally and arbitrarily imposed authority, allowing him to transpose himself freely into the data and to remain open to the results, whatever they might prove to be. Therefore, the historical study of the Christian Church and its founding events is inescapably theological. It possesses, either consciously or unconsciously, theological presuppositions and principles, which it is better to articulate and understand than surreptitiously to hide. It is better for the historian to consider philosophically or theologically the nature of that "objective truth" which he is seeking to discover and explicate in his historical interpretations, than to impose on these interpretations his own subjective and arbitrary criteria of truth. It is at the point of understanding the necessary role of faith and theological judgment in the critical work of the historical theologian that a position dependent upon Baur would differ sharply from the recent work of Wolfhart Pannenberg and his school. Pannenberg apparently believes it possible for the historian to ascertain the revelatory significance of the events of Christian history quite apart from faith, on the basis of reason alone. Not only does this smack of theological fundamentalism, but it also represents in a fashion different from that of the existentialists the reduction of critical historiography to a positivistic model.

Just as the historical study of Christianity entails a theological commitment of one sort or another, by virtue of the nature of historical understanding as well as of Christianity itself, so also, as Baur clearly maintained, Christian faith is dependent in certain specific ways upon historical study. In the first place, the content of Christian faith, although in itself normative or absolutely true for the believer, is *mediated* historically, in the sense that we have access to the dogmatic truths of the Christian faith (e.g., that "God was in Christ reconciling the world to himself") only through the historical witness and tradition of the Church—this *normative* truth is also a *past* truth, mediated to us through an historical continuity. In the second place, the content of Christian faith—that normative historical event of the past—can, among other ways, be *known* historically-critically, and therefore must, among other ways, be instructed and tested by historical-critical study. Such instruction and testing can help to clarify to faith the essential character and shape of those events which it affirms to be true in a normative sense. It can help to distinguish the truth about these events from the mere accretion of tradition. Finally, authentic faith requires the continual prodding and testing of historical criticism, for its certainty is of a different order than the empirical certainties of this world. Historical study, by disclosing the contingency and relativity of all historical events and of our knowledge of the past, renders faith possible. For faith is the acceptance as authoritatively true for oneself of that which is precisely always only probably certain in the historical mode. In this threefold sense, faith is "dependent" upon historical study, although this dependence by no means implies that historical study is the *source* of faith or the *proof* of faith. The *source* and *locus* of faith is subjective religious consciousness, but since its *content* is both mediated historically and knowable historically-critically, *if* and *when* authentic faith is to be found it must be honestly instructed and tested by historical study.

Historical theology rightly understood, then, embraces an internal mediation of faith and historical knowledge; as such, it is a discipline intrinsically proper and necessary to the task of Christian dogmatics. Because Baur recognized this against the separation and external correlation of faith and historical study in the main stream of Protestant theology since Kierkegaard, he is significant for contemporary discussion of the problems with which he dealt. But, as we have seen, Baur tended to dissolve dogmatics as a whole into historical theology, despite his intention to maintain a distinction-in-relation between faith and historical knowledge. An historical theology of our day must resist this temptation. Christian dogmatics, understood as the knowledge of faith, or the science of faith, or the doctrine of faith (*Glaubenslehre*), includes a nonhistorical as well as an historical dimension, for it makes normative claims about certain historically conditioned events. (Its normative claims, however, always remain historically conditioned in character.) Dogmatics reflects the manifold language of faith. Such language is dramatic, aesthetic, parabolic, proclamatory, performatory, ethical, even metaphysical, as well as historical; it contains mythical, poetic, and purely narrative elements. The attempts to isolate the "essence" of religious language or of faith in either a familiar or a unique religious "function" or "model," or perhaps in a religious a priori, have generally not been convincing. It would appear that the distinctiveness of religious language, and therefore of dogmatics, derives from their *object* rather than from a special sort of linguistic usage or from a peculiar faculty of human experience and knowledge. Just as faith is comprised of a multiplicity of languages, so also dogmatics comprises a multiplicity of modes of knowing and the critical or scientific disciplines associated with them. It includes the metaphysical, the psychological, the ethical, and the aesthetic. It also includes the historical, i.e., the historical-critical. For Christian dogmatics especially, the historical mode is essential and does not exist in internal conflict with the other critical disciplines that constitute dogmatics. They cannot be merged into the historical mode or vice versa, but they are intrinsically incomplete without it, just as it is incomplete without them.

In the preceding pages, we have explored some of the strengths and weaknesses in Baur's conception of historical-critical theology. We cannot simply repristinate his achievement in our own day, since our location of an historical theology somewhere between the separation of faith and historical knowledge on the one hand and their identification on the other must be different from his. For we possess a broadened and perhaps richer conception of what constitutes dogmatics and a somewhat more restricted conception of what can be encompassed by historical understanding. Nor, for that matter, are his specific philosophical tools—those of German idealism—still for the most part congenial to us. These are intended as modifications, however, in the context of basic agreement with his conception of the task that lies before us. What Baur did for the theology of his day, by fashioning an authentically mediating historical-critical theology, must be done again, but differently, for ours. Indeed, this would seem to be one of the great theological tasks of our day, since the historical disciplines—as, indeed, all the "scientific" disciplines of the modern world—continue to pose both challenge and opportunity to faith in undiminished intensity. As Baur insisted, to ignore the challenge would be to surrender the effort to articulate the Christian claim in and to the intellectual ethos of our age.

BIBLIOGRAPHY

I. WRITINGS BY FERDINAND CHRISTIAN BAUR

A. BOOKS

This is a complete list, grouped according to subject matter and listed chronologically within groups.

1. STUDIES IN THE HISTORY AND PHILOSOPHY OF RELIGION

Symbolik und Mythologie, oder die Naturreligion des Alterthums. 2 vols. in 3 parts. Stuttgart: J. B. Metzler, 1824–25.

Das manichäische Religionssystem nach den Quellen neu untersucht und entwikelt. Tübingen: Hopfer de l'Orme, 1831.

Die christliche Gnosis, oder die christliche Religions-Philosophie in ihrer geschichtlichen Entwiklung. Tübingen: C. F. Osiander, 1835.

Drei Abhandlungen zur Geschichte der alten Philosophie und ihres Verhältnisses zum Christenthum, ed. EDUARD ZELLER. Leipzig: Fues's Verlag, 1876. Contains: "Apollonius von Tyana und Christus, oder das Verhältniss des Pythagoräismus zum Christenthum" (1832); "Das christliche des Platonismus oder Sokrates und Christus" (1837); "Seneca und Paulus, das Verhältniss des Stoicismus zum Christenthum nach den Schriften Seneca's" (1858).

2. NEW TESTAMENT STUDIES

Die sogenannten Pastoralbriefe des Apostels Paulus aufs neue kritisch untersucht. Stuttgart and Tübingen: J. G. Cotta'schen Verlagshandlung, 1835.

Paulus, der Apostel Jesu Christi. Sein Leben und Wirken, seine Briefe und seine Lehre. Ein Beitrag zu einer kritischen Geschichte des Urchristenthums. 1st ed. Stuttgart: Becher und Müller, 1845. 2d ed., ed. EDUARD ZELLER. 2 vols. Leipzig: Fues's Verlag, 1866–67. (2d. ed. cited in text.)

    Paul the Apostle of Jesus Christ, His Life and Work, His Epistles and His Doctrine. A Contribution to a Critical History of Primitive Christianity. Translated from 2d German ed. by the Rev. A. MENZIES. 2 vols. London and Edinburgh: Williams & Norgate, 1875 (1st ed.), 1876 (2d, identical ed.).

Kritische Untersuchungen über die kanonischen Evangelien, ihr Ver-

hältniss zu einander, ihren Charakter und Ursprung. Tübingen: L. F.
Fues, 1847.
*Das Markusevangelium nach seinem Ursprung und Charakter. Nebst
einem Anhang über das Evangelium Marcions.* Tübingen: L. F. Fues,
1851.
Vorlesungen über neutestamentliche Theologie, ed. FERDINAND FRIED-
RICH BAUR. Leipzig: Fues's Verlag, 1864.

3. STUDIES IN THE HISTORY OF DOGMA

*Die christliche Lehre von der Versöhnung in ihrer geschichtlichen Ent-
wicklung von der ältesten Zeit bis auf die neueste.* Tübingen: C. F.
Osiander, 1838.
*Die christliche Lehre von der Dreieinigkeit und Menschwerdung Gottes
in ihrer geschichtlichen Entwicklung.*
Vol. I: *Das Dogma der alten Kirche bis zur Synode von Chalcedon.*
Tübingen: C. F. Osiander, 1841.
Vol. II: *Das Dogma des Mittelalters.* Tübingen: C. F. Osiander, 1842.
Vol. III: *Die neuere Geschichte des Dogma, von der Reformation bis
in die neueste Zeit.* Tübingen: C. F. Osiander, 1843.
Lehrbuch der christlichen Dogmengeschichte. 1st ed. Stuttgart: Becher's
Verlag, 1847. 2d ed. Tübingen: L. F. Fues, 1858. 3d ed., identical with
2d. Leipzig: Fues's Verlag (L. W. Reisland), 1867. (1st and 3d eds.
cited in text.)
Vorlesungen über die christliche Dogmengeschichte, ed. FERDINAND
FRIEDRICH BAUR.
Vol. I/1: *Das Dogma der alten Kirche von der apostolischen Zeit bis
zur Synode in Nicäa.* Leipzig: Fues's Verlag, 1865.
Vol. I/2: *Das Dogma der alten Kirche von der Synode in Nicäa bis
zum Ende des sechsten Jahrhunderts.* Leipzig: Fues's Verlag, 1866.
Vol. II: *Das Dogma des Mittelalters.* Leipzig: Fues's Verlag, 1866.
Vol. III: *Das Dogma der neueren Zeit.* Leipzig: Fues's Verlag, 1867.

4. STUDIES IN CHURCH HISTORY

Die Epochen der kirchlichen Geschichtschreibung. Tübingen: L. F. Fues,
1852. (Republished in *Ausgewählte Werke,* Vol. II, 1963.)
Geschichte der christlichen Kirche.
Vol. I: *Das Christenthum und die christliche Kirche der drei ersten
Jahrhunderte.* Tübingen: L. F. Fues, 1853 (1st ed.), 1860 (2d ed.),
1863 (3d ed., identical with 2d, published under title *Kirchengeschichte der drei ersten Jahrhunderte*). (3d ed. cited in text. 2d ed.
to be republished in *Ausgewählte Werke,* Vol. III.)
The Church History of the First Three Centuries. Translated from
3d German ed. by the Rev. ALLAN MENZIES. 2 vols. London and
Edinburgh: Williams & Norgate, 1878–79.
Vol. II: *Die christliche Kirche vom Anfang des vierten bis zum Ende
des sechsten Jahrhunderts in den Hauptmomenten ihrer Entwicklung.* Tübingen: L. F. Fues, 1859 (1st ed.), 1863 (2d ed., identical
with 1st). (2d ed. cited in text.)
Vol. III. *Die christliche Kirche des Mittelalters in den Hauptmomen-
tum ihrer Entwicklung,* ed. FERDINAND FRIEDRICH BAUR. 1st ed.
Tübingen: L. F. Fues, 1861. 2d ed. Leipzig: Fues's Verlag (R. Reisland), 1869. (1st ed. cited in text.)

Vol. IV: *Kirchengeschichte der neueren Zeit, von der Reformation bis zum Ende des achtzehnten Jahrhunderts,* ed. FERDINAND FRIEDRICH BAUR. Tübingen: L. F. Fues, 1863.

Vol. V: *Kirchengeschichte des neunzehnten Jahrhunderts,* ed. EDUARD ZELLER. 1st ed. Tübingen: L. F. Fues, 1862. 2d ed. Leipzig: Fues's Verlag (R. Reisland), 1877. (1st ed. cited in text, and to be republished in *Ausgewählte Werke,* Vol. IV.)

5. POLEMICAL WRITINGS

Der Gegensatz des Katholicismus und Protestantismus nach den Principien und Hauptdogmen der beiden Lehrbegriffe. Mit besonderer Rücksicht auf Herrn Dr. Möhler's Symbolik. Tübingen: L. F. Fues, 1834 (1st ed.), 1836 (2d ed.). (2d ed. cited in text.)

Der Kritiker und der Fanatiker, in der Person des Herrn Heinrich W. J. Thiersch. Zur Charakteristik der neuesten Theologie. Stuttgart: Becher's Verlag, 1846.

Die ignatianischen Briefe und ihr neuester Kritiker. Eine Streitschrift gegen Herrn Bunsen. Tübingen: L. F. Fues, 1848.

An Herrn Dr. Karl Hase. Beantwortung des Sendschreibens "Die Tübinger Schule." Tübingen: L. F. Fues, 1855. (To be republished in *Ausgewählte Werke,* Vol. V.)

Die Tübinger Schule und ihre Stellung zur Gegenwart. Tübingen: L. F. Fues, 1859 (1st ed.), 1860 (2d ed.). (2d ed. cited in text, and to be republished in *Ausgewählte Werke,* Vol. V.)

6. NEW EDITIONS

Ausgewählte Werke in Einzelausgaben, ed. KLAUS SCHOLDER. 5 vols. Stuttgart-Bad Cannstatt: Friedrich Frommann Verlag (Günther Holzboog), 1963–.

Vol. I: *Historisch-kritische Untersuchungen zum Neuen Testament.* Introduction by ERNST KÄSEMANN. 1963.

Vol. II: *Die Epochen der kirchlichen Geschichtschreibung (1852), Dogmengeschichtliche Vorreden aus den Jahren 1838–1858.* Introduction by ERNST WOLF. 1963.

Vol. III: *Das Christenthum und die christliche Kirche der drei ersten Jahrhunderte* (2d ed., 1860). Introduction by KLAUS SCHOLDER. Not yet published.

Vol. IV: *Kirchengeschichte des neunzehnten Jahrhunderts* (1862). Introduction by HEINZ LIEBING. Not yet published.

Vol. V: *Für und wider die Tübinger Schule.* Introduction by KLAUS SCHOLDER. Not yet published.

B. JOURNAL ARTICLES

Baur published about eighty articles, ranging from review articles to extensive monographs of several hundred pages in length. The following is a selected list of some of the most important of these, arranged chronologically. Abbreviations are as noted on p. xv.

Review article: G. P. C. Kaiser, *Die biblische Theologie, oder Judaismus und Christianismus nach der grammatisch-historischen Interpretations-Methode, und nach einer freimüthigen Stellung in die kritische-vergleichende Universalgeschichte der Religionen und in die universale Religion* (Erlangen, 1813–1814). *BAT*, II:3 (1818), 656–717.

"Anzeige der beiden academischen Schriften von Dr. F. C. Baur: *Primae Rationalismi et Supranaturalismi historiae capita potiora. Pars I. De Gnosticorum Christianismo ideali. Pars II. Comparatur Gnosticismus cum Schleiermacherianae theologiae indole.* Tub. 1827." *TZT*, I (1828), 220–64.

"Über den wahren Begriff des *glōssais lalein*, mit Rücksicht auf die neuesten Untersuchungen hierüber." *TZT*, IV:2 (1830), 75–133.

"Die Christuspartei in der korinthischen Gemeinde, der Gegensatz des petrinischen und paulinischen Christenthums in der ältesten Kirche, der Apostel Petrus in Rom." *TZT*, V:4 (1831), 61–206. (Republished in *Ausgewählte Werke*, Vol. I, 1963.)

"Über die ursprüngliche Bedeutung des Passahfestes und des Beschneidungsritus." *TZT*, VI:1 (1832), 40–124.

"Apollonius von Tyana und Christus, oder das Verhältniss des Pythagoräismus zum Christenthum. Ein Beitrag zur Religionsgeschichte der ersten Jahrhunderte nach Christus." *TZT*, VI:4 (1832), 3–235. (Republished in *Drei Abhandlungen*, 1876.)

"Der Gegensatz des Katholicismus und Protestantismus nach den Principien und Hauptdogmen der beiden Lehrbegriffe. Mit besonderer Rücksicht auf Herrn Dr. Möhler's *Symbolik*." *TZT*, VII:3, 4 (1833), 1–438. (Published separately as a book in 1834.)

"Über Zweck und Veranlassung des Römerbriefs und die damit zusammenhängenden Verhältnisse der römischen Gemeinde. Eine historisch-kritische Untersuchung." *TZT*, IX:3 (1836), 59–178. (Republished in *Ausgewählte Werke*, Vol. I, 1963.)

"Abgenöthigte Erklärung gegen einen Artikel der *Evangelischen Kirchenzeitung*, herausgegeben von D. E. W. Hengstenberg, Prof. der Theol. an der Universität zu Berlin. Mai 1836." *TZT*, IX:3 (1836), 179–232. (Published separately as an essay in 1836. Republished in *Ausgewählte Werke*, Vol. I, 1963.)

"Das christliche des Platonismus oder Sokrates und Christus." *TZT*, X:3 (1837), 1–154. (Published separately as a monograph, with the additional title, ". . . eine religionsphilosophische Untersuchung," in 1837. Republished in *Drei Abhandlungen*, 1876.)

"Kritische Studien über den Begriff der Gnosis." *TSK*, X:3 (1937), 511–79.

"Über der Ursprung des Episcopats in der christlichen Kirche. Prüfung der neuesten von Hrn. Dr. Rothe hierüber aufgestellten Ansicht." *TZT*, XI:3 (1838), 1–185. (Republished in *Ausgewählte Werke*, Vol. I, 1963.)

"Über die Composition und den Charakter des johanneïschen Evangeliums." *TJ*, III:1, 3, 4 (1844), 1–191, 397–475, 615–700.

"Der Ursprung und Charakter des Lukas-Evangeliums." *TJ*, V:4 (1846), 453–615.

"Über Princip und Charakter des Lehrbegriffe der reformirten Kirche in seinem Unterschied von dem der lutherischen, mit Rücksicht auf A. Schweizer's *Darstellung der reformirten Glaubenslehre*." *TJ*, VI:3 (1847), 309–389.

"Kritische Studien über das Wesen des Protestantismus," *TJ*, VI:4 (1847), 506–581.

"Die Einleitung in das Neue Testament als theologische Wissenschaft. Ihr Begriff und ihre Aufgabe, ihr Entwicklungsgang und ihr innerer Organismus." *TJ*, IX:4 (1850), 463–566; X:1, 2, 3 (1851), 70–94, 222–52, 291–328.

"Rückblick auf die neuesten Untersuchungen über das Markusevangelium." *TJ*, XII:1 (1853), 54–93.

"Das Princip des Protestantismus und seine geschichtliche Entwicklung, mit Rücksicht auf die neuesten Werke von Schendel, Schweizer, Heppe, und die neuesten Verhandlungen über die Unionsfrage." *TJ*, XIV:1 (1855), 1–137.

"Seneca und Paulus, das Verhältniss des Stoicismus zum Christenthum nach den Schriften Seneca's." *ZWT*, I:2, 3 (1858), 161–246, 441–70. (Republished in *Drei Abhandlungen*, 1876.)

"Die Bedeutung des Ausdrucks: *ho huios tou anthrōpou*," *ZWT*, III:3 (1860), 274–92.

C. OTHER PUBLISHED WRITINGS

In addition to the works listed below, Baur published four Latin programma.

KLÜPFEL, K., ed. *Geschichte und Beschreibung der Universität Tübingen.* Tübingen: L. F. Fues, 1849. Baur wrote two chapters in this book: "Die evangelisch-theologische Fakultät vom Jahr 1777 bis 1812," pp. 216–47; and "Die evangelisch-theologische Fakultät vom Jahr 1812 bis 1848," pp. 389–426.

"Predigt zur Vorbereitung auf das Säcularfest der Übergabe der Augsburgischen Confession. . . ." *Feier des dritten Säkularfestes der Übergabe der Augsburgischen Confession auf der Universität Tübingen.* Tübingen: L. F. Fues, 1830. Pp. 93–101.

Primae Rationalismi et Supranaturalismi historiae capita potiora.
Pars I. *De Gnosticorum Christianismo ideali.* Dissertatio inauguralis historico-theologica, quam Deo juvante Munus Professoris Theologiae Evangelicae Ordinarii. Tubingae: Hopferi de l'Orme, 1827.
Pars II. *Comparatur Gnosticismus cum Schleiermacherianae theologiae indole.* Tubingae: Hopferi de l'Orme, 1827.
Pars III. *Exponitur praesertim Arianismi indoles rationalis.* Tubingae: Hopferi de l'Orme, 1828.

"Über die geschichtliche Bedeutung der fünfundzwanzig Jahre 1816–1841." Rede zur Feier des Gedächtnisses der fünfundzwanzigjährigen Regierung seiner Majestät des Königs Wilhelm von Württemberg am 31. Oktober 1841 auf der Universität zu Tübingen. F. F. BAUR, ed. *Gratulationsschrift des Gymnasiums zu Tübingen für die vierte Säcularfeier der Universität Tübingen, 9–11 August 1877.* Tübingen: L. F. Fues, 1877. Pp. 3–22.

Worte der Erinnerung an Dr. Friedrich Heinrich Kern. Tübingen: L. F. Fues, 1842. Baur edited this volume, which includes his speech in honor of Kern.

D. MANUSCRIPTS IN THE UNIVERSITY OF TÜBINGEN LIBRARY

Signatur Md 750 (the *Baur-Nachlass*)

   i.   73 letters to Baur from 22 correspondents, 1823–60

  ii.   142 letters from Baur to 10 recipients, 1823–60

      1. Friedrich August Baur, 64 letters, 1823–55
      2. Caroline Baur, 1 letter, 1854
      3. Louise Christiane Gaupp, 1 letter, 1857
      4. Emilie Becher, draft of an undated letter, winter 1820–21
      5. Albert Baur, 38 letters, 1858–60
      6. Ludwig Friedrich Heyd, 30 letters (all copies of originals in Md 619r), 1824–42
      7. David Friedrich Strauss, 3 letters, 1837–42
      8. Friedrich Theodor Vischer, 1 letter (a copy), 1860
      9. Friedrich August Gottreu Tholuck, draft of an undated letter, 1836
         Emilie Becher, draft and final copy of letter of proposal, 1820

 iii.   8 seminary addresses, 1817–54

 iv.   6 sermons, 1813–57

  v.   5 academic opinions, 1835–42

 vi.   Poem for silver wedding anniversary of Louise Christiane Gaupp

 vii.   Manuscript for "Seneca und Paulus"

viii.   Seminary certificates and a poem, 1816

 ix.   Particulars from Christian Jakob Baur

  x.   Letter from Friedrich August Baur to Eduard Zeller, 1861

 xi.   Miscellany

Signatur Md 619r. 32 letters from Baur to Ludwig Friedrich Heyd, 1824–42

Signatur Md 747, 19, 34. 168 letters from Baur to Eduard Zeller, 1849–1860

Signatur Mh 969. 221 sermons preached by Baur in the Stiftskirche in Tübingen, 1826–60

Signatur Mh 970. Miscellaneous early manuscripts, 1809–26

Signatur Mh II 154–166. 154–165: student notes taken from Baur's lectures. 166 a–q: miscellaneous lecture manuscripts from Baur's hand (including philosophy of religion, New Testament exegesis, Church history, history of dogma, symbolics, Church law, ancient history).

OTHER MATERIALS

1. A few Baur materials are located in the following *Signaturs:* Md 613, Md 750b, Md 750c, Md 753, Md 760, Mi II 53, Mh II 311.

2. Letters from Baur to Christian Märklin are deposited in the Schiller-Nationalmuseum in Marbach, Nos. 20785–20800.

3. Correspondence between Baur and A. Hilgenfeld is in private possession.

PUBLISHED MANUSCRIPTS

Some of the letters in the above collections have been published in the following articles (full details in the secondary bibliography): Barnikol, "Der Briefwechsel zwischen Strauss und Baur"; Barnikol, "Das ideengeschichtliche Erbe Hegels bei und seit Strauss und Baur im 19. Jahrhundert"; Lang, "Ferdinand Baur und David Friedrich Strauss"; Liebing, "Ferdinand Christian Baurs Kritik an Schleiermachers Glaubenslehre"; Rapp, "Baur und Strauss in ihrer Stellung zueinander und zum Christentum."

II. SELECTED SECONDARY BIBLIOGRAPHY

BARNIKOL, ERNST. "Der Briefwechsel zwischen Strauss und Baur," *Zeitschrift für Kirchengeschichte,* 4. Folge X, LXXIII:1/2 (1962), 74–125.

——. "Das ideengeschichtliche Erbe Hegels bei und seit Strauss und Baur im 19. Jahrhundert," *Wissenschaftliche Zeitschrift der Martin-Luther-Universität Halle-Wittenberg,* Gesellschafts- und sprachwissenschaftliche Reihe, X:1 (February 1961), 281–328.

BARTH, KARL. *Die protestantische Theologie im 19. Jahrhundert.* 3d ed. Zürich: Evangelischer Verlag AG., 1960. English translation of eleven chapters by BRIAN COZENS, published under the title, *From Rousseau to Ritschl.* London: SCM Press, 1959.

BAUER, KARL. "Ferdinand Christian Baur als Kirchenhistoriker," *Blätter für Württembergische Kirchengeschichte,* Neue Folge, XXV (1921), 1–38; XXVI (1922), 1–60.

——. "Zur Jugendgeschichte von Ferdinand Christian Baur (1805–1807)," *Theologische Studien und Kritiken,* XCV:3/4 (1923/1924), 303–313.

BAUR, AUGUST. "Ferdinand Christian Baur," *Protestantische Kirchenzeitung für das evangelische Deutschland,* XXXIX:29,30 (July 1892), 661–67, 691–99.

BECKH, HEINRICH. "Die Tübinger historische Schule, kritisch beleuchtet," *Zeitschrift für Protestantismus und Kirche,* Neue Folge, LXXIV (1864), 1–57, 69–95, 133–78, 203–244.

BERGER, SAMUEL. *F. C. Baur: les origines de l'école de Tubingue et ses principes, 1826–1844.* Strasbourg: Berger-Levrault, 1867.

BRUCE, A. B. "Ferdinand Christian Baur and His Theory of the Origin of Christianity and of the New Testament Writings," in *Living Papers Concerning Christian Evidences, Doctrine, and Morals,* Vol. VII. Cincinnati, Chicago, and St. Louis: Cranston & Stowe, 1886.

BULTMANN, RUDOLF. *Theology of the New Testament.* Vol. II. Translated by KENDRICK GROBEL. New York: Charles Scribner's Sons, 1955.

CRITES, STEPHEN D. "The Problem of the 'Positivity' of the Gospel in the Hegelian Dialectic of Alienation and Reconciliation." Unpublished Ph.D. dissertation, Dept. of Religion, Yale University, 1961.

DILTHEY, WILHELM. "Ferdinand Christian Baur," in *Gesammelte Schriften,* Vol. IV, *Die Jugendgeschichte Hegels und andere Abhandlungen zur Geschichte des deutschen Idealismus.* 2d ed. Leipzig and Berlin: B. G. Teubner, 1925. Pp. 403–432. (This essay originally appeared in *Westermanns Monatsheften* in 1865 under the pseudonym of Hoffner.)

DORNER, I. A. *History of Protestant Theology Particularly in Germany, Viewed According to Its Fundamental Movement and in Connection with the Religious, Moral, and Intellectual Life.* Vol. II. Translated by GEORGE ROBSON and SOPHIA TAYLOR. Edinburgh: T. & T. Clark, 1871.

EWALD, HEINRICH. "Ursprung und Wesen der Evangelien," *Jahrbücher der biblischen Wissenschaft,* I (1848), 113 ff.; II (1849), 180 ff.

FRAEDRICH, G. *Ferdinand Christian Baur: der Begründer der Tübinger Schule als Theologe, Schriftsteller, und Charakter.* Gotha: Friedrich Andreas Perthes, 1909.

GEIGER, WOLFGANG. *Spekulation und Kritik: Die Geschichtstheologie Ferdinand Christian Baurs.* München: Chr. Kaiser Verlag, 1964.

HARNACK, ADOLF. *History of Dogma.* Vols. I and VII. Translated from 3d German ed. (1893) by NEIL BUCHANAN. New York: Dover Publications, 1961.

HASE, KARL. *Die Tübinger Schule. Ein Sendschreiben an Herrn Dr. Ferdinand Christian von Baur.* Leipzig: Breitkopf und Härtel, 1855.

HEFNER, PHILIP. "Baur versus Ritschl on Early Christianity," *Church History,* XXXI:3 (September 1962), 259–78.

HEGEL, G. W. F. *Encyclopedia of Philosophy.* Translated by GUSTAV EMIL MUELLER. New York: Philosophical Library, 1959.

———. *Lectures on the Philosophy of Religion.* Vol. I. Translated from 2d German ed. by E. B. SPEIRS and J. B. SANDERSON. London: Routledge & Kegan Paul, 1895.

———. *The Philosophy of History.* Translated by J. SIBREE. New York: Dover Publications, 1956.

HILGENFELD, ADOLF. "Ferdinand Christian Baur nach seiner wissenschaftlichen Entwickelung und Bedeutung," *Zeitschrift für wissenschaftliche Theologie,* XXXVI:I:2 (1893), 222–44.

HIRSCH, EMANUEL. *Geschichte der neuern evangelischen Theologie im Zusammenhang mit den allgemeinen Bewegungen des europäischen Denkens.* Vol. IV, 2d ed. Gütersloh: Verlagshaus Gerd Mohn, 1960. Vol. V. Gütersloh: C. Bertelmanns Verlag, 1954.

HODGSON, PETER C. "The Rediscovery of Ferdinand Christian Baur: A Review of the First Two Volumes of His *Ausgewählte Werke,*" *Church History,* XXXIII:2 (June 1964), 206–214.

LANG, WILHELM. "Baur und Strauss," in *Von und aus Schwaben: Geschichte, Biographie, Litteratur,* Vol. III. Stuttgart: Druck und Verlag von W. Kohlhammer, 1886. Pp. 1–31.

———. "Ferdinand Baur und David Friedrich Strauss," *Preussische Jahrbücher,* CLX (April–June 1915), 474–504; CLXI (July–September 1915), 123–44.

LIEBING, HEINZ. "Ferdinand Christian Baurs Kritik an Schleiermachers Glaubenslehre," *Zeitschrift für Theologie und Kirche,* LIV:2 (1957), 225–43.

———. "Historisch-kritische Theologie: zum 100. Todestag Ferdinand Christian Baurs am 2. Dezember 1960," *Zeitschrift für Theologie und Kirche,* LVII:3 (1960), 302–317.

MACKAY, R. W. *The Tübingen School and Its Antecedents: A Review of the History and Present Condition of Modern Theology.* London: Williams & Norgate, 1863.

Article by HERMANN MULERT, in *Neue deutsche Biographie,* Vol. I. Berlin: Duncker und Humblot, 1952. Pp. 670–71.

PÄLTZ, EBERHARD. "F. C. Baurs Verhältnis zu Schleiermacher." Unpublished doctoral dissertation, University of Jena, 1955. Abstract by the author in *Theologische Literaturzeitung*, LXXXI:9 (September 1956), 570–72.

PATTISON, MARK. "Present State of Theology in Germany," in *Essays by the Late Mark Pattison*, Vol. II, ed. HENRY NETTLESHIP. Oxford: Clarendon Press, 1889. (Originally published in the *Westminster Review*, 1857.)

PFLEIDERER, OTTO. *The Development of Theology in Germany Since Kant, and Its Progress in Great Britain Since 1825.* Translated by J. FREDERICK SMITH. London: Swan Sonnenschein & Co., 1890.

———. "Zu Ferdinand Christian Baur's Gedächtnis," *Protestantische Kirchenzeitung für das evangelische Deutschland*, XXXIX:25 (June 1892), 565–73.

RAPP, ADOLPH. "Baur und Strauss in ihrer Stellung zueinander und zum Christentum," *Blätter für Württembergische Kirchengeschichte*, 3. Folge, LII (1952), 95–149; LIII (1953), 157; LIV (1954), 182–85.

Die Religion in Geschichte und Gegenwart. 1st ed., article by S. A. ECK. Vol. I. Tübingen: J. C. B. Mohr, 1909. Pp. 958–59. 2d ed., article by KARL BAUER. Vol. I. Tübingen: J. C. B. Mohr, 1927. Pp. 817–19. 3d ed., article by M. TETZ. Vol. I. Tübingen: J. C. B. Mohr, 1957. Pp. 935–938.

RITSCHL, ALBRECHT. "Einige Erläuterungen zu dem Sendschreiben: 'Die historische Kritik und das Wunder,'" *Sybels historische Zeitschrift*, VIII (1862), 85–99.

———. *Die Entstehung der altkatholischen Kirche. Eine kirchen- und dogmengeschichtliche Monographie.* 2d ed., revised. Bonn: Adolph Marcus, 1857.

———. "Über geschichtliche Methode in der Erforschung des Urchristenthums," *Jahrbücher für deutsche Theologie*, VI (1861), 429–59.

SCHELLING, F. W. J. *Vorlesungen über die Methode des academischen Studium.* 3d unaltered ed. Stuttgart and Tübingen: J. G. Cotta, 1830.

SCHLEIERMACHER, FRIEDRICH. *The Christian Faith.* Translation of 2d German ed., ed. by H. R. MACKINTOSH and J. S. STEWART. Edinburgh: T. & T. Clark, 1928.

———. *Entwürfe zu einem System der Sittenlehre*, ed. OTTO BRAUN. Leipzig: Feliz Meiner, 1927.

———. *Schleiermachers Sendschreiben über seine Glaubenslehre an Lücke*, ed. HERMANN MULERT. Giessen: Alfred Töpelmann, 1908.

Article by H. SCHMIDT, in *Realencyklopaedie für protestantische Theologie und Kirche.* 2d ed., ed. by J. J. HERZOG and G. T. PLITT, Vol. II. Leipzig: Hinrischs'sche Buchhandlung, 1878. Pp. 163–84, 3d ed., ed. by J. J. HERZOG and ALBERT HAUCK, Vol. II. Leipzig: Hinrischs'sche Buchhandlung, 1897. Pp. 467–83.

SCHNEIDER, ERNST. *Ferdinand Christian Baur in seiner Bedeutung für die Theologie.* München: J. F. Lehmanns Verlag, 1909.

SCHOLDER, KLAUS. "Albert Schweitzer und Ferdinand Christian Baur," in *Albert Schweitzer: Sein Denken und Sein Weg*, ed. H. W. BÄHR. Tübingen: J. C. B. Mohr, 1962. Pp. 184–92.

———. "Ferdinand Christian Baur als Historiker," *Evangelische Theologie*, XXI:10 (1961), 435–58.

SCHWEITZER, ALBERT. *Paul and His Interpreters: A Critical History.* Translated by W. MONTGOMERY. London: Adam & Charles Black, 1912.

SENFT, CHRISTOPH. *Wahrhaftigkeit und Wahrheit: Die Theologie des 19. Jahrhunderts zwischen Orthodoxie und Aufklärung.* Tübingen: J. C. B. Mohr, 1956.

SEYERLEN, RUDOLF. "Ferdinand Christian Baur als akademischer Lehrer und Mensch," *Zeitschrift für wissenschaftliche Theologie,* XXXVI:I:2 (1893), 244–54.

STRAUSS, DAVID FRIEDRICH. *The Life of Jesus Critically Examined.* Translated from 4th German ed. by GEORGE ELIOT. 2d. ed. London: Swan Sonnenschein & Co., 1892.

––––. *Streitschriften zur Vertheidigung meiner Schrift über das Leben Jesu und zur Charakteristik der gegenwärtigen Theologie.* New ed. in one vol. Tübingen: C. F. Osiander, 1841.

TROELTSCH, ERNST. "Adolf v. Harnack und Ferd. Christ. v. Baur," in *Festgabe für D. Dr. A. von Harnack, zum siebzigsten Geburtstag.* Tübingen: J. C. B. Mohr, 1921. Pp. 282–91.

UHLHORN, GERHARD. "Die älteste Kirchengeschichte in der Darstellung der Tübinger Schule," *Jahrbücher für deutsche Theologie,* III (1858), 280–349.

Worte der Erinnerung an Ferdinand Christian von Baur. Tübingen: L. F. Fues, 1861.

Worte der Erinnerung an Dr. Johann Tobias Beck. Tübingen: J. J. Heckenhauer, 1879.

ZELLER, EDUARD. "Ferdinand Christian Baur," in *Allgemeine deutsche Biographie.* Vol. II. Leipzig: Duncker und Humblot, 1875. Pp. 172–79.

––––. "Ferdinand Christian Baur," in *Vorträge und Abhandlungen geschichtlichen Inhalts.* Leipzig: Fues's Verlag (L. W. Reisland), 1865. Pp. 354–434. (First published in the *Preussische Jahrbücher,* 1861.)

––––. "Die historische Kritik und das Wunder," *Sybels historische Zeitschrift,* VI (1861), 356–73.

––––. "Die Tübinger historische Schule," *Sybels historische Zeitschrift,* IV (1860), 90–173. (Reprinted in revised form in *Vorträge und Abhandlungen geschichtlichen Inhalts,* pp. 267–353.)

––––. "Zur Würdigung der Ritschl'schen 'Erläuterung,'" *Sybels historische Zeitschrift,* VIII (1862), 100–116.

INDEX

295

Format by Morris Karol
Set in Linotype Primer
Composed, printed and bound by The Haddon Craftsmen, Inc.
HARPER & ROW, PUBLISHERS, INCORPORATED

DAT